The Princeton Review®

Cracking the

CSET®

By Kate Smith and Riley Dacosta

PrincetonReview.com

Random House, Inc. New York

The Princeton Review, Inc.
111 Speen Street, Suite 550
Framingham, MA 01701
E-mail: editorialsupport@review.com

Terms of Service: The Princeton Review Online Companion Tools ("Online
Companion Tools") for the *Cracking* book series and *11 Practice Tests
for the SAT & PSAT* are available for the two most recent editions of
each book title. Online Companion Tools may be activated only once per
eligible book purchased. Activation of Online Companion Tools more than
once per book is in direct violation of these Terms of Service and may
result in discontinuation of access to Online Companion Tools services.

CSET and CBEST are trademarks of Pearson Education, Inc. or its
affiliate(s).

ISBN: 978-0-375-42954-5
ISSN: 2156-4892

Editor: Selena Coppock
Production Editor: Kathy G. Carter
Production Coordinator: Deborah A. Silvestrini

Printed in the United States of America on
partially recycled paper.

10 9 8 7 6 5 4 3 2 1

Editorial
Robert Franek, VP Test Prep Books, Publisher
Seamus Mullarkey, Associate Publisher
Laura Braswell, Senior Editor
Rebecca Lessem, Senior Editor
Selena Coppock, Editor
Heather Brady, Editor

Random House Publishing Team
Tom Russell, Publisher
Nicole Benhabib, Publishing Manager
Ellen L. Reed, Production Manager
Alison Stoltzfus, Associate Managing Editor

Acknowledgments

Kate Smith:

I would like to express my utmost gratitude to my editor, Selena Coppock, for entrusting me with this project and for being available to me absolutely anytime I needed her, whether day, night, weekend, or holiday, with answers, encouragement, and comic relief. She has ruined me for all other editors.

I would also like to thank some of the people who have given me support and guidance in my education and career: Connie Beringer, Dr. Joanne Rossi, Richard Rossi, Jacqueline Berger, Dr. Margaret Koshland-Crane, Dr. Vincent Fitzgerald, Julie Segedy, Suzi Riley, and Dr. Karen Schwarz.

Finally, I am deeply grateful to my parents, grandmother, and the rest of my family, to my fabulous friends, and to my awesome students, for the love, faith, and inspiration they have all given me.

Riley Dacosta:

I would like to thank The Princeton Review team and in particular Selena Coppock for guidance on this project. Special thanks to Bertha Orr, Gerald Jenkins and Megan Nicole for their support. Additionally, I would like to thank Venessa Henlon, Cheryle Roberts, Rogeair Purnell, Eric Fleming, William Nettles, Robin Dozier, Dr. Alice Ward, and Dr. Clyde Johnson for lending their expertise and suggestions.

Last, I would like to thank William E. Ward for his inspiring dedication and commitment to excellence in teaching and education.

Contents

...So Much More Online!

More Practice...

- Practice your CSET test-taking skills.

- Access three full-length practice CSET exams.

- Take one as a diagnostic test before you work through *Cracking the CSET*.

- Work through the chapters and practice questions found in this book, focusing on the sections where you need specific review.

- Then take the second practice CSET and see how much you improved.

- Take the third practice CSET for additional practice.

- Then, prepare to tackle the real CSET with skill and ease!

Register Your Book Now...

- Go to **PrincetonReview.com/cracking**

- You'll see a welcome page where you should register your book using the serial number. What's a serial number, you ask? It's a unique number assigned to your copy of the book so that you can access online tools. It's printed on either the inside front cover or the inside back cover. Type this combination of letters and numbers into the window on the web page above.

- Next you will see a Sign Up/Sign In page where you will type in your e-mail address (username) and choose a password.

- Now you're good to go!

princetonreview.com/cracking

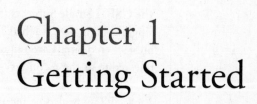

Chapter 1
Getting Started

WHAT IS THE CSET?

CSET stands for **California Subject Examinations for Teachers.** These tests fulfill the subject matter competency requirements for prospective K–12 teachers. The CSET replaces the MSAT, Praxis, SSAT, and CBEST.

A passing score on all three subtests that comprise the CSET: Multiple Subjects (MS) is a requirement for prospective elementary school teachers as part of the teacher credentialing process. Although most elementary schools in California end at fifth grade, the Multiple Subjects teaching credential is designated for grades K–6.

The CSET: Single Subjects (SS) is one way to verify subject matter competence in a single content area, such as Physical Education or Social Science. Generally, Single Subject credentials are required to teach individual subjects in grades 7–12, often referred to as the secondary-level grades.

The CSET may also be required for some teachers who received their teacher training in other states, and it can be taken by current educators adding authorizations or demonstrating No Child Left Behind (NCLB) compliance.

Who Writes the CSET?

The CSET was developed by the California Commission on Teacher Credentialing (CTC) and is administered by National Evaluation Systems, Inc. (NES). Test materials are aligned with current California K–12 Student Academic Content Standards.

Official information about the CSET, including test dates and locations, registration deadlines and requirements, and a practice test, can be found online at www.cset.nesinc.com. Here's additional contact information for the CSET Program:

Address: CSET Program
            Evaluation Systems
            Pearson
            P.O. Box 340789
            Sacramento, CA 95834-0789

Phone: 1-800-205-3334 or 1-916-928-4003
            Monday–Friday 9:00 A.M.–5:00 P.M. PST
            (except for U.S. holidays)
            Saturday test days only 6:30 A.M.–3:00 P.M. PST
            (Automated Information System available 24 hours daily)

Fax: 1-866-483-6460 or 1-916-928-6110

What's on the CSET: Multiple Subjects Exam?
The CSET: Multiple Subjects consists of three subtests.

- Subtest I (101)
  Reading, Language, and Literature
  History and Social Science

- Subtest II (102)
  Science
  Math

- Subtest III (103)
  Physical Education
  Human Development
  Visual and Performing Arts

How is the CSET: Multiple Subjects Exam Structured?
- Each test session is five hours long.
- You have the option of sitting for one, two, or all three subtests in one test session.
- Subtest I consists of 52 multiple-choice questions and four constructed-response questions.
- Subtest II consists of 52 multiple-choice questions and four constructed-response questions.
- Subtest III consists of 39 multiple-choice questions and three constructed-response questions.

One thing you should take comfort in is that, compared to most of the standardized tests out there, the CSET is a test taker's dream (if test takers actually dream about such things). First of all, regardless of how many subtests you're taking in one test session, you can work on the questions in any order that you want—yes, that means between subtests as well as within! At the beginning of the test session, you're given the test booklets for all of the subtests you've registered for, and can flip and switch at will. The five hours are entirely yours.

Also, each subtest is divided equally by content area, so you know exactly how many questions there will be on each subject, and in what order. The breakdown of the test is shown in the following table.

CSET: MULTIPLE SUBJECTS			
Subtest	Domains	Number of Multiple-Choice Questions	Number of Constructed-Response Questions (short [focused] responses)
I	Reading, Language, and Literature	26	2
	History and Social Science	26	2
	Subtest Total	52	4
II	Science	26	2
	Mathematics	26	2
	Subtest Total	52	4
III	Physical Education	13	1
	Human Development	13	1
	Visual and Performing Arts	13	1
	Subtest Total	39	3

This is exactly how the test is structured, with no variations. When you take Subtest III, for example, you know that questions 1–13 will be multiple-choice questions on Physical Education, questions 14–26 will be multiple-choice questions on Human Development, and questions 27–39 will be multiple-choice questions on Visual and Performing Arts. These questions will be followed by one constructed-response question related to Physical Education, then one constructed-response question related to Human Development, and finally one constructed-response question related to Visual and Performing Arts.

How is the CSET: Multiple Subjects Exam Scored?

Each subtest is scored independently, which means that your score on any one subtest does not affect your scores on the others. This also means—more good news—that once you pass a subtest, you don't have to retake that one, even if you haven't yet passed one or both of the others.

Your score on each subtest is based on your overall performance on that test. The proportions of the questions are the same on all three subtests.

- multiple-choice questions: 70%
- constructed-response questions: 30%

The multiple-choice questions each have four answer choices, and are machine scored as correct or incorrect. Your multiple-choice score is based strictly on how many questions you answer correctly. There is no penalty for guessing and no point deduction for wrong answers. We'll discuss good specific test-taking strategies later in the book.

Constructed-response questions are open-ended questions requiring written answers. Your responses to these questions will be scored by two or more California educators, who base the scores on several performance characteristics.

- Purpose: How well do you answer the question?
- Subject matter knowledge: How well do you apply your knowledge of the content area?
- Support: How well do you back up your answer?
- Depth and breadth of understanding: How well do you know your stuff?

Then of course, you have raw scores that are weighted and converted to scaled scores; but unless you're absolutely fascinated with that process, all you have to do is focus on the magic number 220. That's the minimum passing score on each subtest.

How Many Subtests Should I Take in One Session?

This is entirely up to you, but here are some factors to consider as you make your decision.

- your reading/writing speed
- your ability to switch gears
- the time it takes you to study and prepare for a test
- the content area knowledge you already possess
- how soon you need to complete your teaching credential requirements

What Is the CSET: Writing Skills Test?

The CSET: Writing Skills test (142) consists of two constructed-response questions, which are also scored by California educators using standardized procedures. It is a separate test, and it can be used only in conjunction with CSET: Multiple Subjects to satisfy the basic skills requirement. We'll cover the CSET: Writing Skills test in more detail later in the book.

WHAT IS THE PRINCETON REVIEW?

The Princeton Review is an international test-preparation company with branches in all major U.S. cities and several cities abroad. In 1981, John Katzman started teaching an SAT prep course in his parents' living room in New York City. Within five years, The Princeton Review had become the largest SAT prep program in the country.

Our phenomenal success in improving students' scores on standardized tests is due to a simple, innovative, and radically effective philosophy: Study the test, not just what the test claims to test. This approach has lead to the development of techniques for taking standardized tests based on the principles the test writers themselves use to write the tests.

The Princeton Review has found that its methods work not just for cracking the SAT, but for any standardized test. We've already successfully applied our system to the GMAT, LSAT, MCAT, and GRE, to name just a few. Obviously you need to be well versed in many subjects to do well on the CSET, but you should remember that any standardized test is partly a measure of your ability to think like the people who write standardized tests. This book will help you brush up on the CSET and prepare for the exam using our time-tested principle: Crack the system by learning how the test is created.

We also offer books and online services that cover an enormous variety of education and career-related topics. If you're interested, check out our website at **PrincetonReview.com.**

Chapter 2
Cracking the
System

HOW TO USE THIS BOOK

Well, for starters, don't skip this chapter. Our goal is to give you the test-taking techniques you need to boost your score on the CSET. You'll have a better idea of what you're doing when you have read and worked through this book, then taken the practice tests that are found online.

After you've taken the practice tests, make sure to read all of the explanations, even the explanations to the questions you answered correctly. You'll often find that your understanding of a question and the best way to have gone about answering it will be much clearer after you've read the explanation. You'll also catch some instances in which you got the question right, but for all the wrong reasons. Most important, many of the explanations contain content information you won't find elsewhere in the book.

WHAT ARE THE BASIC PRINCIPLES OF CRACKING THE SYSTEM?

There will come a time when the studying is over and you are as prepared as you are going to be. You will be sitting in the test center with sealed exam booklets and answer sheets in front of you. The proctor, droning on at the front of the room, will finally finish reading all of those instructions most people don't listen to anyway, and will say, "You may begin the test."

At that moment, what you know isn't going to change. Your head will be crammed with knowledge, but now your score depends on getting what you know onto that answer sheet. If you know how to take a standardized test, you will squeeze every possible drop of what you know onto that answer sheet, and your score will reflect your efforts.

In this chapter, we're going to walk you through our best strategies for cracking both multiple-choice and constructed-response questions.

Pace Yourself

A big part of scoring well on an exam is working at a consistent pace. The worst mistake made by inexperienced or unsavvy test takers is that they come to a question that stumps them, and rather than just skip it, they panic and stall. Time stands still when you're working on a question you cannot answer, and it's possible for test takers to waste five minutes on a single question because they are too stubborn to cut their losses.

Don't make that mistake. Tests are like marathons; you do best when you work through them at a steady pace. You can always come back to a question you don't know. When you do, very often you will find that your previous mental block is gone, and you will wonder why the question perplexed you the first time around. Even if you still don't know the answer, you will not have wasted valuable time you could have spent on easier questions.

Pacing is especially important on the CSET, because you have the option of taking one or more subtests in one test session. It's essential that you map out your time in advance.

Five hours is allotted for each CSET: Multiple Subjects test session, regardless of how many subtests you take. To begin with, you should divide the total number of minutes equally by the number of subtests you are taking.

- One subtest: 300 minutes
- Two subtests: 150 minutes for each test
- Three subtests: 100 minutes for each test

Now, you may work on the questions in any order you like, but because the multiple-choice questions comprise 70% of your overall score, making those your first priority is a no-brainer. You definitely don't want to start with the constructed-response questions and spend more time on them than you intend to, leaving you without enough time to get through the multiple-choice questions.

The CSET official guide says that each of the constructed-response questions is designed to take about 10–15 minutes to complete. So let's work our way backward to determine how much time to spend on the multiple-choice questions. Let's expand, and because Subtest III is slightly shorter than either Subtest I or Subtest II, we'll just use the length of those two tests as the average: 52 multiple-choice questions and four constructed-response questions each.

If you are taking…

- One subtest: 300 minutes
  Constructed-response questions: 40–50 minutes
  Multiple-choice questions: 250–260 minutes
- Two subtests: 150 minutes each
  Constructed-response questions on each test: 40–50 minutes
  Multiple-choice questions on each test: 100–110 minutes
- Three subtests: 100 minutes each
  Constructed-response questions on each test: 40–50 minutes
  Multiple-choice questions on each test: 50–60 minutes

Now that you have a baseline, you can adjust and plan accordingly. In the first scenario, you'd have a pretty disproportionate amount of time to designate to the multiple-choice questions, but only you know if you'll need the time more there, or whether you'll want to allot more time for the constructed-response questions.

Study

One of the best ways to improve your speed on the test is to know the material. When a question is about material that you are truly familiar with, it will be ridiculously easy. You'll not only get the points, you'll buy time. Just brushing up on basic facts and concepts will speed you up. If, for example, you haven't so much as glanced at the periodic table since that 8:00 A.M. freshman chemistry class with old Professor What's-His-Name, 10 minutes spent looking it over will do you a world of good.

MULTIPLE-CHOICE QUESTIONS

There Is No Guessing Penalty on the CSET!

It's essential that you remember this fact, which is why it appears here first. Unlike some other standardized tests, you lose no credit for an incorrect multiple-choice answer on the CSET, and therefore, you *must* answer every single question, even if you are at the point at which you have to guess randomly. You can only help yourself by guessing, and you can only hurt yourself by leaving a question unanswered. Even if time is running out and you don't have enough time to read through the question, just bubble in an answer anyway. Because there is no guessing penalty, you must answer **every** question. Answer every question. Answer every question. Are you going to answer every question? Good. Then let's move on.

The Two-Pass System

The **two-pass system** is The Princeton Review's term for judicious skipping. It means working through the test once (the first pass) to gather up all the quick, easy points, and then going back (the second pass) to work on the time-consuming, difficult questions you skipped initially.

In the first pass, follow your instincts. There is no magic number of questions to answer on your first pass. You might answer five questions on your first pass or you might answer 30. The main point of the two-pass system is to gather up the easy points quickly and efficiently first. Deciding whether a question is first pass or not is a snap decision. Five seconds is the absolute longest you should think about whether a question is first pass or not. Use the five-second rule:

> If it takes more than five seconds to decide if it's a first or second pass question, it automatically becomes a second pass question. Skip it.

After finishing your first pass, you should be left with the medium and tough questions, the questions you didn't like at first glance. On the first pass, you undoubtedly answered some questions you wish you'd left for later. That's no cause for alarm. On the second pass, you'll find some questions that turn out to be easier than you'd expected. If you've done the first pass well, what you're left with are mostly the tougher questions.

And if you are staying mindful of your time, you can still skip to your heart's content. There's no law that says you can't do a third or even a fourth pass. Skip questions that look like they'll eat up your time without giving you anything back. At a certain point, you'll know it's time to just make your best guess and move on.

Process of Elimination (POE)

You are probably already acquainted with **process of elimination** (POE) in its simplest form: Cross out answers you know are wrong. The Cracking the System approach to POE isn't really different, just more intense.

You'll find that on a number of questions, the right answer will jump out at you. It will be based on a book you've read and remember well, or a math concept you're particularly good at. When that happens, you'll pounce on the right answer, fill in the correct bubble, and move on.

Other times, however, the question topic will be unfamiliar and the answer choices may only ring vague bells. That's when POE should be a reflex. Through POE, you can take advantage of what partial knowledge you have. You may not know the information that leads you directly to the answer, but you could know information that tells you what the answer definitely is *not*. Let's look at an example.

The first important cash crop in the American colonies was:

A.   cotton.

B.   corn.

C.   tobacco.

D.   fresh fruit.

Here's How to Crack It

Let's look at the answer choices one at a time. You may think you don't know the answer, but it's what you know about the answer choices judged against the question that counts. It's what you know about the answer choices that allows you to use POE.

    A.   cotton

The cotton gin was not invented until the late eighteenth century. Cross it out.

    D.   fresh fruit

Ridiculous! You know that fruit would hardly have remained fresh during the long sea journey from the colonies back to England. Cross this one out, too.

By using POE, you've narrowed down your choice to two possibilities. At this point, if you're still stumped, or pressed for time, you can make a guess. But now, instead of having a 25% chance of getting the right answer, you're up to 50%. That's a huge difference. The answer, by the way, is C.

———————————————◯———————————————

And in case this wasn't clear, you can—and should—physically cross out wrong answers. The test booklet is yours to mark up as much as you like. As you eliminate answers, make sure you cross them out. When answers are crossed out, you are less likely to mistakenly choose them (don't forget that the test session can take up to five hours; even the most attentive brain might wander). Finally, circle the answer choice you do choose. That way, if you make a mistake bubbling, it will be easy to fix.

Bubbling

Since we're on the subject, let's just take a quick once-over. **Bubbling** is the art of transferring your answers onto the score sheet. When you bubble, be sure to fill in the oval completely so that you'll receive the credit you deserve. If you follow our advice (and you should), you should be skipping around—so pay special attention to where you bubble. As you skip around different questions on your answer sheet, don't forget to keep track of the question numbers you are bubbling. It's a horrible feeling to get to question 55 and realize you've just bubbled the answer for 54. Check your work regularly.

Types of Questions

The directions for the multiple-choice section simply ask you to select the "best" answer choice for each question. That's code for "More than one of the answer choices might fit in some way or another, but we're looking for the one that makes the most sense." The test uses a variety of question types, though, and if you recognize the different types, you'll save yourself time and the possibility of choosing the wrong answer even when you know the right one.

Standard Questions

The majority of multiple-choice questions are pretty straightforward, like this one:

> The first president of the United States was:
>
> A.   George Washington.
>
> B.   Abraham Lincoln.
>
> C.   Franklin D. Roosevelt.
>
> D.   Mickey Mouse.

In some cases (like this one), you can use common sense to choose the right answer. If you don't know the answer, then use POE to get yourself closer.

Component Questions

Here and there, you'll run into a question that has more than one component. In this case, look for the answer choice that fits all parts of the question, not just one. Remember this phrase: *Part* wrong is *all* wrong. If there's *anything* that is somewhat wrong in the answer choice, even if there is other information that is correct, that answer choice cannot be right. Here's an example.

> George Washington, Abraham Lincoln, and Franklin D. Roosevelt were all:
>
> A.   mice.
>
> B.   born in the nineteenth century.
>
> C.   Democrats.
>
> D.   United States presidents.

Here's How to Crack It

The answer choice you need is one that relates correctly to all parts of the question, which, in this case, are three names. Sometimes, you'll know the correct answer, but other times, you'll have to work at it. If you need to use POE for this type of question, go through the answer choices one by one, like a checklist.

Let's just pretend that you don't know the answer to this one. Quickly check each answer against the components of the question. Answer choice A does not relate to any of the question components, so cross that out. Answer choice B relates to Abraham Lincoln and Franklin D. Roosevelt, but not George Washington, so cross that out. Answer choice C relates only to Franklin D. Roosevelt, so cross that one out as well. Even if you didn't know the answer, based on POE, you've successfully ruled out everything but answer choice D.

CONSTRUCTED-RESPONSE QUESTIONS

You may be wondering why the CSET labels these as **constructed-response questions** and not simply essay questions. Actually, it's a good thing they don't, because that might throw you off track. The constructed-response questions are not supposed to be five-paragraph essays. The test guide tells you that each constructed-response question should take 10–15 minutes. How many people do you think can plan and write a full five-paragraph essay in under 15 minutes?

Here's what they *do* expect of you.

The Prompt

For one thing, they expect you to answer the question. If you write a great response that does not address the prompt, you'll get a lousy score. Most prompts on the constructed-response questions have more than one component. Your first priority is to take apart the prompt and make sure you know exactly what's being asked of you. Let's look at an example of a typical constructed-response prompt:

The American colonies declared their independence from England in 1776.

Using your knowledge of this time period in U.S. history, prepare a response in which you

1. identify two factors that led to this decision;
2. select one of the factors you have identified; and
3. explain how that factor contributed to the event.

After you've read the prompt, take a minute to reword it into questions. Make a list:

1. What are two reasons the colonies wanted independence from England?
2. Which reason am I going to write about?
3. How did that reason contribute to the colonies' decision to declare independence from England?

As a general rule, you can answer the first two questions together in one paragraph. They're really just historical or subject-matter facts; you'll just want to make sure that you write them in complete, well-constructed sentences. The third question is the one you'll need to spend most of your time on, as you should write one or two paragraphs to fully answer it. This is the place where you can synthesize ideas and explore the prompt. We have a few tips and tricks to help you.

Brainstorm

Take about one or two minutes to write down as many things as you can think of that relate to the question. Depending on the content area, you should try to come up with information and ideas about the following items:

- names
- dates
- places
- concepts
- vocabulary

Then sort out the results of your brainstorm. Some of what you write down will become your main point(s), some will be facts that can be used as evidence to support your conclusions, and some will be garbage.

As you will see in the practice tests, the CSET constructed-response questions are very specific. Many questions require you to use terms that are content area-specific. The educators who score your responses are looking for these terms, and they want to know that you know what the terms mean. When you use them, define or explain them. Take particular care to define any such terms that appear in the question. The introductory paragraph is a good place to include any definitions.

Use the Multiple-Choice Section to Your Advantage

Remember: This is an open-book test. There's nothing to stop you from going back through the test booklet and skimming the multiple-choice questions. Sometimes, you'll run into questions that might relate to the material that was covered in the constructed-response questions. You might find key terms, names, and dates. It's worth a shot if you're having trouble getting started or if you want more facts to back up your ideas.

The Format

Remember the following three things as you write your response:

- Start strong.
- Make it clear.
- Keep it neat.

Start Strong

If your essay looks neat, the scorer will start feeling relaxed and optimistic. It's up to you to write a brilliant beginning that will set the tone and sustain the reader's positive attitude. Put a lot of care into writing the first few sentences, and don't make any mistakes. Try to have a variety of sentence structures and be sure to double-check spelling and punctuation. If you're unsure about the spelling of a word, don't use it!

Don't worry so much about the rest of the response; the readers expect a few mistakes. If you try to write the whole response perfectly, you may write too slowly and waste time, or worry too much and write dull, overwrought, and perhaps recondite paragraphs (see how it comes across when you use vocabulary that's too obscure?). All it takes is three or four well-crafted, strong sentences at the start of your essay to convince the reader that you can write a good sentence when you have time to do so. As long as the rest of your response is clear and well organized, the glow of a good beginning can carry over the entire response.

Make It Clear

High-scoring responses are *clear*. They aren't perfect. They aren't moving and profound. They're simply clear. Clarity is your goal.

Keep your sentences as simple as possible. Long sentences get convoluted very quickly and will give your scorers a headache, putting them in a bad mood. Do not antagonize your reader! Remember that good writing does not have to be complicated; some great ideas can be stated simply.

Vocabulary Review
Check out these other titles from The Princeton Review to improve your vocabulary: *WordSmart WordSmart II*

Do not ever use a word if you are unsure of its definition or proper usage. A malapropism might give your scorers a good laugh, but it will not earn you any points, and it will probably cost you.

Do not use contractions or shorthand symbols such as "&" or "w/" or "tho." Get in the habit of using a relatively high level of discourse when you write. You will not impress anyone if your response reads like an email or a text message.

Keep It Neat

Do everything that's reasonably possible to make your responses readable. Your writing doesn't have to be pretty, but it needs to be legible. Think before you write! If your thoughts are clear before you start writing, you will express yourself more clearly in the response; if your thoughts are a mess, your response will be a mess too.

The general appearance of the response is what's most important. An occasional scratch-out is perfectly fine; a scratch-out every third word is a sign that you don't know what you're doing. If you need to cross out, do it neatly. If you are making any major edits—if you want to re-order your paragraphs, for example—make sure you indicate these changes clearly.

If you've ever opened a book and seen nothing but very long paragraphs, you can imagine how scorers think when they see a response without paragraph breaks: "Ugh." Make your paragraphs obvious. Indent twice as far as you normally would. Be sure readers can see the paragraph breaks at first glance.

Some people think it's better to write in cursive than in print. Unless you ordinarily use cursive instead of printing when you write, there's no reason you should. Don't waste time by slowing down your writing, and don't unintentionally make your handwriting indecipherable for the scorer by trying to make it look elegant.

KEY TERMS

two-pass system
process of elimination (POE)
bubbling
constructed-response questions

Summary

o Plan your time management strategy in advance.

o Answer every question. Answer every question. Answer every question.

o In the multiple-choice section, use the two-pass system to collect easy points first.

o Use process of elimination to help you narrow down the choices in multiple-choice questions when you're not sure of the answer.

o Check regularly to make sure you're bubbling the correct oval for the question you are answering.

o In constructed-response questions, make sure you address each part of the prompt.

o Start your written responses strong and error-free.

o Keep your written responses neat and use simple, clear sentence construction.

Subtest I: Reading, Language, and Literature; History and Social Science

Reading, Language, and Literature

History and Social Science

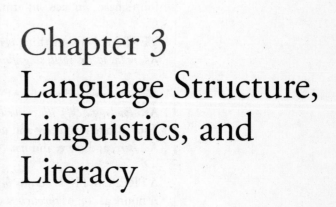

Chapter 3
Language Structure, Linguistics, and Literacy

FIRST, A REFRESHER…

A NOUN's the name of any thing;
As, *school* or *garden*, *hoop* or *swing*.

ADJECTIVES tell the *kind* of noun;
As, *great*, *small*, *pretty*, *white*, or *brown*.
Three of these words we often see
Called ARTICLES—*a*, *an*, and *the*.

Instead of nouns the PRONOUNS stand;
John's head, *his* face, *my* arm, *your* hand.

VERBS tell of something *being done*;
As, *read*, *write*, *spell*, *sing*, *jump*, or *run*.

How things are done the ADVERBS tell;
As, *slowly*, *quickly*, *ill*, or *well*.
They also tell us *where* and *when*;
As, *here*, and *there*, and *now*, and *then*.

A PREPOSITION stands *before*
A noun; as, *in*, or *through*, a door.

CONJUNCTIONS sentences unite;
As, kittens scratch *and* puppies bite.

The INTERJECTION shows surprise;
As, *O*, how pretty! *Ah*, how wise!

From *First lessons in language, or, Elements of English grammar*, by David B. Tower and Benjamin F. Tweed, 1853.

NOW, THE BASICS

The poem above illustrates an important point: English grammar hasn't changed much since the nineteenth century. If you remember anything you learned in your elementary school English classes, you're off to a good start!

So let's begin by brushing up on the two main components of language structure, syntax and semantics, and soldier on from there.

SYNTAX

Syntax is the structure of language: how phrases, sentences, and paragraphs are put together. It's a perfect example of one of those things you know how to *do*, but not how to *explain*. You can probably drive a car without thinking actively about what you're doing, but if someone asked you to explain how the engine worked, could you easily launch into an explanation of alternators, fuel injection, and combustion chambers? By the same token, you may be able to write gorgeous, well-constructed sentences, but could you immediately identify the use of a non-defining relative clause?

The odds of the test asking something that specific, thankfully, are slim to none. Most likely, all you'll need to review are some general terms and concepts.

Parts of a Sentence

Sentence

A **sentence** consists of one or more clauses.

- In 1865, Abraham Lincoln was assassinated.
- Leave the dishes there; I'll clean up later.

Clause

A **clause** is part of a sentence, and must include at least a subject and a predicate.

- They left.
- Aunt Elaine bought Katie a Tonka truck.

Independent Clause

An **independent clause,** or main clause, can stand on its own.

- We'll see you later.
- The painting will be moved to a different museum.

Subordinate Clause

A **subordinate clause,** also known as a relative clause or a dependent clause, cannot stand on its own.

- which proved the defendant's guilt
- because she never showed up

Phrase

A **phrase** is a group of words that form a concept, but cannot stand alone as a sentence.

- out of nowhere
- her blue dress

Grammar Review
Check out The Princeton Review's *Grammar Smart* for additional grammar review.

Subject

A **subject** is a word or group of words defining who or what performs an action or is in a particular state of being.

- *The boy* jumped from the tree.
- *Winning the lottery* did not change their lifestyle.

Predicate

A **predicate** is a verb or verb phrase expressing an action performed or a state of being.

- The cat *meowed*.
- That *was* the last time anyone saw him alive.

Categories of Sentences

Declarative

A **declarative sentence** is the most common type of sentence, and it's named aptly. A declarative sentence states something, generally a fact, an opinion, or an arrangement of some kind. It ends with a period (.).

- I prefer vanilla over chocolate.
- The Boston Americans won the first World Series in 1903.
- The dog needs to go out.

Imperative

An **imperative sentence** is a command or request that ends with a period (.) or an exclamation point (!). This is the hardest type for students to deal with when they learn how to identify the subjects of sentences, because there is actually no subject in an imperative sentence. The subject is actually *you*, but it's not written or spoken; it's implied. *(You) Forget it!*

- Answer the phone.
- Please have the report done by Friday.
- Get in here now!

Interrogative

An **interrogative sentence** asks a question. The auxiliary, or helping, verb or verb phrase comes first, then the subject, followed by the main verb or verb phrase. Naturally, the interrogative form ends with a question mark (?).

- When does his flight arrive?
- How did you like the show?
- Will the author sign copies of her book after the reading?

Exclamatory

An **exclamatory sentence** emphasizes a declarative or imperative statement by using an exclamation point (!).

- I won the contest!
- Look out for that car!
- You're fired!

Types of Sentences

Simple

A **simple sentence** consists of one independent clause. Don't be deceived, though, into thinking that "simple" means that the sentence must be short. An independent clause can have a compound subject or verb, and it can include adjectives and adverbs. The only requirement is that it have no dependent clauses, or other independent clauses joined with a conjunction.

- I went to bed early.
- Heath Ledger, Christian Bale, and Michael Caine all starred in *The Dark Knight*.
- Ron's younger sister and her new boyfriend did their best to be on time for Ron's joint birthday and retirement party.

Compound

A **compound sentence** consists of two or more independent clauses. Just think of taking two or more complete sentences and attaching them together. One way to do that is by using a semicolon (;). The other option is to use a **coordinating conjunction,** the list of which has come to be known as the **fanboys.**

The fanboys: *for, and, nor, but, or, yet, so*.

- The sun is out, yet it's cold.
- Shelbie's boss was away on business Monday, so she spent the day playing solitaire on the computer.
- I don't understand why he's so angry; all I said was that his story was simplistic and trite.

Complex

A **complex sentence** contains one independent, or main, clause, and one or more dependent clauses. To link the dependent clauses to the main clause, use a **subordinating conjunction**. There is a long list of subordinating conjunctions. Some of the more common are *after, until, because, although, since,* and *while*.

- We won't know how Dad is doing until the doctor comes out.
- Even though she cheated on the exam, Sara was not expelled from school.
- I didn't think it was necessary to ask your permission because I knew you'd say yes.

Compound-Complex

Finally, a **compound-complex sentence** consists of at least two independent clauses and at least one dependent clause. To break it down, just start with the compound sentence rule. Take two independent clauses (or two simple sentences) and connect them. Then add a dependent clause to one of the independent clauses, and you've created a compound-complex sentence.

- Since my sister returned from her trip, I've been trying to plan a night out with her, but she's always too busy to return my calls.
- Gary's car emits horrible smoky exhaust; we had to fall far behind to avoid it while we were following him to the restaurant.

Other Conventions

The rest of the "mechanics" of language include **spelling**, **capitalization**, and **punctuation**. Because questions about these will probably be few, there's no need to go into too much detail, so we'll just review a few basic rules. (By the way, that was a compound-complex sentence.)

Spelling

There's an old saying: "German is a language of rules; English is a language of exceptions." Anyone who's suffered through elementary school spelling lessons can attest to that. Luckily, only a tiny percentage of all the words in the English language are used on the exam, and it's unlikely that you'll be asked a standard spelling question. Even if that does happen, as long as you read regularly—novels, newspapers—you should be able to handle any words you encounter.

Capitalization

Keep in mind the basic rules of capitalization. This is obviously not a complete list, but the questions on the test won't be obscure.

- the first word of a sentence
- names and initials of people
- titles preceding names, such as *Mr., Dr., Rev.*
- days of the week, months of the year, holidays
- continents, countries, states, cities, provinces
- the pronoun *I*
- names of languages, nationalities

Punctuation

Once again, there's no reason to go into minute detail—we're not going to bother with the uses of the period and question mark, for instance—but certain concepts and rules bear revisiting.

There are a number of different uses for **commas.**

- to separate a list of items
- to separate phrases and clauses
- to separate independent clauses that are connected by one of the fanboys
- to introduce a direct quote
- to end a direct quote within a framing sentence

Semicolons are often used incorrectly. There are really only two proper uses (other than a couple of obscure optional ones).

- to separate two equally weighted independent clauses, in place of a period *or* a comma and one of the fanboys
- to separate groups of words that are internally separated by commas

There are also two uses for **colons.**

- to set off a list of words or phrases, used for additional explanation, generally after an independent clause
- to introduce a direct quote, although commas are more commonly used

Dashes are used occasionally in place of commas, usually when more emphasis is desired.

Parentheses are used to add information that is related to the sentence but is non-essential to understanding.

Apostrophes can be used in two ways.

- in a contraction, such as *I'm,* to indicate that one or more letters have been omitted from a word
- to show possession, generally before the "s" for singular nouns and after the "s" for plural nouns

So how might the CSET test you on your knowledge of syntax? Let's look at an example.

———————◯———————

Identify the subject in the following sentence:

> Much to the fans' delight, the band's
> new drummer turned out to be far better
> than the previous one.
>
> A.   the fans' delight
>
> B.   the band's new drummer
>
> C.   far better
>
> D.   the previous one

Here's How to Crack It

Rule number one: Don't fall into the "noun trap." Elementary school students begin learning about subjects by identifying nouns, but by now, you should know that nouns can appear anywhere in sentences: in dependent clauses, in prepositional phrases, even in verb phrases. By the same token, you know not to assume that the subject always comes at the beginning of the sentence. Step back, look at the sentence as a whole, and ask yourself, "What is it about?" It's really about the new drummer, so the answer is choice B.

———————◯———————

SEMANTICS

Semantics is commonly used in everyday English to refer to an issue based on words rather than issues. "Your Honor, I didn't *steal* the car; I *borrowed* it. Really, we're just arguing semantics here." Syntax is structure; semantics is meaning. Hold on—don't bother breaking out those vocabulary flashcards. The CSET won't test you on your memorization skills, but on your understanding of how meaning is constructed, and how words relate to each other.

Etymology

Etymology is the study of word origin. If you've ever watched a spelling bee, you know that one of the questions students are allowed to ask is "What is the language of origin?" There's a reason for that, and it's not just to stall for time. Often, English words (or words that have been adopted into the English language) that originate from the same foreign or ancient language have similar construction.

For example, the words *mezzanine*, *pizza* and *paparazzi* all come from the Italian language. One similarity is obvious—the use of the double "z"—but say the words aloud slowly and listen to the vowel sounds. Each "a" sounds like the others, as does each "i." Knowing that the word *mezzanine* is of Italian origin would help a student spell it correctly, as opposed to something like "mezaneen."

However, we also need to look at it the opposite way. Sometimes, the spelling of a word may help determine its origin, and that in turn can lead to an understanding of its meaning. If we know that words which end in "-eur," such as *masseur* and *chauffeur*, are often derivations from the French describing a person with a particular job, when we see a word such as *restaurateur*, the connection of the word ending gives us a clue as to its meaning. We recognize the first part of the word, and the suffix "-eur" helps us put it together: A *restaurateur* is a person who owns a restaurant.

Denotation and Connotation

Denotation refers to the literal definition of a word, while **connotation** refers to an implicit meaning. In other words, the denotative meaning of a word is found in the dictionary. The connotative meaning of a word is a "shade of meaning," used to elicit some kind of emotional response.

- They found a *shady* corner of the park for their picnic.

Here, the word *shady*, in its most literal definition, describes an area that is blocked from direct light. But consider another example.

- No one really liked Bud; there was something *shady* about him.

Does no one like him because he blocks sunlight? Probably not. In this case, it is a connotative meaning of the word *shady*. There is a feeling associated with the word: one of concealment, of dishonesty.

Let's take it one step further. Understanding connotation doesn't just mean determining how a word is used in a sentence. It also means choosing words deliberately in order to evoke a particular emotion. Think about how the sentence changes when we exchange *shady* for similar words.

- No one really liked Bud; there was something *disgraceful* about him.
- No one really liked Bud; there was something *untrustworthy* about him.
- No one really liked Bud; there was something *ignominious* about him.

All three of those words are synonyms for *shady*, yet each one slightly changes the implicit meaning of the sentence.

Here's an example of a CSET question about denotation and connotation.

Which of the following sentences uses a denotative meaning of the underlined word?

A. "Don't give me any of your <u>lip</u>," my mother warned.

B. His teacher secretly felt that he was a little <u>thick</u>.

C. The <u>plot</u> of the story had some major holes in it.

D. After much deliberation, the committee decided to <u>shelve</u> the idea.

Here's How to Crack It

This is a tough type of question because there are so many dictionary-listed meanings for words. However, just because it's in the dictionary doesn't mean it's a literal meaning. The dictionary lists figurative meanings as well. What you want to do here is think as literally as possible, and use POE to eliminate incorrect answers. Picture what's going on. For instance, in choice A, you know that the mother does not think the child is actually going to hand her a lip, right? Choice D may be tricky because "shelving" is a term widely used in this manner, but again, picture it. An *idea* is an abstract concept: Can it actually be placed on a shelf? The best answer here is choice C, because it is a literal meaning of the word "plot."

Context

Looking at words in context is another way to determine a word's meaning. Initially, context is helpful when you're faced with a word that has more than one definition. Children are taught to look at the whole sentence in order to figure out which meaning of the word is used.

- We saw a black *bear* near our campsite. (animal)
- I can't *bear* to see you unhappy. (suffer)

- The tree will *bear* sweet apples once it's grown. (produce)
- *Bear* left at the intersection. (turn)

By upper elementary school, students are also taught to use **context clues** when they run into unfamiliar vocabulary words in their reading. It's an alternative to flipping back and forth between a book and a dictionary. And it makes sense. Imagine a student reading a short story for homework and coming to a word she doesn't recognize. She stops, sets aside the story, opens the dictionary, looks up the word, tries to understand the definition, which often includes more difficult words than the original word and necessitates looking up those words. By the time the poor girl gets back to the reading, she has completely forgotten what the story is about.

Using context clues, on the other hand, keeps the student actively involved in the reading. When she comes to an unfamiliar word, she examines the surrounding text to see if she can determine its meaning based on how it is used in the sentence or paragraph.

Let's look at an example:

- Due to his *opprobrious* conduct at the homecoming game, Rob was benched for the remainder of the season.

Before you balk at the word, think about it for a moment. What clues can you use to determine what it means? Well, there's *conduct*, which (let's assume) you know means *behavior*. That's a start. Next, there is a negative consequence to his behavior. Not only that, but it's a severe consequence—being benched for a game or two is one thing, but missing the rest of the season is extreme. Finally, pretend there's a blank space in place of *opprobrious*, and based on what you've inferred, insert your own word or phrase.

- Due to his *really bad* conduct at the homecoming game, Rob was benched for the remainder of the season.

Then just assume you're right, and move on. Unless you continue reading and realize that your understanding of the word was completely erroneous ("And so, Rob was awarded the school's highest honor for his brave conduct in breaking up that huge brawl—and both legs in the process"), attaching your own meaning to the word made the reading more accessible to you in the moment, and that's what matters. Later, you can look up *opprobrious* and see that it means "outrageously disgraceful or shameful." In other words, "really bad."

You might see a CSET question like this.

Read the sentence below; then choose the best possible definition of the underlined nonsense word.

> Some of Jackie's friends decided to major in <u>schumpology</u>, but due to her phobia, she chose instead to major in a field that wouldn't require her to handle glass.
>
> A. the study of jeans
>
> B. the study of tire tread
>
> C. the study of carpet
>
> D. the study of picture frames

Here's How to Crack It

The test will sometimes use nonsense words in order to make you think about *how* to determine the correct answer, as opposed to just *knowing* the correct answer. This is a context question: They're asking you to look at the sentence as a whole in order to figure out what the nonsense word might mean. There are several context clues here. We see the word *but*, which indicates that she did *not* choose this major. Always keep your eyes peeled for words like "but," which indicate a change in direction. So we find out that Jackie has a phobia, or fear, of glass, which is *why* she does not want to study this subject. Based on these clues, we look at the answers and see that the study of picture frames is the one that would most likely require the handling of glass, so the answer is choice D.

BEYOND THE BASICS

The CSET is also going to test you on other fundamental components of linguistics. These are concepts you may be less familiar with.

Pragmatics

Pragmatics is the study of social language: how people communicate with each other. When a four-year-old child pipes up in a supermarket, "Daddy, that lady is so *old*!" and over the father's stammering apologies, the woman smiles and says, "It's all right; he doesn't know any better," she's right. It's because the child's pragmatic skills aren't developed. Pragmatics covers all aspects of social communication, including these concepts.

- Appropriate use of language for a given situation. This is usually the first aspect to develop—knowing when and how to greet someone, to ask a question, to provide information.
- Varying use of language depending on the situation or the listener. When a child is sitting in his living room watching TV with his parents, and needs to use the bathroom, for him to say, "Be back in a minute," would be fine. But if he's in class and needs to go, he wouldn't say that to the teacher; he'd ask permission.
- Understanding and using verbal and nonverbal signals, such as body language, facial expressions, volume, tone.

Phonology

Phonology is the study of sounds and speech patterns: the distinctions between consonant and vowel sounds, and how they are combined to form words. **Phonological development** is the gradual process in which children develop adult speech patterns. In a child's early speech, the way a word sounds in his brain isn't usually what comes out of his mouth. That's why you'll hear small children say *tar* for *car*, *hagger* for *hamburger*, or *babing suit* for *bathing suit*. These deviations from adult speech are called **phonological processes**.

Phonemes

Phonemes are the smallest units of sound that convey meaning. When you divide words into individual phonemes, use slashes to identify them. Many of them are single letters.

- man   /m/ /a/ /n/
- zip   /z/ /i/ /p/
- get   /g/ /e/ /t/

Some phonemes are letter combinations.

- lash   /l/ /a/ /sh/
- thin   /th/ /i/ /n/
- chop   /ch/ /o/ /p/

You can figure out how to determine whether a pair of letters should be separated into two phonemes or kept as one by sounding the word out by each letter.

- jump   /j/ /u/ /m/ /p/
- play   /p/ /l/ /a/ /y/
- this   /th/ /i/ /s/
- ring   /r/ /i/ /ng/
- lick   /l/ /i/ /ck/

In the first two words, the letter sounds don't change when you say them separately. But read *this* aloud one letter at a time—/t/ /h/ /i/ /s/—and it changes the sound of the word. The same for *ring*. If you separate the last two letters, it might sound more like the "ng" in the word *engine*. And in the last word, the letters "ck" create one sound, "k," which is how the phoneme is identified.

Phonemic Awareness

Phonemic awareness is the understanding that words can be divided into phonemes, and conversely, that phonemes can be blended together to form words. Phonemic awareness is widely considered to be crucial in early reading development. Kindergarten and first-grade teachers use activities like rhyming, clapping out syllables, and filling in missing letters in their instruction.

Morphology

Morphology is the study of units of meaning in language.

Morphemes are the smallest units of meaning in words. It's probably easiest to remember what you learned in school about word construction: root words, prefixes, suffixes, plurals, verb tense. Dividing a word into morphemes means dividing it up into its most basic parts.

One-morpheme words can have one or more syllables, but cannot be broken down into any smaller units of meaning.

- shirt
- love
- giraffe

Other words can be broken down into two or more morphemes.

- hats: hat + s (2)
- unbreakable: un + break + able (3)
- systematically: system + atic + al + ly (4)

The Alphabetic Principle

The **alphabetic principle**, finally, goes back to the very beginning. It refers to the basic understanding of letter-sound awareness, which is the first step in learning to read. Most of it can be figured out with common sense, but you may run into a few particular terms.

- **Alphabetic understanding** is the understanding that in printed words, the letters, representing phonemes, are read left to right.
- A **grapheme** is the term for each of the individual letters and letter combinations that represent the same phoneme. For example, the phoneme /f/ can be represented by more than just the letter "f," as in *fly*; it can also be represented by "ph" as in *phone* and "gh" as in *cough*.
- **Orthography** is the system of using symbols to represent sounds—in English, it is an alphabetic spelling system.

SECOND LANGUAGE ACQUISITION

Most of what we've already covered applies to learners of English both as a first and second language, but there are theories and concepts specifically related to English Language Learners (now referred to in education as ELL, not ESL) that you need to know. This should be basic review for anyone who's been through a teacher credentialing program in California.

Stages of Second Language Acquisition

There are five generally accepted stages of **second language acquisition.**

Preproduction

The **preproduction** stage is also known as the silent period. During this state, students observe, listen, absorb, and develop an understanding of up to 500 words, but may not speak for several months, or may communicate only with gestures and a few basic words.

Early Production

Early production occurs when students understand and can use approximately 1,000 words. They speak in one- to two-word phrases and can demonstrate understanding by answering simple (yes/no, either/or) questions. This stage can last up to six months after preproduction.

Speech Emergence

The **speech emergence** stage can last up to another year; by now, students have usually developed about 3,000 words and are beginning to speak in short sentences, ask simple questions, and engage in basic conversation.

Intermediate Language Proficiency

Intermediate language proficiency is also known as intermediate fluency. At this stage, students have a vocabulary of about 6,000 words. They understand more complex concepts and use longer and more detailed sentences when speaking and writing, though their English is punctuated by frequent grammatical errors. This stage may take up to a year.

Advanced Language Proficiency

Advanced language proficiency is also known as advanced fluency. It takes several years for students to reach this stage, but by this point, their English is comparable to their grade-level native English-speaking peers.

Krashen's Hypotheses

If you are interested in working with English language learners, check out our book *Cracking the TOEFL*.

Researcher and linguist **Dr. Stephen Krashen** is known for his second language acquisition theory, which is broken down into five hypotheses.

The Acquisition-Learning Distinction

In Krashen's acquisition-learning distinction he delineates between the **acquisition** of language and the **learning** of language: Acquisition occurs naturally and subconsciously, while learning is conscious and formal. According to Krashen, acquisition is more important than learning.

The Natural Order Hypothesis

Krashen's **natural order hypothesis** is his belief that the acquisition of grammatical structures in a given language tends to follow a particular order. He does not, though, believe that this should be a basis for the order of teaching grammar.

The Monitor Hypothesis

Aptly named, a **monitor** is a learner's internal editor—when a learner has enough time to edit, is focused on form, and knows the rule, the monitor edits the output. Krashen makes three distinctions:

- **Monitor over-users** try to always use their monitors, and end up so worried about correctness that they prevent fluency.
- **Monitor under-users** either have not consciously learned or choose not to use their conscious knowledge of the language.
- **Optimal monitor** users use the monitor when it is appropriate and does not interfere with communication.

The Input Hypothesis

The **input hypothesis** is the idea that a language acquirer develops competency over time by gradually receiving input one level higher than the learner's current level of competence. If a learner is said to be at level "i," acquisition occurs when he or she receives second language input at "i + 1."

The Affective Filter Hypothesis

Finally, Krashen believes that there are outside **affective** variables that play a role in second language acquisition, such as motivation and self-esteem (which should be high) and anxiety (which should be low). The affective filter can be likened to a brick wall: The higher the filter, the less acquisition will take place.

BICS and CALP

One last theory we'll mention is **Dr. Jim Cummins's** distinction between two types of language.

BICS

BICS stands for **Basic Interpersonal Communications Skills.** This generally refers to social or "playground" language, or low-risk academic language (simple yes/no questions, for example). Learners are socially surrounded and immersed in the second language, which makes it soak in faster—like holding a sponge under water—and they develop conversational fluency long before they develop academic fluency.

CALP

CALP stands for **Cognitive Academic Language Proficiency,** or academic fluency. If BICS is a small "social" sponge immersed in water, CALP is a giant "academic" sponge held under a trickling faucet. It takes several years for learners to acquire the technical and academic language needed to achieve academic proficiency.

KEY TERMS

syntax
sentence
clause
independent clause
subordinate clause
relative clause
dependent clause
phrase
subject
predicate
declarative sentence
imperative sentence
interrogative sentence
exclamatory sentence
simple sentence
compound sentence
coordinating conjunction
fanboys
complex sentence
subordinating conjunction
compound-complex sentence
spelling
capitalization
punctuation
commas
semicolons
colons
dashes
parentheses
apostrophes
semantics
etymology
denotation
connotation

context clues
pragmatics
phonology
phonological development
phonological processes
phonemes
phonemic awareness
morphology
morphemes
alphabetic principle
alphabetic understanding
grapheme
orthography
second language acquisition
preproduction
early production
speech emergence
intermediate language proficiency
  (intermediate fluency)
advanced language proficiency
  (advanced fluency)
Dr. Stephen Krashen
acquisition-learning distinction
natural order hypothesis
monitor
monitor over-users
monitor under-users
optimal monitor users
input hypothesis
affective filter
Dr. Jim Cummins
BICS
CALP

Drill #1

1. What is generally considered a major flaw of the alphabetic principle?

   A. Children whose native written language is not based on letters (that is, Russian, Chinese) are at a disadvantage.

   B. Some children learn the alphabet earlier than others.

   C. Many letters and letter combinations have multiple sounds.

   D. It doesn't take into account the meanings of words.

2. Which of the following words contains exactly two morphemes?

   A. plant

   B. ankle

   C. speakers

   D. loaded

3. In which word can you separate the consonant blend into two phonemes?

   A. lau<u>gh</u>

   B. <u>fl</u>ow

   C. <u>ph</u>one

   D. fea<u>th</u>er

4. In which of the following sentences is the underlined word used correctly?

   A. He left her at the <u>alter</u>.

   B. Make sure you don't <u>altar</u> the meaning of the sentence.

   C. Traffic was diverted around the <u>site</u> of the accident.

   D. The building <u>cite</u> was purchased by Donald Trump.

5. Which of the following is a complex sentence?

   A. Jill played the game of her life, but the team still lost the championship.

   B. You can go out tonight as long as you're home by ten.

   C. Why is Alaska not part of Canada?

   D. I'd hate to lose my scholarship; I'll do anything to raise my grade so that I can stay in school.

ANSWERS AND EXPLANATIONS TO DRILL #1

1. **C** Critics argue that the alphabetic principle is flawed because it is based on the concept that each letter has a corresponding sound, but in English, so many letters and letter combinations have more than one possible sound that children can't count on any kind of consistency.

2. **D** load + ed. Were you fooled by "speakers"? It actually has two suffixes: speak + er + s.

3. **B** /f/ /l/. The consonant sounds don't change when you put the letters together.

4. **C** *Alter* and *altar* are reversed, and *cite* means *quote* or *mention*.

5. **B** The first part of the sentence is an independent clause, and *as long as* is a subordinating conjunction which attaches the dependent clause.

Summary

o   Syntax is the study of structure and form, while semantics is the study of meaning.

o   Pragmatics is the study of social language.

o   Phonology is the study of sound and speech patterns: how letter sounds are combined to form words.

o   Morphology is the study of units of meaning: how words are constructed.

o   There are five stages of second language acquisition.

o   Theories by researchers such as Dr. Stephen Krashen and Dr. Jim Cummins help us to understand how second language development occurs.

Chapter 4
Written and
Non-written
Communication

HIGH STANDARDS

Below is an excerpt from the content standards for English Language Arts, adopted by the California State Board of Education.

1.0 Writing Strategies

Students write clear and coherent sentences and paragraphs that develop a central idea. Their writing shows they consider the audience and purpose. Students progress through the stages of the writing process (e.g., prewriting, drafting, revising, editing successive versions).

Organization and Focus

1.1   Select a focus when writing.

1.2   Use descriptive words when writing.

2.0 Writing Applications
(Genres and Their Characteristics)

Students write compositions that describe and explain familiar objects, events, and experiences. Student writing demonstrates a command of standard American English and the drafting, research, and organizational strategies outlined in Writing Standard 1.0.

Using the writing strategies of grade one outlined in Writing Standard 1.0, students:

2.1   Write brief narratives (e.g., fictional, autobiographical) describing an experience.

2.2   Write brief expository descriptions of a real object, person, place, or event, using sensory details.

THE TIP OF THE ICEBERG

Do you think trying to teach students how to write good sentences is going to be hard? Multiply that by 25, or 50, or 100, and welcome to the world of essays, oral presentations, and research reports! The CSET will test you on your preparedness to teach students how to communicate effectively on and off the page.

Oh, and lest you think that you'll escape the need for such depth of instruction if you plan to teach younger students, take a closer look at the guidelines above: They are excerpted from the content standards for *first grade*.

THE WRITING PROCESS

The writing process is not as simple as assigning an essay and collecting it on the due date. Students need to be taught how to write, and that's your job. You'll use a five-step process to help them learn.

You'll use a five-step process to help them learn: pre-writing, drafting, revising, editing, and publishing.

A sixth step, *evaluating*, is sometimes added.

Pre-writing

Pre-writing is what we used to call brainstorming. In addition to the old standard strategies of note-taking and outlining, teachers now employ a wide variety of techniques to guide students in gathering and developing ideas. **Graphic organizers,** or visual representations of ideas, are very effective. The type of graphic organizer depends on the purpose of the writing. Some examples of pre-writing activities are listed below.

- KWL refers to these questions: *What do we **know**? What do we **want** to know? What have we **learned**?* It is represented by a table with three columns. The first two sections of the chart—answering the first two questions—are filled in as a pre-writing activity, while the last section is completed later.
- A **Venn diagram** is a construction of overlapping circles, used in comparing and contrasting. For students in the lower grades, a two-circle (two-item) diagram is usually used, and it is sometimes extended to a three-circle diagram in the upper grades.
- **Webbing** is very popular in pre-writing. There are many different configurations that teachers and students may use, but the general purpose is to connect and categorize ideas.
- **SQ3R** is a systematic strategy for reading. The acronym stands for the five steps in the process: Survey (or Skim), Question, Read, Recall (or Recite), and Review.

Here's a web that a student might use to collect information about a character.

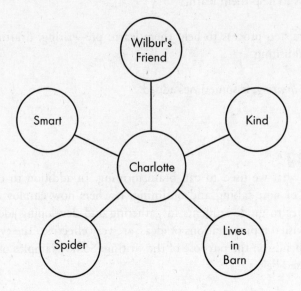

Drafting

Drafting is the step in which students write first drafts. At this point, they just need to focus on getting their ideas down, without worrying about proper essay format or mechanical details.

Revising

Don't get **revising** confused with **editing**, which we'll talk about next. Revising is all about concepts and ideas. Students sometimes have to do two or three revisions, and often at least one of these revisions is done in **peer groups** or **workshops.** These are the types of things to look for in revising:

- thesis strength
- organization/flow
- topic sentences
- supporting sentences/evidence
- transitions between paragraphs
- introduction/conclusion

Editing

Once a student has a well-revised draft, it's time to fix the errors, or start **editing**. As with revising, editing is sometimes done with classmates' help. The following items should be checked and fixed:

- spelling
- capitalization
- punctuation
- sentence structure
- grammar
- subject/verb agreement
- word choice

Publishing

How **publishing** is handled is really up to the teacher. Some simply have students hand in their papers. Others have students make books out of their papers, with covers and illustrations. Some may "publish" student work on a teacher web page. The point of this step is to give the students a sense of completion and pride in their work.

CSET questions about the writing process often come in the form of a paragraph, with one or more questions about the way it is written. That can mean anything from identifying mechanical errors to reorganizing the paragraph to make it flow better. Here's an example.

Read the following draft of an introduction by a fifth grader; then answer the two questions that follow.

¹I've loved hockey for as long as I can remember. ²However, I'm not sure exactly how I turned out to be a hockey fan. ³My father was always a big football fan, my mom loves baseball. ⁴And my brothers and sisters don't like hockey, either.

1. Which sentence has a punctuation error?

    A. Sentence 1

    B. Sentence 2

    C. Sentence 3

    D. Sentence 4

2. Based on what this student has written so far, which of the following sentences would be the best thesis statement?

   A. My favorite team is the Detroit Red Wings.

   B. For many reasons, I think hockey is the best sport there is.

   C. A lot of my friends love hockey as much as I do.

   D. I hope to become a professional hockey player someday.

Here's How to Crack It

The first question is a simple editing question, and it's asking you strictly for punctuation, so focus on that instead of any other issues you see with the sentences. As is, the only sentence with a punctuation error is choice C, sentence 3, which has a **comma splice**—a comma separating two independent clauses without one of the fanboys. The second question seems more subjective, but remember that a correct answer is somewhere in there—it's not just about your opinion. Look at it with a "teacher's eye." A thesis statement lays out the purpose of the paper, and therefore, needs to leave the door open for some substantial material. All of these sentences are logical and grammatically correct, but choice B would be the best thesis because it allows the student to present several solid ideas.

NON-WRITTEN COMMUNICATION

Non-written communication is an important concept. It would make for a pretty boring school year—for students and teachers alike—if every assignment were a written one, not to mention the fact that we wouldn't be doing a very good job of preparing students for real life. Students need the experience of presenting information orally, and teachers can find ways to do that in every grade level. (Remember Show and Tell?)

Oral Presentations

There are many types of **oral presentations** that teachers assign their students, although some are more common than others.

Recitation

Recitation is memorizing a piece of writing and repeating it out loud in front of the teacher and, generally, the class, although some teachers allow students to make recitations privately, for various reasons. Often, a recital is comprised of multiple poem recitations.

Narrative Presentation

A **narrative presentation** is basically an oral presentation of a story. Criteria may include the following:

- sequence of events
- sensory details
- story elements (plot, setting, characters, and so on)

Persuasive Speech

Yes, we start them young! **Persuasive speech** is taught even in the early grades, when students learn to give short persuasive presentations. The prompts are generally simple at first: "Should we be allowed to bring pets to school?" Later, the prompts become more sophisticated: "How can we protect our environment?" No matter what the level, persuasive pieces should include the following basics:

- a clear statement of the speaker's position
- supporting evidence: data, statistics, quotes
- prior knowledge

Response to Literature

A **response to literature** is a very subjective term: It can be just about anything that the teacher or student comes up with as a way to interpret, analyze, or connect to the reading. Responses can include the following:

- monologue/soliloquy
- character analysis
- historical context
- letter
- poem
- song
- summary

Research Report

There's a lot more to a **research report** than just the culminating oral presentations, and we'll get to them in more detail later in this chapter.

Presentation Components

Presentation components include a number of different variables. Obviously, there's more to analyzing and evaluating an oral presentation than grading the information given; if that were the case, you may as well have the students just hand in the written portion. You need to consider other factors, such as the following:

- volume
- pace
- tone
- eye contact
- posture
- gestures
- facial expression
- pronunciation fluency

Make sure that you take into account any factors that may deviate from standard oral English: students who are English language learners, students with differing dialects, students who have hearing or speech problems, and the like.

This is how the CSET might pose a question in that vein.

Mrs. Hasner is evaluating oral presentations in her third-grade class. One of the students, E. J., gave an excellent speech in many respects, but stared at the floor throughout his presentation. What is one possible explanation that, if true, should negate Mrs. Hasner's inclination to mark E. J. down for this component of his speech?

A. E. J. is from a culture in which looking someone in the eye is considered rude.

B. E. J. was nervous in front of the class.

C. E. J. did not have time to rehearse his presentation.

D. E. J. forgot that eye contact was a component that would be graded.

Here's How to Crack It

This is first and foremost a cultural sensitivity question. Watch closely for these! Once you recognize it, the answer, choice A, is obvious. The other three answers may all be true, but they are things that E. J. can be held accountable for within the parameters of the assignment.

RESEARCH STRATEGIES

Let's come back to **research strategies** and look at these in more detail. There are a lot of special considerations when it comes to guiding students in research, so it's important for teachers to be thorough and clear.

Preparation

Preparation is an important tool the students learn gradually, with help from you. Whether the research is for a written or an oral report, students need to be given detailed instructions. It's helpful to provide a series of steps, which can be adjusted by grade level or topic.

Determine the Topic

For the lower grades, a teacher may want to assign a very narrow topic, such as a particular historical figure, animal, or invention. As students get older, the topics become broader and they have more freedom to choose their own directions.

Outline the Main Points

Not unlike a standard essay, a research report should have a clear focus. Again, in the lower grades, a teacher may give the students a few ideas to choose from, while in the upper grades, students are encouraged to determine their own main points.

Identify Resources

Helping the students identify and utilize good resources is the hardest, and most important, step in preparation for the assignment. Except perhaps for the earliest grades, students will be required to draw information from multiple sources. You should provide access to a variety of print materials in the classroom and the school library, and/or guide the students on how to find print resources outside of school. You should provide detailed and carefully constructed instruction on conducting Internet research. This may include limiting the research to Internet sites of your choosing or suggestion, or allowing the students to conduct Internet research only in the classroom or school computer lab.

Interpreting Research

Students need to learn how to interpret their research—that is, determine the validity of the information they collect. *You* know that just because some guy named Geo in Illinois writes a blog about movies, it doesn't necessarily mean he's presenting objective and accurate facts, but your students may not.

To help them evaluate how reliable the research is, teach them about primary and secondary sources.

Primary Sources

A **primary source** is original, firsthand information. Think "straight from the horse's mouth." The following items can be primary sources:

- letters
- speeches
- eyewitness accounts
- government records
- autobiographies
- photographs
- diaries

Secondary Sources

Secondary sources analyze and interpret primary sources. They are one or more steps removed from the primary source and can be the following:

- textbooks
- encyclopedias
- magazine articles
- biographies
- reviews

Citing Sources

Admit it: You just groaned, didn't you? **Citing sources** isn't fun for anyone, but it is necessary, and you'll appreciate it far more as a teacher than you ever did as a student. While formal bibliographies are generally not required until the upper elementary grades at the earliest, even the youngest students should understand the reasoning behind giving credit when using other people's ideas to support their arguments.

At some point in your career, there comes a time when you have to bite the bullet and have "the talk" with your students. It may be difficult and uncomfortable for you and for them, but it's for their own good, and who better to teach them than you? Yes, we're talking about **plagiarism**. Drill, drill, drill into them that plagiarism is the equivalent of stealing, with a healthy dose of cheating sprinkled on top. And be vigilant about checking their sources. *That's* why it's important for you to teach them proper citation methods, so that you can keep them honest.

In the upper elementary and middle school grades, students will begin to learn about two major formats for citations: **APA (American Psychological Association)** and **MLA (Modern Language Association)**. APA is generally used in psychology, education, and other social sciences. MLA is used in literature, arts, and humanities. A citation in either will contain the same basic information, but they differ slightly in the representation, as illustrated below in some of the more common sources your students may use.

Book by One Author

MLA: Author's Last Name, First Name. *Book Title.* Location of Publication: Publisher, Year of Publication.

APA: Author's Last Name, First Initial. (Year of Publication). *Book title.* Location of Publication: Publisher.

Encyclopedia Entry

MLA: "Entry Title." *Encyclopedia Title.* Edition (if stated). Year of Publication.

APA: Author's Last Name, First Initial. (Year of Publication). Entry title. In *Encyclopedia title* (Ed. #, Vol. #, pp. xxx–xxx). Location of Publication: Publisher.

Newspaper Article

MLA: Author's Last Name, First Name. "Article Title." *Newspaper Name* Date (day month year): Pages.

APA: Author's Last Name, First Initial. (year, month day of publication). Article title. *Newspaper Name,* pp. xxx–xxx.

[If a newspaper article or encyclopedia entry has no byline, place the title in the author position.]

Let's take a practice question.

MLA and APA handbooks would most likely agree with which of the following statements regarding proper citations?

A.   Information found on the Internet does not need to be cited.

B.   Direct quotations and paraphrases are the only types of information that should be cited.

C.   Parenthetical acknowledgements are not necessary if there is a complete list of works cited at the end of a research paper.

D.   It is not necessary to use *Anonymous* or *Anon* when a book has no author's name.

Here's How to Crack It

While you may not know each specific rule, you should be able to eliminate some of the answer choices by following the basic principles of citing sources. As a general rule, proper citations require you to account for all information that is borrowed—whether it is direct quotations or simply information and ideas. Though common knowledge statements are not necessary to cite, any specific information that furthers your ideas must be acknowledged. The first three answer choices all violate this premise. Choice A would be the most obvious; just ask Geo from Illinois when he finds out you quoted his *Superman* review without giving him credit. You may not be sure about choice B, but based on standard test-taking sense, you know that any answer with an absolute (here, "the only types") is usually a wrong answer. And if you think about choice C for a moment, you'll realize the major flaw: Yes, there may be a list of works cited, but if you use a quote without a parenthetical reference, how will the reader know which of the works on your list the quote comes from? Once you've eliminated those answers, you know the correct answer is choice D. To cement your confidence in the choice, ask yourself this: How often have you actually seen *Anonymous* or *Anon* in a book citation?

KEY TERMS

writing process
pre-writing
graphic organizers
KWL
Venn diagram
webbing
SQ3R
drafting
revising
editing
peer groups
workshops
editing
publishing
comma splice
non-written communication

oral presentations
recitation
narrative presentation
persuasive speech
response to literature
research report
presentation components
research strategies
preparation
primary source
secondary source
citing sources (citation)
plagiarism
APA
MLA

Drill #2

1. For which of the following essay prompts would a Venn diagram be most useful in pre-writing?

   A. Discuss the importance of setting in *The Cay*.

   B. Analyze the theme of social class in *The True Confessions of Charlotte Doyle*.

   C. Analyze the characters of Jesse and Leslie in *Bridge to Terabithia*.

   D. Discuss the theme of survival in *Island of the Blue Dolphins*.

2. Which would be the most appropriate persuasive speech topic for a second grader?

   A. "Why Bike Safety Is Important"

   B. "Our School Cafeteria"

   C. "How to Take Care of a Dog"

   D. "The Best Way to Study for a Test"

3. Which is a pair of primary sources?

   A. a photocopy of an original newspaper article within a textbook chapter

   B. the biography of a woman and her authentic birth certificate

   C. a video of a speech along with a review of the speech

   D. a letter with a photo enclosed

4. Renee is editing her essay and comes to the following sentence:

   In *Number the Stars*, either Uncle Henrik or Peter have to help Ellen and her family escape.

   What is the type of error in the sentence?

   A. Subject-verb agreement

   B. Punctuation

   C. Capitalization

   D. There is no error.

5. In Richard's essay, he quotes material from a book about legendary punk rockers, written by Todd Oliver and Kristin Pfeifer. It was published in 2002, in New York, by Random House. How would he cite the book in his bibliography using MLA style?

   A. Oliver, Todd & Pfeifer, Kristin (2002). *Punk Paragons*. New York: Random House.

   B. Oliver, T. & Pfeifer, K. (2002). Punk Paragons. New York: Random House.

   C. Oliver, Todd, and Kristin Pfeifer. *Punk Paragons*. New York: Random House, 2002.

   D. Oliver, Todd, and Pfeifer, Kristin. "Punk Paragons," 2002. New York: Random House.

Please turn the page for answers and explanations
for the questions in this drill.

ANSWERS AND EXPLANATIONS TO DRILL #2

1. **C**   A Venn diagram is used to compare and contrast two or more things: In this case, it would be reasonable to use it for the two main characters in the novel.

2. **A**   Again, this is one of those questions that seems subjective, but there are clear wrong answers. Choices B and C sound like informational reports, not persuasive pieces, and choice D just wouldn't be interesting to a second-grade student or her classmates. Choice A is the only option that is both accessible and relevant to the age group.

3. **D**   Choice D is the only pair in which both sources are primary.

4. **A**   In an "either . . . or" construction, when both parts of the subject are singular (Uncle Henrik/ Peter), the verb should be singular. You are assuming that only one or the other is performing the action. Either "Uncle Henrik *has* to help" or "Peter *has* to help."

5. **C**   If you happen to see a question like this on the test, *don't* throw your hands up and guess at random. You don't have to memorize every possible citation type. If you can remember a few basics, you can at least narrow the field. Remember that the title of a book is always italicized or underlined, which in this case immediately cuts your choices down to two. If you also remember that the date comes last in MLA format, you've nailed it.

Summary

o   There are five stages of the writing process: pre-writing, drafting, revising, editing, and publishing.

o   Students are asked to produce a number of different types of oral presentations, including recitations and persuasive speeches.

o   Teachers must guide student research carefully.

o   Knowing how to cite sources properly is vital, in order to properly give credit and to avoid plagiarism.

Chapter 5
Texts

ONCE UPON A TIME

> A young female, smaller than all of her peers, is nonetheless hardworking and trustworthy. One day, an emergency situation arises, and everyone who is bigger and stronger is asked for help. For various reasons—self-absorption, fear, apathy—they refuse, one by one. Finally, she is asked, and though reluctant and unsure of her abilities, she agrees to step up. To everyone's surprise, including her own, her courage and determination (along with an uplifting mantra) carry her through, and she succeeds in saving the day.

Does this story seem vaguely familiar? Or perhaps not so vague—it's the storyline of "The Little Engine That Could."

If you didn't know before that the little engine was female, you do now. You should also know that teachers can, and do, develop entire curriculum units around what seems to be the simplest of stories. The CSET will test you less on your general knowledge of children's literature than on your ability to look at the works you might use in your classroom from many different angles, from character analysis to themes to cultural implications. It's a lot to absorb, so as you study, just remember to stay positive: *I think I can, I think I can, I think I can.*

THE WORKS

No, you don't have to read every book, story, and poem ever written in order to get through the reading, language, and literature section of the CSET. You do, however, need to have some background knowledge of the concepts and conventions of children's literature.

Fiction Genres

The many options within the category of **fiction genres** are the most common types of novels and stories that children read.

Realistic Fiction

Realistic fiction is a broad designation referring to any story that *could* happen in real life. The characters are fictional, but the events in the story are based in the real world.

- *The Secret Garden*, Frances Hodgson Burnett
- *Ramona the Pest*, Beverly Cleary

Science Fiction and Fantasy

The terms **science fiction** and **fantasy** are sometimes used synonymously, but they aren't one and the same. **Science fiction** deals with current or futuristic science and technology, other life forms such as aliens, other planets or universes, and time travel; it refers to fiction that has more of a scientific basis, even if it's far-fetched. **Fantasy**, at the risk of being redundant, is more fantastical. It features witches, wizards, kings, queens, dragons, fairies, mermaids, talking animals, and the like.

- *A Wrinkle in Time*, Madeleine L'Engle (science fiction)
- *The Wizard of Oz*, L. Frank Baum (fantasy)

Fable

Fables are very short stories that teach a **moral** or **lesson**. The characters are usually animals, or sometimes plants or forces of nature, that are **anthropomorphized** (given human qualities).

- "The Tortoise and the Hare"
- "The Wolf in Sheep's Clothing"

Myth and Legend

Myths revolve around heroic, immortal, or extra-human characters. They take place either in other worlds or in other parts of the world, in the distant past, or both. **Legends** overlap with myths in some instances, but legends can also be based on historical figures or events.

- *Odysseus in the Serpent Maze*, Jane Yolen and Robert J. Harris (myth)
- *John Henry: An American Legend*, Ezra Jack Keats (legend)

Folktale

Folktales originated in the early stages of civilization and were passed along orally, which left room for a great deal of shifting and modification by the tellers. This is actually another broad designation, as there are many different categories within the genre. Some folktales are humorous; some have morals; they can be religious, or romantic, or magical. The name itself is the explanation of the genre's origins: Folktales were stories that sprung from folks' imaginations.

- "The People with Five Fingers: A Native Californian Creation Tale," John Bierhorst
- "Anansi the Spider: A Tale from the Ashanti," Gerald McDermott

Mystery

Mystery stories entail solving a puzzle. They usually involve some kind of crime, or **whodunit**, and a detective or sleuth, professional or amateur, who tries to solve it. There is often a cast of colorful characters who may or may not be suspects in the crime.

- *The Westing Game*, Ellen Raskin
- *From the Mixed-Up Files of Mrs. Basil E. Frankweiler*, E. L. Konigsburg

Historical Fiction

Most teachers take advantage of **historical fiction** as a valuable teaching tool. Historical events can be too distant or removed for children to really understand, and reading stories about people and children living through those events makes history more accessible to them.

- *Number the Stars*, Lois Lowry (the Holocaust)
- *Johnny Tremain*, Esther Forbes (the American Revolution)

STORY ELEMENTS

Students are taught to write and to analyze stories based on four major **story elements.**

- Plot
- Character
- Setting
- Theme

Freytag's Pyramid

When children are just beginning to grasp the concept of a story, they learn that all stories have a beginning, a middle, and an end. Later, they're able to dissect plots with more sophistication. One widely adopted system of analysis is **Freytag's Pyramid,** which divides a plot into five parts.

- **Exposition:** setting the stage
- **Rising action:** building the plot
- **Climax:** the turning point
- **Falling action:** the aftermath
- **Resolution:** the conclusion

Theme

The **theme** is the main idea of a work, sometimes called the author's purpose or the moral. Teachers often plan theme units, in which students study several different works with similar themes.

Themes are generally broad, but their treatment can run the gamut from simple to complex. For instance, in a kindergarten-level story, the theme *be yourself* might come in the form of a young girl who likes to wear clothes that are different from the clothes of all the other girls. In a sixth-grade novel, *be yourself* could be presented as the story of a boy who doesn't feel comfortable with his family's religion.

Religion and culture are often inherent in themes. In each of the *be yourself* stories, the theme would change significantly if one of those elements changed: if the protagonists were Caucasian or African American, Jewish or Buddhist.

Perspective

In later studies of literature, **perspective,** or point of view, can become much more complex, but for grade school students, a few suffice.

First Person

A **first-person narrative** is easily identified by the use of *I* and *me* in the narration. (Be sure to make the distinction between the narration and the dialogue: When people speak, they speak in first person.) The **narrator** is a person, animal, creature, or even an object, who tells the story through his or her own eyes and ears. The reader is limited, then, to knowing only what the narrator knows.

Third-Person Limited

In a **third-person limited narrative**, the story still follows one main character, but it is told more from the perspective of a close observer, as if the narrator were shadowing the main character. Instead of first-person pronouns, the narrator uses the character's name and the third-person pronouns *he* or *she, him* or *her* and the corresponding plurals. Again, though, because the narration is centered on one character, the reader still primarily sees and hears only what happens in that character's presence.

Third-Person Omniscient

If the third-person limited narrator is a shadow, the **third-person omniscient narrator** is a ghost, able to move from person to person, room to room, city to city. All of the characters are referred to by name and by third-person pronouns, but while there still may be one or a few main characters, the narrator can see them all—and show them to the reader—at any time.

Poetry

As with prose, the use of **poetry** in the classroom varies significantly based on age. In elementary and middle school, some types of poems are used more frequently than others.

- **Lyric poems** describe a speaker's thoughts or feelings.
- **Narrative poems** are long poems that tell stories.
- **Haiku** have a specific structure and capture a fleeting moment in nature.
- **Odes** celebrate or praise.
- **Elegies** mourn.
- **Ballads** are song-like narrative poems, often of folk origin.
- **Concrete poems** use words to form a shape representative of the poem's subject.

Here's an example of a concrete poem:

A flock
     of geese
        elegantly
          soars through
            the clouds
              as we tilt
                our faces
                  toward the
                    skies.
                 and sunny
              warmth
            them to
          drawing
        harmony,
      timed
     perfectly
   beat in
Their wings

Let's try a question.

Read the following passage from _Heidi,_ by Johanna Spyri, and answer the question that follows.

"Oho!" thought Sebastian, laughing to himself, "the little miss has evidently been up to more mischief." Then, drawing the boy inside he said aloud, "I understand now, come with me and wait outside the door till I tell you to go in. Be sure you begin playing your organ the instant you get inside the room; the lady is very fond of music."

Sebastian knocked at the study door, and a voice said, "Come in."

"There is a boy outside who says he must speak to Miss Clara herself," Sebastian announced.

Clara was delighted at such an extraordinary and unexpected message.

"Let him come in at once," replied Clara; "he must come in, must he not," she added, turning to her tutor, "if he wishes so particularly to see me?"

Whose perspective is this story told from?

A. First person: Clara

B. First person: Sebastian

C. Third-person limited

D. Third-person omniscient

Here's How to Crack It

In the passage, the characters are all referred to by name or by third-person pronouns, which means that you can quickly use POE (review that on page 11 if you need a refresher) to rule out choices A and B. Now, though, you have to pay attention to what else is going on in the passage. Initially, you might assume that the narration closely follows Sebastian, because you hear his thoughts in the first paragraph. But suddenly, in the fourth paragraph, the proverbial ghost passes through the wall. One minute, you're in the hallway with Sebastian, and in the next sentence you're in the room with Clara. And not only do you hear her speak, you are provided access to her thoughts as well (she is "delighted"). With close reading, you can determine that the answer is actually choice D, third-person omniscient.

LITERARY DEVICES

If all you remember about creative elements in literature and poetry is how to spell onomatopoeia, there are a few other things you should probably revisit. Basic elements like **rhyme** and **repetition** really bear no examples, but here are some others.

Simile

A **simile** is the comparison of two dissimilar things using *like* or *as*.

- David is as sharp as a tack.
- The calm water looks like glass.

Metaphor

A **metaphor** is also a comparison of two dissimilar things, though without the use of *like* or *as*.

- In a crisis, Taria is a rock.
- A blanket of snow covered the earth.

There are more complex forms, including **extended metaphor,** which uses a symbol to represent something else throughout a long passage or entire work. "O Captain! My Captain!" by Walt Whitman is a classic example: On the surface, the poem is about a captain who has successfully navigated his ship through a storm, but dies just before reaching port. However, the poem is actually an extended metaphor: The captain represents Abraham Lincoln, the ship is America, the storm is the Civil War, and his sudden death is…well, his sudden death.

Personification

Personification is the assigning of human qualities to non-humans: animals, plants, inanimate objects, and the like.

- The wind whispered in the night.
- Every time Sam dove into the pile, the leaves leaped and danced in the air.

Alliteration

Alliteration is the repetition of initial consonant sounds.

- Little Lucy loves lavender and lilacs.
- Zach zigged and zagged around the zoo.

Hyperbole

Hyperbole is exaggeration. Hyperboles can sometimes be confused with similes, because they often use *like* or *as*.

- I'm so tired, I could sleep for a month!
- To Charlie, his father seemed as tall as a skyscraper.

Imagery

The tendency may be to assume that **imagery** is limited to the use of visual images, but in actuality, imagery is language that appeals to all of the senses.

- I stroked the papery skin of her hands.
- As she sang, Hillary's high, clear voice wafted through the hall.

Tone

Tone may also be referred to as mood. It's the overall attitude of a piece of writing. Look for words or phrases that evoke emotions.

- Chris trudged out into the bleak, gray dawn.
- The puppy bounded eagerly into Lindsey's arms.

Onomatopoeia

And of course, **onomatopoeia** is the term for words that represent sounds. Pretty much every animal sound is included in this group, as well as words such as *slap, crack, swish, click,* and *murmur.*

Now that we have reviewed literary devices, let's tackle a practice question.

Read this poem by Emily Dickinson and answer the question that follows.

A door just opened on a street—
    I, lost, was passing by—
An instant's width of warmth disclosed
    And wealth, and company.

The door as sudden shut, and I,
    I, lost, was passing by,—
Lost doubly, but by contrast most,
    Enlightening misery.

The speaker in the poem can best be
characterized as:

A.   peaceful.

B.   lonely.

C.   nervous.

D.   delighted.

Here's How to Crack It

By scanning the answers, you can determine that this is a *tone,* or *mood,* question. First, isolate any "feeling" words in the poem: *lost, warmth, enlightening, misery.* At first glance, that list proves troublesome. The words seem to contradict each other. The only answer you can really eliminate using POE at this point is choice C, *nervous.* When you look back at the poem, you discover a few things. One, the word *lost* is used three times, which gives it more weight. Two, the word *warmth* is part of a section depicting a scene from which the speaker is excluded. Three, the word *enlightening* is used here in conjunction with the word *misery,* as a way to prove that the speaker is now more acutely aware of his or her unhappiness. This eliminates choices A and D. To be sure, you can go back to the repetition of the word *lost* to verify that your instinct is correct: The answer is choice B, *lonely.*

KEY TERMS

fiction genres
realistic fiction
science fiction
fantasy
fables
moral (lesson)
anthropomorphized
myths
legends
folktales
mystery
whodunit
historical fiction
story elements
plot
character
setting
theme
Freytag's Pyramid
exposition
rising action
climax
falling action
resolution
perspective

first-person narrative
narrator
third-person limited narrative
third-person omniscient narrative
poetry
lyric poems
narrative poems
haiku
odes
elegies
ballads
concrete poems
rhyme
repetition
simile
metaphor
extended metaphor
personification
alliteration
hyperbole
imagery
tone
onomatopoeia

Drill #3

Read the following fable; then answer the two questions that follow.

The Wind and the Sun were arguing over which of them was stronger. Soon they saw a traveler coming down the road, and the Sun said: "Aha! Here is a way to decide our dispute. Whichever of us can make that traveler take off his cloak shall be regarded as the stronger." The Sun hid behind a cloud, and the Wind began to blow as hard as it could onto the traveler. But the harder he blew, the tighter the traveler wrapped his cloak around him, until at last the Wind had to give up in despair. Then the Sun came out and shone in all his glory upon the traveler, who soon grew warm and took off his cloak.

1. What is the moral of the fable?

   A. Be careful what you wish for.

   B. Kindness gets better results than cruelty.

   C. Birds of a feather flock together.

   D. Do not judge a book by its cover.

2. Which of the following elements most clearly reflects the style of traditional fables?

   A. the extended metaphor

   B. the argument between two characters

   C. the use of personification

   D. the one-sided dialogue

Read the following sentence; then answer the question that follows.

The icy rain sliced Lynn's cheeks like razor blades.

3. Which two literary devices does this sentence employ?

   A. simile and onomatopoeia

   B. simile and alliteration

   C. metaphor and personification

   D. metaphor and imagery

4. Which of the following is a narrative poem?

   A. "The Road Not Taken" by Robert Frost

   B. "The Tyger" by William Blake

   C. "Paul Revere's Ride" by Henry Wadsworth Longfellow

   D. "Boa Constrictor" by Shel Silverstein

5. Which is an example of hyperbole?

   A. Claire's laugh echoed throughout the school campus.

   B. In the dark room, the shadows looked like menacing monsters.

   C. Everyone always said that Jules was as sweet as pie.

   D. Our cat hacked up a hairball the size of Cleveland.

ANSWERS AND EXPLANATIONS TO DRILL #3

1. **B** The Sun did with gentleness what the Wind could not do with brute force.

2. **C** One of the main characteristics of fables is the use of non-human characters. None of the other answers is specifically indicative of a fable.

3. **A** Look for what there *isn't* in the sentence rather than what there *is*. There is no alliteration, which rules out choice B; there is no metaphor, which rules out choices C and D. There is a very clear simile, though, and the word slice is onomatopoeia.

4. **C** Yes, you may run into a question or two that does specifically test your content knowledge. If you are familiar with all of the pieces, or at least the one that you know fits the bill, then you'll have no problem. If not, use POE to narrow down your choices based on what you do know. A narrative poem is long and tells a story: You can eliminate any of the other three poems if you recognize that they don't meet the criteria.

5. **D** Choice A is improbable, but not impossible. Choices B and C are simple similes. Choice D is an extreme exaggeration. And...pretty gross.

Summary

o   Students read a wide variety of fiction genres.

o   There are four story elements: plot, character, setting, and theme.

o   Freytag's Pyramid divides a plot into five parts.

o   The three most common perspectives are first person, third-person limited, and third-person omniscient.

o   Students learn to classify and write poems of different types.

o   Writers employ literary devices to make their work more meaningful and interesting.

Chapter 6
United States and
World History

MAPS AND TABLES AND CHARTS, OH MY

Use the map below to answer the two questions that follow.

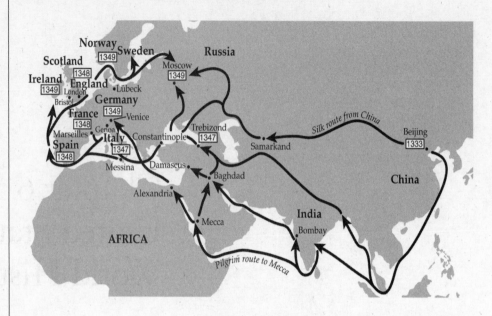

1333–1349 C.E.

1. The map above shows:

    A. the expansion of the Roman Empire.

    B. major routes of the Crusades.

    C. the spread of the Bubonic Plague.

    D. explorations by Ferdinand Magellan.

2. If you have absolutely no idea what this map represents, you should:

    A. eliminate as many wrong answers as possible.

    B. try to get the answer from someone else's test.

    C. hope for an earthquake.

    D. cry.

PICK YOUR BATTLES

There's no easy way to break it to you: To fully prepare for the history and social science part of the exam, you'd have to study everything from the dawn of mankind to what happened in California state legislature yesterday. Just read through the official CSET Subtest I description: It would make a Rhodes scholar hyperventilate. To help you prepare, we recommend the following books for content:

- *Cracking the AP World History Exam*
- *Cracking the AP U.S. History Exam*
- *Cracking the AP U.S. Government & Politics Exam*

The other important thing to do is to focus your energy on the types of questions you'll face and the skills you'll need to answer them.

PROCESS OF ELIMINATION

Obviously, applying the process of elimination is a skill you should be utilizing throughout the test, but it will prove especially valuable in the area of history, so it bears repeating. The trick is not to get hung up on what you *don't* know. Focus instead on what you *do* know. Using whatever scattered facts and concepts you remember from your education and your preparation for this test will help you to narrow down the answer choices. If you can eliminate even one or two answers, you're in much better shape than you were before.

MAPS

Map questions require you to look at a map and answer one or more questions. Watch out because map questions can be a bit tricky, though. These types of questions require some basic outside knowledge of history and geography.

Let's take the map at the beginning of this chapter as an example. Look at the clues you have available to you. One major clue is the map's **date range:** 1333–1349 c.e. (Common Era, formerly known as a.d.; b.c.e. is Before the Common Era). Based on that range, what can you rule out? Well, hopefully you know a bit about the Roman Empire, which developed in the first centuries of the Common Era. That is much too early for this map. Also, the Crusades lasted for several centuries, while this map spans only 16 years. At this point, you're down to two choices, and you can make an educated guess. Ferdinand Magellan sailed around the tip of South America in the early 1500s, so the answer is C.

Let's look at a few more map questions.

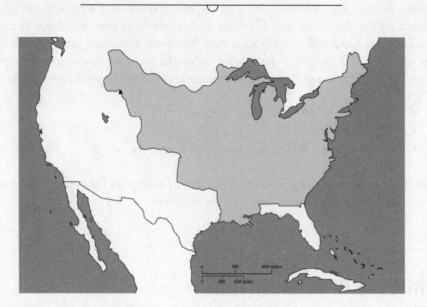

The shaded region on the map above shows the land held by the United States immediately following the:

A. American Revolution.

B. passage of the Northwest Ordinance.

C. Louisiana Purchase.

D. Mexican War.

Here's How to Crack It

Use any or all of what you know to eliminate incorrect answers. The American Revolution occurred when the Thirteen Colonies overthrew the governance of the British Empire. Picture the original colonies and the land they occupied: basically, a somewhat vertical strip along the East Coast. This map indicates far too much land for choice A to be the correct answer. Similarly, the Northwest Ordinance of 1787 allowed only for the creation of up to five states in the area between the Ohio River and the Great Lakes, east of the Mississippi. The shaded region on the map extends too far west, and covers a lot more than five states' worth of land, so choice B cannot be right. The Mexican War resulted in the United States' acquisition of land that would later become Texas, California, and most of the states in between, which rules out choice D. The correct answer is choice C, the Louisiana Purchase.

How about another map question?

African Colonization 1890–1910

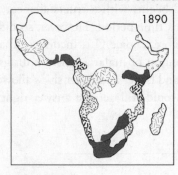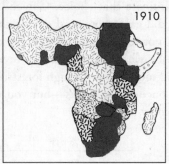

- ☐ Independent
- ■ Britain
- ▨ France
- ▧ Belgium
- ▨ Portugal
- ▦ Italy
- ▨ Germany
- ■ Spain

From the two maps above, what conclusion can you draw about the change in colonization activities between 1890 and 1910?

A.   By 1910, Belgium had become the dominant colonizer on the African continent.

B.   By 1910, more colonized lands were gaining their independence from European colonizers.

C.   While Britain and France expanded their imperial holding between 1890 and 1910, Portugal lost territory during that time period.

D.   Advances in technology and medicine between 1890 and 1910 allowed colonization efforts to shift geographically.

Here's How to Crack It

Yes, there is a lot going on in these maps, but don't let that intimidate you. Rather, let the map do most of the work. According to the 1910 map, the dominant imperial power in Africa was Great Britain, not Belgium, so choice A cannot be the correct answer. As for choice B, there were only two nations in sub-Saharan Africa that remained independent by 1910: Ethiopia and Liberia. Using the map will help you eliminate that choice. Choice C begins with a true statement; Britain and France did gain more land during this time period. However, so did Portugal, though not to the same extent; therefore, choice C is incorrect. That leaves only choice D, which is correct. The invention of malaria-resistant drugs, better methods and tools to cut through forests, and larger and faster ships allowed colonization of once-remote areas—but you would still get the answer right even if you didn't know that.

TABLES

Tables are ordered arrangements of rows and columns, used to present data. The types of tables you'll see in this section of the CSET will consist of names, dates, places, sociological concepts, historical events, and the like. Questions about tables, charts, and graphs are different than questions about maps in that they usually want you only to interpret and analyze the given table, chart, or graph. Some basic outside knowledge could be helpful, sure, but it is not required to reach the correct answer. These types of answers are more about analyzing the information and drawing conclusions.

Look at this example.

Average, highest, and lowest approval ratings, by percentage of all eligible voters, for U.S. presidents, 1953 to 1974			
	Average	Highest	Lowest
Eisenhower	65	79	48
Kennedy	70	83	56
Johnson	55	79	35
Nixon	49	67	24

Which of the following conclusions can be drawn from the information presented in the table above?

A.　Eisenhower was the most consistently popular president in the nation's history.

B.　The difference between Johnson's highest and lowest approval ratings was the greatest for any president during the period in question.

C.　Kennedy received greater congressional support for his programs than did any other president during the period in question.

D.　Nixon's lowest approval rating was the result of the Watergate scandal.

Here's How to Crack It

When you're asked to **draw a conclusion,** the only correct answer is the one that is supported entirely with information from the table. No matter what you remember about history or government or politics, if it's not here, it doesn't count. Once you're clear on this point, you can pick off the wrong answers like flies. Forget choice A—who's talking about the entire nation's history here? Choice C isn't supported here; there's no mention of congressional involvement. And choice D may be true, but there's no evidence in this chart to support the statement. When all you have left is choice B, double-check it. It's actually just a math question, and it's proven true based on the information in the table.

Table questions in the CSET often ask you to select a line that correctly matches two categories. Here's an example.

———————————○———————————

Which line in the table below correctly matches an American president with the year he first took office?

Line	President	Year
1	Thomas Jefferson	1825
2	Abraham Lincoln	1861
3	Franklin D. Roosevelt	1921
4	John F. Kennedy	1965

A. Line 1

B. Line 2

C. Line 3

D. Line 4

Here's How to Crack It

Just as in the map questions, use what you know to eliminate what you don't. Thomas Jefferson was the third president, so you know he was elected well before 1825, when the United States was nearly 50 years old. Therefore, choice A is incorrect. Franklin D. Roosevelt was the president during World War II, which was in the late 1930s–mid 1940s, so choice C is also incorrect. John F. Kennedy was assassinated in 1963, which rules out choice D. Abraham Lincoln was assassinated in 1865, soon after giving his second inaugural address, so choice B is the correct answer.

———————————○———————————

Let's try another one.

Which line in the table below correctly matches a political ideology with one of its major tenets?

Line	Ideology	Tenet
1	Socialism	Goods and services, including those regarding the most basic necessities of life, are produced for profitable exchange.
2	Capitalism	The nation or race is exalted above all else.
3	Communism	A peaceful society would be free from classes and government.
4	Fascism	The ultimate interests of workers best match those of humanity in general.

A. Line 1

B. Line 2

C. Line 3

D. Line 4

Here's How to Crack It

You may not be that familiar with each of the ideologies, but knowing word roots can help you a great deal here. Look at the root of each word, and decide whether the tenet, or belief, seems to fit. The first three are relatively easy to determine; you may not know the root *fascio*, which means *union*, but if you can get enough out of what you do know, it won't matter. In this case, the choice that most clearly matches is choice C. The root of the word *communism* is the same as the root of words like *common* and *communal*. The rejection of social classes and the rule of government fit with the Communist ideology of equality.

CHARTS

Charts and **graphs** ask you to **interpret** information given in various comparisons, usually with numbers, percentages, or timelines. The key with these is not to overanalyze. The questions are very direct: They just want to know that you can interpret a chart. As we mentioned before, outside knowledge that you may have is helpful but not necessary. The correct answer will be indisputably supported by the information provided. They don't want you to think outside the box—literally!

Here's one type of chart you might see.

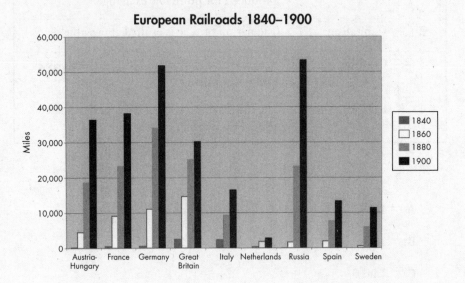

European Railroads 1840–1900

Based on the information in the above chart, which of the following conclusions is accurate?

A.   Russia's Industrial Revolution occurred later than Great Britain's.

B.   Eastern Europe lagged behind western Europe in the development of national railroad systems.

C.   The greatest proportionate growth in miles of rail occurred in Germany between 1880 and 1900.

D.   European nations with the fewest rail miles were located in colder climates.

Here's How to Crack It

First, see which answer choices you can eliminate based on the facts within the chart. Choice B is wrong because the chart shows that eastern Europe exceeded western Europe in miles of railway by 1880. Choice C is also wrong mathematically. That leaves you with choice A and choice D, and some basic common sense may help you determine the correct choice. Think geographically: It's cold in the Netherlands and Sweden, but it's not exactly balmy in Russia either, so choice D is actually a silly answer. Even if you don't know for sure that Russia was still primarily an agricultural nation when Britain was industrializing, it does make sense, and the information in the chart would accurately represent the conclusion. Choice A is the correct answer.

You'll also need to be prepared to interpret graphs.

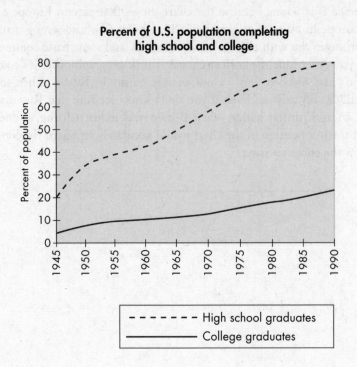

Percent of U.S. population completing high school and college

- - - - - - High school graduates
——— College graduates

Which of the following best accounts for the trend illustrated in the graph above?

A. The Supreme Court decision *Brown vs. the Board of Education* led to increased enrollment in colleges and universities.

B. During the 1960s, increasing numbers of high school graduates rejected the notion that a college education was desirable.

C. Jobs in advanced technical and medical industries generally require postgraduate degrees.

D. Increased affluence beginning in the postwar era allowed people the opportunity to stay in school longer.

Here's How to Crack It

Look for answers that are statistically or factually incorrect based on the information in the graph. The graph clearly indicates that college enrollments increased during the 1960s, so choice B is incorrect. Choice C is actually true, but it has nothing to do with the graph: It addresses postgraduate study, which is not represented here. *Brown vs. the Board of Education* concerned school segregation, and as a teacher, you should be familiar with the case, but that means we can rule it out. Choice D is the correct answer: When the war ended, the Depression-era generation finally had money for luxuries and the leisure time in which to enjoy them. This new level of comfort meant that, in growing numbers of American families, children no longer had to drop out of school to get jobs as a means of survival.

KEY TERMS

date range
C.E./Common Era
B.C.E./Before Common Era
tables
draw a conclusion
charts
graphs
interpret

Drill #4

1. Which of the following is allowed only in the United States Senate, and not in the House of Representatives?

    A.   the vote of impeachment for the president

    B.   the confirmation of Supreme Court justice nominees

    C.   the right to impose taxes

    D.   the power to regulate interstate commerce

2. Colonists who were loyal to King George III of England were often known as:

    A.   Tories.

    B.   Lobsterbacks.

    C.   Minutemen.

    D.   Patriots.

3. What is one major difference between the Inca and the Aztec civilizations?

    A.   The Incans were agrarian; the Aztecs were nomadic.

    B.   The Aztecs built religious monuments while the Incans did not.

    C.   Incans were monotheistic while the Aztecs worshipped many gods.

    D.   The Aztecs developed a system of writing while the Incans did not.

4. The Renaissance did not have a great impact on Spain because:

    A.   language differences prevented the spread of Renaissance thinking.

    B.   Spain was geographically isolated from other parts of Europe.

    C.   the Spanish government strictly censored humanistic ideas and writers.

    D.   there was a great deal of cultural competition between Spain and Italy.

Use the table to answer the question that follows.

	Eligible voters	Registered voters	Votes cast	Turnout, registered voters	Turnout, all eligible voters
1986	178,566,000	118,399,984	64,991,128	54.89%	36.40%
1988	182,778,000	126,379,628	91,594,693	72.48%	50.11%
1990	185,812,000	121,105,630	67,859,189	56.03%	36.52%
1992	189,529,000	133,821,178	104,405,155	78.02%	55.09%
1994	193,650,000	130,292,822	75,105,860	57.64%	38.78%
1996	196,511,000	146,211,960	96,456,345	65.97%	49.08%
1998	200,929,000	141,850,558	73,117,022	70.60%	36.40%

Source: Federal Election Commission

5. The chart above best supports which of the following conclusions?

    A. No more than half of all eligible voters ever participate in federal elections.

    B. The number of registered voters always increases between elections.

    C. Voter turnout for the 1996 presidential election was the lowest for any presidential election during the twentieth century.

    D. Voter turnout for midterm congressional elections is generally lower than it is for presidential elections.

Please turn the page for answers and explanations
for the questions in this drill.

ANSWERS AND EXPLANATIONS TO DRILL #4

1. **B** Only the Senate has the ability to confirm the president's Supreme Court nominees. Both the House and the Senate register votes of impeachment (though impeachment must be initiated by the House). Choices C and D are fundamental rights granted to Congress.

2. **A** Tories were supporters of the king, and many fought for the British during the Revolutionary War.

3. **D** While Aztecs did have a formal system of writing, the Incans instead relied on *quipu*, a rope with different color and size knots, for record keeping. All three of the other choices refer to characteristics in which the two civilizations were very similar: Both were agrarian, not nomadic, societies; religion played a dominant role in all Mesoamerican societies, and architectural monument building was a feature of both the Aztecs and the Incans; and general knowledge about Mesoamerica includes polytheism and the supremacy of the sun god.

4. **C** Before we consider what made Spain different from other European nations, use POE to eliminate answers you know are wrong. For instance, choice A makes no sense. Somehow, the Renaissance spread to England and France, and neither of those nations was Italian-speaking. You also know that choice B is wrong: Spain is *not* isolated. It borders France to the north, and England is geographically farther from Italy than Spain. Choice D is also incorrect because there is no evidence of such cultural competition. During the 700s, Spain and Portugal came under Muslim rule with the invasion of the Moors. For hundreds of decades, Spain fought to free itself of Islamic influence, and what resulted was a strong nation-state with extremely little tolerance for religious dissent. So the Catholic rulers of Spain did not warmly embrace the ideas of the Renaissance.

5. **D** The great thing about this question is that you can actually answer it correctly without even reading the data. Don't believe it? Just read the answer choices. Choice A says "...*ever* participate in federal elections." Ever? Who said anything about ever? We're just talking about 1996 to 1998. Now you know that you can also rule out choice B, which uses the word *always*, for the same reason. And choice C brings up the 1970s—where did they come from? Not from the table, that's for sure. This one is a no-brainer. Literally.

Summary

- Study your history!

- Process of elimination (POE) is especially help-ful in the history/social sciences portion of the test.

- With map questions, use all of the information you know about history and geography to analyze the map and question.

- With table, chart, and graph questions, remember that the answers are there in the figure. You just need to interpret information.

- Don't think outside the box. Use the clues you're given.

Chapter 7
California History

EUREKA!

Currier, Nathaniel, c. 1849

Cute cartoon, but why didn't they just drive?

WE PUT THE "C" IN CSET

Your students go to school in California; therefore, they learn about California history. You will be teaching them California history; therefore, you will be tested on your knowledge of it. There's a lot of history here—far more than can be covered in one book, let alone one chapter. What we can give you here is an overview of what you should know. The CSET divides this section into two time periods:

1.   the pre-Columbian period through the Gold Rush
2.   post-1850

FROM PANGAEA TO GOLD
(Pre-Columbian Period through the Gold Rush)

Geography
In many ways, California's history is defined by its distinctive physical geography.

Mountains
The **Sierra Nevada** mountain range, which runs over 400 miles along the east side of the state, served to isolate much of California from the rest of the country until the mid-nineteenth century. In part because the Sierra Nevada is one of the snowiest regions in the United States, the runoff in streams and rivers provided ample water for life in surrounding areas.

Desert
Most of southeast California is comprised of desert. The largest portion is what we now know as the **Mojave Desert,** which includes the hottest place in the Americas, **Death Valley.** The desert region also helped isolate California from the east and south.

Central Valley
The **Central Valley** is exactly that: a large valley spanning the entire middle section of the state. Due to its Mediterranean climate, fertile soil, and diverse land resources, early tribes in the area developed an agriculture-based culture.

Coast
California's extensive coastline provided protection from foreign conquest in the centuries predating ocean exploration. It also provided an abundance of sea life as a food source for coastal tribes.

American Indians
Several hundred thousand **American Indians,** or Native Americans, comprised of dozens of tribes and hundreds of languages, were indigenous to California before the nineteenth century.

Kinship
California Indian tribes were centered on familial associations. **Kinship networks** formed the basis for leadership, social organization, and economic activity.

Religion

The religious leaders can be classified generally as priests, shamans, and ritualists. California Indian religious communities were divided into two major systems: the **Kuksu** in the north and the **Toloache** in the south. The belief in magic, or supernatural power, was almost universal in California Indian society, and was believed to be both the cause and the effect for everything from health to behavior to natural phenomena.

Economics

California Indians were hunters, trappers, and gatherers. Sources of live game included animals such as deer, elk, rabbits, squirrels, and quail, as well as fish and other sea life in the coastal regions. Other food staples were acorns and other nuts, squash, and corn.

Trade within and among tribes promoted communication and expansion. Basketry was common, and became a widespread skill. California Indians also used redwood trees to make boats, planks, stools, cooking implements, and housing structures. From animal skins, they manufactured clothing and blankets.

Spanish Exploration and Colonization

Spanish explorers and sailors had visited California sporadically since the mid-sixteenth century, when **Hernando Cortes** oversaw the fall of the **Aztec Empire** and established **New Spain,** also known as **Baja California,** which included territory that would later become Mexico and southern California. In 1769, **King Carlos of Spain,** in an attempt to claim **Alta California** before Russian settlers did, ordered the Spanish to send expeditions north and establish missions.

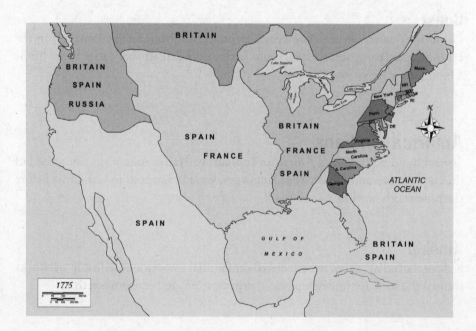

Junipero Serra

Father **Junipero Serra** was a **Franciscan** priest who accompanied one of the first Spanish expeditions. Serra wanted very much to Christianize the California Indians. He established the mission system, building the first nine missions before his death.

The Missions

In all, the Spanish built 21 **missions** between San Diego and San Francisco. No, you probably don't need to memorize all of their names, but there are a few things you should know.

The missions were all constructed similarly; they were almost like small feudal manors, in that they were self-contained communities, gated and surrounded on all sides by the outer perimeter of the buildings. The church was the main building, and there were also living quarters, kitchens, workshops, storerooms, and a large central patio with a fountain.

The California missions were first and foremost in the world in terms of prosperity and functionality. This is due in large part to California's mild climate and bountiful natural resources, but also because Father Serra was persistent in attracting the California Indians to the missions. Many Indians were converted to Christianity and worked in the missions voluntarily; many more were forced to convert. The missionaries taught the natives skills in farming and crafting, and educated them in the Christian religion. Eventually, many of the mission operations depended on Indian labor.

Agriculture

The missionaries and other Spanish settlers introduced a great number of plants and animals to California, including oranges, lemons, apples, figs, wheat, corn, almonds, walnuts, cattle, horses, sheep, and grapes (which ultimately led, of course, to wine vineyards!).

Let's take what we have read about California history and look at a practice problem.

What was one benefit for California Indians living in the missions?

A.   shelter

B.   meals

C.   clothing

D.   all of the above

Here's How to Crack It

Think logically: As a general rule, missionaries converting natives do whatever they can to bring the converts closer to the society and belief structures being offered. These were all advantages the California Indians were afforded. The correct answer is D.

Mexican Rule

In 1821, Mexico won independence from Spain, and four years later, California was officially proclaimed a territory of the **Republic of Mexico.**

Effect on the Missions

In a series of decrees and acts, the Mexican government gradually dismantled the mission system, freeing the Indians and confiscating and plundering the missions, forcing the Franciscans out completely by 1836.

The Rancho Period

To bring more settlers to California, the Mexican government gave out large land grants. **Ranchos,** which were large ranches, dominated the landscape for a period of time in the late 1830s to mid-1840s. Rancheros lived pleasant lives, raised cattle and sheep, rode horses, and employed Indians to work the land and tend the animals. Cattle hides and cattle fat, or **tallow,** which was used to make candles and soap, were major exports.

The Mexican War

Most of the events leading up to the **Mexican War,** which lasted from 1846 to 1848, revolved around Texas, but its repercussions affected California enormously.

The Bear Flag Revolt

The one major prewar incident that did take place in California was the **Bear Flag Revolt.** As tensions mounted between the United States and Mexico, a group of men, inspired by **John C. Fremont,** an Army major who encouraged rebellion against Mexican rule in California, devised a new flag with a bear and star on it. They declared themselves members of a new **Republic of California,** and captured General Mariano Vallejo. After a few brief skirmishes, word came that the United

States had declared war on Mexico, and the **Bear Flaggers** joined the U.S. efforts. The bear flag, though, became the official flag of California.

The Treaty of Guadalupe Hidalgo

In February 1848, the United States, under President Polk, and Mexico signed the **Treaty of Guadalupe Hidalgo**, which granted the United States Texas, New Mexico, and California for the sum of $15 million.

California's Admission to the Union

California was not immediately granted statehood; it hung in a kind of limbo between Mexican and U.S. rule for over two years, during which California was governed by the U.S. military. In September and October of 1849, forty-eight representatives from cities all over California convened at Colton Hall in Monterey to draw up California's first constitution.

On October 13, 1849, the delegates signed the constitution—in which they had redrawn the state boundaries—knowing that the land California currently occupied was far too vast for Congress to agree to confirm it as a free state. They presented the constitution to then-governor Brigadier General Bennett Riley. In the months following, the people of California ratified the constitution and elected state officials and representatives:

Governor: Peter Burnett
Lieutenant governor: John McDougal
Senators: John Fremont and William Gwin
Representatives: Edward Gilbert and George Wright

The two senators traveled to Washington, D.C., to petition Congress to accept California as a free state, and on September 9, 1850, California became the thirty-first state of the United States. San Jose was the first capital of California, but by 1854, state officials decided on Sacramento as the capital city.

The Gold Rush

Here's a quick rundown of the facts, the figures, and the folks involved in the **Gold Rush**.

In the Beginning

On January 24, 1848, James Marshall discovered small gold nuggets at (John) Sutter's Fort—also known as **Sutter's Mill,** when digging a small canal. In the days that followed, Sutter's workers began to dig for gold in their time off, eventually abandoning their work altogether to search full-time.

In mid-spring, Sam Brannan, a merchant at Sutter's Fort, traveled to San Francisco and ran through the streets shouting that gold had been discovered on the American River. Men in San Francisco, Sacramento, and neighboring areas left their work and flocked to the area to search for gold.

Word Spreads

Within weeks, the news traveled throughout California and into the nearby states, and more men abandoned their jobs to mine for gold. By the fall, word had reached all the way across the country.

In November, a delegate from the California government took a sample to Washington, D.C., and on December 5, 1848, President Polk confirmed the discovery in an address to Congress.

The Forty-Niners

Gold miners came in droves and were nicknamed **forty-niners.** The cartoon at the beginning of this chapter shows how many people, both citizens of the United States and people from other parts of the world, dropped everything and headed to California. Most people traveled by boat at first, though later more land passages were developed. No matter what the method, it was often a difficult journey.

Almost overnight, San Francisco turned into a booming metropolis. Ships poured into the harbors. Tents and shacks were set up as interim resting places for those newly arrived before they headed up to gold country; later, as settlers stayed longer in one place, more permanent housing was erected, and businesses developed by the hundreds. Similar expansions gradually hit Sacramento and other large cities like Stockton, which were close to the **Mother Lode**—the hundred or so miles along the foothills of the Sierra Nevada, which were packed with mining camps.

The Effect on California

The population of the state grew exponentially in a matter of just a few years, and at first, the influx of people proved extremely hazardous. Mining was hard work, subject to accidents and disease, the most common of which was cholera. Also, gold mining was, at first, essentially a free-for-all, which led to theft, fights, murders, and lynchings. The California Indian population was nearly decimated. Mining also took a terrible toll on the environment: The mountains and foothills were ravaged, and the rivers and creeks were filled with silt and debris.

There were some positive effects, though: The timing coincided with California's admission to the Union, and the overflow of settlement camps grew into cities. With immigrants from other states and countries came commerce, trade, and better transportation, including steamships and railroads. By the mid-1860s, San Francisco was the tenth largest city in the United States, and California had become the most ethnically diverse area in the world.

Let's try a question before we move on to the other era of California history.

Of the forty-niners, approximately one in twelve:

A. went back home within a month.

B. died.

C. found enough gold to support his family for ten years.

D. became a farmer.

Here's How to Crack It

Think about what you actually know, and think about what would make sense. First, you know that choice C must be wrong. Very few really struck it rich—thousands upon thousands came; one in twelve would be an awful lot of rich men. The same goes for choice D: Yes, some men may have become farmers, but the cities showed immense and immediate growth, so you can imagine that the vast majority moved to the cities rather than stayed in the farmlands. And if you remember that for most people outside of California, the trip there took several months or more, you can guess that most of them would not have turned around and gone right back home. The answer is choice B. One in twelve men died, either on the trip, by violence in the mining process, or from disease.

...AND ALL THE REST (Post-1850)

Railroads

California had a few short-distance railroads, such as one connecting San Jose and San Francisco, but between the excitement of the gold rush and the impending Civil War, plans for a **transcontinental railroad** began to take shape.

The **Central Pacific Railroad** was an integral part of the country—it was the west half of the railroad that eventually linked the two coasts—and of California. The railroad was the brainchild of engineer **Theodore Judah**, who had built the first short-distance railroads. His associates, who took over after Judah's death in 1863, were known as the **Big Four:** Collis Huntington, Mark Hopkins, Leland Stanford (yes, he's the guy who founded Stanford University), and Charles Crocker.

Crocker took advantage of the thousands of Chinese immigrants who were having difficulty finding work due to racial inequality, and it was these Chinese workers who were largely responsible for constructing the western segment of the transcontinental railroad.

Water

It became apparent soon after the population explosion of the 1850s that water was not going to come easily to California cities and farms. Rainfall was sufficient in the northern part of the state, but almost nonexistent in large areas of central and southern California. Engineer William Hammond Hall's research and studies were instrumental in developing California's irrigation systems.

Oil

In the 1890s and early 1900s, oil wells were dug in southern California and on platforms in the Pacific. Oil is considered to be the foundation of the industrial infrastructure of Los Angeles and much of southern California.

Agriculture

After the gold rush, wheat became a huge industry in California. Vast wheat ranches sprawled across much of the Central and Sacramento Valleys. By the late 1870s, California was exporting wheat all over the world.

With the creation of irrigation ditches came more ranches and fields, with crops of every kind, from grains to fruits to vegetables to cotton. California had solidified its status as an agricultural state.

Labor

Here are some key dates and facts concerning labor in California:

- 1850s: The first California unions developed.
- 1870s and 1890s: Depressions hit the state's workers hard.
- 1880s–1890s: Migrant workers became commonplace.
- 1927: The **Confederation of Mexican Workers** was formed.
- 1933: Cotton pickers in the San Joaquin Valley staged the largest agricultural strike in U.S. history.
- 1975: Due to the efforts of **Cesar Chavez**, the **United Farm Workers Union** won the right to unionize agricultural laborers.

Ethnic/Racial Tensions

Though California has virtually always been a diverse state, there have been periods of particular significance in terms of racial inequality.

Skilled and hardworking Chinese laborers were a great threat to Anglo men in the decades following the gold rush. This situation led to discrimination and even lynchings.

Mexican immigrants were targeted during the Great Depression.

Japanese immigrants and Japanese-born citizens were treated equally unfairly, even before World War II, though after the bombing of Pearl Harbor, over one hundred thousand Californians of Japanese descent were sent to **internment camps.**

During and after World War II, thousands of African Americans came to California seeking work, but encountered discrimination in housing and unions. In 1965, racial tension erupted in riots in the Watts section of Los Angeles.

The Immigration and Nationality Act of 1965 resulted in a substantial increase in the Asian population of California.

Most recently, the 1992 Los Angeles riots, sparked by the acquittal of four police officers accused in the videotaped beating of African American motorist Rodney King, showed that racial tensions still persist.

KEY TERMS

Sierra Nevada
Mojave Desert
Death Valley
Central Valley
American Indians
  (Native Americans)
kinship networks
Kuksu
Toloache
Spanish explorers
Hernando Cortes
Aztec Empire
New Spain (Baja California)
King Carlos of Spain
Alta California
Junipero Serra
Franciscan
missions
Republic of Mexico
ranchos
tallow

Mexican War
Bear Flag Revolt
John C. Fremont
Republic of California
Bear Flaggers
Treaty of Guadalupe Hidalgo
gold rush
Sutter's Mill
forty-niners
Mother Lode
transcontinental railroad
Central Pacific Railroad
Theodore Judah
Big Four
Confederation of Mexican Workers
Cesar Chavez
United Farm Workers Union
internment camps
Immigration and Nationality Act
  of 1965

Drill #5

1. Which of the following was considered to be a negative repercussion of the transcontinental railroad on California?

   A. the discrimination against Chinese laborers

   B. the loss of isolation

   C. the destructive effects of the railroad tracks on farmland

   D. the dramatic reduction of ocean travel

2. What is the name of the Mission Trail?

   A. San Diego de Alcala

   B. Junipero Serra

   C. El Camino Real

   D. Alta California

3. What could the *ranchos* of nineteenth-century California most closely be likened to?

   A. British colonies

   B. feudal manors

   C. African villages

   D. German hamlets

4. *The Grapes of Wrath* by John Steinbeck is written about a family traveling from Oakland to California during what period in history?

   A. the Great Depression

   B. the gold rush

   C. World War II

   D. the Mission Period

5. How many of the Japanese Californians sent to internment camps during World War II were U.S. citizens?

   A. 1/10

   B. 1/4

   C. 1/2

   D. 2/3

ANSWERS AND EXPLANATIONS TO DRILL #5

1. **B** Discrimination against the Chinese began well before their work on the railroad; in fact, that is considered one of the reasons they were desirable for the work. As for the farmland, the amount of land used for the railroad versus the sheer size of California is just not proportional. Choice D is simply wrong.

2. **C** El Camino Real means "The King's Highway," and is still a main road in many stretches along the original mission trail.

3. **B** *Ranchos*, like feudal manors, were all-inclusive mini-societies.

4. **A** If you haven't read *The Grapes of Wrath*, pick it up sometime. And in this case, you can still rule out a couple of the answers: No family would have been traveling from Oklahoma to California during the Mission Period, and during the gold rush, men left their families and traveled alone.

5. **D** Sad but true.

Summary

o   California's history was shaped in large part by its geography.

o   For centuries, American Indians were California's only residents.

o   Spanish missionaries built a series of missions along California's coastline.

o   California's admission to the Union coincided with the gold rush, which in turn contributed to a huge population boom.

o   California has been at the forefront of many major U.S. developments and issues.

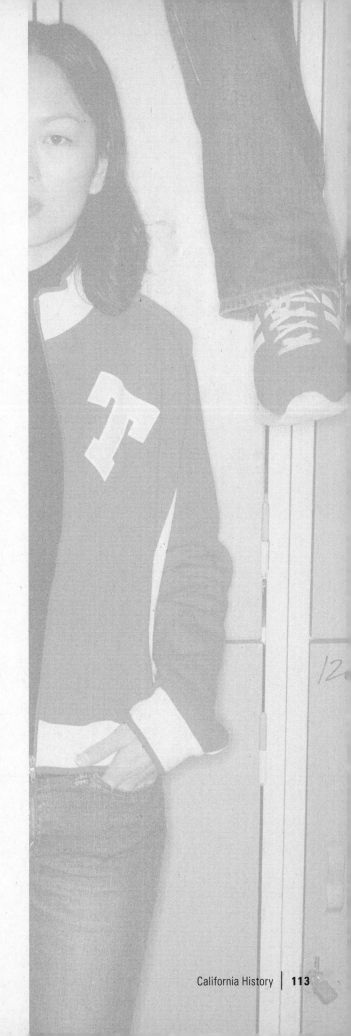

Subtest II: Science and Math

Science

Math

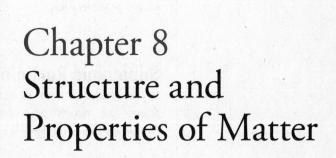

Chapter 8
Structure and
Properties of Matter

INTRODUCTION TO MATTER

Matter Defined

Although organisms exist in many diverse forms, they all have one thing in common. They are all made up of **matter.** Objects that take up space and have mass are known as matter. Matter is made up of **elements,** which by definition are substances that cannot be broken down into simpler substances by chemical means. Everything in the physical world is made up of microscopic matter comprised of **atoms** or **molecules.**

Subatomic Particles

If you break down an element into smaller pieces, you'll eventually come to the atom—the smallest unit of an element that retains its characteristic properties. Atoms are the building blocks of the physical world.

Within atoms, there are even smaller subatomic particles called **protons, neutrons,** and **electrons.**

Let's take a look at a typical atom:

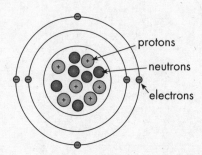

Protons and neutrons are particles that are packed together in the core of an atom called the **nucleus.** You'll notice that protons are positively charged (+) particles, whereas neutrons are uncharged particles.

Electrons, on the other hand, are negatively charged (–) particles that spin around the nucleus. Electrons are quite small compared to protons and neutrons. In fact, for our purposes, electrons are considered massless. Most atoms have the same number of protons and electrons, making them electrically neutral. Some atoms have the same number of protons but differ in the number of neutrons in the nucleus. These atoms are called **isotopes.**

PHYSICAL PROPERTIES OF MATTER

All matter is categorized as being in the **solid** phase, the **liquid** phase, or the **gas** phase.

The solid phase is characterized by the inability of the material to conform to the shape of the container that holds it and an inability of the material to expand to fill the available volume.

The liquid phase is characterized by the ability of the material to conform to the shape of the container that holds it, but an inability of the material to expand to fill the available volume.

The gas phase is characterized by the ability of the material to take the shape of the container that holds it and the ability of the material to expand to fill the available volume.

Matter can undergo **physical changes** and **chemical changes.** The CSET requires that you be familiar with both of these concepts. Physical changes are changes in state, such as the evaporation of water. During evaporation, water goes from being a liquid (for example, water in your cat's water bowl) to a gas (water vapor, and kitty is thirsty again). Chemical changes occur when bonds are broken and new bonds are formed between different atoms. Examples of chemical changes include rusting of metal, ripening of fruit, mixing of ingredients in cake batter to become a new type of matter, photosynthesis, and many more.

Matter has physical, thermal, electrical, and chemical properties. These specific properties can include **color** (the human eye response to light as reflected by matter), **density** (the amount of mass contained in a given substances), **hardness** (the resistance to penetration by a given substance, and **conductivity** (the ability to transmit heat [thermal] or current [electrical]).

Thermal Properties of Matter

When heated or cooled, matter undergoes phase changes. That is, matter can actually change states. Generally, the most common progression of phase changes observed when a substance is heated is solid to liquid to gas. The reverse progression occurs when cooling is in progress—gas to liquid to solid. In a phase change, the initial properties of the matter substance remain constant and unchanged.

Electrical Properties of Matter

Matter is classified as a **conductor** or **non-conductor.** Conductors have a high number of free electrons, while non-conductors do not.

Chemical Properties of Matter

Matter can react with other types of matter when chemically combined. These products can be either liberated (**exothermic**) or absorbed (**endothermic**).

The Periodic Table

The **periodic table** is a method of classifying chemical elements. The location of a substance on the periodic table determines how it will react to another substance.

Each element is represented by its one- or two-letter chemical symbol. Above each chemical symbol is the **atomic number** (number of protons) for that element. Below each chemical symbol is that element's **atomic weight**. There's no need for you to memorize the periodic table for the CSET. However, it may serve you well to be familiar with the location of the more popular elements: H, O, and Fe.

The layout of the periodic table demonstrates recurring (periodic) chemical properties. Elements are listed in order of increasing atomic number (the number of protons in the atomic nucleus). Rows are arranged so that elements with similar properties fall into the same columns (groups or families). There are 18 columns in the periodic table (numbered 1 through 18) and many different categories within the table. These columns and categories are a useful shorthand for knowing a bit of information about an element based on its location.

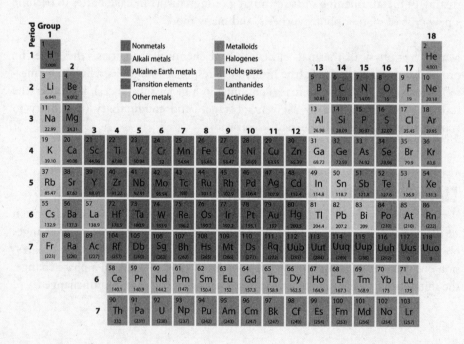

Each horizontal row in the periodic table is called a **period.** The outermost electrons of every atom in a period have the same principal **quantum number,** or **shell number.** Each vertical column in the periodic table is a **group.** Every member of a group has the same number of valence electrons and may be expected to have similar chemical properties to other members of the group.

In general, elements from the same groups will not react, while elements from different groups may. Remember that the more separated or distinguished the groups are, the greater potential for reaction.

Compounds

When two or more different types of atoms are combined in a fixed ratio, they form a chemical **compound.** You'll sometimes find that a compound has different properties from those of its elements. For instance, hydrogen and oxygen exist in nature as gases. Yet, when they combine to make water they often pass into a liquid state. When hydrogen atoms get together with oxygen atoms to form water, a **chemical reaction** occurs.

$$2H_2 \ (g) + O_2 \ (g) \ \rightarrow \ 2H_2O \ (l)$$

The atoms of a compound are held together by **chemical bonds,** which may be ionic bonds, covalent bonds, or hydrogen bonds.

An **ionic bond** is formed between two atoms when one or more electrons are transfered from one atom to the other. In this reaction, one atom loses electrons and becomes positively charged and the other atom gains electrons and becomes negatively charged. The charged forms of the atoms are called ions. For example, when Na reacts with Cl, charged ions, Na^+ and Cl^-, are formed.

A **covalent bond** is formed when electrons are shared between atoms. If the electrons are shared equally between the atoms, the bond is called **nonpolar covalent.** If the electrons are shared unequally, the bond is called **polar covalent.** When two pairs of electrons are shared, the result is a double covalent bond. When three pairs of electrons are shared, the result is a triple covalent bond.

A **hydrogen bond** is a weak chemical bond that forms when a hydrogen atom that is covalently bonded to one electronegative atom is also attracted to another electronegative atom.

Evaporation is an example of:

A.   photosynthesis.

B.   matter undergoing a chemical change.

C.   a covalent bond.

D.   matter undergoing a physical change.

Here's How to Crack It

Hopefully the correct answer jumps out at you on this one. You know that photosynthesis is the process by which plants turn water and sunlight into energy, so choice A must be incorrect. Choice C is completely nonsensical in this context, so cross that one out. Choices B and D are left, but you remember that chemical changes occur when bonds are broken and new bonds are formed between different atoms, while a physical change is a change in state (liquid to gas, for example). So choice D must be the correct answer.

WATER, ACIDS, AND BASES

Water

One of the most important substances in nature is water. Did you know that 70 percent of your body weight consists of water? Water is considered a unique molecule because it plays an important role in chemical reactions.

Let's take a look at one of the properties of water. Water has two hydrogen atoms joined to an oxygen atom.

In water molecules, the hydrogen atoms have a partial positive charge and the oxygen atom has a partial negative charge. Molecules that have partially positive and partially negative charges are said to be polar. Water is therefore a polar molecule. The positively charged ends of the water molecules strongly attract the negatively charged ends of other polar compounds. Likewise, the negatively charged ends strongly attract the positively charged ends of neighboring compounds. These forces are most readily apparent in the tendency of water molecules to stick together as in the formation of water beads or raindrops.

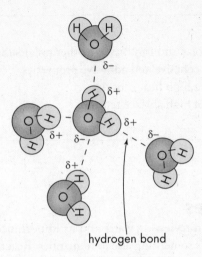

hydrogen bond

Water molecules are held together by hydrogen bonds. Although hydrogen bonds are individually weak, they are collectively strong when present in large numbers. Because it can react with other polar substances, water makes a great solvent; it can dissolve many kinds of substances. The hydrogen bonds that hold water molecules together contribute to a number of special properties.

As previously mentioned, water molecules have a strong tendency to stick together. That is, water exhibits cohesive forces. These forces are extremely important to life. For instance, when water molecules evaporate from leaves, they "pull" neighboring water molecules. These, in turn, draw up the molecules immediately behind them, and so on all the way down the plant vessels. The resulting chain of water molecules enables water to move up a stem.

Water molecules also like to stick to other substances—that is, they are adhesive. Have you ever tried to separate two glass slides stuck together by a film of water? They're difficult to separate because of the water sticking to the glass surfaces. These two forces taken together—**cohesion** and **adhesion**—account for the ability of water to rise up the roots, trunks, and branches of trees. Water has a high surface tension because of the cohesiveness of its molecules. Since this phenomena occurs in thin vessels, it's called **capillary action.**

Another remarkable property of water is its **heat capacity.** What's heat capacity? In plain English, heat capacity refers to the ability of a substance to store heat. For example, when you heat an iron kettle, it gets hot pretty quickly. Why? Because it has a low specific heat. It doesn't take much heat to increase the temperature of the kettle. Water, on the other hand, has a high heat capacity. You have to add a lot of heat to get an increase in temperature. Water's ability to resist temperature changes is one of the things that helps keep the temperature in our oceans fairly stable. It's also why organisms that are composed mainly of water, like human beings, are able to keep a constant body temperature.

Let's review the unique properties of water:

- Water is polar and can dissolve other polar substances.
- Water has cohesive and adhesive properties.
- Water has a high heat capacity.
- Water has a high surface tension.

Acids and Bases

Now, we have just been reviewing water and its importance in the way is reacts to watery solution. There's something else to remember. Reactions are also influenced by whether the solution in which they occur is **acidic, basic,** or **neutral.**

A solution is acidic if it contains a lot of hydrogen ions (H^+). That is, if you dissolve an acid in water, it will release a lot of hydrogen ions. When you think about acids, you usually think of substances with a sour taste, like lemons. For example, if you squeeze a little lemon juice into a class of water, the solution will become acidic. That's because lemons contain citric acid.

Bases, on the other hand, do not release hydrogen ions when added to water. They release a lot of hydroxide ions (OH^-) These solutions are said to be **alkaline.** Bases usually have a slippery consistency. Common soap, for example, is composed largely of bases.

The acidity or alkalinity of a solution can be measured with a **pH scale.** The pH scale is numbered from 1 to 14. The midpoint, 7, is considered neutral pH. The concentration of hydrogen ions in a solution indicates whether it is acidic, basic, or neutral. If a solution contains a lot of hydrogen ions, then it will be acidic and have a low pH. Here's the trend:

An increase in H^+ ions causes a decrease in the pH.

Notice from the scale below that stronger acids have lower pHs. If a solution has a low concentration of hydrogen ions, it will have a high pH.

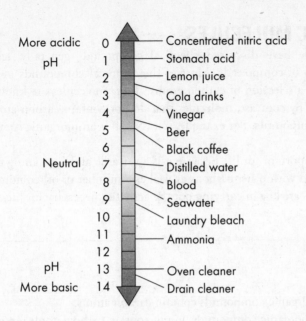

More acidic — pH 0 — Concentrated nitric acid
pH 1 — Stomach acid
2 — Lemon juice
3 — Cola drinks
4 — Vinegar
5 — Beer
6 — Black coffee
Neutral 7 — Distilled water
8 — Blood
9 — Seawater
10 — Laundry bleach
11 — Ammonia
12
pH 13 — Oven cleaner
More basic 14 — Drain cleaner

Just one more thing to remember: The pH scale is not a linear scale—it's logarithmic. That is, a change of one pH number actually represents a tenfold change in hydrogen ion concentration. For example, a pH of 3 is actually ten times more acidic than a pH of 4. This is also true in the reverse direction: A pH of 4 represents a tenfold decrease in acidity compared to a pH of 3.

Your doctor says that your diet is too acidic and it's causing stomach distress. What should you drink with lunch that day?

A. distilled water

B. coffee

C. beer

D. lemonade

Here's How to Crack It

Choice D, lemonade, probably sounds like a terrible idea if you're looking to eliminate acid from your diet, right? So cross out that one. From the scale that you saw before, you remember that coffee has a pH of 5 and beer has a pH of about 4.5, while neutral is 7. So choice A is correct, distilled water with a pH of 7, neutral.

ORGANIC MOLECULES

Now that we have discussed chemical compounds generally, let's turn to a special group of compounds. Most of the chemical compounds in living organisms contain a selection of carbon atoms. These molecules are known as **organic compounds**. By contrast, molecules that do not contain carbon atoms are called **inorganic compounds**. For example, salt (NaCl) is an inorganic compound.

Carbon is important for life because it is a versatile atom, meaning that it has the ability to bind with other carbons as well as a number of other atoms. The resulting molecules are key in carrying out the activities necessary for life.

To review:

- Organic compounds contain carbon atoms.
- Inorganic compounds do not contain carbon atoms (except carbon dioxide).

Next, let's take a look at four classes of organic compounds central to life on earth:

- carbohydrates
- proteins
- lipids
- nucleic acids

Carbohydrates

Organic compounds that contain carbon, hydrogen, and oxygen are called **carbohydrates**. They usually contain these three elements in a ratio of 1:2:1, respectively.

Most carbohydrates are categorized as either **monosaccharides, disaccharides,** or **polysaccharides.** The term *saccharides* is a fancy word for sugar. The prefixes mono-, di-, and poly- refer to the number of sugars in the molecule. Mono means "one," di- means "two," and poly means "many." A monosaccharide is therefore a carbohydrate made up of a single type of sugar molecule.

Monosaccharides: The Simplest Sugars

Monosaccharides, the simplest sugars, serve as an energy source for cells. While there are many different types of monosaccharides, the two most common sugars are glucose and fructose. Both of these monosaccharides are six-carbon sugars with the chemical formula $C_6H_{12}O_6$. **Glucose,** the most abundant monosaccharide, is the most popular sugar around. Plants produce it by capturing sunlight for energy, while cells break it down to release stored energy. Glucose can come in two forms: a-glucose and B-glucose, which differ simply by a reversal of the H and OH on the first carbon. **Fructose,** the other monosaccharide you should be familiar with is a common sugar in fruits.

One last thing. Glucose and fructose can be depicted as either straight chains or rings. Both of them are pretty easy to spot; just look for the six carbon molecules. These are the two different forms.

Ring form of glucose

Straight-chain
form of glucose

Ring form of fructose

Straight-chain
form of fructose

Disaccharides

What happens when two monosaccharides are brought together? The hydrogen (–H) from one sugar molecule combines with the hydroxyl group (–OH) of another sugar molecule. What do H and OH add up to? Water (H_2O)! So a water molecule is removed from the two sugars. The two molecules of monosaccharide are chemically linked and form a disaccharide.

Maltose is an example of a disaccharide:

Glucose   Glucose

Maltose

Maltose is formed by linking two glucose molecules—forming a **glycosidic bond.** This process is called **dehydration synthesis,** or **condensation.** During this process, a water molecule is lost.

Now what if you want to break up the disaccharide and form two monosaccharides again? Just add water! That's called **hydrolysis.**

Polysaccharides

Polysaccharides are made up many repeated units of monosaccharides. Therefore, a polysaccharide is a kind of **polymer,** a molecule with repeating subunits of the same general type. Common polysaccharides you should be familiar with include **starch, cellulose,** and **glycogen.** Polysaccharides are often storage forms of sugar or structural components of cells. For instance, animals store glucose molecules in the form of glycogen in the liver and muscle cells. Plants stockpile a-glucose in the form of starch in structures called **plastids.** On the other hand, cellulose, which is made up of B-glucose, is a major part of the cell wall in plants. Its function is to lend structural support. Chitin, a polymer of B-glucose molecules, serves as a structural molecule in the walls of fungus and in the exoskeletons of arthropods.

Here's something to think about: Why can't humans digest cellulose? The glycoside bond in polymers that have a-glucose can easily be broken down by humans but the glycoside bond in polymers containing B-glucose polymers, such as cellulose, cannot. This is because the bonds joining the glucose subunits in cellulose are different than those in starch. Starch is composed of a-glucose subunits held together by 1-4 glycoside linkages, while cellulose contains B-glucose subunits held together by 1-4 linkages.

———————————————◯———————————————

Of the choices below, which is the simplest sugar, which serves as an energy source for cells?

A.   carbohydrate

B.   polysaccharide

C.   monosaccharide

D.   disaccharide

Here's How to Crack It
Carbohydrates are organic compounds that contain carbon, hydrogen, and oxygen, but they are not the simplest sugars, so eliminate choice A. From your reading, you recall that "saccharide" is a fancy word for sugar and the prefixes poly-, mono-, and di- indicate the number of sugars in the molecule. From words like monotone, monologue, you know that mono means "one" and it stands to reason that the simplest sugar is the one that hasn't come together with any other molecules yet, so the correct answer is choice C, monosaccharide.

———————————————◯———————————————

Proteins
Amino acids are organic molecules that serve as the building blocks of proteins. They contain carbon, hydrogen, oxygen, and nitrogen atoms. There are 20 different amino acids commonly found in proteins. You should remember that every amino acid has four important parts: an **amino group** ($-NH_2$), a **carboxyl group** (−COOH), a **hydrogen atom,** and an **R group.**

Here is a typical amino acid:

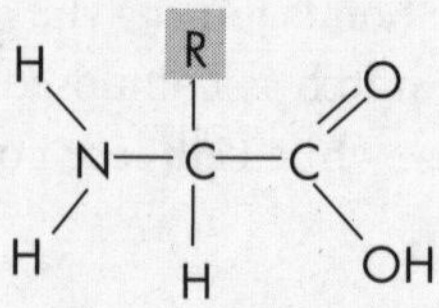

Amino acids differ only in the R group, which is also called the **side chain**. The R group associated with an amino acid could be as simple as a hydrogen atom (as in the amino acid glycine) or as complex as a carbon skeleton (as in the amino acid arginine).

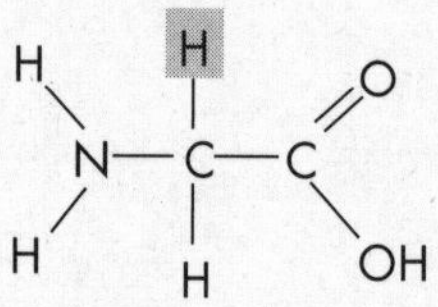

Glycine

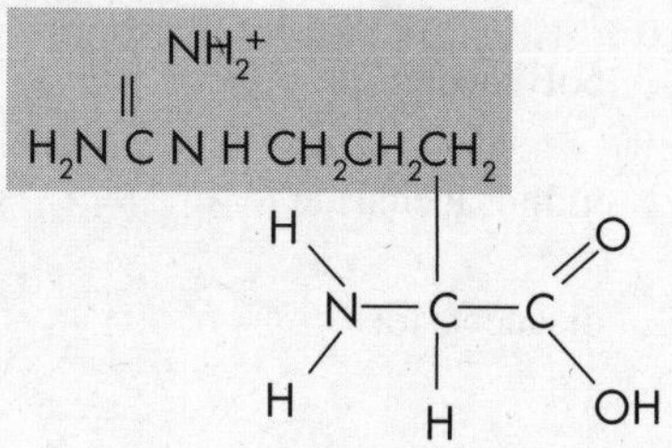

Arginine

It's a good idea to identify the functional groups of the different structures. Functional groups are the distinctive groups of atoms that play a large role in determining the chemical behavior of the compound they are a part of. For example, an organic acid has a functional group, the carboxyl group (COOH) that releases hydrogen ions in water. This makes the solution acidic. When it comes to spotting an amino acid, simply keep an eye out for the amino group (NH_2), and then look for the carboxyl molecule (COOH). The most common functional groups of organic compounds are as follows:

Functional Group	Structural Formula	Molecular Formula
Amino		$-NH_2$
Alkyl		$-C_nH_{2n+1}$
Methyl		$-CH_3$
Ethyl		$-C_2H_5$
Propyl		$-C_3H_7$
Carboxyl		$-COOH$
Hydroxyl	$-O-H$	$-OH$
Aldehyde		$-CHO$
Keto (carbonyl)		$-CO$
Sulfhydryl (thiol)	$-S-H$	$-SH$
Phenyl		$-C_6H_5$

Polypeptides

When two amino acids join, they form a **dipeptide.** The carboxyl group of one amino acid combines with the amino group of another amino acid. Here's an example:

Here's the
peptide bond

This is the same process we saw earlier: dehydration synthesis. Why? Because a water molecule is removed to form a bond. By the way, the bond between two amino acids has a special name—**a peptide bond.** If a group of amino acids is joined together in a "string," the resulting organic compound is called a **polypeptide.** Once a polypeptide string twists and folds on itself, it forms a three-dimensional structure called a **protein.**

Lipids

Like carbohydrates, **lipids** consist of carbon, hydrogen, and oxygen atoms, but not in the 1:2:1 ratio typical of carbohydrates. The most common examples of lipids are fats, oils, phospholipids, and **steroids.** Let's talk about the simple lipids—**neutral fats.** A typical fat consists of three fatty acids and one molecule of **glycerol.** If you see the word *triglyceride* on the test, it's just a fancy word for *fat.*

Glycerol —

Ester Linkage

Fatty Acid 1 (saturated)

Fatty Acid 2 (monounsaturated)

Fatty Acid 3 (saturated)

To make a triglyceride, each of the carboxyl groups (–COOH) of the three fatty acids must react with one of the three hydroxyl groups (–PH) of the glycerol molecule. This happens by the removal of a water molecule. So, the creation of a fat requires the removal of three molecules of water. Once again, what have we got? You probably already guessed it—dehydration synthesis! The linkage now formed between the glycerol molecule and the fatty acids is called **ester linkage**. A fatty acid can be **saturated**, which means it has a single covalent bond between each pair of carbon atoms or it can be **unsaturated**, which means adjacent carbons are joined by double bonds instead of single bonds. A **polyunsaturated** fatty acid has many double bonds within the fatty acid.

Lipids are important because they function as structural components of cell membranes, sources of insulation, and a means of energy storage.

Phospholipids

Another special class of lipids is known as **phospholipids**. Phospholipids contain two fatty acid "tails" and one negatively charged phosphate "head." Take a look at a typical phospholipid.

Typical Phospholipid

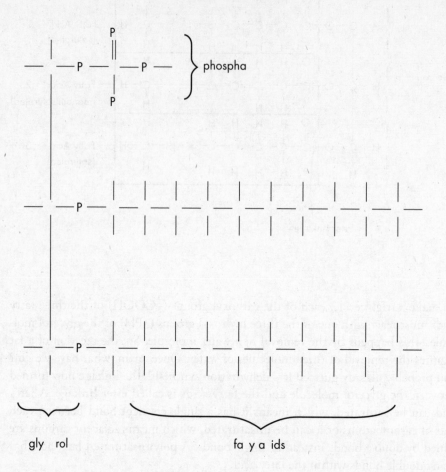

gly rol   fa y a ids

A Chemistry Lesson at the Salad Bar!
You deal with phospholipid separation every time you shake salad dressing before serving it.

Phospholipids are extremely important, mainly because of some unique properties they possess, particularly with regard to water.

Interestingly enough, the two fatty acid tails are **hydrophobic** (water-hating). In other words, just like oil and vinegar, fatty acids and water don't mix. The reason for this is that fatty acid tails are nonpolar, and nonpolar substances don't mix well with polar ones, such as water.

On the other hand, the phosphate head of the lipid is **hydrophilic** (water-loving) meaning that it does mix well with water. Why? It carries a negative charge, and this charge draws it to the positively charged end of a water molecule. A molecule is **amphipathic** if it has both a hydrophilic region and a hydrophobic region. A phospholipid is amphipathic.

This arrangement of the fatty acid tail and the phosphate group head provides phospholipids with a unique shape. The two fatty acid chains orient themselves away from the water, while the phosphate portion orients itself toward the water.

One class of lipids is known as steroids. All steroids have a basic structure of four linked carbon rings. This category includes cholesterol, vitamin D, and a variety of hormones. Take a look at a typical steroid.

Nucleic Acids

The fourth class of organic compounds is the **nucleic acids.** Like proteins, nucleic acids contain carbon, hydrogen, oxygen, and nitrogen but nucleic acids also contain phosphorus. Nucleic acids are molecules made up of simple units called **nucleotides.** There are two kinds of nucleic acids you should be familiar with: **deoxyribonucleic acid** (DNA) and **ribonucleic acid** (RNA).

KEY TERMS

matter

elements

atoms

molecules

protons

neutrons

electrons

nucleus

isotopes

solid liquid gas

physical change

chemical change

color

density

hardness

conductivity

conductor

non-conductor

exothermic

endothermic

periodic table

atomic number

atomic weight

period

quantum number (shell number)

group

compound

chemical reaction

chemical bonds

ionic bonds

covalent bonds

hydrogen bonds

nonpolar covalent

polar covalent

cohesion

adhesion

capillary action

heat capacity

acidic

basic

neutral

alkaline

pH scale

organic compounds

inorganic compounds

carbon

carbohydrates

monosaccharide

disaccharide

polysaccharide

glucose

fructose

glycosidic bond

dehydration synthesis
  (condensation)

hydrolysis

polymer

starch

cellulose

glycogen

plastids

amino acids

amino group

carboxyl group

hydrogen atom

R group (side chain)

dipeptide

peptide bond

polypeptide

protein

lipids

steroids

neutral fats

glycerol

ester linkage

saturated

unsaturated

polyunsaturated

phospholipids

hydrophobic

hydrophilic

amphipathic

nucleic acids

nucleotides

deoxyribonucleic acid (DNA)

ribonucleic acid (RNA)

Drill #6

Each group of questions below is followed by four suggested answers or completions. Select the one that is best in each case.

1. Which of the following organic molecules is a major storage carbohydrate used to store energy in plants?

   A. cellulose

   B. maltose

   C. fructose

   D. glycogen

2. A solution with a pH of 10 is how many times more basic than a solution with a pH of 8?

   A.   2

   B.   4

   C.   10

   D. 100

3. The conversion of lactose to glucose and galactose involves the addition of which of the following molecules to the lactose molecule?

   A. O_2

   B. H_2

   C. ATP

   D. H_2O

4. A scientist is studying a type of matter called WC22. All that scientists know about WC22 is that it's unable to expand to fill the available volume, but it's able to conform to the shape of the container that holds it. What type of matter must WC22 be?

   A. liquid

   B. solid

   C. gas

   D. conductor

5. Which of the following is something that plants produce by capturing sunlight for energy and cells break it down to release stored energy?

   A. fructose

   B. glucose

   C. disaccharides

   D. photosynthesis

ANSWERS AND EXPLANATIONS TO DRILL #6

1. **D** There are only two major storage forms of carbohydrates, starch and glycogen. Starch is the storage form of sugars in plants. Cellulose (A) is a structural component of the cell wall. Choices B and C (maltose and fructose) are monosaccharides.

2. **D** A change of pH equals a tenfold change in hydrogen ion concentration. Therefore, if the pH changes from 8 to 10 (a pH change of 2), the resulting solution is 10×10, or 100, times more basic.

3. **D** For lactose to be hydrolyzed to glucose and galactose, a water molecule must be added. The other species—O_2, H_2, and ATP—will not hydrolyze lactose.

4. **A** WC22 must be a liquid, as the liquid phase of matter is characterized by the ability of the material to confirm to the shape of the container that holds it, but an inability of the material to expand to fit the available volume.

5. **B** Glucose is the most abundant monosaccharide, the most popular sugar around, and plants produce it by capturing sunlight for energy, while cells break it down to release stored energy. Don't be thrown off by photosynthesis, choice D, which is described in the question. Glucose is what plants produce during photosynthesis, so choice B is correct.

Summary

- Everything in the world is made up of matter comprised of atoms or molecules.

- Within atoms are protons, neutrons, and electrons.

- Matter can be a gas, a liquid, or a solid.

- Matter can undergo physical changes and chemical changes.

- The periodic table is a useful tool for organizing all elements.

- Solutions can be acidic, basic, or neutral and the acidity or alkalinity of a solution is measured with a pH scale.

- Most of the chemical compounds in living organisms contain a selection of carbon atoms, also known as organic compounds. Molecules without carbon atoms are inorganic compounds.

- Most carbohydrates are categorized as either monosaccharides, disaccharides, or polysaccharides.

- Amino acids are organic molecules that serve as the building blocks of proteins.

Chapter 9
Principles of
Motion and Energy

Subtest II will test your knowledge of the principles of motion and energy. Like the content in the last chapter, you need to know about a bunch of different topics, but not in extreme depth. Think of this as a shallow review—let's go over the basics and review some math and science topics that you probably haven't seen in years. Fear not, we've got you covered.

To successfully tackle this section, you need to review the following:

Principles of Motion and Energy
- Description of object motion based on speed, velocity, and acceleration
- Forces such as gravity, magnetism, and friction
- Forms of energy, including solar, chemical, electrical, magnetic, nuclear, sound, light, and electromagnetic
- Heat, thermal energy, and temperature as well as measurement systems
- Transfer of heat by conduction, convection, and radiation
- Sources of light
- Optical properties of waves including light, sound, and reflection
- Conservation of energy resources for renewable and nonrenewable natural resources

MOTION BASICS

The basics of motion are seen in everyday life. **Motion** is any physical movement or change in position or place. Motion may be characterized by **position**, the location of an object; **displacement**, the distance an object has moved; **speed**, the time-rate of displacement or object movement; **velocity**, the direction of speed; and **acceleration**, the rate of velocity change.

POSITION, DISTANCE, AND DISPLACMENT

Position is an object's relation to a coordinate axis system. **Distance** is a scalar that represents the total amount traveled by an object. **Displacement** is an object's change in position. It's the vector that points from the object's initial position to its final position, regardless of the path actually taken. Since displacement means change in position, it's generically denoted Δs, where Δ denotes *change in* and s means spatial location. (The letter p is not used for position because it's reserved for another quantity: **momentum**.)

Let's try a problem.

In a track-and-field event, an athlete
runs exactly once around an oval track,
a total distance of 500 m. Find the
runner's displacement for the race.

A.   0 m

B.   500 m

C.   1,000 m

D.   2,000 m

Here's How to Crack It

If the runner returns to the same position from which she left, then her displacement is zero.

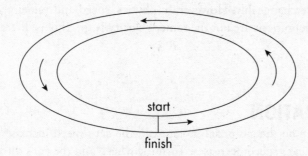

The *total* distance covered is 500 m, but the net distance—the displacement—is 0. Don't be tricked into picking 500 m, choice B, because you didn't read the question carefully. The correct answer is choice A.

SPEED AND VELOCITY

When we're in a moving car, the speedometer tells us how fast we're going; it gives us our speed. But what does it mean to have a speed of say, 10 m/s? It means that we're covering a distance of 10 meters every second. By definition, **average speed** is the ratio of the total distance traveled to the time required to cover that distance:

$$\text{average speed} = \frac{\text{total distance}}{\text{time}}$$

The car's speedometer doesn't care in what direction the car is moving (as long as the wheels are moving forward). You could be driving north, south, east, west, whatever; the speedometer would make no distinction. 55 miles per hour, north and 55 miles per hour, east register the same on the speedometer: 55 miles per hour.

However, we will also need to include direction in our descriptions of motion. We just learned about displacement, which takes both distance (net distance) and direction into account. The single concept that embodies both speed and direction is called **velocity**, and the definition of average velocity is

$$\text{average velocity} = \frac{\text{displacement}}{\text{time}}$$

$$\bar{v} = \frac{\Delta s}{\Delta t}$$

(The bar over the **v** means average.) Because Δs is a vector, $\bar{v}$ is also a vector, and because Δt is a positive scalar, the direction of $\bar{v}$ is the same as the direction of Δs. The magnitude of the velocity vector is called the object's speed, and is expressed in units of meters per second (m/s).

Note the distinction between speed and velocity. In everyday language, they're often used interchangeably. However, in physics, speed and velocity are technical terms whose definitions are not the same. Velocity is speed plus direction.

ACCELERATION

When you step on the gas pedal in your car, the car's speed increases; step on the brake and the car's speed decreases. Turn the wheel, and the car's direction of motion changes. In all of these cases, the velocity changes. To describe this change in velocity, we need a new term: **acceleration.** In the same way that velocity measures the rate-of-change of an object's position, acceleration measures the rate-of-change of an object's velocity. An object's average acceleration is defined as follows:

$$\text{average acceleration} = \frac{\text{change in velocity}}{\text{time}}$$

$$\bar{a} = \frac{\Delta v}{\Delta t}$$

The units of acceleration are meters per second, per second: $[a]$ = m/s^2. Because $\Delta \mathbf{v}$ is a vector, $\bar{a}$ is also a vector; and because Δt is a positive scalar, the direction of $\bar{a}$ is the same as the direction of $\Delta \mathbf{v}$.

Furthermore, if we take an object's original direction of motion to be positive, then an increase in speed corresponds to a positive acceleration, while a decrease in speed corresponds to a negative acceleration (deceleration).

Note that an object can accelerate even if its speed doesn't change. (Again, it's a matter of not allowing the everyday usage of the word *accelerate* to interfere with its technical, physics usage.) This is because acceleration depends on Δ**v**, and the velocity vector **v** changes if (1) speed changes, or (2) direction changes, or (3) both speed and direction change. For instance, a car traveling around a circular racetrack is constantly accelerating even if the car's speed is constant, because the direction of the car's velocity vector is constantly changing.

Let's tackle a sample problem.

A car is traveling in a straight line along a highway at a constant speed of 80 miles per hour for 10 seconds. What is its acceleration?

A.   0

B.   80

C.   600

D.   3,600

Here's How to Crack It
This is another example of a tricky question that requires careful reading. Since the car is traveling at a constant velocity, its acceleration is zero. If there's no change in velocity, then there's no acceleration. Choice A is correct.

GRAVITY AND FORCE
Gravity's value at Earth's surface, denoted g, is approximately expressed below as the standard average.

$$g = 9.81 \text{ m/s}^2 = 32.2 \text{ ft/s}^2$$

This means that, ignoring air resistance, an object falling freely near Earth's surface increases its velocity with 9.81 m/s (22 mph) for each second of its descent.

An interaction between two bodies—a push or a pull—is called a **force**. If you lift a book, you exert an **upward force** (created by your muscles) on it. If you pull on a rope that's attached to a crate you create a **tension** in the rope that pulls the crate. When a skydiver is falling through the air, the earth is exerting a downward pull called **gravitational force,** and the air exerts and upward force called **air resistance**. When you stand on the floor, the floor provides an upward, supporting force called the **normal force**. If you slide a book across a table, the table exerts a **frictional force** against the book, so the book slows down and then stops. Static cling provides a directly observable example of the **electrostatic force**. Protons and neutrons are held together in the nuclei of atoms by the **strong nuclear force,** and radioactive nuclei decay through the action of the **weak nuclear force.**

NEWTON'S LAWS

Sir Isaac Newton began the modern study of principles associated with these concepts. Three of the laws that Newton stated in *Principia* are known as **Newton's Laws of Motion**. They form the basis for dynamics—that is, why things move the way they do.

The First Law

Newton's First Law says that an object will continue in its state of motion unless compelled to change by a force impressed upon it. That is, unless an unbalanced force acts on an object, the object's velocity will not change: If the object is at rest, then it will stay at rest; and if it is moving, then it will continue to move at a constant speed in a straight line.

Basically, no force means no change in velocity. This property of objects, their natural resistance to changes in their state of motion, is called **inertia**. In fact, the First Law is often referred to as the **Law of Inertia**.

The Second Law

Newton's Second Law predicts what will happen when a force *does* act on an object: The object's velocity will change; the object will accelerate. More precisely, it says that its acceleration, **a**, will be directly proportional to the strength of the total—or *net*—force ($\mathbf{F}_{net}$) and inversely proportional to the object's mass, *m*:

$$\mathbf{F}_{net} = m\mathbf{a}$$

This is the most important equation in mechanics!

The **mass** of an object is the quantitative measure of its inertia; intuitively, it measures how much matter is contained in an object. Two identical boxes, one empty and one full, have different masses. The box that's full has the greater mass, because it contains more stuff; more stuff, more mass. Mass is measured in **kilograms**, abbreviated kg. (Note: An object whose mass is 1 kg weighs about 2.2 pounds.) It takes twice as much force to produce the same change in velocity of a 2 kg object than of a 1 kg object. Mass is a measure of an object's inertia, its resistance to acceleration.

The Third Law

The Third Law is commonly remembered as to every action, there is an equal, but opposite, reaction. More precisely, if Object 1 exerts a force on Object 2, then Object 2 exerts a force back on Object 1, equal in strength but opposite in direction. These two forces, $F_{1\text{-on-}2}$ and $F_{2\text{-on-}1}$, are called an **action/reaction pair**.

Let's try a problem.

Newton's Third Law of motion states that for every action, there is an equal and opposite reaction. Which of the following is the best example of the application of this law?

A.   Less energy is used to roll a wheelbarrel over ice than to roll it over sand.

B.   A paper airplane thrown across a classroom remains in motion until it bumps into the force of a student's head.

C.   When swimming, your hands push the water behind you and the water pushes you in the forward direction.

D.   More fuel is needed to drive a car 35 miles when the trunk is full of sandbags, than when the trunk is empty.

Here's How to Crack It

Choices A and D are obviously wrong—they have nothing to do with Newton's Third Law. Choice B might sound familiar, because it's an example of Newton's First Law. Don't fall for that trap. That leaves the only correct example of an action (pushing water behind you) and its reaction (being propelled forward), choice C.

WEIGHT

Mass and **weight** are not the same thing—there is a clear distinction between them in physics—but they are often used interchangeably in everyday life. The weight of an object is the gravitational force exerted on it by Earth (or by whatever planet it happens to be on). Mass, by contrast, is an intrinsic property of an object that measures its inertia. An object's mass does not change with location. Put a baseball in a rocket and send it to the Moon. The baseball's weight on the Moon is less than its weight here on Earth (because the Moon's gravitational pull is weaker than Earth's due to its much smaller mass), but the baseball's mass would be the same.

FRICTION

When an object is in contact with a surface, the surface exerts a contact force on the object. The component of the contact force that's parallel to the surface is called the **friction force** on the object. Friction, like the normal force, arises from electrical interactions between atoms that comprise the object and those that comprise the surface.

We'll look at two main categories of friction: (1) **static friction** and (2) **kinetic (sliding) friction**. If you attempt to push a heavy crate across a floor, at first you meet with resistance, but then you push hard enough to get the crate moving. The force that acted on the crate to cancel out your initial pushes was static friction, and the force that acts on the crate as it slides across the floor is kinetic friction. Static friction occurs when there is no relative motion between the object and the surface (no sliding); kinetic friction occurs when there *is* relative motion (when there's sliding).

Let's try a problem.

On a chilly winter day, Selena rubs her hands together while waiting at the bus stop. As she rapidly rubs them against each other, her hands become warm. What is this an example of?

A.   Newton's First Law

B.   static friction

C.   Newton's Third Law

D.   friction between surfaces converting kinetic energy into thermal energy

Here's How to Crack It

You can eliminate choices A and C immediately—this question isn't about inertia or a force acting on an object outside itself. With choice B, the word "friction" might catch your eye and entice you—don't fall for it! As we covered before, static friction occurs when there is no relative motion between the object and the surface, so choice B must be wrong. Choice D is the perfect explanation, and the correct answer.

SIMPLE MACHINES

Simple machines are an important piece in learning about motion and energy. There are six classical simple machines:

1.   A **lever** is a rigid object that is used with a **fulcrum** (pivot point) to multiply the mechanical force (**effort**) that can be applied to another object (**load**). This leverage is called **mechanical advantage.** An example of a lever is a teeter-totter.
2.   A **wheel and axle** is a modified first-class lever that rotates in a circle around a center point (fulcrum). The larger wheel (or outside) rotates around the smaller wheel (**axle**). Examples include bicycle wheels, ferris wheels, and gears.
3.   A **pulley** is a device that changes the direction of the tension force in the cords that slide over them. These are often seen on ships, where they are called "blocks."
4.   An **inclined plane** is basically a ramp. If you've ever loaded furniture into and out of a moving truck, you know that placing an inclined plane from the road to the truck bed makes life a lot easier.

5. A **wedge** is a triangular-shaped tool that is really a compound inclined plane. It can be used to separate two objects or portions of an object, lift an object, or hold an object in place. Examples include nails (split and separate the material into which they are driven; the shafts may then hold fast due to friction) and doorstops.

6. A **screw** is a shaft with some type of helical groove or thread formed on its surface. It is basically an inclined plane wrapped around a shaft. Examples include a drill bit, a nut and bolt, and a cork screw.

A simple machine is a mechanical device that changes the direction or magnitude of force. In general, these simple machines are the building blocks from which more complicated machines are composed. For example, wheels, levers, and pulleys are used together in the mechanism of a bicycle. Simple machines are used to accomplish difficult tasks through manipulating and leveraging small forces.

Let's try a simple machine practice problem.

Sean uses his wooden paint stirrer to pry open a fresh can of paint by wedging the wooden stick beneath the top, then pressing his body weight down (force) on the other end of the stick, with the paint can's outer lip acting as a fulcrum. What type of simple machine has Sean created?

A. wedge

B. screw

C. lever

D. inclined plane

Here's How to Crack It

Don't fall for the trap of choice A—just because the word "wedge" appears in the question doesn't make this simple machine a wedge. The paint-stirring stick isn't a triangular tool, and choice A is definitely wrong. Choices B and D don't even apply to this situation. If you visualize the situation, it's clear that Sean has created a lever—the fulcrum multiplies his force so that the paint can's lid (the load, in this situation) will pop off. Choice C is correct.

ENERGY

It wasn't until more than one hundred years after Newton's studies that the idea of energy became incorporated into physics. Today it permeates every branch of the subject.

It's difficult to give a precise definition of energy; there are different forms of energy because there are different kinds of forces. The CSET focuses on the following forms of energy:

- **Solar energy** is radiant light and heat from the Sun, and it is used along with secondary solar-powered resources such as wind, wave power, and hydroelectricity. One example of solar energy is the use of solar panels to harness energy that can be used even when it's nighttime.
- **Chemical energy** is the interrelation of work and heat with chemical reactions. Natural gas, coal, and petroleum are examples of stored chemical energy.
- **Electrical energy** is associated with conservative Coulomb forces (electrostatic interaction between electrically charged particles). Examples include batteries and lightning.
- **Magnetic energy** and electrical energy are related by Maxwell's equations (equations can be combined to show that light is an electromagnetic wave). Magnets align with magnetic fields. One example of magnetic energy in action includes the compass.
- **Nuclear energy** is released by the splitting (**fission**) or merging (**fusion**) of atoms. Examples include nuclear power plants and atomic and hydrogen bombs.
- **Sound energy** is the same thing as sound waves. Sound is a traveling wave that is an oscillation of pressure transmitted through a solid, liquid, or gas. One example is an opera singer hitting a high note and shattering a glass.
- **Energy of light** is also known as **luminous energy.** This is not the same as radiant energy. The human eye can see light only in the visible spectrum and has different sensitivities to light of different wavelengths within the spectrum. Examples include the way in which you process the physical world.
- **Electromagnetic energy** is a phenomenon that takes the form of self-propagating waves in a vacuum or matter. Examples include radio waves, micro waves, X-rays, gamma rays, and much more.

All energy can be put into one of two categories: potential and kinetic.

Potential energy is energy of position—gravitational energy. Examples include chemical, mechanical, nuclear, gravitational, and electrical energy.

Kinetic energy is energy of motion—of waves, objects, substances, and molecules. Examples include radiant, thermal, motion, and sound energy.

Energy can come into a system or leave it via various interactions that produce changes. One of the best definitions we know reads as follows:

> **Force** is the agent of change, **energy** is the measure of change, and **work** is the way of transferring energy from one system to another.

And one of the most important laws in physics (the **Law of Conservation of Energy,** also known as the **First Law of Thermodynamics**) says that if you account for all its various forms, the total amount of energy in a given process will stay constant; that is, it will be conserved. For example, electrical energy can be converted into light and heat (this is how a light bulb works), but the amount of electrical energy coming into the light bulb equals the total amount of light and heat given off. Energy cannot be created or destroyed; it can only be transferred (from one system to another) or transformed (from one form to another).

WORK

When you lift a book from the floor, you exert a force on it, over a distance; when you push a crate across a floor, you also exert a force on it, over a distance. The application of force over a distance, and the resulting change in energy of the system that the force acted on, give rise to the concept of work. When you hold a book in your hand, you exert a force on the book (normal force), but since the book is at rest, the force does not act through a distance, so you do no work on the book. Although you did work on the book as you lifted it from the floor, once it's at rest in your hand, you are no longer doing work on it.

> If a force **F** acts over a distance d, and **F** is parallel to **d**, then the work done by **F** is the product of force and distance: $W = Fd$.

Notice that, although work depends on two vectors (**F** and **d**), work itself is not a vector. Work is a scalar quanity.

Let's try a problem.

A man pushes against a rock for 15 minutes to move it out of his driveway, but the rock never budges.

Work is defined as the force it takes to actually move an object. Using this definition, how much work did the man do?

A.   none

B.   more than was necessary

C.   15 minutes' worth

D.   enough to tire him out

Here's How to Crack It

Choices B, C, and D might seem appealing, but they are wrong. Focus on the definition of work to solve this problem. The man actually did no work, even though he is completely exhausted from the effort.

POWER

Simply put, **power** is the rate at which work gets done (or energy gets transferred, which is the same thing). Suppose you and I each do 1000 J of work, but I do the work in 2 minutes while you do it in 1 minute. We both did the same amount of work, but you did it more quickly; you were more powerful. Here's the definition of power:

$$\text{Power} = \frac{\text{Work}}{\text{time}} \qquad \text{(in symbols)} \quad \rightarrow \quad P = \frac{W}{t}$$

The unit of power is the joule per second (J/s), which is renamed the **watt**, and symbolized W (not to be confused with the symbol for work, W). One watt is 1 joule per second: 1 W = 1 J/s.

FORMS OF ENERGY

Heat

Energy can present in the form of **heat.** But **temperature** is best characterized as a measure of the aggregate atomic or molecular activity pertaining to a particular object. Measurements of temperature may be calculated using such devices as thermometers, thermocouples, and optical methods.

When heated to a certain temperature, a mercury or alcohol **thermometer** will use principles of expansion properties. Fluids, when heated, will expand or contract to an exact amount which can then be read by the identifiers on the thermometer.

A **thermocouple** is also a temperature sensor. A small electrical signal is produced by metals that are joined together.

Optical methods may be used for certain solids (such as metals). For example, some metals will begin to glow when heated. Color plays a major role in this with warmer temperatures exhibiting a dull red, which may progress to a yellow/white and at the highest temperatures appear as a blueish white.

TRANSFER OF HEAT

Conduction, radiation, and **convection** are different ways in which the transfer of heat may occur. Conduction refers to instances in which heat flows from a hotter object to a cooler one. Radiation refers to heat transfer in a vacuum where there is no possibility of conduction. The heat radiates or emits from the heated object into a space area. Convection involves the heating and circulation of a substance that changes density when it is heated.

Light Sources

The CSET requires that you know about light sources including the Sun, light bulbs, and excited atoms. The light given off by the Sun enables photosynthesis (more below). We can also produce light, as in light bulbs. The basic idea behind light bulbs is simple. Electricity runs through the filament. Because the filament is so thin, it offers some resistance to the electricity, and this resistance converts electrical energy into heat. The heat is enough to make the filament white hot, and the "white" part is light. That is how an **incandescent light** bulb works. A fluorescent light bulb works differently. A **fluorescent bulb** has electrodes at both ends of a fluorescent tube, and a gas containing argon and mercury vapor inside the tube. A stream of electrons flows through the gas from one electrode to the other.

These electrons bump into the mercury atoms and excite them. As the mercury atoms move from the excited state back to the unexcited state, they give off ultraviolet photons. These photons hit the phosphor, coating the inside of the fluorescent tube, and this phosphor creates visible light. Light sources emanate from wavelengths (meaning color). **Polychromatic** refers to a mixture of colors, or a white light source. Single-color sources are known as **monochromatic.**

Light and Matter Interaction

Vision, photosynthesis, and **photoemission** are modes of light and matter interaction. Vision (light in the visible spectrum) interacts with the human eye, producing electrical signals that the brain is able to read and decipher as color. We perceive color in an object because of the way the object reflects the light reaching it. For example, we see bananas as yellow because bananas absorb all the colors of the spectrum except yellow. Photosynthesis is the process by which organisms (plants and bacteria) use energy in the form of light and convert it to chemical form (oxygen and reduced carbon compounds). Photoemission refers to the interaction of light with certain types of materials. Electrons are emitted by the lighted material.

Let's try a problem.

Which of the following is an explanation for why we perceive a red apple as red?

A. The apple reflects all the colors of the spectrum except for red, which is absorbed.

B. The apple absorbs all the other colors of the spectrum, but reflects red.

C. The apple reflects green and blue, the other two primary colors, but absorbs red.

D. The apple absorbs green, blue, and red.

Here's How to Crack It

Primary colors have nothing to do with anything here, so scratch out choice C immediately. Choice A gets the information that we know about light and color backward. We see color because that color is reflected back to us, not absorbed. So you can eliminate choice A. Choice B gets the information right exactly—this is the correct answer. Choices C and D maintain that we see colors that are absorbed by the object, rather than reflected by the object, so cross them off.

Waves

Waves are designated as **transverse** or **longitudinal.** A transverse wave has a wave disturbance, or amplitude perpendicular or transverse to the direction of propagation. However, in a longitudinal wave, wave disturbances are parallel to the direction of propagation. One way to think about a wave's energy is simply a disturbance traveling through medium at speeds that depend on the medium.

Waves are reflected or refracted. **Reflection** occurs when all or part of a wave bounces off a surface and is redirected to another surface. **Refraction** refers to a wave's penetration of a surface.

Frequency is one way to measure sound waves. The frequency is the number of complete cycles of a sound wave within one second. One cycle per second is called 1 **hertz.** Human ears can detect sounds from about 20 hertz (the lowest sound) to about 20,000 hertz (the highest sound). Below 20 hertz, humans feel only the vibration of the sound. Above 20,000 hertz, they can't hear the sound at all (but dogs can!). All sound travels at the same speed, regardless of frequency.

MAGNETS

The CSET will likely have a few questions about magnetic properties, so let's do a quick review of magnets.

A **magnet** is a material or object that produces a magnetic field. This magnetic field is a force that pulls or repels other magnets, depending on their magnetism. A magnet pulls unlike charges and repels like charges. In short, opposites attract. The magnetic force surrounding a magnet isn't uniform. Each end of a magnet has a great concentration of force, while the center of a magnet has a weak magnetic force. The two ends of a magnet are called the **poles**, much like the poles on Earth.

A **compass** works because its needle is a freely rotating magnet. The painted end, or **needle,** of a compass is drawn to the north (magnetic) pole of Earth to align itself in a northerly direction. It seems confusing, but the needle labeled "N" in a compass is actually a magnet of the opposite charge (S)—it is drawn to north because opposites attract. The area to which the needle points is called the **North**

Magnetic Pole, which is close to the geographic North Pole (but not the exact same place).

Let's tackle a magnetism question of the type you may encounter on the CSET.

Magnets are often made of polarized metal bars, especially bars made of iron. Magnets are attracted only to certain types of metal. Typically, metals that make good magnets are also attracted to magnets. Based on this information, which of the following is a magnet most likely attracted to?

A. copper penny

B. aluminum can

C. plastic wrap

D. iron fillings

Here's How to Crack It

Choice C is obviously wrong—plastic is not magnetic, even in the best of science fiction movies. The passage states that magnets are often made of iron and also that the materials used to make magnets are also attracted to magnets. Thus, it can be inferred that magnets and iron attract and choice D is correct.

KEY TERMS

motion
position
displacement
speed
velocity
acceleration
position
distance
momentum
average speed
force
upward force
tension
gravitational force
air resistance
normal force
frictional force
electrostatic force
strong nuclear force
weak nuclear force
Newton's Laws of Motion
inertia
Law of Inertia
mass
kilogram
action/reaction pair
mass
weight
friction force
static friction
kinetic (sliding) friction
simple machine
lever
fulcrum
effort
load
mechanical advantage

wheel and axle
pulley
inclined plane
wedge
screw
force
energy
work
Law of Conservation of Energy
    (First Law of Thermodynamics)
power
watt
heat
temperature
thermometer
thermocouple
optical methods
conduction
radiation
convection
incandescent light
fluorescent light
photosynthesis
photoemission
waves
transverse waves
longitudinal waves
reflection
refraction
frequency
Hertz
magnet
pole
compass
needle
North Magnetic Pole

Drill #7

Each of the questions below is followed by four suggested answers or completions. Select the one that is best in each case.

1. Which of the following is/are true?

   I.   If an object's acceleration is constant, then it must move in a straight line.

   II. If an object's acceleration is zero, then its speed must remain constant.

   III. If an object's speed remains constant, then its acceleration must be zero.

   A.   I and II only

   B.   I and III only

   C.   II only

   D.   III only

2. A baseball is thrown straight upward. What is the ball's acceleration at its highest point?

   A.   0

   B. $\frac{1}{2}g$, downward

   C. g, downward

   D. $\frac{1}{2}g$, upward

3. A person standing on a horizontal floor feels two forces: the downward pull of gravity and the upward supporting force from the floor. These two forces:

   A.   have equal magnitudes and form an action/reaction pair.

   B.   have equal magnitudes but do not form an action/reaction pair.

   C.   have unequal magnitudes and form an action/reaction pair.

   D.   have unequal magnitudes and do not form an action/reaction pair.

4. Which of the following statements is true?

   A.   A white shirt absorbs all colors of light.

   B.   A blue shirt absorbs blue light.

   C.   A black shirt reflects all colors of light.

   D.   A red shirt reflects red light.

5. Below is a figure of a science experiment in which three donut-shaped magnets were stacked on a pole.

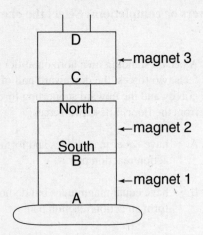

Based on the figure, which of the following represent(s) north poles?

A. A only

B. B only

C. B and C

D. A, B, and C

Please turn the page for answers and explanations
for the questions in this drill.

ANSWERS AND EXPLANATIONS TO DRILL #7

1.   **C**   Statement I is false since a projectile experiencing only the constant acceleration due to gravity can travel in a parabolic trajectory. Statement II is true: Zero acceleration means no change in speed (or direction). Statement III is false: An object whose speed remains constant but whose velocity vector is changing direction is acceleration.

2.   **C**   The baseball is still under the influence of Earth's gravity. Its acceleration throughout the entire flight is constant, equal to g downward.

3.   **B**   Because the person is not accelerating, the net force he feels must be zero. Therefore, the magnitude of the upward normal force from the floor must balance that of the downward gravitational force. Although these two forces have equal magnitudes, they do not form an action/reaction pair because they both act on the same object (namely, the person). The forces in an action/reaction pair always act on different objects.

4.   **D**   The color of an object is determined by the colors of light reflected. Choice D is correct because a red shirt must reflect red light.

5.   **C**   We know that opposite poles attract and like poles repel. In the diagram, we see that B is attracted to the south pole (above it), so B must be north and A must be south. We can see that C is repelled by a north pole (thus the gap), so C must be north and D is south. Thus, the north poles are B and C, and choice C is the correct answer.

Summary

o   The basics of motion are seen in everyday life.

o   Average speed is the ratio of the total distance traveled by the time required to cover that distance.

o   Velocity is a concept that embodies both speed and direction. Average velocity = displacement / time.

o   Acceleration measures the rate of change of an object's velocity.

o   Force is an interaction between two bodies.

o   Gravity on Earth's surface is 9.81 m/s^2 and denoted by the letter g.

o   Newton's Laws of Motion are the basis of dynamics.

o   The weight of an object is the gravitational force exerted on it by Earth.

o   The mass is the intrinsic property of an object that measures its inertia.

o   Friction force is the component of the contact force that is parallel to the surface.

o   There are two main categories of friction: static and kinetic.

o   There are six types of simple machines and from those simple machines, all more complex machines are made.

o   All energy is either potential or kinetic.

o   Energy is a measurement of change; work is the way of transferring energy from one system to another.

o   Power is the rate at which work gets done.

o   Temperature is a measure of the aggregate atomic or molecular activity pertaining to a particular object.

o   Conduction, radiation, and convection are different ways in which the transfer of heat may occur.

o   The Sun, incandescent light bulbs, and fluorescent bulbs are three different sources of light.

o   All waves are either transverse or longitudinal. They can be reflected or refracted.

o   In the world of magnets, as in the singing of Paula Abdul, opposites attract.

Chapter 10
Structure and
Function of Living
Organisms

This chapter covers the structure of living organisms and their function. The CSET requires that you be familiar with the concepts listed below.

> ## Structure of Organisms and Their Function
> - Levels of organization and related functions in plants and animals including organ systems
> - Structures and related functions of plants and animals such as reproductive, respiratory, circulatory, and digestive functions
> - Principles of chemistry underlying the function of biological systems including carbon, water and salt, DNA, and photo-synthesis

LIVING THINGS

All living things—plants and animals—are composed of **cells.** According to the cell theory, the cell is life's basic unit of structure and function. In other words, the cell is the smallest unit of living material that can carry out all the activities necessary for life. Cells are studied using different types of microscopes.

WHAT ARE THE DIFFERENT TYPES OF CELLS?

For centuries, scientists have known about cells. However, it wasn't until the development of the electron microscope that scientists were able to figure out what cells do. We now know that there are two distinct types of cells: **eukaryotic cells** and **prokaryotic cells.** A eukaryotic cell contains a membrane-bound structure called a **nucleus** and **cytoplasm,** filled with tiny structures called **organelles** (literally "little organs"). Examples of eukaryotic cells are fungi, plant cells, and animal cells.

A prokaryotic cell, which is a lot smaller than a eukaryotic cell, lacks both a nucleus and membrane-bound organelles. An example of a prokaryotic cell is bacteria. The genetic material in a prokaryote is one continuous, circular DNA molecule that lies free in the cell in an area called the **nucleoid.** In addition to a plasma membrane, most prokaryotes have a cell wall composed of peptidoglycan. Prokaryotes may also have ribosomes (although smaller than those found in eukaryotic cells) as well as a **flagellum,** a long fiber that helps them move.

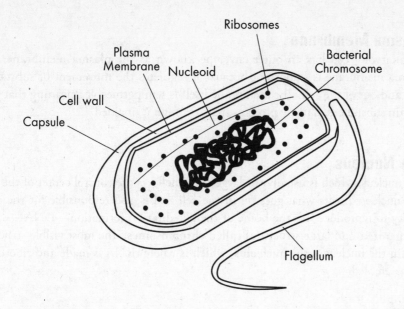

Ribosomes

Plasma Membrane

Nucleoid

Bacterial Chromosome

Cell wall

Capsule

Flagellum

Organelles

A eukaryotic cell is like a microscopic factory. It's filled with organelles, each of which has its own special task. Let's take a tour of a eukaryotic cell and focus on the structure and function of each organelle. Here's a picture of a typical animal cell and its principal organelles:

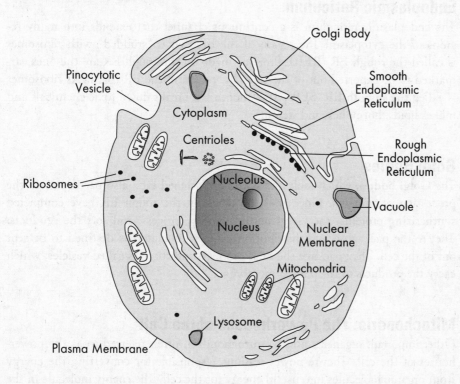

Golgi Body

Pinocytotic Vesicle

Smooth Endoplasmic Reticulum

Cytoplasm

Centrioles

Rough Endoplasmic Reticulum

Ribosomes

Nucleolus

Vacuole

Nucleus

Nuclear Membrane

Mitochondria

Plasma Membrane

Lysosome

Plasma Membrane

A eukaryotic cell has an outer envelope known as the **plasma membrane.** The plasma membrane is important because it regulates the movement of substances into and out of the cell. The membrane itself is semipermeable, meaning that only certain substances, namely proteins, pass through it unaided.

The Nucleus

The nucleus, which is usually the largest organelle, is the control center of the cell. The nucleus directs what goes on in the cell and is also responsible for the cell's ability to reproduce. It's the home of the hereditary information—DNA—which is organized into large structures called **chromosomes.** The most visible structure within the nucleus is the **nucleolus,** which is where rRNA is made and ribosomes are assembled.

Ribosomes

The **ribosomes** are the sites of protein synthesis. Their job is to manufacture all the proteins required by the cell or secreted by the cell. Ribosomes are round structures composed of RNA and proteins. They can be either free floating in the cell or attached to another structure called the **endoplasmic reticulum (ER).**

Endoplasmic Reticulum

The endoplasmic reticulum is a continuous channel that extends into many regions of the cytoplasm. The region of the ER that is "studded" with ribosomes is called the **rough ER (RER).** Proteins made on the rough ER are the ones earmarked to be exported out of the cell. The region of the ER that lacks ribosomes is called the **smooth ER (SER).** The smooth ER breaks down toxic chemicals and makes lipids, hormones, and steroids.

Golgi Bodies

The **Golgi bodies,** which look like stacks of flattened sacs, also participate in the processing of proteins. Once the ribosomes on the rough ER have completed synthesizing proteins, the Golgi bodies modify, process, and sort the products. They're the packaging and distribution centers for materials destined to be sent out of the cell. They package the final products in little sacs called **vesicles,** which carry the products to the plasma membrane.

Mitochondria: The Powerhouses of the Cell

Other important organelles are the **mitochondria,** often referred to as the powerhouses of the cell. They're power stations responsible for converting the energy from organic molecules into useful energy for the cell. The energy molecule in the cell is **adenosine triphosphate (ATP).**

The mitochondrion is usually an easy organelle to recognize because it has a unique oblong shape and a characteristic double membrane consisting of an inner portion and an outer portion.

Since mitochondria are the cell's powerhouses, you're most likely to find more of them in cells that require a lot of energy. Muscle cells, for example, are rich in mitochondria.

Lysosomes

Throughout the cell are small, membrane-bound structures called **lysosomes.** These tiny sacs carry digestive enzymes, which they use to break down old, worn-out organelles, debris, and large ingested particles. The lysosomes make up the cell's cleanup crew, helping to keep the cytoplasm clear of unwanted flotsam.

Centrioles

The **centrioles** are small, paired, cylindrical structures that are found within **microtubule organizing centers (MTOCs).** Centrioles are most active during cellular division. When a cell is ready to divide, the centrioles produce microtubules, which pull the replicated chromosomes apart and move them to opposite ends of the cell. Although centrioles are common in animal cells, they are not found in plant cells.

Vacuoles

In Latin, the term *vacuole* means "empty cavity." But **vacuoles** are far from empty. They are fluid-filled sacs that store water, food, wastes, salts, and pigments.

Peroxisomes

Peroxisomes are organelles that detoxify various substances, producing hydrogen peroxide as a byproduct. They also contain enzymes that break down hydrogen peroxide (H_2O_2) into oxygen and water. In animals, they are common in the liver and kidney cells.

Cytoskeleton

Have you ever wondered what actually holds the cell together and enables it to keep its shape? The shape of a cell is determined by a network of fibers called the **cytoskeleton.** The most important fibers you'll need to know are **microtubules** and **microfilaments.**

Microtubules, which are made up of the protein **tubulin,** participate in cellular division and movement. These small fibers are an integral part of three structures:

centrioles, cilia, and flagella. We've already mentioned that centrioles help chromosomes separate during cell division. Cilia and flagella, on the other hand, are threadlike structures best known for their locomotive properties in single-celled organisms. The beating motion of cilia and flagella structures propels these organisms through their watery environments.

Though we usually associate such structures with microscopic organisms, they aren't the only ones with cilia and flagella. As you probably know, these structures are also found in certain human cells. For example, the cells lining your respiratory tract possess cilia that sweep constantly back and forth (beating up to 20 times per second), helping to keep dust and unwanted debris from descending into your lungs. And every sperm cell has a flagellum, which enables it to swim through the female reproductive organs to fertilize the waiting ovum.

Microfilaments, like microtubules, are important for movement. These thin, rod-like structures are composed of the protein actin. They are involved in cell mobility, and play a central role in muscle contraction.

Want More Practice?
Download free CSET practice exams at www.princetonreview.com/cracking

---

If you were inside a cell and giving directions to the location where water, food, wastes, salt, and pigments are stored, you would be talking about the:

A.   nucleus.

B.   ribosomes.

C.   vacuoles.

D.   centrioles.

Here's How To Crack It

After your careful review of the cell and its different sections, this one should be a breeze. Choice A, the nucleus, can't be right because the nucleus is the brain center of the cell—that's not where waste and water is stored. Choice B, the ribosomes, are the sites of protein synthesis, and choice D, the centrioles, facilitate cell division, which is not what the question asks about. The correct answer must be choice C, vacuoles. Go back and review this section if those concepts are confusing.

Plant Cells Versus Animal Cells

Plant cells contain most of the same organelles and structures seen in animal cells, with several key exceptions. Plant cells, unlike animal cells, have a protective outer covering called the **cell wall** (made of cellulose). A cell wall is a rigid layer just outside of the plasma membrane that provides support for the cell. It is found in plants, protists, fungi, and bacteria. In fungi, the cell wall is usually made of **chitin.** In addition, plant cells possess **chloroplasts** (organelles involved in photosynthesis). Chloroplasts contain chlorophyll, the light-capturing pigment that gives plants their characteristic green color. Another difference between plant and animal cells is that most of the cytoplasm within a plant cell is usually taken up by a large vacuole that crowds the other organelles. In mature plants, this vacuole contains the **cell sap.** Plant cells also differ from animal cells in that plant cells do not contain centrioles.

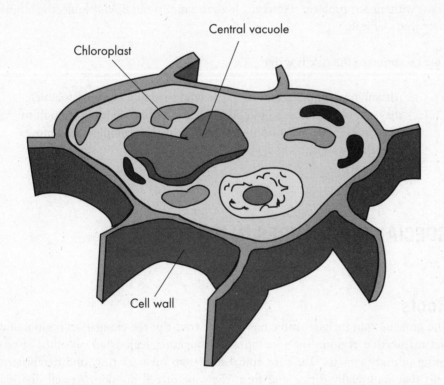

Chloroplast

Central vacuole

Cell wall

To help you remember the differences among prokaryotes, plant cells, and animal cells, we've put together this simple table.

STRUCTURAL CHARACTERISTICS OF DIFFERENT CELL TYPES			
Structure	**Prokaryote**	**Plant Cell**	**Animal Cell**
Cell Wall	Yes	Yes	No!
Plasma Membrane	Yes	Yes	Yes
Organelles	No!	Yes	Yes
Nucleus	No!	Yes	Yes
Centrioles	No!	No!	Yes
Ribosomes	Yes	Yes	Yes

Transport: The Traffic across Membranes

We've talked about the structure of cell membranes. Now let's discuss how molecules and fluids pass through the plasma membrane. What are some of the patterns of membrane transport? The ability of molecules to move across the cell membrane depends on two things: (1) the semipermeability of the plasma membrane and (2) the size and charge of particles that want to get through.

First let's consider how cell membranes work. For a cell to maintain its internal environment, it has to be selective in the materials it allows to cross its membrane. Since the plasma membrane is composed primarily of phospholipids, lipid-soluble substances cross the membrane without any resistance. Why? Because "like dissolves like." Generally speaking, the lipid membrane has an open-door policy for substances that are made up of lipids. These substances can cross the plasma membrane without any problem. However, if a substance is not lipid-soluble, the bilipid layer won't let it in.

One exception to the rule is water:

> Although water molecules are polar (and therefore not lipid-soluble), they can rapidly cross a lipid bilayer because they are small enough to pass through gaps that occur as a fatty acid chain momentarily moves out of the way.

SPECIAL STRUCTURES IN PLANTS

Roots

The growing root includes three regions: the **root tip**, the **elongation region**, and the **maturation region**. The root tip and elongation regions are the sites of ongoing primary growth. The **root apical meristem** includes tiny, undifferentiated cells that continually divide and form the zone of cell division. As cell division in the root apical meristem continues, the new cells left behind grow rapidly in length and push the root tip along. As the cells absorb water, elongation occurs. Tiny **root hairs,** extensions of the epidermal cells, form and provide an increased surface area through which water and dissolved minerals can move into the plant.

All roots have an **epidermis** (an outer protective covering), a **cortex** (a middle region which stores starch and other minerals), and a **stele** (the inner cylinder, which contains xylems and phloems). How do water and minerals enter the root? They travel through the root cortex either by the **apoplast** (porous cell walls) or **symplast** (through plasmodesmata). Once water and minerals reach the inner layer of the cortex, called the **endodermis,** they must cross the **endodermal cells,** tightly packed cells that regulate the selective passage of water and minerals into the vascular tissue, in order to reach the root's interior.

Leaves

Leaves play an important role in photosynthesis. But did you know that leaves are sometimes modified for other purposes?

Here's a list of some of the other functions of leaves:

- Leaves can be modified to form **spines,** as in a cactus. This adaptation is great for protection.
- Leaves can be adapted for water storage. Fleshy leaves allow plants to survive particularly harsh environments where the water supply is intermittent or undependable.
- Leaves can also be modified to trap prey. Insectivorous plants have specialized leaves that digest insects. Because they grow in soils deficient of essential nutrients, especially nitrogen, these plants are forced to eat insects. There are basically two general forms of these adaptations:
    1. Some leaves have tiny hairs that act like bear traps. For example, an insect brushing against the hairs in a Venus flytrap triggers the leaves to snap shut.
    2. Other leaves are adapted to form a "slippery slope" that traps insects. In a pitcher plant, for example, once an insect gets inside, it can't get out. It slips down into the bell-shaped interior of the leaf, where it drowns in a mixture of water and enzymes. These enzymes then finish the job by digesting the insect.

Flowering Plants

Let's take a look at what you do need to know about flowering plants.

Flowering plants have several organs: the **stamen, pistil, sepals,** and **petals.**

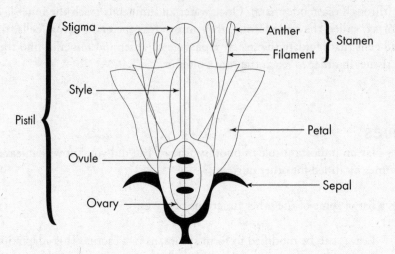

The male parts are collectively called the stamen, and the female parts are called the pistil. The sepals are the green, leaf-like structures that cover and protect the flower, while the brightly colored petals attract potential pollinators. Let's review each of these structures.

The Stamen

The stamen consists of the **anther** and the **filament.** The anther is the structure that produces pollen grains. These **pollen grains,** called **microspores,** are the plant's male gametophytes, or sperm cells. Pollen grains are produced and released into the air. The filament is the thin stalk that holds up the anther.

The Pistil

The pistil includes three structures: the **stigma, style,** and **ovary.** The stigma is the sticky portion of the pistil that captures the pollen grains. The style is a tubelike structure that connects the stigma with the ovary.

The ovary is the structure in which fertilization occurs. Within the ovary are the **ovules,** which contain the plant's equivalent of the female gametophytes. In a fertilized plant, the ovary develops into the fruit. Apples, pears, and oranges are all fertilized ovaries of flowering plants. The female gametes of plants are known as **megaspores.** They undergo meiosis to produce eight female nuclei, including one **egg nucleus** and two **polar nuclei.**

Double Fertilization

Now that we've seen both the male and the female organs in plants, let's take a look at how they actually reproduce. Flowering plants carry out a process called **double fertilization.** When a pollen grain lands on the stigma, it germinates and grows a thin pollen tube down the style, which meets up with the ovary. The pollen grain then divides into two **sperm nuclei.** One sperm nucleus (n) fuses with an egg nucleus (n) to form a zygote (2n). This zygote will eventually form a plant. The other sperm nucleus (n) will fuse with two polar nuclei (2n) in the ovary to form the **endosperm** (3n). The endosperm will not develop into a plant. Rather, it will serve as food for the plant embryo. Double fertilization produces two things: a plant and food for the plant.

Let's review the steps involved in double fertilization:

- Grains of pollen fall onto the stigma. The pollen grains grow down the style into the ovary.
- The pollen grains (microspores) meet up with megaspores in the ovule. Microspores fertilize the megaspores.
- One microspore unites with an egg nucleus and eventually develops into a complete plant.
- The other microspore unites with two polar nuclei and develops into food for the plant, often in the form of a fruit.

As the embryo germinates, different parts of the plant begin to develop. The **cotyledons** are the first embryo leaves to appear. They temporarily store all the nutrients for the plant. The **epicotyl** is the part at the tip of the plant. This portion becomes the stems and leaves. The **hypocotyl** is the stem below the cotyledons. This portion becomes the roots of the plant. In some embryos, root development begins early, and the well-defined embryonic root is referred to as a **radicle.**

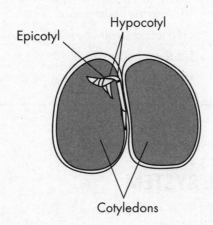

Epicotyl

Hypocotyl

Cotyledons

What triggers sexual reproduction in plants? Plants flower in response to changes in the amount of daylight and darkness. This is called **photoperiodism.** Plants fall into three main groups: **short-day plants, long-day plants,** and **day-neutral plants.** Although you'd think that plants bloom based on the amount of sunlight, they actually flower according to the amount of uninterrupted darkness.

Short-day plants require a long period of darkness, whereas long-day plants need short periods of darkness. Short-day plants usually bloom in late summer or fall when daylight is decreasing. Long-day plants, on the other hand, flower in late spring and summer when daylight is increasing. Day-neutral plants don't flower in response to daylight changes at all. They use other cues such as water or temperature.

The light receptor involved in photoperiodism is a pigment called **phytochrome.** In short-day plants, it inhibits flowering, whereas in long-day plants it induces flowering.

Vegetative Propagation

Flowering plants don't always reproduce via fertilization. In some cases, flowering plants can reproduce asexually. This process is known as **vegetative propagation.** That means parts of the parent plant—such as the roots, stems, or leaves—can produce another plant. Some examples of plant parts that can reproduce this way include **tubers, runners,** and **bulbs.** For instance, suppose you wanted to make white potatoes without fertilization. All you'd have to do is cut out the eyes of a potato, the tubers, and plant them. Each of the eyes will develop into a separate potato plant. **Grafting** is another way plants can be reproduced asexually.

Here's a list of the different types of vegetative propagation:

VEGETATIVE PROPAGATION		
Types	**Description**	**Examples**
Bulbs	Short stems underground	Onions
Runners	Horizontal stems above the ground	Strawberries
Tubers	Underground stems	Potatoes
Grafting	Cutting a stem and attaching it to a closely related plant	Seedless oranges

THE DIGESTIVE SYSTEM

The Purpose of the Digestive System

All organisms need nutrients to survive. But where do the nutrients—the raw building blocks—come from? That depends on whether the organism is an autotroph or heterotroph. As you may recall, autotrophs make their own food through photosynthesis, and all of the building blocks—CO_2, water, and sunlight—come from their immediate environment. Heterotrophs, on the other hand, can't make their own food; they must acquire their energy from outside sources.

When we talk about digestion, we're talking about the breakdown of large food molecules into simpler compounds. These molecules are then absorbed by the body to carry out cell activities. In fact, everything we'll discuss in this section revolves around three simple questions:

1. What do organisms need from the outside world in order to survive?
2. How do they get those things?
3. What do they do with them once they get them?

Multicellular organisms have come up with a variety of ways of getting their nutrients. In simple animals, food is digested through **intracellular digestion**—that is, digestion occurs within food vacuoles. For example, a hydra encloses the food it captures in a food vacuole. Lysosomes containing digestive enzymes then fuse with the vacuole and break down the food. More complex animals have evolved a digestive tract and digest food through **extracellular digestion.** That is, the food is digested in a gastrovascular cavity. For example, in grasshoppers, food passes through specialized regions of the gut: the **mouth, esophagus, crop** (a storage organ), **stomach, intestine, rectum,** and **anus.**

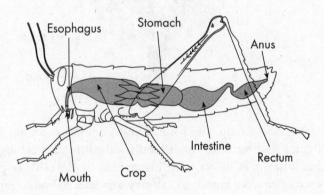

The Human Digestive System

The human digestive tract consists of the mouth, esophagus, stomach, **small intestine, large intestine,** and **accessory organs** (liver, pancreas, gall bladder, and salivary glands). Four groups of molecules must be broken down by the digestive tract: **starch, proteins, fats,** and **nucleic acids.**

The Mouth

The first stop in the digestive process is the mouth, or **oral cavity.**

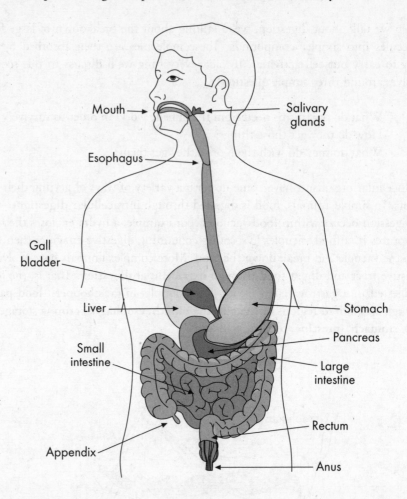

Mouth — Salivary glands

Esophagus

Gall bladder

Liver — Stomach

Small intestine — Pancreas

Large intestine

Appendix — Rectum

Anus

When food enters the mouth, mechanical and chemical digestion begins. The chewing, softening and breaking up of food is called mechanical digestion. The mouth also has **saliva** in it. Saliva, which is secreted by the **salivary glands,** contains an important enzyme known as **salivary amylase.** Salivary amylase begins the chemical breakdown of starch into maltose.

Once chewed, the food, now shaped into a ball called a **bolus,** moves through the **pharynx** and into the esophagus. Food moves through the esophagus in a wave-like motion known as **peristalsis.**

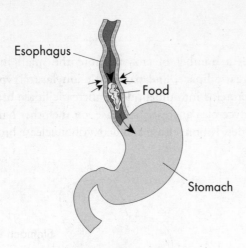

Esophagus

Food

Stomach

Peristalsis

The waves of contraction push the food toward the stomach.

The Stomach

Once food has been chewed, it moves from the esophagus to the stomach. The stomach is a thick, muscular sac that has several functions:

- It temporarily stores the ingested food.
- It partially digests proteins.
- It kills bacteria.

The stomach secretes **gastric juices,** which contain digestive enzymes and hydrochloric acid (HCl). One of the most important enzymes is **pepsin,** which breaks down proteins into smaller peptides. Pepsin works best in an acidic environment. When HCl is secreted, it lowers the pH of the stomach and activates pepsinogen into pepsin to digest proteins. The stomach also secretes mucus, which protects the stomach lining from the acidic juices. Finally, HCl kills most bacteria.

Food is also mechanically broken down by the churning action of the stomach. Once that's complete, this partially digested food, now called **chyme,** is ready to enter the small intestine.

The Small Intestine

The small intestine has three regions: the duodenum, the jejunum, and the ileum. The chyme moves into the first part of the small intestine, the duodenum, through the **pyloric sphincter.** The small intestine is very long—about 23 feet in an average man. In the small intestine, all three food groups are completely digested. The walls of the small intestine secrete enzymes that break down proteins (peptidases) and carbohydrates (maltase, lactase, and sucrase).

The Pancreas

The **pancreas** secretes a number of enzymes into the small intestine: **trypsin, chymotrypsin, pancreatic lipase,** and **pancreatic amylase**. Trypsin and chymotrypsin break down proteins into dipeptides. Pancreatic lipase breaks down lipids into fatty acids and glycerol. Pancreatic amylase, on the other hand, breaks down starch into disaccharides. Ribonuclease and deoxyribonuclease break down nucleic acids into nucleotides.

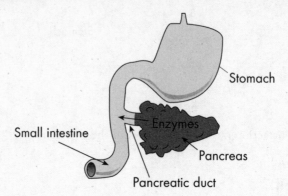

These enzymes are secreted into the small intestine via the **pancreatic duct.**

Another substance that works in the small intestine is called **bile.** Bile is not a digestive enzyme. It's an **emulsifier,** meaning that it mechanically breaks up fats into smaller fat droplets. This process makes the fat globules more accessible to pancreatic lipase. Bile enters the small intestine by the bile duct, which merges with the pancreatic duct.

Here's something you should memorize:

> Bile is made in the **liver** and stored in the **gall bladder.**

Once food is broken down, it is absorbed by tiny, fingerlike projections of the intestine called **villi** and **microvilli.** Villi and microvilli are folds that increase the surface area of the small intestine for food absorption. Within each of the villi is a capillary that absorbs the digested food and carries it into the bloodstream. Within each villus are also lymph vessels, called **lacteals,** which absorb fatty acids.

Don't forget that hormones are also involved in the digestive system: **gastrin** (which stimulates stomach cells to produce gastric juice), **secretin** (which stimulates the pancreas to produce bicarbonate and digestive enzymes), and **cholecystokinin** (which stimulates the secretion of pancreatic enzymes and the release of bile).

Here's a summary of the pancreatic enzymes:

THE PANCREATIC ENZYMES AND THE FOODS THEY DIGEST	
Pancreatic Enzymes	**Food Substance**
pancreatic amylase, pancreatic lipase, trypsin, chymotrypsin	starch fat protein
proteolytic enzymes, maltase, lactase	proteins carbohydrates

The Large Intestine

The **large intestine** is much shorter and thicker than the small intestine. The large intestine has an easy job: It reabsorbs water and salts. The large intestine also harbors harmless bacteria that are actually quite useful. These bacteria break down undigested food and in the process provide us with certain essential vitamins, like **vitamin K**. The leftover undigested food, called **feces**, then moves out of the large intestine and into the rectum.

In food digestion, what begins the chemical breakdown of starch into maltose?

A.   salivary amylase

B.   bolus

C.   esophagus

D.   oral cavity

Here's How To Crack It

Don't be misled by choice D (oral cavity) and think, "That's the first step in the digestive process! That must be the answer." Be sure to read each question on the CSET carefully so that you don't make a careless error. From your careful review of the digestive process, you know that the esophagus is the tube that leads food to the stomach and bolus is the name of food once it is chewed, so choices B and C must be wrong. That leaves only choice A, salivary amylase. Even if you didn't come up with "salivary amylase" off the top of your head, the process of elimination can lead you to the correct answer.

THE RESPIRATORY SYSTEM

The Purpose of the Respiratory System

All cells need oxygen for aerobic respiration. For simple organisms, such as platy-helminthes, no special structures are needed because the gases can easily diffuse across every cell membrane. In other multicellular organisms, however, the cells are not in direct contact with the environment. These organisms must find other ways of getting oxygen into their systems. For some animals, such as segmented worms, gas exchange occurs directly through their skin. Others, such as insects, have special tubes called **tracheae.** Air enters these tubes through tiny openings called **spiracles.** Among vertebrates, the respiratory structures you should be familiar with are **gills** (used by many aquatic creatures) and **lungs.**

The Human Respiratory System

Air enters the human body through the nose or mouth.

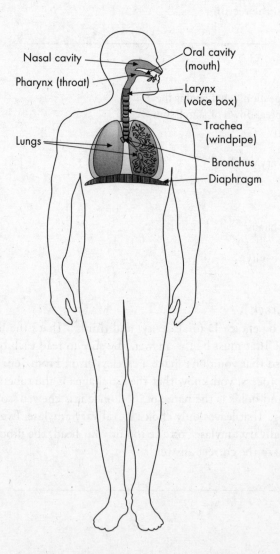

The nose cleans, warms, and moistens the incoming air and passes it through the **pharynx** (throat) and **larynx** (voice box). Next, air enters the trachea. A special flap called the **epiglottis** covers the trachea when you swallow, preventing food from going down the wrong pipe. The trachea also has cartilage rings to help keep the air passage open as air rushes in.

The trachea then branches into two bronchi: the **left bronchus** and the **right bronchus.** These two tubes service the lungs. In the lungs, the passageways break down into smaller tubes known as **bronchioles.** Each bronchiole ends in a tiny air sac known as an **alveolus.** These sacs enable the lungs to have an enormous surface area: about 100 square meters. Let's take a look at one of these tiny air sacs:

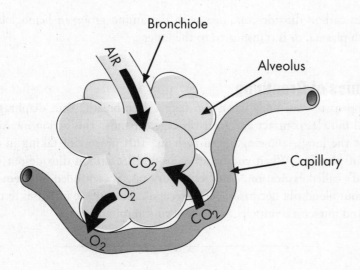

You'll notice that alongside the alveolus is a **capillary.** Oxygen and carbon dioxide diffuse across the membrane of both the alveolus and capillary. Every time you inhale, you send oxygen to the alveoli. Oxygen then diffuses into the capillaries. The capillaries, on the other hand, have a high concentration of carbon dioxide. Carbon dioxide then diffuses into the alveoli. When you exhale, you expel the carbon dioxide that diffused into your lungs. Gas exchange occurs via passive diffusion.

Transport of Oxygen

Oxygen is transported throughout the body by the iron-containing protein **hemoglobin** in red blood cells. Hemoglobin transports 97 percent of the oxygen while the other 3 percent is dissolved in the **plasma** (the fluid of the blood). The percent O_2 saturation of hemoglobin is highest where the concentration of oxygen is greatest. Oxygen binds to hemoglobin in oxygen-rich blood leaving the lungs and dissociates from hemoglobin in oxygen-poor tissues.

Transport of Carbon Dioxide

We've just mentioned that carbon dioxide can leave the capillaries and enter the lungs. However, carbon dioxide can travel in many forms. Most of the carbon dioxide enters red blood cells and combines with water to eventually form **bicarbonate ions** (HCO_3^-). Here's a summary of the reaction:

$$_+ \ CO_2 \qquad + \qquad H_2O \qquad \rightarrow \qquad H_2CO_3 \qquad \rightarrow \qquad H^+$$
$$HCO_3^-$$

| Carbon dioxide Bicarbonate ion | Water | Carbonic Acid | Hydrogen ion |

Sometimes carbon dioxide combines with the amino group in hemoglobin and mixes with plasma, or is transported to the lungs.

Mechanics of Breathing

What happens to your body when you take a deep breath? Your diaphragm and intercostal muscles contract and your rib cage expands. This action increases the volume of the lungs, allowing air to rush in. This process of taking in oxygen is called **inspiration**. When you breathe out and let carbon dioxide out of your lungs, that's called **expiration**. Your respiratory rate is controlled by **chemoreceptors**. As your blood pH decreases, chemoreceptors send nerve impulses to the **diaphragm** and intercostal muscles to increase your respiratory rate.

Hemoglobin transports 97 percent of the oxygen that is transported throughout your body. What happens to the other 3 percent?

A.   It is dissolved in the lipids.

B.   It is dissolved in the plasma.

C.   It is lost.

D.   It forms bicarbonate ions.

Here's How To Crack It

You can cross off choice A immediately, as lipids aren't related to the respiratory system at all. Choice C is too vague; it must be wrong. Bicarbonate ions probably sound familiar, but don't be thrown off by that choice. The correct choice is B; the other 3 percent of oxygen that is not transported by hemoglobin is dissolved in plasma (the fluid of the blood).

THE CIRCULATORY SYSTEM

The Purpose of the Circulatory System

Most organisms need to carry out two tasks: (1) supply their bodies with nutrients and oxygen, and (2) get rid of wastes. Many simple aquatic organisms have no trouble moving materials across their membranes since their metabolic needs are met by diffusion. Larger organisms, on the other hand, particularly terrestrial organisms, can't depend on diffusion. They therefore need special circulatory systems to accomplish internal transport.

There are two types of circulatory systems: an **open circulatory system** and a **closed circulatory system**. In an open circulatory system, blood is carried by open-ended blood vessels that spill blood into the body cavity. In arthropods, for example, blood vessels from the heart open into internal cavities known as **sinuses**. Other organisms have closed circulatory systems. That is, blood flows continuously through a network of blood vessels. Earthworms and some mollusks have a closed circulatory system, as do vertebrates.

The Human Circulatory System

The heart is divided into four chambers, two on the left and two on the right. The four chambers of the heart are the **right atrium**, the **right ventricle**, the **left atrium**, and the **left ventricle**. Let's take a look at a picture of the heart:

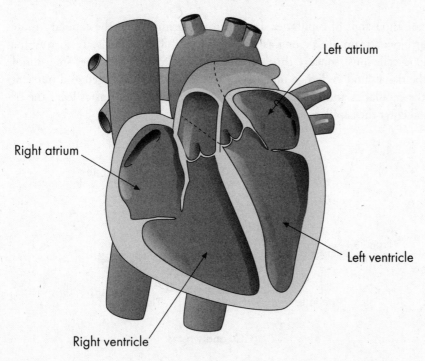

Left atrium

Right atrium

Left ventricle

Right ventricle

The heart pumps blood in a continuous circuit. Since blood makes a circuit in the body, it doesn't matter where we begin to trace the flow of blood. For our purposes, we'll begin at the point in the circulatory system where the blood leaves the heart and enters the body: the left ventricle. When blood leaves the left ventricle it will make a tour of the body. We call this **systemic circulation.**

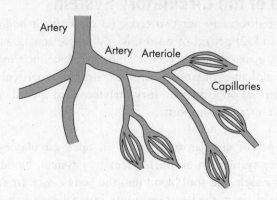

Systemic Circulation

Blood leaves the heart through the **aortic semilunar valve** and enters a large blood vessel called the **aorta.** The aorta is the largest artery in the body. The aorta then branches out into smaller vessels called **arteries.**

Arteries always carry blood away from the heart. Just remember "A" stands for "away" from the heart. They're able to carry the blood because arteries are thick-walled, elastic vessels. The arteries become even smaller vessels called **arterioles,** and then the smallest vessels called **capillaries.**

There are thousands of capillaries. In fact, some estimate that the capillary routes in your bloodstream are as long as 100 kilometers! These vessels are so tiny that red blood cells must squeeze through them in single file. Capillaries intermingle with the tissues and exchange nutrients, gases, and wastes. Oxygen and nutrients leave the capillaries and enter the tissues; carbon dioxide and wastes leave the tissues and enter the capillaries.

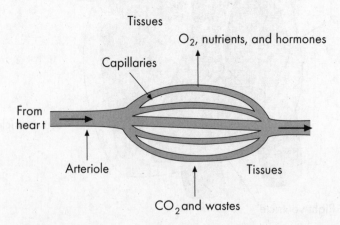

Before we take a look at the next stage of circulation, let's recap the pathway of blood through the body:

- Blood leaves the heart's left ventricle via the aorta.
- It travels through the arteries to the arterioles, and eventually to the capillaries.
- Gas and nutrient/waste exchange occurs between the blood and the tissues through the capillary walls.

Back to the Heart

After exchanging gases and nutrients with the cells, blood has very little oxygen left. Most of its oxygen was donated to the cells through the capillary walls. Since the blood is now depleted of oxygen, it is said to be **deoxygenated.** To get a fresh supply of oxygen the blood now needs to go to the lungs.

But the blood doesn't go *directly* to the lungs. It must first go back to the heart. As the blood returns to the heart, the vessels get bigger and bigger.

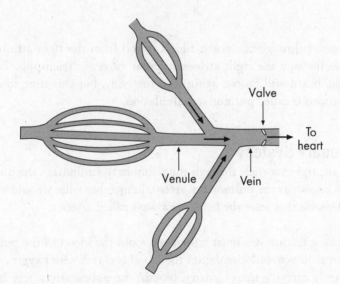

From the capillaries, blood travels through vessels called **venules** and then through larger vessels called **veins.** Veins always carry blood *toward* the heart. Veins are thin-walled vessels with valves that prevent the backward flow of blood.

Blood eventually enters the heart's right atrium via two veins known as the **superior vena cava** and the **inferior vena cava.**

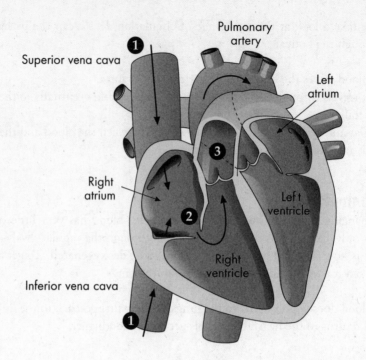

Blood now moves through the heart. Blood travels from the right atrium to the right ventricle through the **right atrioventricular valve** (or **tricuspid**). From the right ventricle, blood will go out again into the body, but this time toward the lungs. This process is called **pulmonary circulation**.

The Pulmonary System

Blood leaves the right ventricle through the pulmonary semilunar valve and enters a large artery known as the **pulmonary artery**. Remember what we said about arteries? Blood vessels that leave the heart are always called arteries.

There's one major feature you must remember about the blood in the pulmonary system. Whereas in systemic circulation the blood was rich with oxygen, the pulmonary artery is carrying deoxygenated blood. The pulmonary artery branches into the right and left pulmonary arteries which lead, respectively, to the right and left lungs. These arteries become smaller arterioles and then once again capillaries.

We just said that these vessels carry deoxygenated blood. In the lungs, the blood will pick up oxygen and dump carbon dioxide. Sounds familiar? It should. It's just like the gas exchange we discussed in the respiratory system. In the lungs, the blood fills with oxygen, or becomes **oxygenated**. The blood returns to the heart via the **pulmonary veins** and enters the left atrium.

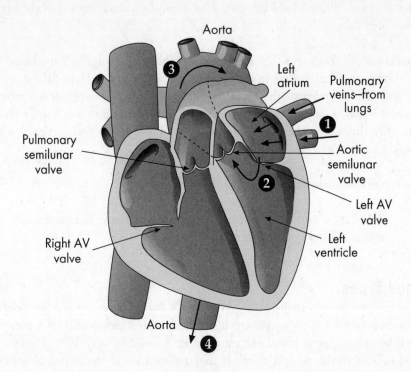

Blood then moves to the left ventricle through the **left atrioventricular valve** (or **bicuspid** or **mitral valve**). Now we've completed our tour of the heart. Let's recap the events in pulmonary circulation:

- Deoxygenated blood leaves the right ventricle via the pulmonary artery.
- The pulmonary artery branches into the right and left pulmonary arteries, carrying the blood to the lungs.
- Blood travels from the arteries to the arterioles, and eventually to the capillaries.
- Gas exchange occurs between the capillaries and alveoli in the lungs.
- Once the blood is oxygenated, it returns to the heart through the pulmonary veins.

The Contents of Blood

Now let's take a look at blood itself. Blood consists of two things:

- plasma
- cells and cell fragments suspended in the fluid

Blood carries three types of cells: **red blood cells** (also called **erythrocytes**), **white blood cells** (also called **leukocytes**), and **platelets.** Red blood cells are the oxygen-carrying cells in the body. They contain hemoglobin, the protein that actually carries the oxygen (and carbon dioxide) throughout the body. Mature red blood cells lack a nucleus. White blood cells fight infection by protecting the body against foreign organisms.

Platelets are cell fragments that are involved in blood clotting. When a blood vessel is damaged, platelets stick to the collagen fibers of the vessel wall. The damaged cells and platelets release substances that activate clotting factors, and a series of reactions occur. First, a prothrombin activator converts prothrombin (a plasma protein) to thrombin. Then thrombin converts fibrinogen to fibrin threads, which strengthen the clot.

Here's something you should remember for the test:

> All of the blood cells are made in the **bone marrow**. The bone marrow is located in the center of the bones.

Blood Types

There are four blood groups: **A, B, AB,** and **O.** Blood types are pretty important and are based on the type of antigen(s) found on red blood cells. If a patient is given the wrong type of blood in a transfusion, it could be fatal! Why? Because red blood cells in the blood will clump if they are exposed to the wrong blood type. For example, if you've got blood type A (that is, your red cells carry the A antigen) and you receive a blood transfusion of blood type B, your blood will clump. That's because your blood contains **antibodies,** an immune substance that will bind and destroy the foreign blood.

What is important to remember about the different blood types is that type O blood is the universal donor and that type AB is the universal recipient.

Use the diagram below to answer the question that follows.

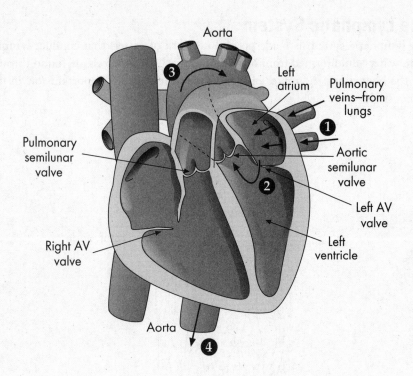

Which chamber of the heart labeled
in the diagram above is primarily
responsible for pumping blood to most
of the organs and tissues of the body?

A. left atrium

B. left ventricle

C. right atrium

D. right ventricle

Here's How To Crack It

This is yet another question that requires simple memorization. You know that
blood makes a tour of the body, called systemic circulation, but where does that
tour begin? Like a band kicking off a tour in their hometown, blood starts its tour
in the left ventricle (choice B) and then takes the show on the road.

THE LYMPHATIC AND IMMUNE SYSTEM

The Lymphatic System

The **lymphatic system** is made up of a network of vessels that conduct **lymph,** a clear, watery fluid formed from interstitial fluid. Lymph vessels are found throughout the body along the routes of blood vessels. It plays an important role in fluid homeostasis.

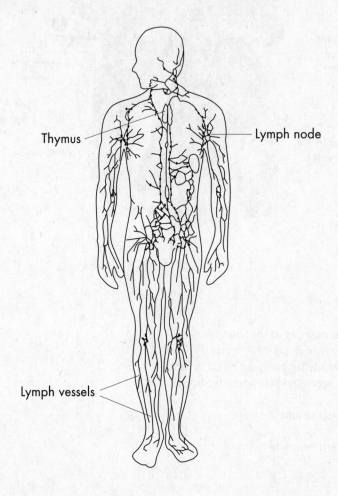

Thymus

Lymph node

Lymph vessels

The lymphatic system has three functions:

- It collects, filters, and returns fluid to the blood by the contraction of adjacent muscles.
- It fights infection using lymphocytes, cells found in lymph nodes.
- It removes excess fluid from body tissue.

Sometimes a lymph vessel will form a **lymph node,** a mass of tissue found along the course of a lymph vessel. A lymph node contains a large number of lymphocytes:

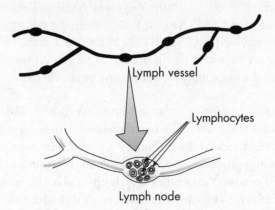

Lymph vessel

Lymphocytes

Lymph node

Lymphocytes are important in fighting infection. They multiply rapidly when they come in contact with an **antigen,** or foreign substance recognized by the immune system. (We'll talk about this in a second.) The lymph nodes swell when they're fighting an infection. That's why when you have a sore throat, one of the first things a doctor does is touch the sides of your throat to see if your lymph nodes are swollen, a probable sign of infection.

The Immune System

The **immune system,** generally speaking, is one of the body's defense systems. It is a carefully and closely coordinated system of specialized cells, each of which plays a specific role in the war against bodily invaders. As we mentioned above, foreign molecules—be they viral, bacterial, or simply chemical—that can trigger an immune response are called antigens. The appearance of antigens in the body stimulates a defense mechanism that produces antibodies.

The body's first line of defense against foreign substances is the skin and mucous lining of the respiratory and digestive tracts. If these defenses are not sufficient, other nonspecific defense mechanisms are activated. These include **phagocytes** (which engulf antigens), **complement proteins** (which lyse [disintegrate] the cell wall of the antigen), **interferons** (which inhibit viral replication and activate surrounding cells that have antiviral actions), and **inflammatory response** (a series of events in response to antigen invasion or physical injury).

Types of Immune Cells

The primary cells of the immune system are lymphocytes—T-cells and B-cells. The plasma membrane of cells has **major histocompatibility complex markers (MHC markers)** that distinguish between self and nonself cells. When **T-lymphocytes** encounter cells infected by pathogens, they recognize the foreign antigen-MHC markers on the cell surface. T-cells are activated, multiply, and give rise to clones. Some T-cells become **memory T-cells,** whereas others become **helper T-cells.** Helper T-cells activate **B-lymphocytes** and other T-cells in responding to the infected cells. Memory T-cells recognize bacteria or viruses that they have encountered before. Other T-cells, **cytotoxic T-cells,** recognize and kill infected cells. The activation of T-cells is referred to as a **cell-mediated response.** T-cells are made in the bone marrow, but mature in the thymus.

In antibody-mediated immunity (humoral immunity), when B-lymphocytes encounter antigen-presenting cells (like **macrophages**) with foreign MHC markers, they are activated and produce clones. Some B-cells become memory cells that can rapidly divide and can produce plasma cells after an infection has been overcome. These plasma cells produce **antibodies** that bind to the antigens that originally activated them. Helper T-cells are also involved and produce interleukins. Both memory T- and memory B-cells are responsible for long-term immunity.

AIDS

Acquired immunodeficiency syndrome (AIDS) is a devastating disease that interferes with the body's immune system. AIDS essentially wipes out the helper T-cells, preventing the body from defending itself. Those afflicted with AIDS do not die of AIDS itself but rather of infections that they can no longer fight off due to their compromised immune systems.

One thing to remember about the immune cells and blood cells: All blood cells, white and red, are produced in the bone marrow. To summarize:

- T-lymphocytes actually fight infection and help the B-lymphocytes proliferate.
- B-lymphocytes produce antibodies.

THE EXCRETORY SYSTEM

The Purpose of the Excretory System

As you already know, all organisms must get rid of wastes. We'll now focus primarily on how organisms get rid of **nitrogenous wastes** (products containing nitrogen) and regulate water. When cells break down proteins, one of the byproducts is **ammonia** (NH_3), a substance that is toxic to the body. Consequently, organisms had to develop ways of converting ammonia to a less poisonous substance. Some animals convert ammonia to **uric acid,** while others convert ammonia to **urea.** Some examples of excretory organs among invertebrates are **nephridia** (found in earthworms) and **Malpighian tubules** (found in arthropods).

The Human Excretory System

In humans, the major organ that regulates excretion is the **kidney**. Each kidney is made up of a million tiny structures called **nephrons**. Nephrons are the functional units of the kidney. A nephron consists of several regions: the **Bowman's capsule**, the **proximal convoluted tubule**, the **loop of Henle**, the **distal convoluted tubule**, and the **collecting duct**.

Here's an illustration of a nephron:

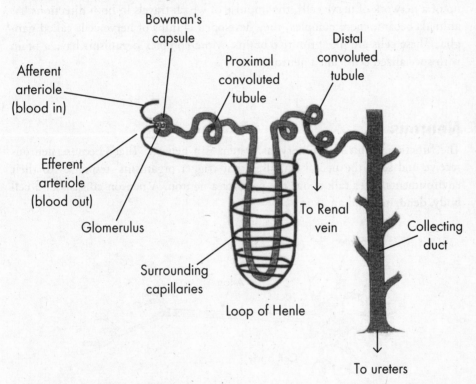

How does a nephron work? Let's trace the flow of blood in a nephron. Blood enters the nephron at the Bowman's capsule. A blood vessel called the **renal artery** leads to the kidney and branches into arterioles, then tiny capillaries. A ball of capillaries that "sits" within a Bowman's capsule is called a **glomerulus**. Blood is filtered as it passes through the glomerulus, and the plasma is forced out of the capillaries into the Bowman's capsule. This plasma is now called a **filtrate**.

The filtrate travels along the entire nephron. From the Bowman's capsule, the filtrate passes through the proximal convoluted tubule, then the loop of Henle, then the distal convoluted tubule, and finally the collecting duct. As it travels along the tube, the filtrate is modified to form urine.

What happens next? The concentrated **urine** moves from the collecting ducts into the **ureters**, then into the **bladder**, and finally out through the **urethra**.

THE NERVOUS SYSTEM

The Purpose of the Nervous System

All organisms must be able to react to changes in their environment. As a result, organisms have evolved systems that pick up and process information from the outside world. The task of coordinating this information falls to the nervous system. The simplest nervous system is found in the hydra. It has a **nerve net** made up of a network of nerve cells, the impulse of which travels in both directions. As animals became more complex, they developed clumps of nerve cells called **ganglia.** These cells are like primitive brains. More complex organisms have a brain with specialized cells called **neurons.**

Neurons

The functional unit in the nervous system is a neuron. That's because neurons receive and send the neural impulses that trigger organisms' responses to their environments. Let's talk about the parts of a neuron. A neuron consists of a **cell body, dendrites,** and an **axon.**

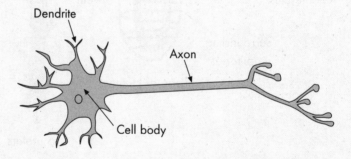

The cell body contains the nucleus and all the usual organelles found in the cytoplasm. Dendrites are short extensions of the cell body that receive stimuli. The axon is a long, slender extension that transmits an impulse from the cell body to another neuron or to an organ. A nerve impulse begins at the top of the dendrites, passes through the dendrites to the cell body, and moves down the axon.

Types of Neurons

Neurons can be classified into three groups: **sensory neurons, motor (effector) neurons,** and **interneurons.** Sensory neurons receive impulses from the environment and take them to the body. For example, sensory neurons in your hand are stimulated by touch. A motor neuron transmits the impulse to muscles or glands to produce a response. The muscle responds by contracting or the gland responds by secreting a substance (for example, a hormone). Interneurons are the links between sensory neurons and motor neurons. They're found in the brain and spinal cord:

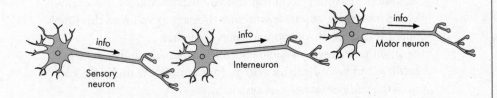

How Neurons Communicate

There are billions of neurons running throughout the body, firing all the time. More often than not, one or more neurons are somewhat "connected." This means that one neuron has its dendrites next to another neuron's axon. In this way, the dendrites of one cell can pick up the impulse sent from the axon of another cell. The second neuron can then send the impulse to its cell body and down its axon, passing it on to yet another cell.

Parts of the Nervous System

The nervous system can be divided into two parts: the **central nervous system** and the **peripheral nervous system.**

All of the neurons within the brain and spinal cord make up the central nervous system. All of the other neurons lying outside the brain and the spinal cord—in our skin, our organs, and our blood vessels—are collectively part of the peripheral nervous system. Although both of these systems are really part of one system, we still use the terms *central* and *peripheral.*

So keep them in mind:

- The central nervous system includes the neurons in the brain and spinal cord.
- The peripheral nervous system includes all the rest.

The peripheral nervous system is further broken down into the **somatic nervous system** and the **autonomic nervous system.**

- The somatic nervous system controls voluntary activities. For example, the movement of your eyes across the page as you read this line is under the control of your somatic nervous system.
- The autonomic nervous system controls involuntary activities. Your heartbeat and your digestive system, for example, are under the control of the autonomic nervous system.

The interesting thing about these two systems is that they sometimes overlap. For instance, you can control your breathing if you choose to. Yet most of the time you do not think about it: Your somatic system hands control of your respiration over to the autonomic system.

The autonomic system is broken down even further to the **sympathetic nervous system** and the **parasympathetic nervous system.** These two systems actually work antagonistically.

The sympathetic system controls the **fight-or-flight response,** which occurs when an organism confronted with a threatening situation prepares to fight or flee (thus "fight" or "flight"). To get ready for a quick, effective action, whether that be brawling or bolting, the sympathetic nervous system raises your heart and respiration rates, causes your blood vessels to constrict, increases the levels of glucose in your blood, and produces goose bumps on the back of your neck. It even reroutes your blood sugar to your skeletal muscles in case you need to make a break for it. After the threat has passed, the parasympathetic nervous system brings the body back to **homeostasis**—that is, back to normal. It lowers your heart and respiratory rates and decreases glucose levels in the blood.

The flowchart below will give you a nice overview of the different parts of the nervous system:

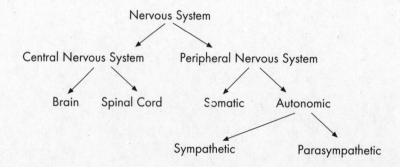

Parts of the Brain

The brain can also be divided into parts. Here's a summary of the major divisions within the brain.

DIVISIONS WITHIN THE BRAIN	
Parts of the Brain	**Function**
Cerebrum	Controls all voluntary activities; receives and interprets sensory information; largest part of the human brain
Cerebellum	Coordinates muscle activity and refinement of movement
Hypothalamus	Regulates homeostasis and secretes hormones; regulates the pituitary gland
Medulla	Controls involuntary actions such as breathing, swallowing, heartbeat, and respiration
Pons	Connects parts of the brain with one another and contains the respiratory center
Midbrain	Center for visual and auditory reflexes (pupil reflex and blinking)
Thalamus	Main sensory relay center for conducting information between the spinal cord and cerebrum

DNA: THE BLUEPRINT OF LIFE

All living things possess an astonishing degree of organization. From the simplest single-celled organism to the largest mammal, millions of reactions and events must be coordinated precisely for life to exist. This coordination is directed from the nucleus of the cell, by **deoxyribonucleic acid,** or **DNA.**

> DNA is the hereditary blueprint of the cell.

The DNA of a cell is contained in structures called chromosomes. The chromosomes consist of DNA wrapped around proteins called histones. When the genetic material is in a loose form in the nucleus, it is called **euchromatin,** and its genes are active, or available for transcription. When the genetic material is fully condensed into coils, it is called **heterochromatin,** and its genes are generally inactive. Situated in the nucleus, chromosomes direct and control all the processes necessary for life, including passing themselves, and their information, on to future generations.

Structure of DNA

The DNA molecule consists of two strands that wrap around each other to form a long, twisted ladder called a **double helix.** The structure of DNA was brilliantly deduced in 1956 by two scientists named James Watson and Francis Crick.

DNA is made up of repeated subunits of **nucleotides.** Each nucleotide has a **five-carbon sugar,** a **phosphate,** and a **nitrogenous base.** Take a look at the nucleotide below. This particular nucleotide contains a nitrogenous base called **adenine:**

The name of the pentagon-shaped sugar in DNA is **deoxyribose.** Hence, the name *deoxyribo*nucleic acid.

The Importance of DNA

Enzymes are proteins that are essential for life. This is true not only because they help liberate energy stored in chemical bonds, but also because they direct the construction of the cell. This is where DNA comes into the picture.

DNA's main role is directing the manufacture of proteins. These proteins, in turn, regulate everything that occurs in the cell. But DNA does not *directly* manufacture proteins. Instead, DNA passes its information to an intermediate molecule known as **ribonucleic acid (RNA).** These RNA molecules carry out the instructions in DNA, producing the proteins that determine the course of life.

The flow of genetic information is therefore

$$DNA \rightarrow RNA \rightarrow proteins$$

This is the central doctrine of molecular biology.

DNA is the hereditary blueprint of the cell. By directing the manufacture of proteins, DNA serves as the cell's blueprint. But how is DNA inherited? For the information in DNA to be passed on, it must first be copied. This copying of DNA is known as **DNA replication.**

KEY TERMS

cells
eukaryotic cells
prokaryotic cells
nucleus
cytoplasm
organelles
nucleoid
flagellum
plasma membrane
chromosomes
nucleolus
ribosomes
endoplasmic reticulum (ER)
rough ER
smooth ER
Golgi bodies
mitochondria
adenosine triphosphate (ATP)
lysosomes
centrioles
microtubule organizing centers
  (MTOCs)
vacuoles
peroxisomes
cytoskeleton
microtubules
microfilaments
tubulin
cell wall
chitin
chloroplasts
cell sap
roots
root tip
elongation region
maturation region
root apical meristem
root hairs
epidermis
cortex
stele
apoplast
symplast
endodermis
endodermal cells
spines

stamen
pistil
sepals
petals
anther
filament
pollen grains (microspores)
stigma
style
ovary
ovules
megaspores
egg nucleus
polar nuclei
double fertilization
sperm nuclei
endosperm
cotyledons
epicotyls
hypocotyls
radical
photoperiodism
short-day plants
long-day plants
day-neutral plants
phytochrome
vegetative propagation
tubers
runners
bulbs
grafting
intracellular digestion
extracellular digestion
mouth
esophagus
crop
stomach
intestine
rectum
anus
small intestine
large intestine
accessory organs
starch
proteins
fats

nucleic acids
oral cavity
saliva
salivary glands
salivary amylase
bolus
pharynx
peristalsis
gastric juices
pepsin
chime
pyloric sphincter
pancreas
trypsin
chymotrypsin
pancreatic lipase
pancreatic amylase
pancreatic duct
bile
emulsifier
liver
gall bladder
villi
microvilli
lacteals
gastrin
secretin
cholecystokinin
vitamin K
feces
tracheae
spiracles
gills
lungs
pharynx
larynx
epiglottis
left bronchus
right bronchus
bronchioles
alveolus
capillary
hemoglobin
plasma
bicarbonate ions
inspiration
expiration

chemoreceptors
diaphragm
open circulatory system
closed circulatory system
sinuses
right atrium
right ventricle
left atrium
left ventricle
systemic circulation
aortic semilunar valve
aorta
arteries
arterioles
capillaries
deoxygenated
venules
veins
superior vena cava
inferior vena cava
right atrioventricular valve
   (tricuspid)
pulmonary circulation
pulmonary artery
oxygenated blood
pulmonary veins
left atrioventricular valve (bicuspid,
   or mitral valve)
red blood cells (erythrocytes)
white blood cells (leukocytes)
platelets
blood types
antibodies
lymphatic system
lymph
lymph node
lymphocytes
antigen
immune system
phagocytes
complement proteins
interferons
inflammatory response
major histocompatibility complex
   markers (MHC markers)
T-lymphocytes
memory T-cells

helper T-cells

B-lymphocytes

cytotoxic T-cells

cell-mediated response

macrophages

antibodies

acquired immunodeficiency
  syndrome (AIDS)

nitrogenous wastes

ammonia

uric acid

urea

nephridia

Malpighian tubules

kidney

nephrons

Bowman's capsule

proximal convoluted tubule

loop of Henle

distal convoluted tubule

collecting duct

renal artery

glomerulus

filtrate

urine

ureters

bladder

urethra

nerve net

ganglia

neurons

cell body

dendrites

axon

sensory neurons

motor (effector) neurons

interneurons

central nervous system

peripheral nervous system

somatic nervous system

autonomic nervous system

sympathetic nervous system

parasympathetic nervous system

fight-or-flight response

homeostasis

cerebrum

cerebellum

hypothalamus

medulla

pons

midbrain

thalamus

deoxyribonucleic acid (DNA)

euchromatin

heterochromatin

double helix

nucleotides

five-carbon sugar

phosphate

nitrogenous base

adenine

deoxyribose

ribonucleic acid (RNA)

Drill #8

Each group of questions below is followed by four suggested answers or completions. Select the one that is best in each case.

1. A major difference between bacterial cells and animals cells is that bacterial cells have:

    A. a plasma membrane.

    B. ribosomes, which are involved in protein synthesis.

    C. a cell wall.

    D. a nuclear membrane.

2. The nucleolus is:

    A. the site at which rRNA is formed.

    B. a channel inside the cytoplasm that is the site of lipid synthesis.

    C. a polymer of the protein tubulin that is found in cilia, flagella, and spindle fibers.

    D. a semi-rigid structure that lends support to the cell.

3. Which of the following structures is not part of the pistil?

    A. ovule

    B. ovary

    C. style

    D. anther

4. The digestive enzyme that hydrolyzes molecules of fats into fatty acids is known as:

    A. bile.

    B. lipase.

    C. amylase.

    D. protease.

5. The blood type that is the universal recipient is:

    A. O.

    B. A.

    C. AB.

    D. B.

ANSWERS AND EXPLANATIONS TO DRILL #8

1. **C** Bacterial cells have a cell wall made up of peptidoglycan, while animal cells don't. Choices A and B: Both bacterial cells and animal cells have ribosomes and plasma membranes made of phospholipids. Choice D is wrong because bacterial cells do not have nuclear membranes and vacuoles.

2. **A** Choice A is correct. The nucleolus is the site where rRNA is formed. Choice B is a description of smooth ER, Choice C is a description of microtubules, and choice D is a description of the cell wall.

3. **D** The anther is the male part of the flower. The pistil is the female part of flowering plants. It consists of the ovule, style, ovary (which contains the female gametes), and the stigma (sticky protein that traps pollen trains).

4. **B** Enzymes that digest fats are called lipase (choice B). Choice A, bile, isn't an enzyme; rather, it emulsifies fats. Choice C, amylase digests carbohydrates. After eliminating choices A and C, you're down to two answer choices. You may not know what proteases are, but you should know that lipase digests fats.

5. **C** There are four blood types: A, B, AB, and O. Blood type O is the universal donor, and AB is the universal recipient. Individuals with blood type AB can receive blood from all of the other blood groups without any blood clotting.

Summary

o   All living things are composed of cells.

o   Inside cells are many organelles that perform important, specific tasks. You should memorize these for the CSET.

o   Plants have special structures including roots and leaves.

o   Flowering plants contain both male and female parts and reproduce through a process called double fertilization.

o   In human digestion, food travels from the oral cavity, is broken down by salivary amylase, travels through the pharynx and into the esophagus, then into the stomach, small intestine, large intestine, and is finally expelled as feces.

o   Gills and lungs are respiratory structures among vertebrates.

o   Taking in oxygen is called inspiration; breathing out is called expiration.

o   The two types of circulatory systems are the open circulatory system and the closed circulatory system.

o   In the human body, blood leaves the heart from the left ventricle and then makes a tour of the body that is called systemic circulation.

o   The lymphatic system is important for fluid homeostasis in the body.

o   The immune system is the body's defense system.

o   The excretory system is the body's system to get rid of nitrogenous wastes and to regulate water.

o   The nervous system is an elaborate system that picks up and processes information from the outside world.

Chapter 11
Living and Nonliving Components in Environments (Ecology)

LIVING AND NONLIVING COMPONENTS

Living and nonliving components coexist on earth in a careful balance. Life is the condition that distinguishes active organisms from inorganic matter. Living organisms undergo metabolism, maintain homeostasis, possess a capacity to grow, respond to stimuli, reproduce, and adapt to their environment in successive generations. To maintain homeostasis, all living things require four basic things: food, water, air, and space.

CYCLES IN NATURE

Nutrients such as carbon, oxygen, nitrogen, phosphorus, sulfur, and water all move through the environment in complex cycles known as **biogeochemical cycles.**

As you can probably tell from the collective name of these natural cycles, living organisms, geologic formations, and chemical substances are all involved in these cycles. Keep in mind that when we describe the movement of these inorganic compounds, it's important to understand both the destinations of the compounds and how they move to their destinations. For example, for the CSET, it won't be enough for you to know that water moves from the atmosphere to Earth. You'll need to know the different ways it has of getting there. In other words, you'll need to know that water moves from the atmosphere to Earth's surface through precipitation, either in the form of snow or rainfall.

But, let's talk about a few things that all of these cycles have in common before we go into each one in detail. First of all, the term **reservoir** is used to describe a place where a large quantity of a nutrient sits for a long period of time (in the water cycle, the ocean is an example of a reservoir). The opposite of a reservoir is an **exchange pool,** which is a site where a nutrient sits for only a short period of time (in the water cycle, a cloud is an example of an exchange pool). The amount of time a nutrient spends in a reservoir or an exchange pool is referred to as its **residency time.** In the water cycle, water might exist in the form of a cloud for a few days, but it might exist as part of the ocean for a thousand years! Perhaps surprisingly, living organisms can also serve as exchange pools and reservoirs for certain nutrients; we'll delve into more about this later.

The energy that drives these biogeochemical cycles in the biosphere comes primarily from two sources: the Sun and the heat energy from the mantle and core of Earth. The movements of nutrients in all of these cycles may be via abiotic mechanisms, such as wind, or may occur through biotic mechanisms, such as through living organisms. Another important fact to note is that while the **Law of Conservation of Matter** states that matter can be neither created nor destroyed, nutrients can be rendered unavailable for cycling through certain processes—for example, in some cycles, nutrients may be transported to deep ocean sediments where they are locked away interminably.

Though we won't get into a discussion of trace elements here, you should also know that certain trace elements such as zinc, copper, and iron are necessary in small amounts for living organisms. Trace elements can cycle in conjunction with the major nutrients, but there's still much to be discovered about these elements and their biogeochemical cycles. For the CSET, just know that there are certain trace elements required by living things that cycle, along with the major elements, through the biosphere.

Let's start with perhaps the most famous biogeochemical cycle: the water cycle.

The Water Cycle

As you might imagine, the water that exists in the atmosphere is in a gaseous state, and when it condenses from the gaseous state to form a liquid or solid, it becomes dense enough to fall to Earth because of the pull of gravity. This process is formally known as **precipitation.** When precipitation falls onto Earth, it may travel below ground to become **groundwater,** or it may travel across the land's surface and enter a drainage system, such as a stream or river, that will eventually deposit it into a body of water such as a lake or an ocean. Lakes and oceans are reservoirs for water. In certain cold regions of Earth, water may also be trapped on Earth's surface as snow or ice; in these areas, the blocks of snow or ice are reservoirs.

Water is also cycled through living systems. For example, plants consume water (and carbon dioxide) in the process of photosynthesis, in which they produce carbohydrates. Because all living organisms are primarily made up of water, they act as exchange pools for water.

Water is returned to the atmosphere from both Earth's surface and from living organisms in a process called **evaporation.** Specifically, animals respire and release water vapor and additional gases to the atmosphere. In plants, the process of **transpiration** releases large amounts of water into the air. Finally, other major contributors to atmospheric water are the vast number of lakes and oceans on Earth's surface. Incredibly large amounts of water continually evaporate from their surfaces.

Take a look at the graphic below, which shows all of the forms that water takes in the biosphere and atmosphere.

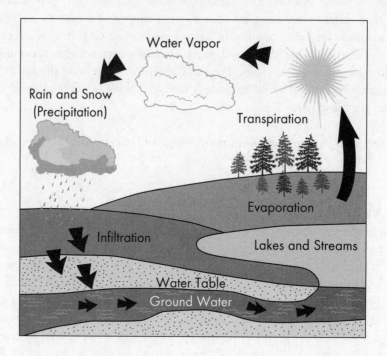

The Carbon Cycle

Now let's talk about carbon. The key events in the carbon cycle are **respiration**, in which animals breathe and give off carbon dioxide (CO_2); and **photosynthesis**, in which plants take in carbon dioxide, water, and energy from the Sun to produce carbohydrates. In other words, living things act as exchange pools for carbon.

When plants are eaten by animal consumers, the carbon locked in the plant carbohydrates passes to other organisms and continues through the food chain (more on this later in the chapter). In turn, when organisms—both plants and animals—die, their bodies are decomposed through the actions of bacteria and fungi in the soil; this releases CO_2 back into the atmosphere.

One aspect of the carbon cycle that you should definitely be familiar with for the exam is this: When the bodies of once-living organisms are buried and subjected to conditions of extreme heat and extreme pressure, eventually this organic matter becomes oil, coal, and gas. Oil, coal, and natural gas are collectively known as fossil fuels, and when **fossil fuels** are burned, or **combusted**, carbon is released into the atmosphere. Finally, carbon is also released into the atmosphere through volcanic action.

There are two major reservoirs of carbon. The first is the world's oceans, because CO_2 is very soluble in water. The second large reservoir of CO_2 is Earth's rocks. Many types of rocks—called carbonate rocks—contain carbon, in the form of calcium carbonate.

The Carbon Cycle

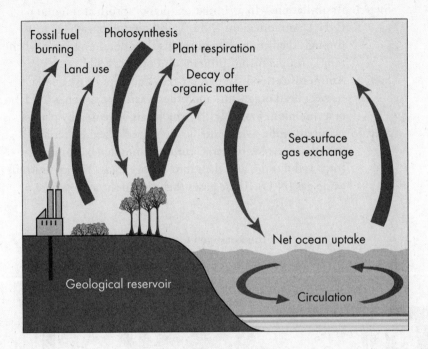

The Nitrogen Cycle

Earth's atmosphere is made up of approximately 78 percent nitrogen (N_2) and 21 percent oxygen (the other components of the atmosphere are trace elements), so as you can see, nitrogen is the most abundant element in the atmosphere. For this reason, it might not seem like living organisms would find it difficult to get the nitrogen they need in order to live. But it is! This is because atmospheric N_2 is not in a form that can be used directly by most organisms. In order to keep this rather complicated cycle straight, let's look at it in steps.

Step 1: **Nitrogen fixation**—In order to be used by most living organisms, nitrogen must be present in the form of ammonia (NH_3) or nitrates (NO_3^-). Atmospheric nitrogen can be converted into these forms, or "fixed," by atmospheric effects such as lightning storms, but most nitrogen fixation is the result of the actions of certain soil bacteria. One important soil bacteria that participates in nitrogen fixation is *Rhizobium*. These nitrogen-fixing bacteria are often associated with the roots of legumes such as beans and clover. In the future we may be able to insert the genes for nitrogen fixation into crop plants, such as corn, and reduce the amount of fertilizer that is used.

Step 2: **Nitrification**—In this process, soil bacteria converts ammonium (NH_4^+) into one of the forms that can be used by plants—nitrate (NO_3).

Step 3: Assimilation—In assimilation, plants absorb ammonium (NH_3), ammonia ions (NH_4^+), and nitrate ions (NO_3^-) through their roots. Heterotrophs then obtain nitrogen when they consume plants' proteins and nucleic acids.

Step 4: Ammonification—In this process, decomposing bacteria convert dead organisms and other waste to ammonia (NH_3) or ammonium ions (NH_4^+), which can be reused by plants.

Step 5: Denitrification—In dentrification, specialized bacteria (mostly anaerobic bacteria) convert ammonia back into nitrites and nitrates and then into nitrogen gas (N_2) and nitrous oxide gas (N_2O). These gases then rise to the atmosphere.

The Nitrogen Cycle

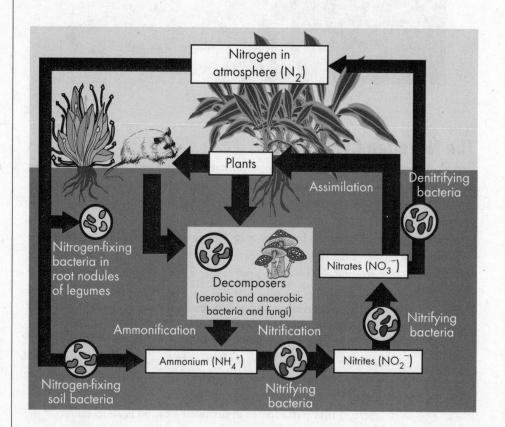

The Phosphorus Cycle

The last biogeochemical cycle we'll talk about is the phosphorus cycle. The **phosphorus cycle** is perhaps the simplest biogeochemical cycle, mostly because phosphorus does not exist in the atmosphere other than in dust particles. Phosphorus is necessary for living organisms because it's a major component of nucleic acids and other important biological molecules. One important idea for you to remember about the phosphorus cycle is that phosphorus cycles are more local than those of the other important biological compounds.

For the most part, phosphorus is found in soil, rock, and sediments; it's released from these rock forms through the process of chemical weathering. Phosphorus is usually released in the form of phosphate (PO_4^{3-}), which is very soluble and can be absorbed from the soil by plants. You should know that phosphorus is also often a limiting factor for plant growth, so plants that have little phosphorus are stunted.

Phosphates that enter the water table and travel to the oceans can eventually be incorporated into rocks in the ocean floor. Through geologic processes, ocean mixing, and upwelling, these rocks from the seafloor may rise up so that their components once again enter the **terrestrial cycle**. Take a look at the phosphorus cycle shown below.

Humans have affected the phosphorus cycle by mining phosphorus-rich rocks in order to produce fertilizers. The fertilizers placed on fields can easily leach into the groundwater and find their way into aquatic ecosystems where they can cause eutrophication and overgrowth of algae.

The Phosphorous Cycle

We are almost done with the chemistry. But we need to discuss one more element before we move on to discuss the biosphere, and that's sulfur.

Sulfur

Sulfur is one of the components that make up proteins and vitamins, so both plants and animals need sulfur in their diets. Plants absorb sulfur when it is dissolved in water, so they can take it up through their roots when it's dissolved in groundwater. Animals obtain sulfur by consuming plants.

Most of Earth's sulfur is tied up in rocks and salts or buried deep in the ocean in oceanic sediments, but some sulfur can be found in the atmosphere. The natural ways that sulfur enters the atmosphere are through volcanic eruptions, certain bacterial functions, and the decay of once-living organisms. When sulfur enters the atmosphere through human activity, it's mainly via industrial processes that produce sulfur dioxide (SO_2) and hydrogen sulfide (H_2S) gases.

All right! It's time to move on to our discussion of the biotic components of Earth. Let's start with a review of how energy moves through ecosystems. First, let's look at a sample question.

Nitrogen from the atmosphere must be incorporated into living organisms to make proteins. Which of the following plants is a vehicle for organisms that add nitrates to the soil?

A. rice

B. lima bean

C. rose

D. Venus flytrap

Here's How To Crack It

Remember that we discussed the nitrogen-fixing bacteria associated with legumes, back in our discussion of the nitrogen cycle? Keep that one in mind and it's obvious that choice B is the correct answer.

FOOD CHAINS AND FOOD WEBS

You might recall that the nonliving components of the environment are known as the **abiotic components.** These include the atmosphere, hydrosphere, and lithosphere. Well, it's time to begin our study of the living, biotic components of Earth. Together, all of the living things on Earth constitute the biosphere.

All living things can be classified by the manner in which they obtain food. You might recall that plants are capable of making their own food through photosynthesis, and that some animals (for example, mice) eat plants. Some animals (for example, humans) eat both plants and animals, and some animals (for example, wolves) eat only other animals. There are actually two fancy terms that are normally used to describe these broad categories of organisms: **Autotrophs** are those organisms that can produce their own organic compounds from inorganic chemicals, while **heterotrophs** obtain food energy by consuming other organisms or products created by other organisms.

Finally, as unpleasant as it might be to think about, some animals feed only on the remains of other plants and animals! All of these different types of living things fall into specific categories.

Producers

Producers are organisms that are capable of converting radiant energy or chemical energy into carbohydrates. The group of producers includes plants and algae, both of which can carry out photosynthesis. The unbalanced overall reaction of photosynthesis is shown below.

$$H_2O + CO_2 + \text{solar energy} \rightarrow CH_2O + O_2$$

While most producers make food through photosynthesis, a few autotrophs make food from inorganic chemicals in anaerobic (without oxygen) environments, through the process of chemosynthesis. Chemosynthesis is carried out by only a few specialized bacteria, called **chemotrophs,** some of which are found in hydrothermal vents deep in the ocean. This unbalanced reaction is shown below.

$$O_2 + H_2S + O_2 + \text{energy} \rightarrow CH_2O + S + H_2O$$

At this point, let's discuss a few other environmental science terms that you may be required to know for the exam. The **net primary productivity (NPP)** is the amount of energy that plants pass on to the community of herbivores in an ecosystem. It is calculated by taking the **gross primary productivity (GPP),** which is the amount of sugar that the plants produce in photosynthesis, and subtracting from it the amount of energy the plants need for growth, maintenance, repair, and reproduction. NPP is measured in kilocalories per square meter per year ($kcal/m^2/y$). In other words, the gross primary productivity of an ecosystem is the rate at which the producers are converting solar energy to chemical energy (or, in a hydrothermal ecosystem, the rate of productivity of the chemotrophs). Perhaps not surprisingly, the net productivity of an ecosystem is a limiting factor for its number of consumers. Let's talk about them next.

Consumers

Consumers are organisms that must obtain food energy from secondary sources, for example, by eating plant or animal matter. There are a number of different types of consumers:

- **Primary consumers** include the herbivores, which consume only producers (plants and algae).
- **Secondary consumers** consume primary consumers.
- **Tertiary consumers** consume secondary consumers.
- **Detritivores** derive energy from consuming nonliving organic matter such as dead animals and fallen leaves.
- **Decomposers** are bacteria or fungi that absorb nutrients from nonliving organic matter such as plant material, the wastes of living organisms, and corpses. They convert these materials into inorganic forms. Generally, fungi and bacteria are decomposers. They serve as the "garbage collectors" in our environment.

Note that one organism may occupy multiple levels of a food chain. By eating a hamburger and bun you are both a primary consumer because you are eating tomatoes and lettuce, and a secondary consumer by eating the beef.

Let's move on and talk about how energy flows through all of these different types of organisms in ecosystems.

Food Chains

As you probably recall, energy flows in one direction through ecosystems: from the Sun to producers, to primary consumers, to secondary consumers, to tertiary consumers. In an ecosystem, each of these feeding levels is referred to as a **trophic level**. With each successive trophic level, the amount of energy that's available to the next level decreases. In fact, only about 10 percent of the energy from one trophic level is passed to the next; most is lost as heat, and some is used for metabolism and anabolism. Interestingly enough, this is why food chains rarely have more than four trophic levels.

Food chains are usually represented as a series of steps, in which the bottom step is the producer and the top step is a secondary or tertiary consumer. In food chains, the arrows depict the transfer of energy through the levels, and in fancier food chains, the relative **biomass** (the dry weight of the group of organisms) of each trophic level will often be represented. Here's a simple food chain.

Food Chain

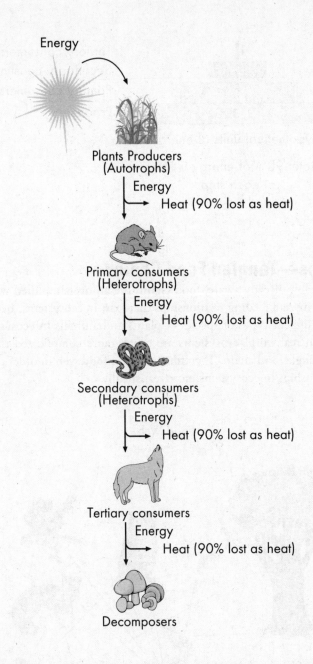

Energy

Plants Producers
(Autotrophs)

Energy
Heat (90% lost as heat)

Primary consumers
(Heterotrophs)

Energy
Heat (90% lost as heat)

Secondary consumers
(Heterotrophs)

Energy
Heat (90% lost as heat)

Tertiary consumers

Energy
Heat (90% lost as heat)

Decomposers

What we're showing here is a typical terrestrial food chain, but keep in mind that there are aquatic food chains as well, with algae and different types of fish.

One final note about food chains: At each successive level in a food chain, much energy is lost. The amount of energy (in kilocalories) available at each trophic level organized from greatest to least is an **energy pyramid.** In other words, the producers have the most energy in an ecosystem; the primary consumers have less energy than producers; the secondary consumers have less energy than the primary consumers; and the tertiary consumers will have the least energy of all.

Energy Pyramid

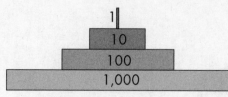

1	Tertiary consumers
10	Secondary consumers
100	Primary consumers
1,000	Producers

Hypothetical units of energy

Note: 90% of energy is lost
at each step

Food Webs—Tangled Food Chains

As you're probably already aware, food chains are an oversimplified way of demonstrating the myriad feeding relationships that exist in ecosystems. Because there are so many different types of species of plants and animals in ecosystems, their relationships in real-world ecosystems are much more complicated than can be depicted in a single food chain. Therefore, we use a **food web** in order to represent feeding relationships in ecosystems more realistically.

Food Web

Again, this is a typical terrestrial food web, but keep in mind that very complicated aquatic food webs exist as well! Let's take a step back for a minute and discuss the setting for food chains and food webs—ecosystems. But first, let's try a question.

Which of the following organisms serve as decomposers in the ecosystem?

A.   bacteria and viruses

B.   fungi and bacteria

C.   viruses and protists

D.   fungi and viruses

Here's How To Crack It

Both fungi and bacteria serve as decomposers, so choice B is correct. Fungi and bacteria break down organic matter. Viruses invade other organisms, but they're not decomposers. Protists are unicellular organisms, such as paramecium and euglena. They're not decomposers either.

THE WORLD'S ECOSYSTEMS

Because different geographic areas on Earth differ so much in their abiotic and biotic components, we can easily place them in broad categories. The two largest categories are broken down in this way: Ecosystems that are based on land are called **biomes,** while those in aqueous environments are known as **aquatic life zones.** Aquatic ecosystems are categorized primarily by the salinity of their water—freshwater and saltwater ecosystems fall into separate categories. Land environments are separated into biomes based on their climate.

Although it might seem that each biome listed in the following table is very distinct, in reality, biomes blend into each other; they do not have distinct boundaries. The transitional area where two ecosystems meet actually has a name—these areas are called **ecotones.** Another important term that you should be familiar with for the exam is **ecozones**: Ecozones (also called **ecoregions**) are smaller regions within ecosystems that share similar physical features.

Information about the Earth's Biomes

Biome	Annual Rainfall, Soil Type	Major Vegetation	World Location
Deciduous forest (temperate and tropical)	75–250 cm, rich soil with high organic content	Hardwood trees	North America, Europe, Australia, and Eastern Asia
Tropical rainforest	200–400 cm, poor quality soil	Tall trees with few lower limbs, vines, epiphytes, plants adapted to low light intensity	South America, West Africa, and Southeast Asia
Grasslands	10–60 cm, rich soil	Sod-forming grasses	North American plains and prairies; Russian steppes; South African velds; Argentinean pampas
Coniferous forest (Taiga)	20–60 cm (mostly in summer), acidic soil due to vegetation	Coniferous trees	Northern North America, northern Eurasia
Tundra	Less than 25 cm, permafrost soil	Herbaceous plants	The northern latitudes of North America, Europe, and Russia
Chaparral (scrub forest)	50–75 cm (mostly in winter), shallow and infertile soil	Small trees with large hard leaves, spiny shrubs	Western North America, the Mediterranean region
Deserts (cold and hot)	Less than 25 cm (sandy soil with a coarse texture)	Cactus, other low-water adapted plants	30 degrees north and south of the equator

Not surprisingly, each biome has specific characteristics that determine the types of organisms that are capable of living in it. Some of these characteristics are the type and availability of nutrients, the ecosystems' temperature, the availability of water, and how much sunlight the region receives. One important law to be familiar with for this test is the **Law of Tolerance**. The Law of Tolerance describes the degree to which living organisms are capable of tolerating changes in their environment. Living organisms exhibit a range of tolerance, and even individuals within a population tolerate changes to their environment differently: This concept is the basis for natural selection, which drives evolution. We'll cover that thoroughly in Chapter 12.

Another important law for you to know is the **Law of the Minimum,** which states that living organisms will continue to live, consuming available materials until the supply of these materials is exhausted.

Environmental **accommodation** and **adaptation** are important phenomena that you should be familiar with. Accommodation is the process by which mental structures and behaviors are modified to adapt to new experiences. For example, dogs were wild at one time and have been domesticated. They are capable of learning specific behaviors and generalizing that knowledge. A dog doesn't instinctively know not to urinate or defecate indoors, but can be taught not to do so. If you trained your dog not to urinate or defecate in your house, and then took him to a friend's home, his modified behavior would carry over to that environment, and he knows that he may not urinate or defecate there, either. He has made a generalization about his environment and can accommodate his surroundings.

An adaptation is a change that an organism must make for survival. It enables the organism (plant or animal) to adjust to different conditions within the environment. Structural adaptation happens over a long period of time, unlike accomodation. Examples of adaptation include behavior adaptation, hibernation, teeth, body covering, and many more. The polar bear is a perfect example of adaptation. Polar bears are closely related to the brown bear, but have adapted for cold temperatures; for moving across snow, ice, and open water; and for retaining heat.

Ecosystem Diversity

The term **biodiversity** is used to describe the number and variety of organisms found within a specified geographic region, or ecosystem. It also refers to the variability among living organisms, including the variability within and between species and within and between ecosystems.

Therefore, when we talk about the biodiversity of an area, we must specifically state the aspect of biodiversity that we're describing, or else the term is too vague to be comprehensible. In general, however, biodiversity in an ecosystem is a good thing. The more biodiversity in a certain species within an ecosystem, the larger and more diverse the species' gene pool is, and the greater its chance of adaptation, and thus survival.

SHARE AND SHARE ALIKE?

When people talk about managing common property resources such as air, water, and land, a paper published in *Science* magazine by Garret Hardin in 1958, called "The Tragedy of the Commons," often comes to mind. In this paper, Hardin referenced a parable from the 1880s in which a piece of open land, a commons, was to be used collectively by the townspeople for grazing their cattle. Each townsperson who used the land continued to add one cow or ox at a time until the commons was overgrazed. Hardin quite eloquently says, "Each man is locked into a system that compels him to increase his herd without limit—in a world that is limited. Ruin is the destination toward which all men rush, each pursuing his own best interest in a society that believes in the freedom of the commons. Freedom in a commons brings ruin to all."

This parable serves as a foundation for modern conservation. **Conservation** is the management or regulation of a resource so that its use does not exceed the capacity of the resource to regenerate itself. This is different from **preservation**, which is the maintenance of a species or ecosystem in order to ensure its perpetuation, with no concern as to its potential monetary value.

Next, we'll show how human economics often influences how we interact with Earth's resources. Ecosystems (both biotic and abiotic) are often referred to as **natural resources**. When we describe something as a *resource*, we are essentially putting an economic value on it; therefore, natural resources are described in terms of their value as **ecosystem capital**.

Some Terms Used to Describe Resources

Let's start by discussing the two main types of resources:

- **Renewable resources** such as plants and animals, can be regenerated quickly.
- **Nonrenewable resources** such as minerals, fossil fuels, and soil, are typically formed by very slow geologic processes, so we consider them incapable of being regenerated within the realm of human existence.

There are a couple more terms you should know before we dive into our review of the major resources available to humans on Earth. The **consumption** of natural resources refers to the day-to-day use of environmental resources such as food, clothing, and housing. On the other hand, **production** refers to the use of environmental resources for profit. An example of this might be a fisherman who sells his fish in a market. Got those terms? Let's move on.

AGRICULTURE

How do resources relate to your dinner? Well, 77 percent of the world's food comes from croplands, 16 percent comes from grazing lands, and 7 percent of the world's food comes from ocean resources. Despite the importance of our crops, and although the population of the United States has increased significantly, fewer people than ever in the history of the United States now farm the land. Why is this? The short answer is that it has a lot to do with increasing urbanization and industrialization. Now that machines are readily available to work the land and harvest crops, farms have become more like factories—currently only 15 percent of the entire workforce of the United States produces the food to feed the entire county—and for exporting. Farms in the United States today are quite a bit larger than farms of the past; the average farm is 400 acres, while in the early twentieth century the average farm size was about 100 acres.

The use of machinery in farming has allowed a farmer to work more land and do so more efficiently; however, one of the drawbacks of the machinery is the amount of fossil fuel needed to power it. As the cost of fuel rises, the cost of food will also rise.

This rise in agricultural productivity can be tied to the new pesticides and fertilizers, expanded irrigation, and the development of new high-yield seed types. However, it has also resulted in a significant decrease in the genetic variability of crop plants, and led to huge problems in erosion.

Traditional Agriculture and the Green Revolution

Throughout most of history, agriculture all over the world was such that each family grew crops for themselves, and families primarily relied on animal and human labor to plant and harvest crops. This process is called **traditional subsistence agriculture,** and it provides enough food for one family's survival. Traditional subsistence agriculture is still practiced in developing nations, and is currently practiced by about 42 percent of the world's population.

Another component of traditional agriculture that's still practiced in many developing countries today is a method called **slash and burn;** this practice actually dates back to early man. In slash and burn, an area of vegetation is cut down and burned before being planted with crops. Then because soils in these developing countries are generally poor, the farmer must leave the area after a relatively short time and find another location to clear. This practice severely reduces the amount of available forest; it is a significant contributor to deforestation.

The **Green Revolution** is generally thought of as the time after the Industrial Revolution when farming became mechanized and crop yields in industrialized nations boomed. Don't confuse the Green Revolution, which is about farming, with the Green Movement, which is about conservation.

Norman Borlaug is considered by many to be the founder of the Green Revolution. He was born in 1914 on a farm in Iowa, and throughout his career, Borlaug collaborated with scientists worldwide on problems of wheat improvement. He worked with India and Pakistan, attempting to find ways to adapt the newly created strains of wheat to these lands. His work has allowed developed and developing countries to produce higher yields of crops on less land, which is quite advantageous; the use of less land saves forests, grasslands, mountainsides, and wetlands from being degraded and also preserves their biodiversity. Borlaug received the Nobel Peace prize in 1970 for his work with high-yield crops.

Fertilizers and Pesticides

One factor that contributed to the Green Revolution was an increase in the use of fertilizers and pesticides. Interestingly, when the non-native settlers (the first white settlers) planted their first corn crops, certain tribes of Native Americans taught them to plant a fish along with the corn seed; the fish acted as a natural fertilizer for the crops. As you can see, manures and other organic materials have been used as fertilizers by farmers for many years. However, the development of inorganic (chemical) fertilizers brought about the huge increases in farm production seen during the Green Revolution. It's estimated that if chemical fertilizers were suddenly no longer used, then the total output of food in the world would drop about 40 percent!

Of course, there are downsides to the widespread use of chemical fertilizers, and these include the following: the reduction of organic matter and oxygen in soil; the fact that these fertilizers require large amounts of energy to produce, transport, and supply; and the fact that once they are washed into watersheds, they are dangerous pollutants.

Similarly, the increased use of pesticides in the Green Revolution has significantly reduced the number of crops lost to insects, fungi, and other pests, but these chemicals have also had an effect on ecosystems in and surrounding farms. It's estimated that the average insect pesticide will be useful for only 5–10 years before its target insect evolves to become immune to its effects; therefore, new pesticides must constantly be developed. However, even with this constant development, crop loss due to pests has not decreased since 1970, although the use of pesticides has tripled!

Because the use of pesticides is so prevalent in the United States, Congress passed the **Federal Insecticide, Fungicide, and Rodenticide Act (FIFRA)** in 1947 and amended it in 1972. This law requires the EPA to approve the use of all pesticides in the United States.

Irrigation

Another major contributor to the increased crop yields seen in the Green Revolution was advanced irrigation techniques, which allowed crops to be planted in areas that normally would not have enough precipitation to sustain them. However, repeated irrigation can cause serious problems, including a significant buildup of salts on the soil's surface that make the land unusable for crops. To combat this **salinization** of the land, farmers have begun flooding fields with massive amounts of water in order to move the salt deeper into the soil. The drawback to this, however, is that the large amounts of water can waterlog plant roots, which will kill the crops. This process also causes the water table of the region to rise.

Genetically Engineered Plants

The third and last significant contributor to the Green Revolution was the introduction of genetically engineered plants. When genetically engineered plants were first introduced to the public, they were met with hostility and fear. This is in part because many people feared the eventual creation of hybrid humans and other genetic abominations.

Arguably, one of the most important developments in the genetic modification of plants has been the creation of golden rice, which contains vitamin A and iron. The introduction of this rice addresses two of the serious health problems that are seen in developing nations: vitamin A deficiency, which can result in blindness and other serious health problems; and iron deficiency, which leads to anemia. This is just one example of the potentially multitudinous uses of genetic engineering in solving global hunger problems!

So far, the only empirical problem that has arisen as a result of the introduction of genetically engineered plants has been that pollen from these plants can spread, and hybrids between genetically engineered and non-genetically engineered plants can arise. This is a concern for some, since it may result in a loss of certain indigenous plant strains, such as the blue corn of Mexico.

Genetically engineered plants enable us to develop foods with higher nutritional value, and they also have the potential to enable us to decrease the amount of pesticides we use. For example, one particular strain of cotton has been genetically modified in such a way that it produces a pesticide in its leaves—but only at times when the insect population is a problem. Some other potential benefits of genetically engineered plants include producing their own nitrogen (which is often hard for plants to derive from the soil) or tolerating higher levels of salt in the soil. As you know, this latter development would allow plants to grow in areas where over-irrigation previously rendered the soil unusable.

Monotonous Monoculture

Believe it or not, three grains provide more than half of the total calories that are consumed worldwide! These three crops are rice, wheat, and corn, and the phenomenal increase in the yield of these crops was a result of genetic engineering. Genetic engineers discovered a way to cause plants to divert more of their photosynthetic products (called **photosynthate**) to becoming grain biomass rather than plant body biomass.

It's estimated that, of the roughly 30,000 plant species that could possibly be used for food, only 10,000 have been used historically, with any regularity. Today 90 percent of the caloric intake worldwide is supplied by just fourteen plant species and eight terrestrial animal species! In other words, today's agriculture represents a major reduction in agricultural biodiversity.

On a smaller scale, much of the farming that occurs today is characterized by **monoculture.** In monoculture, just one type of plant is planted in a large area. As we discussed earlier, this has proved to be an unwise practice for numerous reasons. **Plantation farming,** which is practiced mainly in tropical developing nations, is a type of industrialized agriculture in which a monoculture cash crop, such as bananas, coffee, or vegetables, is grown and then exported to developed nations.

Soil Degradation

Great Plains droughts in the 1930s were the major causative factors that created the Dust Bowl, but also, farming practices used at that time contributed to the destruction of the land.

In an effort to address the Dust Bowl and other agricultural problems, the United States Soil and Conservation Service (today it's called the National Resources Conservation Service) was established, and it passed the Soil Conservation Act in 1935. Conservation districts were set up by the Service and these franchises provided education to farmers.

Today, farmers can protect soil from degradation in numerous ways. The practice of **contour plowing,** in which rows of crops are plowed across the hillside, prevents the erosion that can occur when rows are cut up and down on a slope. **Terracing** also aids in preventing soil erosion on steep slopes. Terraces are flat platforms that are cut into the hillside to provide a level planting surface; this reduces the soil runoff from the slope. Additionally, **no-till methods** are quite beneficial; in no-till agriculture, farmers plant seeds without using a plow to turn the soil. Soil loses most of it carbon content during plowing, which releases carbon dioxide gas into the atmosphere.

Finally, **crop rotation** can provide soils with nutrients when legumes are part of the cycle of crops in an area. An alternate to crop rotation is **intercropping** (also called **strip cropping**), which is the practice of planting bands of different crops across a hillside. This type of planting can also prevent some erosion by creating an extensive network of roots. As you might be aware, plant roots hold the soil in place and reduce or prevent soil erosion.

The Livestock Business

Perhaps not surprisingly, the introduction of all these new agricultural techniques has significantly affected the livestock business. As long as the grazing area is sufficient for the number of animals, livestock grazing is a sustainable practice. If, however, grass is consumed by animals at a faster rate than it can re-grow, land is considered **overgrazed**. Overgrazing is harmful to the soil because it leads to erosion and soil compaction. One solution to the problem of overgrazing is similar to crop rotation—animals can be rotated from site to site. Another solution involves the overall control of herd numbers.

Various tracts of public lands are available for use as rangeland, and cooperation between government agents, environmentalists, and ranchers can help avoid problems of overgrazing on these lands.

Another problem that arises from the large number of grazing animals worldwide is the large amount of animal waste produced. Instead of this waste being used as a natural fertilizer, it has instead become the most widespread source of water pollution in the United States. Grazing animals also consume 70 percent of the total grain crop consumed in the United States, making them expensive food stuff.

The law that describes the degree to which living organisms are capable of tolerating changes in the environment is called the:

A. Law of Adaptation.

B. Law of Accommodation.

C. Law of Tolerance.

D. Law of Ecosystem.

Here's How To Crack It

This question is a great example of how, sometimes, the answer is right under your nose. Read the question carefully and you will see that choice C, Law of Tolerance (the correct answer) is staring you in the face. Adaptation and accomodation are certainly important parts of the study of ecology, but they are not the correct answers here.

ECONOMICS AND RESOURCE UTILIZATION

The study of how people use limited resources to satisfy their wants and needs is called **economics.** As you can imagine, some of those needs are tangible (food and shelter are two examples) while others are intangible (the beauty of a forest and clean air are two examples). A resource can have both tangible and intangible properties.

A forest has value for supplying jobs and wood (tangible) as well as for its beauty and ability to remove CO_2 from the air (intangible). When private citizens, governments, and corporations make a decision on how to use a forest, they must weigh the benefits (more jobs and lumber) against the cost of cutting down the trees (less recreation space, the loss of biodiversity, and loss of CO_2 removal). This process is called **cost-benefit analysis.** It may be easy to assign a monetary value to the tangible properties (like the amount of lumber in the forest), but how do you assign a monetary value to the intangible properties (like the beauty of a forest)? While cost-benefit analysis helps make decisions on how to use resources, you can see that the process is very difficult, and it can lead to different estimates by different groups.

Economists also want to figure out the cost of each step in a process. From our forest example, what is the cost to the economy of adding one more acre to the forest; or what is the benefit to us if we add one more acre to the forest? The additional costs are termed **marginal costs,** and the added benefits are called **marginal benefits.** It is important to remember that resources are not free and unlimited. Some resources must be expended in order for us to use them. While we may benefit from more acres to hike in, the lumber company will suffer from not having as many trees to cut. In other words, marginal benefits and costs help us understand tradeoffs. By preserving a forest, we trade more hiking space with less profit for local economies.

KEY TERMS

biogeochemical cycles
reservoir
exchange pool
residency time
Law of Conservation of Matter
water cycle
precipitation
groundwater
evaporation
transpiration
carbon cycle
respiration
photosynthesis
fossil fuels
combusted
nitrogen fixation
nitrification
assimilation
ammonification
dentrification
phosphorus cycle
terrestrial cycle
sulfur
abiotic components
autotrophs
heterotrophs
producers
chemotrophs
net primary productivity (NPP)
gross primary productivity (GPP)
consumers
primary consumers
secondary consumers
tertiary consumers
detritivores
decomposers
trophic level
food chains
biomass
energy pyramid

food web
biomes
aquatic life zones
ecotones
ecozones (ecoregions)
Law of Tolerance
Law of the Minimum
accommodation
adaptation
biodiversity
conservation
preservation
natural resources
ecosystem capital
renewable resources
nonrenewable resources
consumption
production
traditional subsistence agriculture
slash and burn
Green Revolution
Norman Borlaug
Federal Insecticide, Fungicide, and
 Rodenticide Act (FIFRA)
salinization
photosynthate
monoculture
plantation farming
contour plowing
terracing
no-till methods
crop rotation
intercropping (strip cropping)
overgrazed
economics
cost-benefit analysis
marginal costs
marginal benefits

Drill #9

Directions: Each of the questions or incomplete statements below is followed by five suggested answers or completions. Select the one that is best in each case.

1. Which organisms in the food chain are producers?

   A. birds

   B. insects

   C. grass

   D. mice

2. When two species live in the same habitat and use exactly the same resources, which of the following will probably occur?

   A. The two species can live together indefinitely.

   B. One of the species will eventually die.

   C. One species will evolve into a parasite.

   D. The two species do not interact.

3. Organisms use different resources in the same habitat, and in this way avoid competition. This is referred to as:

   A. the Law of Tolerance.

   B. hunting and gathering.

   C. predator-prey relationship.

   D. resource partitioning.

4. Which of the following correctly describes the process of smelting?

   A. separating the desired metal from other elements in the ore

   B. cleaning up drainage from mines

   C. detoxifying harmful chemicals

   D. removing ore from underground mines

5. In a very polluted river it costs $3 per kilogram to remove the first 80 percent of the pollution. It costs $25 per kilogram to remove the last 20 percent of the pollutant. This phenomenon is correctly referred to as:

   A. cost-benefit analysis.

   B. external costs.

   C. marginal costs.

   D. marginal benefit.

Please turn the page for answers and explanations
for the questions in this drill.

ANSWERS AND EXPLANATIONS TO DRILL #9

1. **C** A producer is an organism that is capable of converting radiant or chemical energy into carbohydrates. The only example of this is choice C, grass.

2. **B** This concept is called competitive exclusion. The idea behind competitive exclusion is that two species who share the same niche cannot infinitely exist in the same ecosystem; eventually one will prove to be more fit and out-compete the other.

3. **D** Different species can use slightly different parts of the habitat to avoid direct competition with other species. For example, there are five species of warblers that can live in the same pine tree. They can coexist because each species feeds in a different part of the tree: the trunk, at the ends of the branches, and at other sites.

4. **A** Smelting is a process that separates a desired ore from other materials in mined ore. It is usually accomplished by heating the ore and ladling off the desired molten element.

5. **C** Cost-benefit analysis (A) is the comparison of the benefit of an action relative to the costs of that action. External costs (B) are the costs that occur after someone purchases something. For example, after you buy a car, the cost of gasoline is an external cost. Marginal benefits (D) are the tradeoff between how much we gain by buying forest land (for example) or using the money to do some other beneficial activity. Marginal costs (C) are the costs of each step in a process. Thus, choice C is the correct answer.

Summary

o   All living things require four basic things: food, water, air, and space.

o   Nutrients move through the environment in biogeochemical cycles including the water cycle, the carbon cycle, the nitrogen cycle, and the phosphorous cycle.

o   Energy flows in one direction through the ecosystem: from the Sun to producers to primary consumers to secondary consumers to tertiary consumers to decomposers, in a system called the food chain.

o   Ecosystems based on land are called biomes; those based in aqueous environments are aquatic life zones.

o   Biodiversity is the variety of organisms in a specified region or ecosystem.

o   Renewable resources and nonrenewable resources are the two main types of resources available.

o   Conservation is the regulation of a resource so that its use doesn't exceed the capacity to regenerate itself. Preservation is the regulation of a resource to ensure its perpetuation.

o   Norman Borlaug is considered by many to be the founder of the Green Revolution.

o   Economics is the study of how people use limited resources.

Chapter 12
Life Cycle,
Reproduction,
and Evolution

LIFE CYCLE

How does a tiny, single-celled egg develop into a complex, multicellular organism? By dividing, of course. The cell will change shape and organization many times by going through a succession of stages. This process is called **morphogenesis.** In order for the human sperm to fertilize an egg it must dissolve the **corona radiata,** a dense covering of follicle cells that surrounds the egg. Then the sperm must penetrate the **zona pellucida,** the zone below the corona radiata.

When an egg is fertilized by a sperm, it forms a **diploid cell** called a **zygote.**

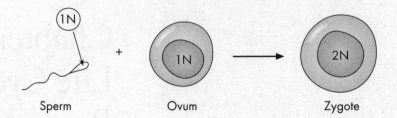

| Sperm | Ovum | Zygote |

Fertilization triggers the zygote to go through a series of rapid cell divisions called **cleavage.** What's interesting at this stage is that the embryo doesn't grow. The cells just keep dividing to form a solid ball called a **morula.**

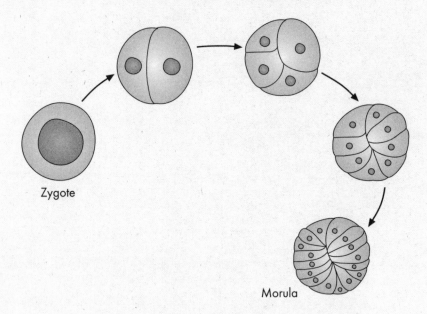

One cell becomes two cells, two cells become four cells, and so on.

Blastula

The next stage is called **blastula.** As the cells continue to divide, they press against each other and produce a fluid-filled cavity called a **blastocoel.**

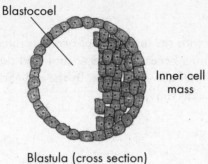

Blastocoel

Inner cell mass

Blastula (cross section)

Gastrula

During **gastrulation**, the zygote begins to change its shape. Cells now migrate into the blastocoel and differentiate to form three germ layers: the **ectoderm**, **mesoderm**, and **endoderm**.

- The outer layer becomes the ectoderm.
- The middle layer becomes the mesoderm.
- The inner layer becomes the endoderm.

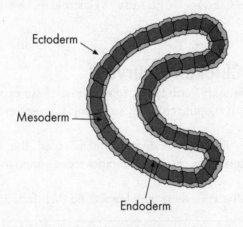

Ectoderm

Mesoderm

Endoderm

Gastrula (cross-section)

Each germ layer gives rise to various organs and systems in the body. Here's a list of the organs that develop from each germ layer.

- The ectoderm produces the **epidermis** (the skin), the eyes, and the nervous system.
- The endoderm produces the inner linings of the digestive tract and respiratory tract, as well as accessory organs such as the pancreas, gall bladder, and liver. These are called "accessory" organs because they are offshoots of the digestive tract, as opposed to the channels of the tract itself.
- The mesoderm gives rise to everything else. This includes bones and muscles as well as the excretory, circulatory, and reproductive systems.

Organogenesis

The **neurula** stage begins with the formation of two structures: the **notochord**, a rod-shaped structure running beneath the nerve cord, and the **neural tube** cells, which develop into the central nervous system. By the end of this stage, we're well on our way to developing a nervous system.

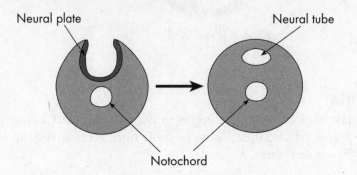

The *order* of the stages and the various events is extremely important. For our purposes, think of the order of embryological development in this way:

$$\text{Zygote} \rightarrow \text{Cleavage} \rightarrow \text{Blastula} \rightarrow \text{Gastrula} \rightarrow \text{Organogenesis}$$

What About Chicken Embryos?

In addition to the primary germ layers, some animals have **extraembryonic membranes.** An average developing chicken, for example, possesses these membranes.

There are basically four extraembryonic membranes: the **yolk sac, amnion, chorion,** and **allantois.** These extra membranes are common in birds and reptiles.

You should be familiar with these membranes and their functions:

FUNCTIONS OF EXTRAEMBRYONIC MEMBRANES	
Extraembryonic membrane	**Function**
Yolk sac	Provides food for the embryo
Amnion	Forms a fluid-filled sac that protects the embryo
Allantois	Is involved in gas exchange; stores uric acid
Chorion	Surrounds all the other extraembryonic membranes

Fetal Embryo

The fetal embryo also has extraembryonic membranes during development: the amnion, chorion, allantois, and yolk sac. The **placenta** and the **umbilical cord** are outgrowths of these membranes. The placenta is the organ that provides the fetus with nutrients and oxygen and gets rid of the fetus's wastes. The placenta develops from both the chorion and the uterine tissue of the mother. The umbilical cord is the organ that connects the embryo to the placenta.

Development of an Embryo

During embryonic development, some tissues determine the fate of other tissues in a process called **induction**. Certain cells, called **organizers**, release a chemical substance (a **morphogen**) that moves from one tissue to the target tissue. It is now known that development involves many episodes of embryonic induction.

Homeotic genes control the development of the embryo. Some homeotic genes, called homeobox genes, consist of homeoboxes (short, nearly identical DNA sequences) that encode proteins that bind to DNA; these proteins tell cells in various segments of the developing embryo what type of structures to make. Interestingly, homeobox genes are shared by almost all eukaryotic species. Hox genes, which are a subset of homeobox genes, specify the position of body parts in the developing embryo. Mutations in Hox genes result in the conversion of one body part into another. For example, in *Drosophila,* a specific Hox mutation results in a leg developing where an antenna would normally be.

The cytoplasm can also have an influence on embryonic development. For example, chicken and frog embryos contain more yolk in one pole (the vegetal pole) versus the other pole (the animal pole). This causes cells within the animal pole to divide more, and thus to be smaller than those of the vegetal pole. Because of the distribution of the yolk, cleavage of the egg does not produce eggs that develop normally. If the egg is divided into an animal and vegetal pole, development does not proceed normally.

Which of the following processes produces embryonic germ layers?

A. gastrulation

B. cleavage

C. blastulation

D. organogenesis

Here's How to Crack It

The process that produces embryonic germ layers is gastrulation. Cleavage (choice B) is the mitotic division of the zygote after fertilization. Blastulation (choice C) is the hollow ball of cells produced by cleavage of a fertilized ovum. Organogenesis (choice D) is the process by which organs develop. Therefore, choice A is the correct answer.

REPRODUCTION

Reproduction can be either **sexual** or **asexual**. You're probably most familiar with sexual reproduction, as it is how humans procreate. But asexual reproduction is an important piece in the puzzle, also.

Asexual Reproduction

Asexual reproduction is reproduction that does not involve meiosis or fertilization. Only one parent is involved in asexual reproduction, and the technical definition refers to reproduction without the fusion of gametes. This form of reproduction is the primary one used for single-celled organisms such as the archaea, bacteria, and protists, as well as many plants and fungi. A few types of asexual reproduction include budding (when cells split and result in a "mother" and "daughter" cell, with buds eventually breaking off from the parent, like hydra); mitotic sporogenesis (the spreading of spores by water or air, which is the way that some fungi and algae reproduce); and binary fission (used by all prokaryotes, resulting in the reproduction of a living prokaryotic cell by division into two parts each of which has the potential to grow to the size of the original cell).

Sexual Reproduction

Sexual reproduction in animals involves the production of eggs and sperm.

Since the ovaries release hormones, they are considered endocrine glands. The **ovaries** have two main responsibilities:

- They manufacture **ova**.
- They secrete **estrogen** and **progesterone**, sex hormones that are found in females.

The hormones secreted by the ovaries are involved in the menstrual cycle.

The Menstrual Cycle

Phase 1: The Follicular Phase

In phase 1, the anterior pituitary secretes two hormones: **follicle-stimulating hormone (FSH)** and **luteinizing hormone (LH)**. The FSH stimulates several follicles in the ovaries to grow. Eventually, one of these follicles gains the lead and dominates the others, which soon stop growing. The one growing follicle now takes command.

Because the follicle is growing in this phase, the phase itself is known as the **follicular phase.** Remember that during all this time the follicle is releasing estrogen. Estrogen helps the uterine lining to thicken and eventually causes the pituitary to release LH. This increase in estrogen causes a sudden surge in luteinizing hormone. This release of LH is known as a **luteal surge.** LH triggers **ovulation**—the release of the follicle from the ovary.

There are thus three hormones associated with the follicular phase:

- Follicle-stimulating hormone (FSH) originates in the pituitary gland.
- Estrogen originates in the follicle.
- Luteinizing hormone (LH) originates in the pituitary gland.

The luteal surge makes the follicle burst and release the ovum. The ovum then begins its journey into the **fallopian tube,** which is also known as the **oviduct.** This crucial event in the female menstrual cycle is known as ovulation. Once the ovum has been released, the follicular phase ends and the ovum is ready to move on to the next phase.

In addition to the growth of the follicle, the follicular phase involves the thickening of the **uterine walls,** or **endometrium.** This happens in preparation for the implantation of a fertilized cell. The entire follicular phase lasts about 10 days.

Phase 2: The Luteal Phase

By the end of the follicular phase, the ovum has moved into the fallopian tube and the follicle has been ruptured and left behind in the ovary. However, the ruptured follicle (now a fluid-filled sac) continues to function in the menstrual cycle. At this stage, it condenses into a little yellow blob called the **corpus luteum,** which is Latin for "yellow body."

The corpus luteum continues to secrete estrogen. In addition, it now starts producing the other major hormone involved in female reproduction, progesterone. Progesterone is responsible for readying the body for pregnancy. It does this by promoting the growth of glands and blood vessels in the endometrium. Without progesterone, a fertilized ovum cannot latch onto the uterus and develop into an embryo. We can therefore think of progesterone as the hormone of pregnancy.

After about 13 to 15 days, if fertilization and implantation have not occurred, the corpus luteum shuts down. Once it has stopped producing estrogen and progesterone, the final phase of the menstrual cycle begins.

Phase 3: The Flow Phase, or Menstruation

Once the corpus luteum turns off, the uterus can no longer maintain its thickened walls. It starts to reabsorb most of the tissue that the progesterone encouraged it to grow. However, since there is too much to reabsorb, a certain amount is shed. This "sloughing off," or bleeding, is known as **menstruation**.

With the end of menstruation, the cycle starts all over again, readying the body for fertilization. Let's recap some of the major steps:

- In the follicular phase, the pituitary releases FSH, causing the follicle to grow.
- The follicle releases estrogen, which helps the endometrium to grow.
- Estrogen causes the pituitary to release LH, resulting in a luteal surge.
- This excess LH causes the follicle to burst, releasing the ovum during ovulation.
- The shed follicle becomes the corpus luteum, which produces progesterone.
- Progesterone, the "pregnancy hormone," enhances the endometrium, causing it to thicken with glands and blood vessels.
- If fertilization does not occur after about two weeks, the corpus luteum dies, leading to menstruation—the sloughing off of uterine tissue.

If pregnancy occurs, the extraembryonic tissue of the fetus releases **human chorionic gonadotropin (HCG)**, which helps maintain the uterine lining.

Take a look at the following diagram. Familiarize yourself with the parts of the female reproductive system and pay special attention to the different sites of the stages we've just discussed.

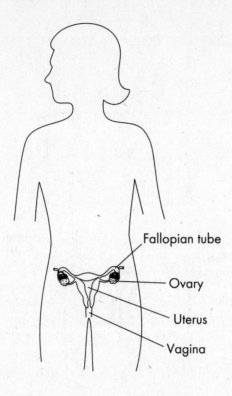

Female Reproductive System

Remember:

- The follicles (and thus the ova) are contained in the ovaries.
- Hormones are released from the ovaries and the pituitary gland.
- Fertilization occurs in the fallopian tube.
- The fertilized ovum implants itself in the uterus.

The Male Reproductive System

Now let's discuss the hormones in the male reproductive system. **Testosterone**, along with the cortical sex hormones, is responsible for the development of the sex organs and secondary sex characteristics. In addition to the deepening of the voice, these characteristics include body hair, muscle growth, and facial hair, all of which indicate the onset of **puberty**. Testosterone also has another function. It stimulates the testes, the male reproductive organs, to manufacture **sperm cells**. Testosterone does this by causing cells in the testes to start undergoing meiosis.

Take a look at the male reproductive system.

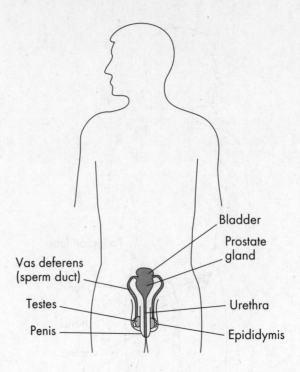

Male Reproductive System

Sperm and male hormones are produced in the testes. The main tissues of the testes, called the **seminiferous tubules,** are where spermatogonia undergo meiosis. The spermatids then mature in the **epididymis.** The **interstitial cells,** which are supporting tissue, produce testosterone and other androgens. Sperms then travel through the **vas deferens** and pick up fluids from the **seminal vesicles** (which provide them with fructose for energy) and the **prostate gland** (which provides an alkaline fluid that neutralizes the vagina's acidic fluids). Semen is transported to the vagina by the penis.

Unlike the female reproductive system, the male reproductive system continues to secrete hormones throughout the life of the male. FSH targets the seminiferous tubules of the testes, where it stimulates sperm production. LH stimulates interstitial cells to produce testosterone.

Cell Division

Every second, thousands of cells are dying throughout our bodies. Fortunately, the body replaces them at an amazing rate. In fact, epidermal, or skin, cells die off and are replaced so quickly that the average 18-year-old grows an entirely new skin every few weeks. The body keeps up this unbelievable rate thanks to the mechanisms of **cell division.**

Cell division is only a small part of the life cycle of a cell. Most of the time, cells are busy carrying out their regular activities. Let's now look at how cells pass their genetic material to their offspring.

The Cell Cycle

Every cell has a life cycle—the period from the beginning of one division to the beginning of the next. The cell's life cycle is known as the **cell cycle**. The cell cycle is divided into two periods: **interphase** and **mitosis.** Take a look at the cell cycle of a typical cell:

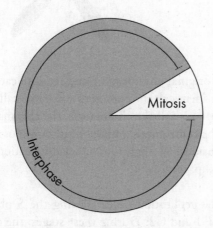

Notice that most of the life of a cell is spent in interphase.

Interphase: The Growing Phase

Interphase is the time span from one cell division to another. We call this stage interphase (*inter-* means between) because the cell has not yet started to divide. Although biologists sometimes refer to interphase as the "resting stage," the cell is definitely not inactive. During this phase, the cell carries out its regular activities. All the proteins and enzymes it needs to grow are produced during interphase.

Interphase can be divided into three stages: **G1, G2,** and **S phase.**

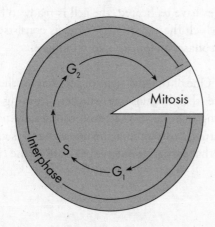

Want More?
For in depth coverage of these topics, check out *Cracking the AP Biology Exam* from The Princeton Review.

The most important phase is the S phase. That's when the cell replicates its genetic material. The first thing a cell has to do before undergoing mitosis is to duplicate all of its chromosomes, which contain the organism's DNA "blueprint." During interphase, every single chromosome in the nucleus is duplicated.

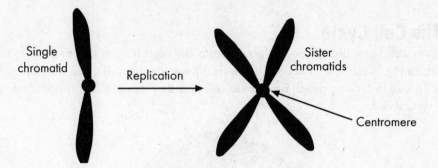

You'll notice that the original chromosome and its duplicate are still linked, like Siamese twins. These identical chromosomes are now called **sister chromatids** (each individual structure is called a chromatid). The chromatids are held together by a structure called the **centromere**. Although the chromosomes have been duplicated, they are still considered a single unit. Once duplication has been done, we're ready for the big breakup: mitosis.

We've already said that replication occurs during the S phase of interphase, so what happens during G1 and G2? During these stages, the cell produces proteins and enzymes. For example, during G1, the cell produces all of the enzymes required for DNA replication. By the way, "G" stands for "gap," but we can also associate it with "growth."

Let's recap:

- The cell cycle consists of two periods: interphase and mitosis.
- During the S phase of interphase, the chromosomes replicate.
- Growth and preparation for mitosis occur during the G1 and G2 stages of interphase.

Mitosis: The Dance of the Chromosomes

Once the chromosomes have replicated, the cell is ready to begin mitosis. Mitosis is the period during which the cell divides. Mitosis consists of a sequence of four stages: **prophase, metaphase, anaphase,** and **telophase.**

Stage 1: Prophase. One of the first signs of prophase is the disappearance of the nucleolus. In prophase, the chromosomes thicken, forming coils upon coils, and become visible. (During interphase, the chromosomes are not visible. Rather, the genetic material is scattered throughout the nucleus and is called **chromatin**. It is only during prophase that we can properly speak about the chromosomes.)

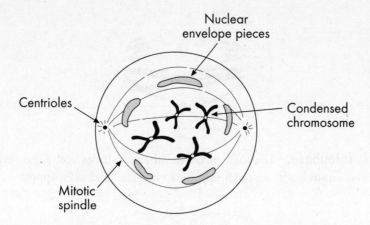

Nuclear envelope pieces

Centrioles

Condensed chromosome

Mitotic spindle

Now the cell has plenty of room to "sort out" the chromosomes. Remember centrioles? During prophase, these cylindrical bodies found within microtubule organizing centers (MTOCs) start to move away from each other, toward opposite ends of the cell. The centrioles will spin out a system of microtubules known as the **spindle fibers.** These spindle fibers will attach to a structure on each chromatid called a **kinetochore.** The kinetochores are part of the centromere.

Stage 2: Metaphase. The next stage is called metaphase. The chromosomes now begin to line up along the equatorial plane, or the **metaphase plate,** of the cell. That's because the spindle fibers are attached to the kinetochore of each chromatid.

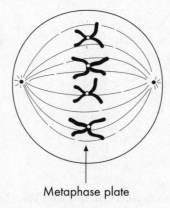

Metaphase plate

Stage 3: Anaphase. During anaphase, the sister chromatids of each chromosome separate at the centromere and migrate to opposite poles. The chromatids are pulled apart by the microtubules, which begin to shorten. Each half of a pair of sister chromatids now moves to opposite poles of the cell.

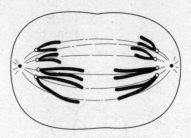

Stage 4: Telophase. The final phase of mitosis is telophase. A nuclear membrane forms around each set of chromosomes and the nucleoli reappear.

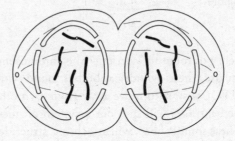

The nuclear membrane is ready to divide. Now it's time to split the cytoplasm in a process known as **cytokinesis.** Look at the figure below and you'll notice that the cell has begun to split along a **cleavage furrow** (which is produced by actin microfilaments):

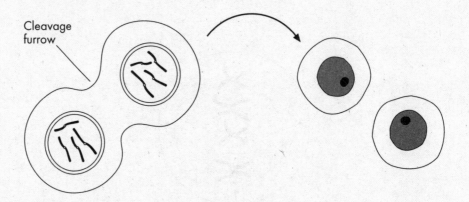

Cleavage furrow

A cell membrane forms about each cell and they split into two distinct daughter cells. The division of the cytoplasm yields two daughter cells.

Here's one thing to remember: Cytokinesis occurs differently in plant cells. The cell doesn't form a cleavage furrow. Instead, a partition called a **cell plate** forms down the middle region.

Stage 5: Interphase. Once the daughter cells are produced, they reenter the initial phase—interphase—and the whole process starts over. The cell goes back to its original state. Once again, the chromosomes become invisible, and the genetic material is called chromatin.

But How Will I Remember All That? For mitosis, you may already have your own mnemonic. If not, here's a table with a mnemonic we created for you.

IPMAT	
Interphase	I is for **Interlude**
Prophase	P is for **Prepare**
Metaphase	M is for **Meet**
Anaphase	A is for **Apart**
Telophase	T is for **Tear**

Purpose of Mitosis. Mitosis has two purposes:

- to produce daughter cells that are identical copies of the parent cell
- to maintain the proper number of chromosomes from generation to generation

For our purposes, we can say that mitosis occurs in just about every cell except sex cells. When you think of mitosis, remember: Like begets like. That is, hair cells beget other hair cells; skin cells beget other skin cells; and so on.

Haploids versus Diploids

Every organism has a certain number of chromosomes. For example, fruit flies have 8 chromosomes, humans have 46 chromosomes, and dogs have 78 chromosomes. It turns out that most eukaryotic cells in fact have two full sets of chromosomes—one set from each parent. Humans, for example, have two sets of 23 chromosomes, giving us our grand total of 46.

A cell that has both sets of chromosomes is a **diploid cell,** and the zygotic chromosome number is given as "2n." That means we have two copies of each chromosome. For example, we would say that for humans the diploid number of chromosomes is 46.

If a cell has only one set of chromosomes, we call it a **haploid cell.** This kind of cell is given the symbol "n." For example, we would say that the haploid number of chromosomes for humans is 23.

Remember:

- *Diploid* refers to any cell that has two sets of chromosomes.
- *Haploid* refers to any cell that has one set of chromosomes.

Flashcards
You might want to make some flashcards to help with memorization of all this cellular vocabulary.

Why do we need to know the terms *haploid* and *diploid*? Because they are extremely important when it comes to sexual reproduction. As we've seen, 46 is the normal diploid number for human beings. We can say, therefore, that human cells have 46 chromosomes. However, this isn't entirely correct.

Human chromosomes come in pairs called **homologues.** So while there are 46 of them altogether, there are actually only 23 *distinct* chromosomes. The **homologous chromosomes** that make up each pair are similar in size and shape and express similar traits. This is the case in all sexually reproducing organisms. In fact, this is the essence of sexual reproduction: Each parent donates half its chromosomes to its offspring.

Gametes

Although most cells in the human body are diploid (that is, filled with pairs of chromosomes), there are special cells that are haploid (unpaired). These haploid cells are called **sex cells,** or **gametes.** Why do we have haploid cells?

As we've said, an offspring has one set of chromosomes from each of its parents. A parent, therefore, contributes a gamete with one set that will be paired with the set from the other parent to produce a new diploid cell, or zygote.

Let's try a problem.

What occurs in sexual reproduction?

A. Each parent donates half its chromosomes to its offspring.

B. Each parent donates two full sets of chromosomes.

C. Each parent donates 46 chromosomes.

D. Each parent donates a diploid cell.

Here's How to Crack It

Don't be thrown by this question—it's a bit tricky. You know from your review that humans have 46 chromosomes—two full sets, one from each parent. Choices B and C must be wrong, because parents cannot donate all of their chromosomes to the child. Choice D is a bit confusing because it talks about a diploid, which is any cell that has two sets of chromosomes. This choice doesn't fit at all, so cross it off. So we're left with A, the correct answer: In sexual reproduction, each parent donates half its chromosomes to its offspring.

EVOLUTION

All of the organisms we see today arose from earlier organisms. This process, known as **evolution,** can be described as a change in a population over time. Interestingly, however, the driving force of evolution, **natural selection,** operates on the level of the individual. In other words, evolution is defined in terms of populations but occurs in terms of individuals.

Natural Selection

What is the basis of our knowledge of evolution? Much of what we now know about evolution is based on the work of **Charles Darwin.** Darwin was a nineteenth-century British naturalist who sailed the world in a ship named the HMS *Beagle.*

Darwin developed his theory of evolution based on natural selection after studying animals in the Galapagos Islands.

Darwin concluded that it was impossible for the finches and turtles of the Galapagos simply to "grow" longer beaks or necks. Rather, the driving force of evolution must have been natural selection. Quite simply put, this means that nature would "choose" which organisms survive on the basis of their fitness. For example, on the first island Darwin studied, there must once have been short-necked turtles. Unable to reach the higher vegetation, these turtles eventually died off, leaving only those turtles with longer necks. Consequently, evolution has come to be thought of as "the survival of the fittest": Only those organisms most fit to survive will survive.

Darwin elaborated his theory in a book entitled *On the Origin of Species.* In a nutshell, here's what Darwin observed:

- Each species produces more offspring than can survive.
- These offspring compete with one another for the limited resources available to them.
- Organisms in every population vary.
- The offspring with the most favorable traits or variations are the most likely to survive and therefore produce more offspring.

Artificial Selection

Artificial selection is similar to natural selection, except, as its name implies, it's artificial. It's a man-made phenomenon of deliberate breeding for certain traits or certain combinations of traits. Today, this phenomenon is quite prevalent, with mixed breed dogs such as the Labradoodle (Labrador Retriever and Standard Poodle). The Labradoodle is a product of artificial selection, as this is a man-made mixed breed dog that is bred for its combination of both Lab and Poodle qualities. Not only is this new breed highly intelligent and friendly, but it is also full of energy and a good watchdog.

Keep in mind that there is no real difference in the genetic processes underlying artificial and natural selection. Charles Darwin coined the term "artificial selection" as an illustration of natural selection. He noted that many domesticated animals and plants had special properties that were developed by intentional breeding to create and promote desirable characteristics. The bi-product of this type of breeding is a decrease in the proliferation of plants and animals with less desirable characteristics.

Evidence for Evolution

In essence, nature "selects" which living things survive and reproduce. Today, we find support for the theory of evolution in several areas:

- **Paleontology,** or the study of fossils. Paleontology has revealed to us both the great variety of organisms (most of which, including trilobites, dinosaurs, and the woolly mammoth, have died off) and the major lines of evolution.
- **Biogeography,** or the study of the distribution of flora (plants) and fauna (animals) in the environment. Scientists have found related species in widely separated regions of the world. For example, Darwin observed that animals in the Galapagos have traits similar to those of animals on the mainland of South America. One possible explanation for these similarities is a common ancestor. As we'll see below, there are other explanations for similar traits. However, when organisms share multiple traits, it's pretty safe to say that they also shared a common ancestor.
- **Embryology,** or the study of the development of an organism. If you look at the early stages in vertebrate development, all the embryos look alike! All vertebrates—including fish, amphibians, birds, and even humans—show fishlike features called gill slits.

- **Comparative anatomy,** or the study of the anatomy of various animals. Scientists have discovered that some animals have similar structures that serve different functions. For example, a human's arm, a dog's leg, a bird's wing, and a whale's fin are all the same append-ages, though they have evolved to serve different purposes. These structures, called **homologous structures,** also point to a common ancestor.

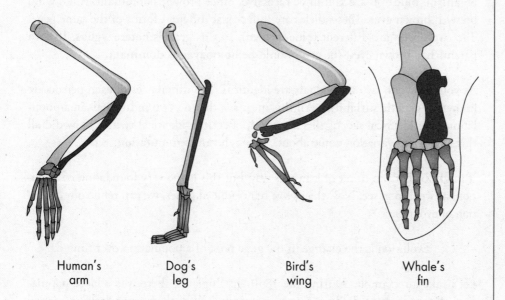

Human's arm   Dog's leg   Bird's wing   Whale's fin

In contrast, sometimes animals have features with the same function but that are structurally different. A bat's wing and an insect's wing, for example, are both used to fly. They therefore have the same func-tion, but have evolved totally independently of one another. These are called **analogous structures.** Another classic example of an analogous structure is the eye. Though scallops, insects, and humans all have eyes, these three different types of eyes are thought to have evolved entirely independently of one another. They are therefore analogous structures.

- **Molecular biology.** Perhaps the most compelling proof of all is the similarity at the molecular level. Today, scientists can examine the nucleotide and amino acid sequences of different organisms. From these analyses, we've discovered that organisms that are closely related have a greater proportion of sequences in common than distantly related species. For example, most of us don't look much like chim-panzees. However, by some estimates, as much as 99% of our genetic code is identical to that of a chimp.

Genetic Variability

Different **alleles** are passed from parents to their progeny. An allele is an alternative form of a gene (one member of a pair) that is located at a specific position on a specific chromosome. For example, you might have an allele for brown eyes from your mother and an allele for blue eyes from your father. In this coupling, brown is considered **dominant**, as it masks blue eyes when both are present in the same organism. Blue eyes are said to be **recessive**. Since brown is dominant, you'll wind up with brown eyes. These alleles are in fact just different forms of the same gene. The two alleles are different (blue, brown), so this gene is **heterozygous.** If both parents had brown eyes, the gene would be **homozygous dominant.**

As you know, no two individuals are identical. The differences in each person are known as **genetic variability.** All this means is that no two individuals in a population have identical sets of alleles (except, of course, identical twins). How did all this wonderful variation come about? Through **random mutation.**

It might be hard to think of it in this way, but this is the very foundation of evolution, as we'll soon see. Now that we've reintroduced genes, we can refine our definition of evolution:

> Evolution is the change in the gene pool of a population over time.

Let's take an example. During the 1850s in England, there was a large population of peppered moths. In most areas, exactly half of them were dark, or carried "dark" alleles, while the other half carried "light" alleles. All was fine in these cities until air pollution, due primarily to the burning of coal, changed the environment. What happened?

Imagine two different cities: one that was unpolluted, City 1, in the south of the country, and the other that was heavily polluted, City 2, in the north. Prior to the Industrial Revolution, both of these cities had unpolluted environments. In these environments, dark moths and light moths lived comfortably side by side. For simplicity's sake, let's say our proportions were a perfect fifty-fifty, half dark and half light. At the height of the Industrial Revolution, City 2, our northern city, was heavily polluted, whereas City 1, our southern city, was nearly the same as before.

In the north, where all the trees and buildings were thick with soot, the light moths didn't stand a chance. They were impossible for a predator to miss! As a result, the predators gobbled up light-colored moths just as fast as they could reproduce, sometimes even before they reached an age where they *could* reproduce. However, the dark moths were just fine. With all the soot around, the predators couldn't even see them; they continued doing their thing—above all, *reproducing*. And when they reproduced, they had more and more offspring carrying the dark allele.

After a few generations, the peppered moth gene pool in City 2 changed. Although our original moth gene pool was 50 percent light and 50 percent dark, excessive predation changed that. By about 1950, the gene pool reached 90 percent dark and only 10 percent light. This occurred because the light moth didn't stand a chance in an environment where it was so easy to spot. The dark moths, on the other hand, multiplied just as fast as they could.

In the southern city, you'll remember, there was very little pollution. What happened there? Things remained pretty much the same. The gene pool was unchanged, and the population continued to have roughly equal proportions of light moths and dark moths.

Causes of Evolution

The allele frequency remains constant in a population unless something happens to alter the gene pool. In the case above, the pollution in City 2 altered the frequency of certain alleles in the peppered moth population.

Individuals in a population are always competing, whether it's for food, water, shelter, mates, or something else. When a population is subjected to environmental change, or "stress," those who are better equipped to compete are more likely to survive. As we saw above, this process is called natural selection. In other words, nature "chooses" those members of a population best suited to survive. These survivors then have offspring that will carry many of the alleles that their parents carried, making it more likely that they, too, will survive.

As time goes on, more and more members of the population resemble the better competitors, while fewer resemble the poorer competitors. Over time, this will change the gene pool. The result is evolution.

Wait a second—didn't we say earlier that *random mutation* was the foundation of evolution? In fact, we did. Yet our example seems to say that the **environment** caused evolution. The truth lies somewhere between these two.

For natural selection to operate, there must be variation in a population. In this case, the variation was due to a mutation. By the way, what other possible sources of variation exist in a population? Sexual reproduction is a major factor in genetic variability. Meiosis, through crossing-over, produces new genetic combinations, as does the union of different haploid gametes to produce a diploid zygote.

Now let's go back to our moths. Why did the dark moths in the north survive? Because they were dark-colored. But how did they become dark-colored? The answer is, through random mutation. One day, a moth was born with a dark-colored shell. As long as a mutation does not kill an organism before it reproduces (most mutations, in fact, do), it may be passed on to the next generation. Over time, this one moth had offspring. These, too, were dark. The dark- and the light-colored moths lived happily side by side until something from the outside—in our example, the environment—changed all that.

The initial variation came about by chance. This variation gave the dark moths an edge. However, the edge did not become apparent until something made it apparent. In our case, that something was the intensive pollution due to the burning of coal. The abundance of soot made it easier for predators to spot the light-colored moths, thus effectively removing them from the population.

Eventually, over long stretches of time, these two different populations might change so much that they could no longer reproduce together. At that point, we would have two different species, and we could say, definitively, that the moths had evolved. As a consequence of random mutation and the pressure put on the population by an environmental change, evolution occurred.

Types of Selection

The situation with the moths is an example of **directional selection**. One of the phenotypes was favored at one of the extremes of the normal distribution.

In other words, directional selection "weeds out" one of the phenotypes. In our case, dark moths were favored and light moths were practically eliminated. Here's one more thing to remember: Directional selection can happen only if the appropriate allele—the one that is favored under the new circumstances—is already present in the population.

Two other types of selection are **stabilizing selection** and **disruptive selection**. Stabilizing selection means that organisms in a population with extreme traits are eliminated.

This type of selection favors organisms with common traits. It "weeds out" the phenotypes that are less adaptive to the environment. A good example is birth weight in human babies. If babies are abnormally small or abnormally large, they have a low rate of survival. The highest rate of survival is found among babies with an average weight. Disruptive selection, on the other hand, does the reverse. It favors both the extremes and selects against common traits. For example, females are "selected" to be small and males are "selected" to be large in elephant seals. You'll rarely find a female or male of intermediate size. Artificial selection, on the other hand, refers to the process by which a breeder *chooses* which traits to favor. A good example is how farmers breed seedless grapes.

Remember that there are three types of selection:

- directional selection
- stabilizing selection
- disruptive selection

Species

A dog and a bumblebee obviously cannot come together to produce offspring. They are therefore different **species.** However, a poodle and a Great Dane could reproduce (at least in theory). We would not say that they are different species; they are merely different breeds.

Let's get back to our moths. We said above that evolution occurred when they could no longer reproduce. In fact, this is simply the endpoint of that particular cycle of evolution: **speciation.** Speciation refers to the emergence of new species. The type of evolution that our peppered moths underwent is known as **divergent evolution.**

Divergent evolution results in closely related species with different behaviors and traits. As with our example, these species often originate from a common ancestor. More often than not, the "engine" of evolution is cataclysmic environmental change, such as pollution in the case of the moths. Geographical barriers, new stresses, disease, and dwindling resources are all factors in the process of evolution.

Convergent evolution is the process in which two unrelated and dissimilar species come to have similar (analogous) traits, often because they have been exposed to similar selective pressures. Examples of convergent evolution include aardvarks, anteaters, and pangolins. They all have strong, sharp claws and long snouts with sticky tongues to catch insects, yet they evolved from three completely different mammals.

There are two types of speciation: **allopatric speciation** and **sympatric speciation.** Allopatric speciation simply means that a population becomes separated from the rest of the species by a geographical barrier so that they can't interbreed. An example would be a mountain that separates two populations of ants. In time, the two populations might evolve into different species. If, however, new species form without any geographic barrier, it is called sympatric speciation. This type of speciation is common in plants. Two species of plants may evolve in the same area without any geographic barrier.

Although kangaroos, koalas, and opossums are very different mammals, they are all marsupials—that is, they have a maternal pouch. The process of similar traits arising in diverse species is an example of:

A. divergent evolution.

B. convergent evolution.

C. disruptive selection.

D. genetic variability.

Here's How to Crack It

These marsupials were exposed to the same environmental conditions and developed similar structures (pouches) because of it. This is an example of convergent evolution. Divergent evolution (A) refers to two species that branched out from a common ancestor. Genetic variability (D) is too broad a term for this question. Disruptive selection (C) refers to a situation in which extreme phenotypes are favored in a population.

KEY TERMS

morphogenesis

corona radiata

zona pellucida

diploid cell

zygote

fertilization

cleavage

morula

blastula

blastocoel

gastrulation

ectoderm

mesoderm

endoderm

epidermis

neurula

notochord

neural tube

extraembryonic membranes

yolk sac

amnion

chorion

allantois

placenta

umbilical cord

induction

organizers

morphogen

homeotic genes

sexual reproduction

asexual reproduction

budding

mitotic sporogenesis

binary fission

ovaries

ova

estrogen

progesterone

follicle-stimulating hormone (FSH)

luteinizing hormone (LH)

follicular phase

luteal surge

ovulation

fallopian tube (oviduct)

ovulation

fallopian tube (oviduct)

uterine walls (endometrium)

corpus luteum

menstruation

human chorionic gonadotropin (HCG)

testosterone

puberty

sperm cells

seminiferous tubules

epididymis

interstitial cells

vas deferens

seminal vesicles

prostate gland

cell division

cell cycle

interphase

mitosis

G1

G2

S phase

sister chromatids

centromere

prophase

metaphase

anaphase

telophase

chromatin

spindle fibers

kinetochore

metaphase plate

cytokinesis

cleavage furrow

cell plate

diploid cell

haploid cell

homologues

homologous chromosomes

sex cells (gametes)

evolution

natural selection

Charles Darwin

artificial selection

paleontology

biogeography

embryology

comparative anatomy

homologous structures

analogous structures

molecular biology

alleles

dominant

recessive

heterozygous

homozygous dominant

genetic variability

random mutation

environment

directional selection

stabilizing selection

disruptive selection

species

speciation

divergent evolution

convergent evolution

allopatric speciation

sympatric speciation

Drill #10

1. The phases of mitosis are:

    A. telophase then anaphase then metaphase then prophase then interphase.

    B. telophase then metaphase then prophase then anaphase then interphase.

    C. interphase then prophase then metaphase then anaphase then telophase.

    D. interphase then prophase then metaphase then telophase then anaphase.

2. Which of the following is derived from embryonic endoderm?

    A. epidermis of skin

    B. muscular system

    C. stomach

    D. pancreas

3. The reduction in cell size from zygote to blastula in mammals is most likely due to:

    A. the loss of DNA in the embryo.

    B. decreases in the amount of cytoplasm per cell.

    C. feedback inhibition.

    D. the haploid nuclei of the embryo.

4. The greatest degree of genetic variability would be expected among organisms that reproduce via:

    A. budding.

    B. sporulation.

    C. sexual recombination.

    D. vegetative propagation.

5. Which of the following statements is true regarding mutations?

    A. Mutations are irreversible.

    B. Mutations are generally lethal to populations.

    C. Mutations serve as a source for genetic variation in a population.

    D. Mutations affect only certain gene loci in a population.

ANSWERS AND EXPLANATIONS TO DRILL #10

1. **C** Use the handy IPMAT mnemonic and tricks of thinking Interlude, Prepare, Meet, Apart, Tear to remember that the phases of mitosis are interphase then prophase then metaphase then anaphase then telophase.

2. **D** The pancreas is derived from the endoderm. The epidermis of skin (A) is derived from the ectoderm. The muscular system (B) and stomach (C) are derived from the mesoderm.

3. **B** The reduction of the cell size is most likely due to decreases in the amount of cytoplasm in each cell since the embryo does not enlarge during this stage. The embryo does not suffer a loss of DNA (A). Feedback inhibition (C) is not responsible for the reduction in cell size. The cells within the zygote are diploid not haploid (D).

4. **C** Genetic variability is usually due to a mutation during meiosis (sexual reproduction). Choices A, B, and D are all examples of asexual reproduction. They create identical offspring.

5. **C** One way to get genetic variability is by mutations. Mutations are not irreversible (A). They can revert (or back mutate). Mutations are not common (there are low rates) in a population (B). Mutations can influence any gene locus in a population (D).

Summary

o   A single-celled egg develops into a complex, multicellular organism by dividing and going through many stages in a process called morphogenesis.

o   Organisms reproduce sexually or asexually, depending on their reproductive organs.

o   Sexual reproduction involves the meeting of eggs and sperm.

o   Asexual reproduction can occur in a few different ways, including budding, spreading spores, and binary fission.

o   The cell cycle has two periods: interphase (growing) and mitosis (dividing).

o   Charles Darwin developed the evolutionary theories of natural selection and artificial selection.

Chapter 13
Earth and
Space Science

THE SOLAR SYSTEM AND UNIVERSE (ASTRONOMY)

Our **solar system** consists of the **Sun** and other celestial objects bound to it by **gravity**. It includes planets, moons, and other small bodies. The planet names in order from the Sun are **Mercury, Venus, Earth, Mars, Jupiter, Saturn, Uranus,** and **Neptune**. Until 2006, **Pluto** was considered a planet, but that year it was reclassified as merely a **dwarf planet**.

Asteroids, which are smaller bodies than the planets, also orbit the Sun. Asteroids are sometimes referred to as minor planets. Asteroids are comprised of carbonaceous or rocky-metallic materials.

Comets are distinctly different from asteroids in that they have significant amounts of ices and water. A comet is a small solar system body that orbits the Sun and exhibits a visible coma, or tail. Comets leave a trail of debris behind them.

Earth rotates on its own axis. It rotates once upon its axis every 24 hours with the actual time of day varying at points on its surface. Therefore, at one point on Earth it may be a particular time, say 9:00 A.M., and at another point on Earth it may be 9:00 P.M. relative to the hemispheric location of the point. For our daily purposes, Earth is viewed as a grid with latitude and longitude lines. **Longitudinal lines** are designated by linear forms from pole to pole, and there are 360 of these around Earth in one-degree increments. Each hour a given location on Earth's surface rotates through 15 degrees of longitude.

The Sun is in a fixed position in the sky. At dawn it appears before the eastern horizon and it sets below the western horizon at dusk. To an observer, the Sun appears to rise higher and higher in the sky each hour during the day.

The Sun is not unique in that it is really only one of billions of stars in what is known as the Milky Way galaxy. A **galaxy** is a large collection of stars which contains stars, hydrogen, dust particles, and various other gases. Galaxies are located light years away from Earth. Classification of galaxies is made according to appearance. An **irregular system** has no form. A **spiral system** tends to resemble a pinwheel. **Elliptical systems** appear round with spiral-like arms. The universe is composed of countless galaxies, many of which may yet remain unknown.

Stars are luminous balls made of plasma that is held together by its own gravity. They are made largely of hydrogen. The nearest star to planet Earth is the Sun.

Asteroids are comprised of:

A.   carbonaceous or rocky-metallic
      materials.

B.   ice, water, and a visible tail.

C.   stars, hydrogen, dust particles, and
      gases.

D.   hydrogen and helium.

Here's How to Crack It

You must simply memorize the information for this question, but you can cross off choices that seem familiar and go from there, if necessary. Choice D is describing the Sun—hydrogen and helium. Choice B should stick out immediately with the mention of a tail—that's a comet, like a sperm cell in the solar system. Cross off that one. Stars, hydrogen, dust particles, and gases are simply too much material to be an asteroid, so choice C must be wrong (and it's describing a galaxy). That leaves only choice A, carbonaceous or rocky-metallic materials. Indeed, that's what asteroids are comprised of.

STRUCTURE AND COMPOSITION OF EARTH (GEOLOGY)

What Is Earth Made Of?

Planet Earth is made up of three concentric zones of rocks that are either solid or liquid (molten). The innermost zone is the **core**. The core has two parts: a solid inner core and a molten outer core. The inner core is composed mostly of nickel and iron, and is solid due to tremendous pressures. The outer core is composed mostly of iron and sulfur, and is semisolid due to lower pressures. Surrounding the outer core is the **mantle,** which is made mostly of solid rock. The mantle has an area, called the asthenosphere, which is slowly flowing rock. The **lithosphere,** a thin, rigid layer of rock, is the outermost layer of Earth. The lithosphere contains the rigid upper mantle and the **crust,** the solid surface of Earth.

Earth's Layers

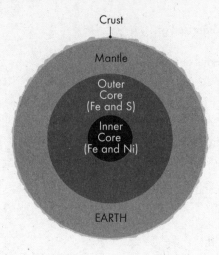

Lithosphere

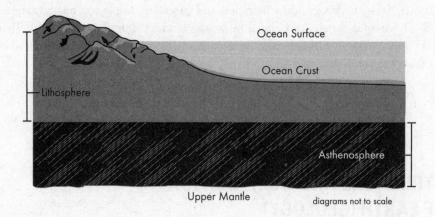

diagrams not to scale

Tectonic Plates

Because the lithosphere floats atop the asthenosphere like a cracker on a layer of pudding, it can move and break into large pieces, or **tectonic plates.** There are a dozen or so tectonic plates in the lithosphere that move independently of one another. The plates are made up of both mantle and crust. The majority of the land on Earth sits above six giant plates; the remainder of the plates lie under the ocean as well as the continents.

Some plates consist only of ocean floor, such as the Nazca plate, which lies off the west coast of South America, while others contain both continental and oceanic material. One example of the latter is the North American plate, where the United States is located; this plate extends out to the mid-Atlantic ridge. There is even a plate that is located exclusively within the Asian continent; its boundaries nearly coincide with those of Turkey. The largest plate is the **Pacific plate**—it primarily consists of ocean floor, but also includes Mexico's Baja Peninsula and southwestern California. The major plates of Earth are shown on the map below.

Earth's Plates

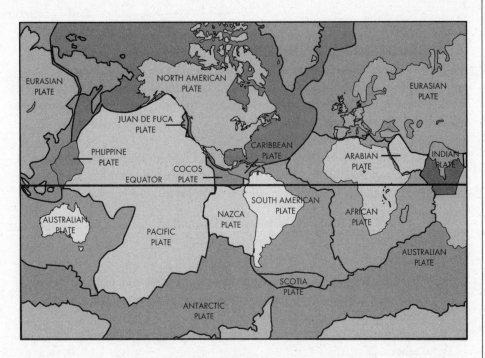

The edges of the plates are called **plate boundaries** and the places where two plates abut each other is where events like sea floor spreading and most volcanoes and earthquakes occur. There are three types of plate boundary interactions:

- **Convergent boundary.** Two plates are pushed toward each other. One of the plates will be pushed deep into the mantle.
- **Divergent boundary.** Two plates are moving away from each other. This causes a gap that can be filled with **magma** (molten rock) and when it cools new crust is formed.
- **Transform fault boundary.** Two plates slide from side to side relative to each other—like when you rub your hands back and forth. These are also called transform boundaries.

So, what happens when plates collide? It depends on what types of plates collide, and where. Converging ocean-ocean and converging ocean-continent boundaries often result in **subduction,** in which a heavy ocean plate is pushed below the other plate and melts as it encounters the hot mantle. Converging continent-continent boundaries result in the uplifting of plates to form large mountain chains, like the Himalayas (which were created by a collision between the plate carrying India and the Asian plate), the Urals, the Alps, and the Appalachian Mountains.

One important result of plate movement is the creation of volcanoes and earthquakes. Let's examine those next.

Volcanoes and Earthquakes

Volcanoes are mountains formed by magma from Earth's interior. **Active volcanoes** are those that are currently erupting or have erupted within recorded history, while **dormant volcanoes** have not been known to erupt. It's thought that **extinct volcanoes** will never erupt again.

Volcanoes form where tectonic plates meet. At these junctures, breaks occur in Earth's crust and magma flows out. If no outlet is available as the plates push together, pressure builds up until it is relieved in an explosion—a volcanic eruption.

Active volcanoes are categorized by the kind of tectonic event that produces them. There are three types:

- **Rift volcanoes** occur when plates move away from each other. When a rift volcano erupts, new ocean floor is formed as magma fills in where the plates have separated.
- **Subduction volcanoes** occur where plates collide and slide over each other.
- **Hot spot volcanoes** do not form at the margin of plates. Instead, they are found over "hot spots," which are areas where magma can rise to the surface through the plates. The Hawaiian Islands are thought to have formed over a hot spot.

Earthquakes are the result of vibrations (often due to plate movements) deep in Earth that release energy. They often occur as two plates slide past one another at a transform boundary. The **focus** of the earthquake is the location at which it begins within Earth, and the initial surface location is the **epicenter.** The size, or magnitude, of earthquakes is measured by using an instrument known as a **seismograph,** which was devised by Charles Richter in 1935. The Richter scale measures the amplitude of the highest S-wave of an earthquake. Each increase in Richter number corresponds to an increase of approximately 33 times the energy of the previous number.

The 2004 Indian Ocean undersea earthquake, known by the scientific community as the Sumatra-Andaman earthquake, occurred on December 26, 2004, and was the second largest earthquake ever recorded. The earthquake generated a giant wave called a **tsunami** that was among the deadliest disasters in modern history, killing well over 240,000 people. During this earthquake, an estimated 1,200 km (750 miles) of faultline slipped about 15 m (50 ft.) along the subduction zone where the India Plate is subducted under the Burma Plate. The slip did not happen instantaneously, but took place in two phases that occurred over a period of several minutes.

The Rock Cycle

Rocks are all around us, in the soil, buildings, and the ore used in industry. So, where do all those rocks come from? The answer: other rocks. The oldest rocks on Earth are 3.8 billion years old, while others are only a few million years old. This means that rocks have to be recycled. The process that does this is the **rock cycle.** In the rock cycle, time, pressure, and Earth's heat interact to create three basic types of rocks.

- **Sedimentary rocks** are formed as sediment (eroded rocks and the remains of plants and animals) builds up and is compressed. One place this can occur is at a subduction zone where ocean sediments are pushed deep into Earth and compressed by the weight of rock above it. An example of a sedimentary rock is limestone.
- **Metamorphic rock** is formed as a great deal of pressure and heat is applied to rock. As sedimentary rocks sink deeper into Earth, they are heated by the high temperatures found in Earth's mantle. An example of a metamorphic rock is slate.
- **Igneous rock** results when rock is melted (by heat and pressure below the crust) into a liquid and then resolidifies. The molten rock (magma) comes to the surface of Earth. When it emerges, it is called **lava.** Solid lava is igneous rock. An example of an igneous rock is basalt.

The diagram below illustrates the rock cycle.

The Rock Cycle

California is the site of more
earthquakes than New York because of

A.   New York's location on the
     Pacific plate.

B.   California's location on the
     Pacific plate.

C.   California's location near the
     Scotia plate.

D.   subduction.

Here's How to Crack It

Choice A should look wrong immediately, as New York is nowhere near the Pacific Ocean. Cross off that one and keep Choice B until you know more. As we read earlier in this section, California is not located near the Scotia plate, so you can eliminate choice C. Subduction is the phenomenon in which a heavy ocean plate is pushed below the other plate and melts as it encounters hot mantle—definitely not the answer to this question. That leaves just choice B, which is correct. California experiences earthquakes because of its location on the Pacific plate.

Soil

One very important but often underappreciated player in Earth's interdependent systems is soil. Soil plays a huge and crucial role in the lives of plants, animals, and other organisms that live in the biosphere. It acts as a crucial link between the **abiotic** (the nonliving components of the world) and the **biotic** (that's right, the living components of the world). Soil also plays an active role in the cycling of nutrients. Let's take a moment to review the major characteristics of soil.

Soil Is More than Just Dirt

Although it may be tempting to think of soil as simply "dirt," soil is actually a complex, ancient material teeming with living organisms. Some soil is hundreds of years old! In just one gram of soil, there may be as many 50,000 protozoa, as well as bacteria, algae, fungi, and larger organisms such as earthworms and nematodes. About one half of the volume of soil is made up of mineral materials, and about 5 percent is organic matter (both living and dead). The pores between the grains of minerals in soil are filled with air or water and, as a rule, the size of the particles that make up the soil determines the size of the pores between the soil particles.

Soils can be categorized based on numerous physical and chemical features including color and texture. The United States Department of Agriculture (USDA) divides soil textures into three large groups. The category with the smallest particles is **clay,** which has particles that are less than 0.002 mm in diameter. The next largest is **silt,** with particles 0.002–0.05 mm in diameter, and **sand** is the coarsest soil, with particles 0.05–2.0 mm in diameter. Sand particles are too large to easily stick together, and sandy soils have larger pores; which means that they can hold more water. Clays easily adhere to each other and there is little room between particles for water; clay soil is extremely compact.

Another very important characteristic of soil types is soil **acidity** or **alkalinity.** Recall that the pH of a substance ranges from 0–14, and is a measure of the concentration of hydrogen ions. Most soils fall into a pH range of about 4–8, meaning that most soils range in pH from being neutral to slightly acidic. Soil pH is important because it affects the solubility of nutrients, and this in turn determines the extent to which these nutrients are available for absorption by plant roots. If the soil in a region is too acidic or basic, certain soil nutrients will not be able to be used by the regional plants.

Where Does Soil Come From?

Basically, soil is a combination of organic material and rock that has been broken down by chemical and biological weathering. Therefore, it should not be surprising to learn that the types of minerals found in soil in a particular region will depend on the identity of the base rock of that region.

Water, wind, and living organisms are all prominent agents of weathering, and all weathering processes are placed into the following three rather broad categories:

- **Physical weathering** (also known as **mechanical weathering**) is any process that breaks rock down into smaller pieces without changing the chemistry of the rock. The forces responsible for physical weathering are typically wind and water.
- **Chemical weathering** occurs as a result of chemical interactions between water and other atmospheric gases, and the bedrock of a region.
- **Biological weathering** takes place as the result of the activities of living organisms.

Soil is made up of distinct layers with very different characteristics. Let's discuss those next.

Soil Layers

Soil is comprised of distinctive layers known as **horizons,** which vary considerably in content.

- The **O horizon** is the uppermost horizon of soil. It is primarily made up of organic material, including waste from organisms, the bodies of decomposing organisms, and live organisms. The dark, crumbly material that results from the decomposition of organic material forms **humus.**
- The **A horizon** lives below the O layer. This layer is made up of weathered rock and some organic material that has traveled down from the O layer. The A layer, often referred to as **topsoil,** plays an important role in plant growth. This is the zone of **leaching.**
- The **B horizon** lies below the A horizon. The B layer receives all of the minerals that are leached out of the A horizon as well as organic materials that are washed down from the topsoil above. This is the zone of **illuviation.**
- The **C horizon** is the bottommost layer of soil. It is composed of larger pieces of rock that have not undergone much weathering.
- The **R horizon** is the bedrock, which lies below all of the other layers of soil.

We touched on soil in Chapter 11, but let's now discuss soil in the context of geology.

Soil Problems for (and Caused by) Humans

In order to be able to grow all of the foods that humans consume, we must have enough **arable**—suitable for plant growth—soil to meet our agricultural needs. Soil fertility refers to soil's ability to provide essential nutrients, like nitrogen (N), potassium (K), and phosphorus (P), to plants. Humus (remember: it's in the O layer!) is also an extremely important component of soil because it is rich in organic matter.

Soils composed of roughly the same amount of all three textures (remember: clay, silt, and sand) are described as being **loamy,** and these types of soil are considered the best for plant growth. Another important characteristic of soil for agricultural purposes is the extent to which it **aggregates,** or clumps. The most fertile soils are aggregates (look: it's a noun, too!) of soils of different textures bound together with organic material.

Monoculture. Unfortunately, certain agricultural activities can change the texture of soil; for example, repeated plowing tends to break down soil aggregates, leaving "plow pan" or "hard pan," which is hard, unfertile soil.

While communities traditionally planted many different types of crops in a field, in modern agriculture the **monoculture,** or the planting of just one type of crop in a large area, predominates. Over the history of agriculture, a significant decrease in the genetic diversity of crop species has taken place. This creates numerous problems. First of all, a lack of genetic variation makes crops more susceptible to pests and diseases. Second, the consistent planting of one crop in an area eventually leaches the soil in that area of the specific nutrients that the plant needs in order to grow. One way of preventing this phenomenon is to practice **crop rotation**, in which different crops are planted in the area in each growing season.

Other problems with modern agriculture include its reliance on large machinery (which can damage soil), and the fact that as an industry, agriculture is a huge consumer of energy. Energy is consumed both in the production of pesticides and fertilizers, and in the use of fossil fuels to run farm machinery.

The past 50 years or so have seen a huge increase in worldwide agricultural productivity, and this is largely due to the mechanization of farming that resulted from the Industrial Revolution. The boom in agricultural productivity is known as the **Green Revolution,** and unfortunately it has since had many detrimental environmental effects. For example, the use of chemical pesticides resulted in the emergence of new species of insects that were pesticide-resistant. Recently, the introduction of genetically modified plants has enabled researchers to take steps in solving the problem of pesticide-resistant insect species.

Another drawback to the Green Revolution resulted from the dramatic increase in irrigation worldwide; over-irrigated soils undergo salinization. In **salinization,** the soil becomes water-logged and when it dries out, salt forms a layer on its surface; this eventually leads to **land degradation**. In order to combat this problem, researchers have developed **drip irrigation**, which allots an area only as much water as is necessary, and delivers the water directly to the roots.

Soil Erosion. The small rock fragments that result from weathering may be moved to new locations in the process of erosion, and bare soil (soil upon which no plants are growing) is more susceptible to erosion than soil that's covered by organic materials.

Because of the constant movement of water and wind on Earth's surface, the **erosion** of soil is a continual and normal process. However, when erosion removes valuable topsoil or deposits soil in undesirable places, it can become a problem for humans. Eroded topsoil usually ends up in bodies of water, posing a problem for both farmers, who need healthy soil for planting, and people who rely on bodies of water to be uncontaminated with soil runoff (soil can contaminate the water with pesticides and other harmful chemicals).

The most significant portion of erosion caused by humans results from logging and slash-and-burn agriculture. The removal of plants in an area makes the soil much more susceptible to the agents of erosion.

EARTH'S ATMOSPHERE (METEOROLOGY)

In the broadest definition, the **atmosphere** is a layer of gases that's held close to Earth by the force of gravity. The layer of gases that lies closest to Earth is the **troposphere**; it extends from the surface of Earth to about 10–20 km (5–10 miles). The troposphere is where all of the weather that we experience takes place; this layer contains the majority of atmospheric water vapor and clouds. Generally the troposphere is vertically well mixed and (with the exception of periods of temperature inversions) it gradually becomes colder with an increase in altitude (by about 6.5°C/km).

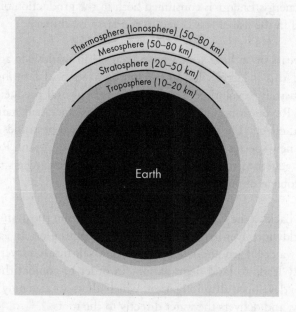

You've probably heard about the troposphere before in the news because of the **greenhouse effect.** The troposphere contains certain gases called **greenhouse gases,** the most important of which are H_2O and CO_2. As the Sun's rays strike Earth, some of the solar radiation is reflected back into space; however, greenhouse gases in the troposphere intercept and absorb a lot of this radiation.

The Greenhouse Effect

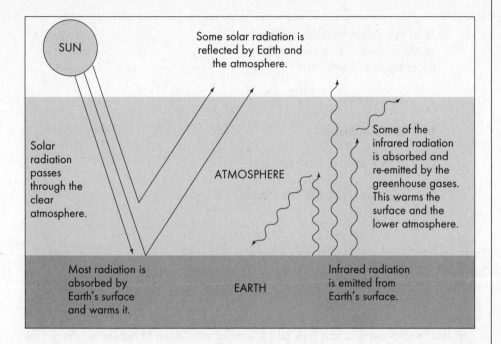

Crowning the troposphere is the **tropopause**, which is a layer that acts as a buffer between the troposphere and the next layer up, the stratosphere. In this buffer zone, the atmospheric temperature no longer decreases with altitude; instead the temperature begins to *increase* with altitude.

The **stratosphere** sits on top of the tropopause and extends about 20–50 km above Earth's surface. Unlike the troposphere, its gases are not very well mixed and, as in the tropopause, the temperature in the stratosphere increases as the distance from Earth increases. This warming effect is due to a thin band of **ozone** (O_3) that exists in this layer. The ozone traps the high-energy radiation of the Sun, holding some of the heat and protecting the troposphere and Earth's surface from this radiation.

Above the stratosphere are two layers called the mesosphere and the thermosphere (ionosphere). The **mesosphere** extends about 80 km above Earth's surface and is the area where meteors usually burn up.

The **thermosphere** is the thinnest gas layer; it is located about 110 km above Earth and is where auroras take place. It's also the layer of the atmosphere where space shuttles orbit! The thermosphere is also known as the **ionosphere** because of the ionization that takes place in this region; this region also absorbs most of the energetic photons (solar wind) from the Sun. Interestingly, the thermosphere also reflects radio waves, which is what makes long-distance radio communication possible.

What human activity/activities has/have increased the levels of erosion in the upper layers of Earth's soil?

A. crop rotation

B. land degradation

C. urbanization and deforestation

D. under-cultivation of agricultural fields

Here's How to Crack It

Crop rotation (choice A) is actually a phenomenon that prevents soil problems caused by humans, so eliminate this choice. Choice B, land degradation, is the same thing as erosion, so don't fall for that trick choice—cross it off. Choice C certainly seems correct, but let's take a gander at Choice D before we decide for sure. Under-cultivation of agricultural fields is the opposite of what causes erosion, so cross that one off. Choice C is the correct answer.

Climate

Earth's atmosphere has physical features that change day to day as well as patterns that are consistent over a space of many years. The day-to-day properties such as wind speed and direction, temperature, amount of sunlight, pressure, and humidity are referred to as **weather**. The patterns that are constant over many years (30 years or more) are referred to as **climate**. The two most important factors in describing climate are average temperature and average precipitation amounts. **Meteorologists** are scientists who study weather and climate.

The weather and climate of any given area is the result of the Sun unequally warming Earth (and the gases above it) as well as the rotation of Earth.

Air Circulation in the Atmosphere

The motion of air around the globe is the result of solar heating, the rotation of Earth, and the physical properties of air, water, and land. There are three major reasons that Earth is unevenly heated:

- More of the Sun's rays strike Earth at the equator in each unit of surface area than strike the poles in the same unit area.
- Earth's axis points regions tilt toward or away from the Sun. When pointed toward the Sun, those areas receive more direct or intense light than when pointed away. This causes the seasons.
- Earth's surface at the equator is moving faster than the surface at the poles. This changes the motion of air into major prevailing winds, belts of air that distribute heat and moisture unevenly.

Solar energy warms Earth's surface. The heat is transferred to the atmosphere by radiation heating. The warmed gases expand, become less dense, and rise creating vertical currents called **convection currents.** The warm currents can also hold a lot of moisture compared to the surrounding air. As these large masses of warm moist air rise, cool air flows along Earth's surface into the area where the warm air was located. This flowing air, or **horizontal airflow,** is one way that surface winds are created.

As warm moist air rises into the cooler atmosphere, it cools to the **dew point,** the temperature at which water vapor condenses into liquid water. This condensation creates clouds. If condensation continues and the drops get bigger, they can no longer be held up by gravity and they fall as **precipitation** (which can be frozen or liquid). The cold dry air is now denser than the surrounding air. This air mass then sinks to Earth's surface where it is warmed and can gather more moisture, thus starting the **convection cell** rotation again.

Convection Cell

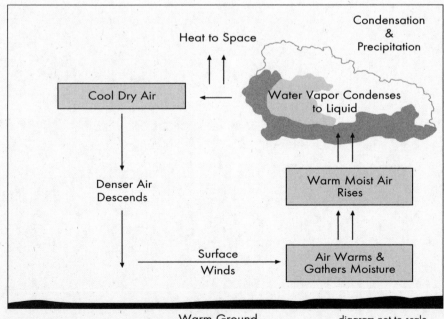

On a local level this phenomena accounts for land and sea breezes. On a global scale these cells are called **Hadley cells.** A large Hadley cell starts its cycle over the equator, where the warm moist air evaporates and rises into the atmosphere. The precipitation in that region is one cause of the abundant equatorial rain forests. The cool dry air then descends about 30 degrees north and south of the equator, forming the belts of deserts seen around Earth at those latitudes.

Hadley Cell

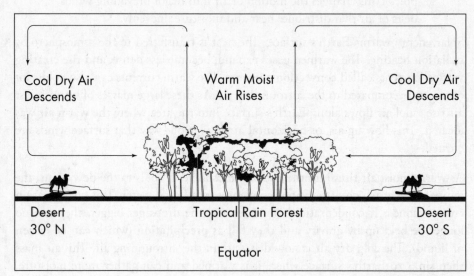

Cool Dry Air
Descends

Warm Moist
Air Rises

Cool Dry Air
Descends

Desert
30° N

Tropical Rain Forest

Desert
30° S

Equator

diagram not to scale

Seasons

The motion of Earth around the Sun—and the fact that Earth is tilted on its axis by 23.5 degrees—together create the seasons that we experience on Earth. When Earth is in the part of its orbit in which the Northern Hemisphere is tilted toward the Sun, the northern half of the planet receives more direct sunlight for longer periods of time each day than does the Southern Hemisphere. This means that when the Northern Hemisphere is experiencing summer, the Southern Hemisphere is experiencing winter.

Interestingly, because of Earth's tilt, the Sun rises and sets just once a year at the North and South Poles. Approximately six months of the year at the poles is day-time, while the other six months is dark, and considered nighttime.

Seasons

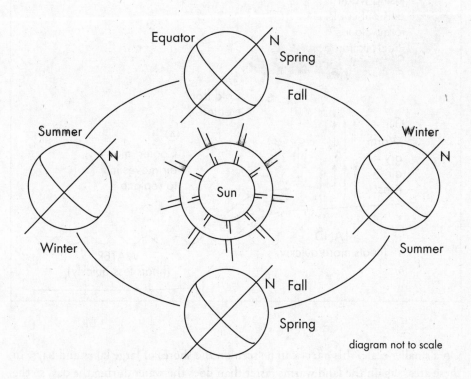

diagram not to scale

Weather Events

Monsoons, which occur primarily in coastal areas, are caused by the fact that land heats up and cools down more quickly than water does. In a monsoon, hot air rises from the heated land, and a low-pressure system is created. The rising air is quickly replaced by cooler moist air that blows in from over the ocean. As this air rises, it cools, and the moisture it carries is released in a steady seasonal rainfall. This process happens in reverse in the dry season, when masses of air that have cooled over the land blow out over the ocean. Check out the illustration below.

How a Monsoon Forms

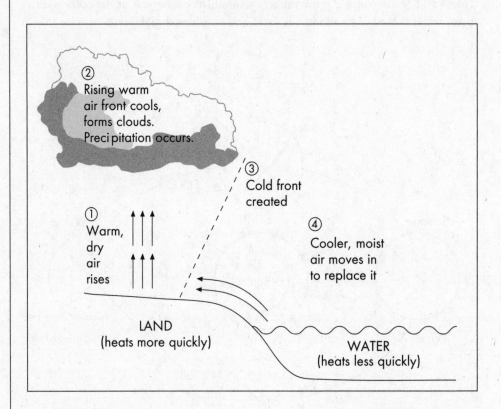

On a smaller scale, this effect can be seen on the shores of large lakes and bays. In these areas, again the land warms faster than does the water during the day, so the air mass over the land rises. Air from over the lake moves in to replace it, and this creates a breeze. At night, the reverse happens; the land cools more quickly than the water and the air over the lake rises. The air mass from the land moves out over the lake to replace the rising air, and this creates a breeze as well. If you live in San Francisco, you may have experienced this small-scale monsoon effect!

As we mentioned above, the air that moves in from over the ocean or a large body of water contains large amounts of water. An air mass may be forced to climb in altitude—if, for instance, it encounters an obstruction such as a mountain. When the air mass rises, it will cool and water will precipitate out on the ocean side of the mountain. By the time the air mass reaches the opposite side of the mountain, it will be virtually devoid of moisture. This phenomenon, known as the **rain shadow effect,** is responsible for the impressive growth of the Olympic rainforest on the Washington State coast. Interestingly, the Olympic rainforest receives up to 5 m of rain per year, while the opposite side (the leeward side) receives less than 50 cm of rain per year.

How the Rainshadow Effect Works

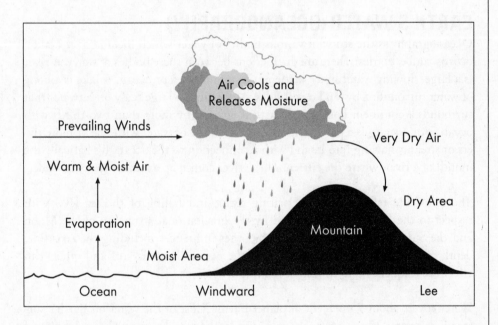

Crucial meteorological phenomena that you should know about are **trade winds.** So named for their ability to quickly propel trading ships across the ocean, trade winds are steady and strong and can travel at a speed of about 11 to 13 mph. They occur in somewhat predicable patterns, but they may cause local disturbances when they blow over very warm ocean water. When this occurs, the air warms and forms an intense, isolated, low-pressure system, while also picking up more water vapor from the ocean surface. The wind circles around this isolated low-pressure air area (counterclockwise in the Northern Hemisphere and opposite in the Southern Hemisphere). The low pressure system will continue to move over warm water, increasing in strength and wind speed; this will eventually result in a tropical storm.

Certain tropical storms are of sufficient intensity to be classified as **hurricanes.** Hurricanes can have winds with speeds in excess of 130 km/hr. The rotating winds of a hurricane remove water vapor from the ocean's surface, and heat energy is created by the condensing water vapor. This addition of heat energy continues to contribute to the increase in wind speed, and some hurricanes have winds traveling at speeds of nearly 400 km per hour! A major hurricane contains more energy than that released during a nuclear explosion, but since the force is released more slowly, the damage is generally less concentrated. Another important note about these types of storms is that they are referred to as hurricanes in the Atlantic Ocean, but they are called **typhoons** or cyclones when they occur in the Pacific Ocean. Go figure!

EARTH'S WATER (OCEANOGRAPHY)

Oceanography is the study of various bodies of water which include rivers, lakes, oceans, and estuaries. There are distinctions between these bodies of water. A **river** is a large, flowing water body that empties into the sea or ocean. A **lake** is a body of water surrounded by land on all sides. An **ocean** is a large body of saltwater that surrounds a continent land mass. Earth is covered by more than two-thirds with oceans. An **estuary** is a partly enclosed coastal body of water with one or more rivers or streams flowing into it, and with a connection to the ocean. It's basically the mouth of a river, where the current of the river comes up against the ocean's tide.

The term **tide** refers to the alternating rising and falling of the sea level with respect to the land and is produced by the gravitational attraction of the Moon and the Sun. Tides are also affected by other influences including the coastline, depth of a body of water, topography of the ocean. These factors and others can affect the frequency and timing of the tide arrival.

Water covers about 75 percent of planet Earth. Most of the water on Earth's surface is saltwater. On average, the saltwater in the world's oceans has a salinity of about 3.5 percent. This means that for every 1 liter (1,000 ml) of seawater, there are 35 grams of salts (mostly, but not entirely, sodium chloride) dissolved in it. In fact, one cubic foot of seawater would evaporate to leave about 1 kg of sea salt! However, **seawater** is not uniformly saline throughout the world. The planet's freshest seawater is in the Gulf of Finland, part of the Baltic Sea. The most saline open sea is the Red Sea, where high temperatures and confined circulation result in high rates of surface evaporation.

Freshwater is water that contains only minimal quantities of dissolved salts, especially sodium chloride. All freshwater ultimately comes from precipitation of atmospheric water vapor, which reaches inland lakes, rivers, and groundwater bodies directly, or after melting of snow or ice. Let's start with a discussion of freshwater before discussing the world's oceans.

Freshwater

Freshwater is deposited on the surface of Earth through precipitation. Water that falls on Earth and doesn't move through the soil to become groundwater moves along Earth's surface, via gravity, and forms small streams, and then eventually larger ones. The size of the stream continues to increase as water is added to it, until the stream becomes a river, and the river flows until it reaches the ocean. The land area that drains into a particular stream is known as a **watershed**, or drainage basin.

As water moves into streams, it carries with it sediment and other dissolved substances, including small amounts of oxygen. Turbulent waters are especially laden with dissolved oxygen and carbon dioxide, such as those found at the source, or head waters, of a stream. As a general rule, the more turbulent the water, the more dissolved gases it will contain.

As you probably know, freshwater that travels on land is largely responsible for shaping Earth's surface. Erosion occurs when the movement of water etches channels into rocks. The moving water then carries eroded material farther downstream.

Because of obstructions on land, moving water does not move in a straight line; instead it follows the lowest topographical path, and as it flows, it cuts farther into its banks to eventually form a curving channel. As the water travels around these bends, its velocity decreases and the stream drops some of its sedimentary load.

Rivers drop most of their sedimentary load as they meet the ocean because their velocity decreases significantly at this juncture. At these locations, landforms called **deltas** (which are made of deposited sediments) are created. Another important freshwater body that you should know about is the estuary. As we mentioned before, estuaries are sites where the "arm" of the sea extends inland to meet the mouth of a river. Estuaries are often rich with many different types of plant and animals species, because the freshwater in these areas usually has a high concentration of nutrients and sediments. The waters in estuaries are usually quite shallow, which means that the water is fairly warm and that plants and animals in these locations can receive significant amounts of sunlight.

Some of Earth's most important ecologically diverse ecosystems are the areas along the shores of fresh bodies of water known as **wetlands**. Types of wetlands include marshes, swamps, bogs, prairie potholes (which exist seasonally), and flood plains (which occur when excess water flows out of the banks of a river and into a flat valley).

A myriad assortment of plants and animal species are usually found in estuaries because:

A. landforms of deposited sediments are located there.

B. the freshwater in these areas has a high concentration of nutrients and sediments.

C. seawater isn't uniformly saline throughout the world.

D. the rain shadow effect encourages such assortments.

Here's How To Crack It

Remember that an estuary is where the "arm" of the sea extends inland and meets the mouth of a river. These areas are rich with different plants and species because the freshwater there has a high concentration of nutrients and sediments. Choice B is correct. Why are the others wrong? Choice A describes a delta, so cross off that one. Choice C presents a true statement—seawater isn't uniformly saline throughout the world—but that doesn't explain why many plants and animals are found in estuaries. The rain shadow effect is responsible for the growth of the Olympic rainforest on the Washington state coast, but this doesn't have anything to do with estuaries. You can cross off choice D.

The World's Oceans

Before we get into our review of the world's oceans, let's consider another aquatic ecosystem (besides wetlands and estuaries) that's an important source of biodiversity—this one is a saltwater ecosystem. Certain landforms that lie off coastal shores are known as **barrier islands**. Because barrier islands are created by the buildup of deposited sediments, their boundaries are constantly shifting as water moves around them. These spits of land are generally the first hit by offshore storms, and they are important buffers for the shoreline behind them.

In tropical waters, a very particular type of barrier island, called a **coral reef**, is quite common. These barrier islands are formed not from the deposition of sediments, but from a community of living things. The organisms that are responsible for the creation of coral reefs are cnidarians that secrete a hard, calciferous shell; these shells provide homes and shelter for an incredible diversity of species, but they are also extremely delicate and thus very vulnerable to physical stresses, changes in light intensity, and changes in water temperature.

Like freshwater bodies, oceans are divided into zones based on changes in light and temperature. They're listed below:

- The **coastal zone** consists of the ocean water closest to land. Usually it is defined as being between the shore and the end of the continental shelf.
- The **euphotic zone** is the photic, upper layers of water. The euphotic zone is the warmest region of ocean water; this zone also has the highest levels of dissolved oxygen.
- The **bathyal zone** is the middle region; this zone receives insufficient light for photosynthesis and is colder than the euphotic zone.
- The **abyssal zone** is the deepest region of the ocean. This zone is marked by extremely cold temperatures and very low levels of dissolved oxygen, but very high levels of nutrients because of the decaying plant and animal matter that sinks down from the zones above.

Ocean Zones

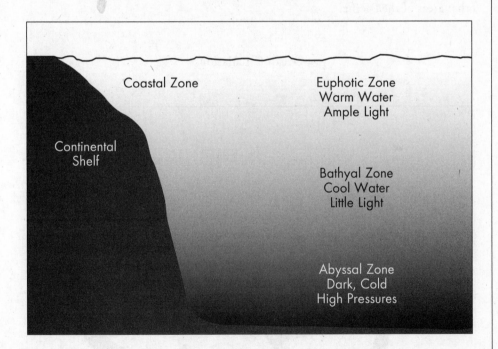

Both freshwater and saltwater bodies experience a seasonal movement of water from the cold and nutrient-rich bottom to the surface. These **upwellings** provide a new nutrient supply for the growth of living organisms in the photic regions. Therefore, they are followed by an almost immediate exponential growth in the population of organisms in these zones, especially the single-cell algae, which may form blooms of color called algal blooms. These algae can also produce toxins that may kill fish and poison the beds of filter feeders, such as oysters and mussels. One fairly notorious recurring toxic algal bloom is referred to as **red tide;** this is caused by a proliferation of dinoflagellates.

Ocean currents play a major role in modifying conditions around Earth that can affect where certain climates are located. As the Sun warms water in the equatorial regions of the globe, prevailing winds, differences in salinity (saltiness), and Earth's rotation set ocean water in motion. For example, in the Northern Hemisphere, the Gulf Stream carries Sun-warmed water along the east coast of the United States and as far as Great Britain. This warm water displaces the colder, denser water in the polar regions, which can move south to be rewarmed by the equatorial Sun. Northern Europe is kept 5 to 10°C warmer than if the current was not present.

Oceanographers also study a major current, the **ocean conveyor belt,** which moves cold water in the depths of the Pacific Ocean while creating major upwellings in other areas of the Pacific.

Ocean Circulation

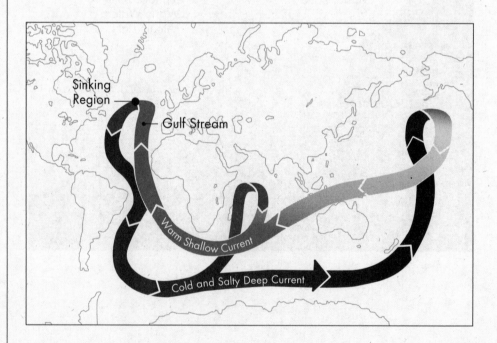

KEY TERMS

solar system
Sun
gravity
Mercury
Venus
Earth
Mars
Jupiter
Saturn
Uranus
Neptune
Pluto
dwarf planet
asteroids
comets
longitudinal lines
galaxy
irregular system
spiral system
elliptical system
stars
core
mantle
lithosphere
crust
tectonic plates
Pacific plate
plate boundaries
convergent boundary
divergent boundary
magma
transform fault boundary
subduction
active volcanoes
dormant volcanoes
extinct volcanoes
rift volvanoes
subduction volcanoes
hot spot volcanoes
earthquakes
focus
epicenter
seismograph
tsunami
rock cycle
sedimentary rocks
metamorphic rocks

igneous rocks
lava
abiotic
biotic
clay
silt
sand
acidity
alkalinity
physical weathering
  (mechanical weathering)
chemical weathering
biological weathering
horizons
O horizon
humus
A horizon
topsoil
leaching
B horizon
illuviation
C horizon
R horizon
arable
loamy
aggregates
monoculture
crop rotation
Green Revolution
salinization
land degradation
drip irrigation
erosion
atmosphere
troposphere
greenhouse effect
greenhouse gases
tropopause
stratosphere
ozone
mesosphere
thermosphere
ionosphere
weather
climate
meteorologists
convection currents

horizontal airflow

dew point

precipitation

convection cell

Hadley cells

monsoons

rain shadow effect

trade winds

hurricanes

typhoons

oceanography

river

lake

ocean

estuary

tide

seawater

freshwater

watershed

deltas

wetlands

barrier islands

coral reef

coastal zone

euphotic zone

bathyal zone

abyssal zone

upwellings

red tide

ocean conveyor belt

Drill #11

Each group of questions below is followed by four suggested answers or completions. Select the one that is best in each case.

1. Inner planets that orbit the Sun consist of:

   A. Mercury, Venus, Earth, and Mars.

   B. Mercury, Venus, and Pluto.

   C. Earth.

   D. Earth and Venus.

2. Asteroids are minor planets that are:

   A. rocky, or metallic objects.

   B. collections of hydrogen gas.

   C. similar in structure to elements of Earth.

   D. non-orbital artifices.

3. Meteoroids are:

   A. non-orbital artifices.

   B. large bodies.

   C. small bodies.

   D. soft, liquid-like material.

4. Tides are most affected by:

   A. the location of the water body.

   B. the surrounding land temperature.

   C. the time of the day.

   D. the pull of gravity on Earth's force.

5. A researcher is preparing to study the effects of logging on the streams and lakes in the Amazon rainforest. Which of the following types of information would be a primary source of data to the researcher?

   A. blog posts about logging methods and potential environmental damage

   B. topographic maps of the Amazon rainforest, showing areas of clear-cutting and streams

   C. a *Newsweek* article about logging methods

   D. reports by an environmental-political group on the silting of a stream caused by logging in a forest in the Pacific Northwest

ANSWERS AND EXPLANATIONS TO DRILL #11

1. **A** Mercury, Venus, Earth, and Mars are known as inner planets in our solar system.

2. **A** Asteroids are known as minor planets that orbit the Sun in the asteroid belt between Mars and Jupiter. They are made of rocky and metallic objects. Hydrogen is found in planets. Asteroids are not substantially similar to Earth's surface and they are orbital.

3. **C** Meteoroids are small bodies, smaller than asteroids, and are very tiny. They travel through space. The other answers are incorrect because they do not meet the definition of a meteoroid.

4. **D** Tides are affected by gravity and its pull in the Earth-Moon-Sun system and the movement of those bodies within the system.

5. **B** Remember that primary sources are also known as direct sources, and they are generally sources that experienced the phenomenon, were around during the time of study, or have first-hand knowledge of the situation. Secondary sources are generally commenting on, citing, or referencing primary sources. The blog post, *Newsweek* article, and report written by an environmental-political group are all considered secondary sources.

Summary

o The solar system consists of the Sun and other celestial objects bound to it by gravity.

o Since 2006, the planet names in order from the Sun are Mercury, Venus, Earth, Mars, Jupiter, Saturn, Uranus, and Neptune.

o The nearest star to planet Earth is the Sun.

o Planet Earth is in the Milky Way galaxy and is made up of three concentric zones of rocks that are either solid or liquid (molten).

o The majority of the land on Earth sits above six tectonic plates. The movements of these plates sometimes cause earthquakes.

o Volcanoes, which are mountains formed by magma from Earth's interior, form where tectonic plates meet.

o Soil plays a crucial role in the lives of plants and animals, and soil erosion is an increasingly major problem as the mechanization of farming increases.

o The atmosphere is the layer of gases that's held close to Earth by gravity.

o Seawater is salty, but varies in levels of salinity; freshwater contains only minimal quantities of dissolved salts.

Chapter 14
Number Sense

NUMBERS

Numbers like –1, –400, –10,000 are **integers.** 0 is an integer.

But $\frac{1}{2}$, –0.089, and 5.78 are *not* integers; these are **fractions** and **decimals.**

An integer is any number that is not a fraction or a decimal.

Positive numbers, numbers larger than 0, can be integers.

Numbers like 73, 1, and 5 are integers.

Negative numbers, which are numbers smaller than 0, can be integers.

Whole numbers are all the positive integers and 0.

Every integer is also considered a **rational number.** A rational number is any number that can be expressed as the quotient (for example, *a/b*) of two integers, with the denominator *b* not equal to zero. We'll cover numerators and denominators in detail later in this chapter.

Since every integer is considered a rational number, then every integer is also considered a **real number.** Real numbers include both rational numbers, such as 12 and –16/126, and irrational numbers, such as pi and the square root of 5. A real number can also be given by an infinite decimal representation, such as 1.246835..., where the digits continue in some way.

The easiest way to visualize integers is to put them on a **number line.** You probably remember these. Here is a number line:

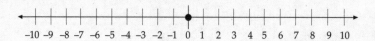

Moving to the right the numbers become larger; moving to the left the numbers become smaller.

Here is the number line that will be used in this book:

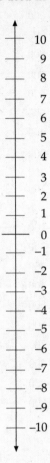

The ends of a number line go on forever, because there is no end to the numbers in the world. The way to express this is to write the symbol ∞, which represents **infinity**. By making the number line vertical, it's easy to see which numbers are larger. Just like using a measuring stick, any number that's higher up is bigger.

No matter where you are on the number line, any number *above* another *is* the larger of the two. This is always true, no matter whether the numbers are positive (larger than 0), negative (less than 0), or even 0.

Why is −1 bigger than −10? If you owe someone $1, you have more money for yourself than if you owe someone $10. Owing someone money is a good way to think about negative numbers. Look on the number line and see which number is higher. This will help when you have any kind of confusion over which of two numbers is larger. Think about −100 and −1,000. Put them both on your own number line.

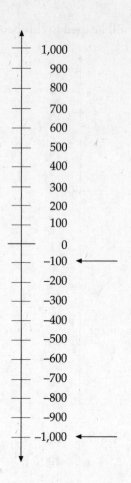

Which number is higher? –100. So this is the larger number.

The CSET requires that you be familiar with the concept of **ordering integers**, which is what we've just discussed. Basically, you know how to order integers when you know what order they appear in on the number line. That is, you understand their respective locations on the number line. Let's use an example to illustrate what we mean.

7, –12, –2, –1

Arrange the integers listed above in the correct order from least to greatest.

A. 7, –2, –1, –12

B. 7, –1, –2, –12

C. –12, –1, –2, 7

D. –12, –2, –1, 7

Here's How to Crack It

Keep in mind that ordering integers is all about their location on the number line. The biggest negative number has the lowest value (–12). So you can eliminate choices A and B immediately. The next number in order will be the next "biggest" negative number, –2. So the correct answer is choice D, with the four numbers correctly ordered from farthest down the number line, all the way up to the positive side of the number line, 7.

The **absolute value** of a number is its distance from zero. For example, the distance on the number line from 0 to –100 is 100 spaces. Even though these 100 spaces are on the negative part of the line, you refer to them as the absolute value of –100, which is positive 100. The absolute value of any number is always positive, whether the number itself is positive or negative. The way to write the absolute value of –100 is this:

$$|{-100}| = 100$$

The absolute value of 7 is $|7| = 7$.

Note that when negative numbers are written, they have a negative sign next to them, like –5, but when positive numbers are written, most won't have a positive sign; it will be just the number.

Digits

Digits are the integers 0 through 9. The places in a number are called **digit places.** For instance, 357 is a three-digit number, because it takes up three digit places; 200 is also a three-digit number, though you need only two digits, 2 and 0, to write it. It is a three-digit number because it takes up three digit places. Each digit place has a name. In the number 357, 7 is called the **units digit,** or the **ones digit.** The **tens digit** is 5, and the **hundreds digit** is 3.

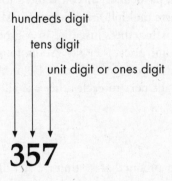

Calculations with Integers

For any calculation with any type of number, you will use an **algorithm**. Simply put, an algorithm is a process that performs a sequence of operations.

A standard algorithm is conventionally taught for solving particular mathematical problems. These methods generally include carrying, borrowing, long division, and long multiplication using a standard notation (much of which we just reviewed) and standard formulas for average, area, and volume. Similar methods also exist for procedures such as square root and other functions, but have fallen out of the general mathematics curriculum in favor of calculators or software.

Addition

When you add positive integers, you combine them to form a larger number. **Addition** is putting integers together to get their **sum**. Sum is the result of addition.

Subtraction

Subtraction is the **inverse (reverse) operation** of addition. If you had 7 pieces of gum, and your friend took 2 of them, you would be left with 5. That's subtraction.

Multiplication

You may not have looked at it this way before, but **multiplication** is actually just an outgrowth of addition. It's a way of saving time. The result of multiplication is called the **product**.

Look at it this way: If you were to add 5 and 5 and 5 and 5, you would end up with 20.

$$5 + 5 + 5 + 5 = 20$$

But that takes a long time, particularly if you wanted to add twenty 5s together, or a hundred 5s. That's where multiplication comes in. Multiplication can shorten the work of adding four 5s together. Just like in a grocery store when you get four cans of soup for the same price, they say "Soup, four times." You can say "5, four times" or 4 times 5 or 4•5 or 4 × 5 or even (4)(5). A big dot, an ×, and the numbers in parentheses right next to each other are all different ways of saying "multiply by."

$$4 \times 5 = 20$$

The product of 4 times 5 is 20.

Distributive Law. Now say you had 54 relatives, and the holidays were coming up, and you had to buy each and every one of them a present. Now say you didn't have a whole lot of money and you decided to get each of them something lame, like a $3 washcloth. To figure out if it's even worth doing this, you want to figure out how much it is going to cost you. So what, as an officially math smart person, do you do? You multiply 54 people by $3. Here you can use something called the **distributive law,** or the **distributive property.** This law says that multiplying 54 by 3 is the same as multiplying 4 by 3 and adding it to 50 times 3. You are separating the 54 into two easier pieces.

$$
\begin{array}{r} 4 \\ \times\ 3 \\ \hline 12 \end{array}
\qquad
\begin{array}{r} 50 \\ \times\ 3 \\ \hline 150 \end{array}
\qquad
\begin{array}{r} 150 \\ +\ 12 \\ \hline 162 \end{array}
$$

4 times 3 is 12.

50 times 3 is 150.

54 times 3 equals 162.

Excellent job, but probably not worth it for the washcloths, right? Now let's get back to that distributive law. What does the distributive law mean, really?

Officially, the distributive law says that: $a(b + c) = ab + ac$.

What this means is that 5×12 is equal to 5 times 12 broken down in the easiest way you know. Like $7 + 5$, or $6 + 6$, or $10 + 2$.

$$5(10\ +\ 2)\ =$$

$$(5\ \times\ 10)\ +\ (5\ \times\ 2)$$

$$\text{or}$$

$$50\ +\ 10$$

Together these equal 60. Just like $5 \times 12 = 60$. Check your times tables.

You can also test this by getting out a lot of matchsticks or something else you have a lot of and making twelve groups of 5 or five groups of 12 and counting them all up. You should get 60 each time.

The distributive law also means that if I said to you, "Hey! What is 5×2 plus 5×3?" You could just say, "Please *try* to challenge me a little bit. That's obviously a fancy way to say 5 times 5, which I know is 25."

$$(5 \times 3) + (5 \times 2) = 15 + 10 = 25$$

Commutative Law. Another law of multiplication is the **commutative law,** or **commutative property.** You already know it—really. Remember back a few lines when we said you could count out five groups of 12 or twelve groups of 5?

Officially, the commutative law of multiplication is this:

$$a \times b = b \times a$$

What it means is $2 \times 5 = 5 \times 2$. And both of these things equal 10.

So you now know practical math, as well as math theory. Impressive.

Factors. There are some other things you might want to think about that have to do with multiplication. You know that $2 \times 3 = 6$. But did you also know that both 3 and 2 are **factors** of 6? A factor of a number is any number that can be multiplied by another number to get that first number. Since you can multiply 2 by some other number and get 6 as a product, 2 is a factor of 6. The factors of 6 are 1, 2, 3, and 6.

$$
\begin{array}{cc}
\text{Factors} & \text{Factors} \\
1 & 2 \\
\times\, 6 & \times\, 3 \\
\hline
6 & 6
\end{array}
$$

How about the factors of 18? They are 1, 2, 3, 6, 9, and 18.

There are some numbers so huge it would take forever to list all their factors. And there are other numbers that have only two factors in the world, 1 and the numbers themselves. These numbers are called **prime numbers.** For instance, list the factors of 2: 1 and 2. And that's it. So 2 is a prime number. Check out some other numbers. Is 3 prime? Is 4?

Yes, 3 is prime, $1 \times 3 = 3$. There are no other factors of 3. No, 4 is not prime: $1 \times 4 = 4$ and $2 \times 2 = 4$ so there are three factors of 4: 1, 2, and 4.

Prime numbers are positive.

There's one crazy thing about prime numbers. 1 is not a prime number. Why not? Because some mathematician said so.

Division

Division is the process of breaking down numbers into smaller groups.

It can look like this $10 \div 5$, this $5\overline{)10}$, and this $\dfrac{10}{5}$

If you see the $\div$ sign between two numbers, the number that comes *before* the $\div$ is being divided by the number that comes *after* the $\div$.

If you see the $\overline{)}$ sign, the number *inside* the box thing is being divided by the number *outside* the box thing.

If you see the — sign, the number on *top* is being divided by the number on the *bottom*.

If you had 40 chocolate bars and you wanted to separate them into 2 equal groups, one for before dinner and one for after dinner, how many would be in each group? (We're just going to assume here that you are really hungry for something sweet.) There are 20 in each group. What you just did was divide 40 by 2.

How about if you wanted to divide 2 into 2 groups? Or 5 into 5 groups? There would be 1 in each group, right? That's why any number, no matter how gigantic or tiny, divided by itself, is always equal to 1.

How about if you wanted to divide 1,765,432 radios among 1 person. You're thinking, "Among 1 person? Is she crazy? You can't divide among one person, the one person would get all of them." Exactly right, you would have to give the one person all 1,765,432 radios. That is why any number divided by 1 is equal to itself.

More Review
For more math review, check out *MathSmart* and *MathSmart II* from The Princeton Review.

Division is useful. Think about it. You might need to know how much each person will get if you divide your $100 among your 5 family members. What you are asking in that case is how many times 5 will go into 100. Like all the math you've been doing, you are going to do it piece by piece.

$$5\overline{)100}$$

First you ask yourself, "How many 5s are there in the number 1?" Well, there aren't any; 1 is too small, so you move to include the next digit place. Now ask yourself, "How many 5s are there in the number 10?" There are two 5s that make up the number 10, so write 2 on top of your division sign, in the tens place since that is the digits place you are working with.

$$5\overline{)\overset{2}{100}}$$

Since there is still a 0 left, ask yourself, "How many 5s are there in 0?" And you figure there are none, so you write 0 above the units place.

$$5\overline{)\overset{20}{100}}$$

Twenty dollars is the result. That's how much money you could spend on each family member, if you had $100, and 5 family members, and you felt like buying each one a present.

Notice that 5 times 20 is 100 and 20 goes into 100, 5 times. This is because division is the inverse calculation of multiplication (and subtraction is the inverse calculation of addition).

How about if you had to divide into a more complex number? For instance, what if you had 578 hot dogs, and you had to divide them among 34 screaming kids in a day camp?

$$34\overline{)578}$$

You approach this problem the same way as the simpler-looking problem, but you need to figure this time how many 34s will fit in a 5? Too small, so how many 34s will fit in a 57?

Here is where approximating can make your life a lot easier. If you had two (use 30 because it is easier to approximate with than 34) you would have 60, so it must be less than 2 and you are going to write down 1 in the tens place.

$$34\overline{)578}^{\,1}$$

Below you are going to use your excellent subtraction skills. Write down 34 below the 57. This is because what you are really doing is multiplying 34 by the 1 on top, and sticking it under the 57 to find the difference.

$$34\overline{)578}^{\,1}$$
$$34$$

Now you subtract the 34 from the 57. You get 23.

$$34\overline{)578}^{\,1}$$
$$\underline{34}$$
$$23$$

And you drop down the next digit of that 578, which is 8.

$$34\overline{)578}^{\,1}$$
$$\underline{34}$$
$$238$$

Take a guess how many 34s will fit into 238? There are about three 30s in every hundred, and you have a little more than two 100s here, so you can try a little more than 6, for instance 7. Multiply 7 by 34 and put your result under the 238.

$$34\overline{)578}^{\,17}$$
$$\underline{34}$$
$$238$$
$$238$$

There is nothing left over when you divide this time, which means it has divided in evenly. There will be no leftover hot dogs. And you don't have any digits left in 578, so you're done. Each screaming kid will get 17 hot dogs. By the way, the number you are dividing into, in this case 578, is called the **dividend**. The number you are dividing by, in this case 34, is called the **divisor**. And the result, the 17 hot dogs each kid is going to get, is called the **quotient**.

Question: Why is it that when you multiply the 17 by the 34 you get the number of hot dogs you started with, 578?

Answer: Because just as you saw with the $20 fitting 5 times into 100, division is the inverse of multiplication.

Whenever you have a number that divides evenly into another number, the way you divided 34 into 578 and got the whole number 17 as your quotient, you know that 578 is **divisible** by both 17 and 34.

That means that 17 and 34 are factors of 578. It's all connected. The most convenient thing about this is that now you have a tidy way to check your answers in division.

Multiply the quotient by the divisor and see if you get the dividend; if this works, you are right on target. This also gives you an opportunity to get more practice in perfecting your multiplication skills. Whoopee, right?

Now you can try a simple division problem, and work on it as it gets more complex.

There are 4 friends over at your house, and you have a box with 36 shirts in it. If you gave everybody an equal number of shirts, how many would each friend get?

Here's How to Crack it

Think about it for a second. What are you dividing up? The shirts, right? So the 36 shirts will be your dividend.

And what are you dividing by? The number of groups, which in this case equals the number of friends. How many groups of shirts will there be? There will be 4.

You have $4\overline{)36}$.

How many groups of 4 are there in 36? The answer is 9.

Take a minute to remember that division is the inverse of multiplication. Then remember the multiplication tables for 4 times 9. Since your quotient times your divisor will always give you your dividend, knowing your multiplication tables backward and forward will make your life much easier once you are done memorizing.

Okay, you give each friend 9 shirts, no big deal. But say for a minute that you notice that 5 of your favorite shirts were stashed in the pile by someone clearly not looking out for your best interests. Of course you want to keep them, but you still want to divide up the shirts that are left among your friends. What do you do?

As always, one step at a time.

First take your favorite shirts out of the pile and put them back in your closet. Then divide what is left among your friends.

36 shirts − 5 favorite shirts = 31 shirts left

Then, divide the number you get by the 4 friends.

$$4\overline{)31}$$

By approximating, you know that each person won't get 9 shirts, right? Because you are starting with fewer shirts than the last time you divided, each person is going to get fewer shirts. Since 9 is too many, try 8.

$$\begin{array}{r} 8 \\ 4\overline{)31} \\ 32 \end{array}$$

But 32 is bigger than 31. So you can't give them 8 each; there aren't enough shirts; there are only 31. Try 7.

$$\begin{array}{r} 7 \\ 4\overline{)31} \\ 28 \end{array}$$

Well, there are enough shirts to give each person 7, but that means there will be some left over. You give away only 28 if you give each of your 4 friends 7 shirts.

$$4 \times 7 = 28$$

If you give away 28 shirts, how many will be left over out of those 31?

$$\begin{array}{r} 31 \\ -28 \\ \hline 3 \end{array}$$

You have 3 extra shirts. In math you are going to call this the **remainder.** The remainder is what is left over if something doesn't divide evenly. That means you are trying to divide a number by another number that isn't one of its factors (remember factors?). The answer to this shirt question is 7 remainder 3. Generally it is written as 7 r3. If you want to read that out loud, say "seven remainder three."

Negative Numbers

Adding Negative Numbers

With whole numbers you can say, "Well 3 is like having 3 baseballs or 3 bananas or whatever." But what is a good way to visualize –3?

Think of –3, or any negative number, as the number owed. For instance, if you have no money in your pockets, *and* you owe your best friend $3, it is like having –3. And that's how you can think about adding them. Say you had –3 and someone came along and gave you $5. Since $3 of those $5 would be absorbed by the money you owe your friend—if you're being prompt and honest, and for the problem's sake we'll assume you are—then all you end up with is $2 for yourself.

$$\begin{array}{r} 5 \\ + (-3) \\ \hline 2 \end{array}$$

Subtracting Negative Numbers

Think back to that situation in which you owed your friend $3. And let's say you still haven't paid her back. Your brother comes along and reminds you that you also owe him $5. You now have a grand total of –$8. "But don't worry," he says, "since you painted my house for me last week, I am going to wipe out that debt." That means you have – $8 –(–$5). You are back up to where you started. You owe only $3.

$$\begin{array}{r} -8 \\ - (-5) \\ \hline -3 \end{array}$$

Order of Operations

Now that you know addition, subtraction, division, and multiplication (for positive and negative numbers), what happens when you're asked to perform a few of these operations in a single question?

Let's try an example. Say that you wanted to find the result of the following expression:

$$6 + 10 \div 5 - 3 \times 2 + (3 \times 5)$$

There are a number of different operations that you must perform in order to simplify this expression. In fact, you'll see many CSET questions that ask you to use many different operations to solve a problem. To simplify the expression correctly, you must perform these operations in a particular order. This method is called the **order of operations.** Just remember one thing:

PEMDAS

Most people know this as "Please Excuse My Dear Aunt Sally" (though no one seems to remember the story behind that phrase). This acronym stands for the following math operations: **P**arentheses, **E**xponents, **M**ultiplication, **D**ivision, **A**ddition, and **S**ubtraction. In a complex expression, the first thing you solve should be the operation inside parentheses; next, reduce any term with exponents; then, perform all multiplication and division at the same time, going from left to right in the expression; finally, perform all addition and subtraction, again going from left to right in the expression.

Most CSET questions are designed to give you a clear understanding of the order in which you must perform operations. However, if you're unsure of exactly the order in which to solve a problem, be sure to use the rules of PEMDAS. Let's go back to the previous expression and solve it using the rules of PEMDAS:

$$6 + 10 \div 5 - 3 \times 2 + (3 \times 5)$$

Step 1: Solve all work inside the parentheses. $3 \times 5 = 15$, so our problem now looks like this:

$$6 + 10 \div 5 - 3 \times 2 + 15$$

Step 2: Since the problem has no exponents, move along to multiplication and division, moving from left to right in the expression:

$$6 + 2 - 6 + 15$$

Step 3: Finish the problem by using addition and subtraction, moving from left to right in the expression:

$$8 - 6 + 15$$

$$2 + 15$$

17

FRACTIONS

A **fraction** is a number that names a part of a whole or a part of a group. Fractions are most easily recognized when they use the **fraction bar.** The fraction bar, that line between the 2 numbers, shows that division is taking place.

$$\frac{6}{3}$$

In some cases the numbers will divide evenly, like $\frac{6}{3}$. In other cases, however, these numbers will not divide evenly, like $\frac{5}{2}$ or $\frac{2}{3}$. They leave remainders.

All these types of numbers are called fractions whether they express division or part over whole. Fractions are actually pretty great.

A fraction is made up of two parts: the top, also called the **numerator,** and the bottom, also called the **denominator.** In the fraction $\frac{5}{2}$, 5 is the numerator, and 2 is the denominator. The numerator represents the part, and the denominator represents the whole.

For positive numbers, when the numerator (top) of the fraction is a number larger than the denominator (bottom), like $\frac{5}{2}$, the value of the fraction is greater than 1. You already know that because you know that $\frac{5}{2}$ = 5 ÷ 2 = 2 r1. People in math call this an **improper fraction.** The part is 5 and the whole is 2. Think of it as cutting up apples into 2 pieces, and having 5 of these pieces. Five halves is more than 1 apple.

For positive numbers, when the numerator of the fraction is smaller than the denominator, like $\frac{2}{3}$, the value of the fraction is less than 1. This is because 3 can't fit into 2 even one time. This is called a **proper fraction**. It's like cutting up an apple into 3 pieces, and having only 2 of these parts.

And remember dividing a number by itself? What if you cut an apple into 3 pieces and you had all 3 of them? You would have the whole apple, wouldn't you.

When the numerator and the denominator have the same value, like $\frac{3}{3}$, the fraction is exactly equal to 1.

What about when your fraction has a denominator of 1? Any number over 1 is equal to that number. For instance, $\frac{3}{1}$ equals 3. Think about if you had an apple divided into 1 piece; in other words, a whole apple. What if you had 3 of them? Exactly as it seems; you would have 3 apples.

Remember: You can never divide 0 into any number, so the denominator of a fraction can never be 0.

What about when you divide 0 by something else? Well a fraction with the numerator 0 is always equal to 0, no matter what number it has for a denominator. If you had 0 apples cut up into 3 pieces, you would have 0 sets of pieces.

Fractions Smaller Than 1

Lots of math deals with fractions that are smaller than 1. We could think back to the apple and figure that you took a small bite, and maybe the apple consisted of 5 more bites exactly that size, or 6 bites total. So the bite you took was $\frac{1}{6}$, or 1 bite out of a possible 6. The 1 bite represents the part of the apple, and the 6 bites represent the whole. It's back to what we said before—fractions represent part over whole. You say, "one sixth." This number is less than 1, because it is less than the whole of the apple.

Reducing Fractions

Reducing a fraction means dividing *both* the numerator and the denominator by the same number to get a simpler fraction. Use the fraction $\frac{20}{100}$. Look at both the numerator and the denominator. What is a factor of both these numbers? They are both even, so 2 will divide evenly into both of them.

Divide the 20 by 2, and the 100 by 2, and get $\frac{10}{50}$

$$\frac{20 \div 2}{100 \div 2} = \frac{10}{50}$$

Since both 10 and 50 still have a common factor, you can reduce again.

$$\frac{10 \div 10}{50 \div 10} = \frac{1}{5}$$

This fraction, $\frac{1}{5}$, is the simplest form of the same fraction. You know this because 1 has no other factors, so you couldn't divide it again. Fractions can look entirely different. For instance, $\frac{20}{100}$ and $\frac{1}{5}$ and $\frac{4}{20}$ and $\frac{3}{15}$ still represent the same number. All the fractions in the last sentence are equal.

Adding Fractions

Think for a minute about what it is you are adding when you add fractions. Let's say you have a box of 100 pencils and you give Julie 3 pencils, or $\frac{3}{100}$ of the box, and you give Sam 1 pencil, or $\frac{1}{100}$ of the box. How many pencils have you given away total? 4. Out of how many pencils? 100. So, you've given away $\frac{4}{100}$ of the box of pencils.

$$\frac{3}{100} + \frac{1}{100} = \frac{4}{100}$$

You add the numerators, but not the denominators. The denominator, or the whole, does not change. You are still talking about 100 pencils. Only the number given away has been altered.

But what happens when the denominators of the fractions are different? If, for example, you want to combine $\frac{1}{2}$ of one apple with $\frac{2}{5}$ of another apple, you need to add the fraction $\frac{1}{2}$ to the fraction $\frac{2}{5}$.

$$\frac{1}{2} + \frac{2}{5}$$

How do you add $\frac{2}{5}$ and $\frac{1}{2}$? By changing the denominators so they are the same. This is called finding a **common denominator.**

A common denominator is a number that is divisible by both denominators of the fractions you are adding. In this case, since the denominators of the two fractions you are working with are 2 and 5, you can choose the number 10: 10 is divisible by both 2 and 5. The best common denominators are the numbers that are easiest to work with. For instance, 50 is a common denominator because it is also divisible by 5 and 2, but 10 is a smaller number, so it is easier to use.

To change the fraction $\frac{1}{2}$ into a fraction with a denominator of 10, multiply the fraction by $\frac{5}{5}$. Remember: Any number over itself is equal to 1, and you can multiply any number by 1 without changing the number. Since $\frac{5}{5}$ is equal to 1, you don't change the value of the fraction. It's like reducing in the opposite direction.

$$\frac{1}{2} \times \frac{5}{5} = \frac{5}{10}$$

To make $\dfrac{2}{5}$ into a fraction with a denominator of 10, multiply by $\dfrac{2}{2}$.

$$\frac{2}{5} \times \frac{2}{2} = \frac{4}{10}$$

Now you can add $\dfrac{4}{10}$ and $\dfrac{5}{10}$ the same way you added the fractions in which the denominators started out the same.

$$\frac{4}{10} + \frac{5}{10} = \frac{9}{10}$$

You've got $\dfrac{9}{10}$ of an apple when you combine them.

Finding a common denominator works for fractions larger than 1 in exactly the same way. Try adding $\dfrac{5}{2}$ and $\dfrac{4}{3}$.

$$\frac{5}{2} + \frac{4}{3}$$

The easiest to use common denominator of 2 and 3 is 6.

$$\frac{5}{2} \times \frac{3}{3} = \frac{15}{6} \quad \text{and} \quad \frac{4}{3} \times \frac{2}{2} = \frac{8}{6}$$

You have $\dfrac{15}{6} + \dfrac{8}{6} = \dfrac{23}{6}$.

One way to find a common denominator is to multiply the denominators of a fraction addition problem together. This way, you can be sure that your common denominator is divisible by both.

Sometimes in math, people use the **lowest common denominator**. Look at it this way: You have $\dfrac{3}{4}$ of a box of erasers and your co-teacher has $\dfrac{1}{6}$ of a box of erasers. You're trying to figure out if together you have 1 whole box of erasers to give to your students as a class prize. So you want to add the two fractions, $\dfrac{3}{4}$ of a box and $\dfrac{1}{6}$ of a box.

$$\frac{3}{4} + \frac{1}{6}$$

As you know, you want to find a common denominator to solve this problem. Of course, one way to find the common denominator would be to multiply the 2 original denominators together: $4 \times 6 = 24$.

$$\frac{18}{24} + \frac{4}{24} = \frac{22}{24}$$

Reduce $\frac{22}{24}$ and you get $\frac{11}{12}$. You and your co-teacher don't quite have 1 whole box. You are a little bit short.

Here's another way to figure out the same problem. Your denominators, 4 and 6, are factors of 24, but they are also factors of a smaller number: 12. How would you know to look for 12? Try fooling around with the larger denominator. First see if 6 could serve as the denominator. It can't, because 4 is not a factor of 6. Try multiplying 6 by 2. You get 12. Well, what about 12? Sure, because 4 and 6 are both factors of 12.

Multiply $\frac{3}{4}$ by $\frac{3}{3}$ to get 12 as your denominator.

$$\frac{3}{4} \times \frac{3}{3} = \frac{9}{12}$$

Multiply $\frac{1}{6}$ by $\frac{2}{2}$ to get 12 as your denominator.

$$\frac{1}{6} \times \frac{2}{2} = \frac{2}{12}$$

Now add.

$$\frac{9}{12} + \frac{2}{12} = \frac{11}{12}$$

Because fractions can look different and mean the same thing, this is the same addition problem as $\frac{18}{24} + \frac{4}{24} = \frac{22}{24} = \frac{11}{12}$. Same answer, smaller denominator to start, and you skip the step of reducing. Which is the better way to do it, lowest common denominator or regular old common denominator? Whichever one you feel more comfortable using.

Let's try a fraction problem.

Of the following fractions, which is smallest?

A. $\dfrac{3}{5}$

B. $\dfrac{4}{9}$

C. $\dfrac{7}{13}$

D. $\dfrac{2}{9}$

Here's How to Crack It

The trick here is approximation. Choice A is greater than $\dfrac{1}{2}$, and choices B and C are just under $\dfrac{1}{2}$. To be around $\dfrac{1}{2}$, the numerator in choice D would have to be 4 or 5 ($\dfrac{4}{9}$ or $\dfrac{5}{9}$) and 2 is far below that. So choice D, $\dfrac{2}{9}$, is the smallest fraction.

Mixed Numbers

Some fractions are presented as **mixed numbers.** A mixed number is a number that contains both an integer and a fraction, like $4\dfrac{2}{3}$. You can look at $4\dfrac{2}{3}$ as representing 4 cans of peas with an additional $\dfrac{2}{3}$ of a can of peas.

One of the easier ways to work with a number like this is to treat it as an addition problem.

First turn the integer 4 into a fraction, $\frac{4}{1}$. Then $4\frac{2}{3}$ looks like $\frac{4}{1} + \frac{2}{3}$.

Since $4\frac{2}{3}$ has turned into an addition problem, you need to find a common denominator. Since $\frac{4}{1}$ has a denominator of 1, the denominator of $\frac{2}{3}$, which is 3, will work as a common denominator since it is a multiple of 1. Now, just like in any other fraction addition problem, multiply the fraction $\frac{4}{1}$ by $\frac{3}{3}$.

$$\frac{4}{1} \times \frac{3}{3} = \frac{12}{3}$$

Now you can add.

$$\frac{12}{3} + \frac{2}{3} = \frac{14}{3}$$

So you see, $\frac{14}{3}$ is the same number as $4\frac{2}{3}$. You have converted a mixed number into a regular fraction.

Earlier in this chapter, we spoke about ordering integers. You should also understand how to order mixed numbers, factions, decimals, and percents. The exact same rules apply and you just follow the logic that whatever number is farthest down the number line (negative) is the least, and the highest up the number line (positive) is the greatest.

Let's try a problem.

$4.5, \dfrac{50}{100}, 88\%, -26.2$

Arrange the numbers listed above in the correct order from least to greatest.

A.　$4.5, \dfrac{50}{100}, 88\%, -26.2$

B.　$4.5, 88\%, \dfrac{50}{100}, -26.2$

C.　$-26.2, \dfrac{50}{100}, 88\%, 4.5$

D.　$-25.2, 4.5, 88\%, \dfrac{50}{100}$

Here's How to Crack It

This should be old hat by now. You can eliminate choices A and B immediately, because both choices list 4.5 as the least integer, which cannot be correct since one of the choices is a negative number. Both, $\dfrac{50}{100}$ and 88% $\left(\dfrac{88}{100}\right)$ are less than 1, so choice D can't be correct. So the correct answer is choice C, $-26.2, \dfrac{50}{100}, 88\%,$ 4.5.

DECIMALS

Decimals are just a way to express fractional parts. The thing to understand about decimals is that they are fractions over powers of ten (10; 100; 1,000; 10,000; and so on).

Earlier, digit places were discussed. We talked about digit places to the left of the units digit. Well guess what, there are digit places to the right of the units digit, too—they are called decimal places. The point separating the decimal places from the units or ones digit is called the **decimal point**.

0.57

When there is a zero or no number to the left side of the decimal point it means your decimal has a value less than 1, like the decimal above. To read it aloud you say, "point five seven." The way decimals work is that each decimal place represents one of those fractions over powers of ten. The place just to the right of the decimal point is the **tenths place.**

tenths place

0.5

So the decimal 0.5 could also be written as $\frac{5}{10}$, 0.3 would be $\frac{3}{10}$, and 0.1 would be $\frac{1}{10}$.

The place to the right of the tenths place is the **hundredths place.**

hundredths place

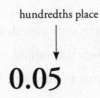

0.05

The decimal 0.05 can also be written as $\frac{5}{100}$. And 0.15 can be written as $\frac{15}{100}$. Going back to the first example, fractionally, 0.57 would be written $\frac{57}{100}$. You have 57 out of a possible 100. When it is written as a decimal, people like to write in the 0 next to the .57 even though they would never think of doing that with a fraction.

How do you see 0.57? Probably the way you view most decimals in the world, as money. It is 57 cents. You have 57 out of a possible 100 cents, since the U.S. monetary system is based on a power of 10 (100 cents to the dollar).

When there is a number to the left of the decimal point, it is like having a mixed number in a fraction. The decimal 34.12 would be written fractionally as $34\frac{12}{100}$ or $34\frac{3}{25}$. Or 34 dollars and 12 cents.

You can probably already figure out what the place just to the right of the hundredths place is called: the **thousandths place**, though you probably won't say any of these decimal places aloud because you would end up spitting all over everything.

thousandths place

0.005

You can write 0.003 as $\frac{3}{1,000}$, 0.035 as $\frac{35}{1,000}$, and 0.123 as $\frac{123}{1,000}$.

You know that money is always written as decimals when there is any change that doesn't make up a whole dollar. This gives you an easy way to approximate with decimals. For instance, if you were trying to add 0.024 and 0.341 you might think to yourself, "Well if I forget about the ends it's just like adding 2 cents to 34 cents so I am going to have around 36 cents or 0.36."

Why is it that you can drop the ends sometimes? The digit 4 at the end of 0.024 represents $\frac{4}{1,000}$, which is a very tiny number. It's as though you cut an apple into 1,000 equal pieces, which would be tiny, and took 4 of them. Now you won't be able to completely ignore these numbers always, but it is always a help to approximate. Approximating takes on a form with decimals called **rounding**.

0.024 gets rounded to 0.02

When you are rounding numbers, you are shortening them according to their decimal places. These are the rules of rounding:

When rounding a number, if the digit to the right of the place you are rounding to is greater than or equal to 5, you take it away and make the digit to the left 1 greater.

> 0.035 rounded to the nearest *hundredth* becomes 0.04
> 0.167 rounded to the nearest *hundredth* becomes 0.17
> 125 rounded to the nearest *tens place* becomes 130

Look at that last one. Sometimes you will be asked to round nondecimal numbers. Rounding appears in the form of a request to round a number to a particular decimal place.

The other rule of rounding is this: If the digit to the right of the place you are rounding to is less than 5, you throw out the numbers to the right and leave the number to the left as it is.

> 0.032 rounded to the nearest *hundredth* becomes 0.03
>
> 1.541 rounded to the nearest *hundredth* becomes 1.54
>
> 323 rounded to the nearest *tens place* becomes 320

Sometimes you will be asked to round off several places. You will have a number that goes to the thousandths place, and you will be asked to round it to the nearest tenth. Just find the digit to the direct right of the place to which you are rounding.

Someone says, "Round 78.6345 to the nearest tenth."

$$78.6345$$

You find the place next to the tenths place, the hundredths place, and the number there is 3. Since 3 is less than 5, you drop it, and leave the 6 in the tenths place as is. Don't worry about the numbers to the right of the 3. If you are rounding the number to the nearest tenth, look only to the direct right of the tenths place.

$$78.6$$

Now you have rounded it to the nearest tenth.

Adding Decimals

You're saying, "What's so great about decimals?"

One of the great things about decimals is that since they are fractions with powers of ten, you don't have to do anything fancy when you add them. Think about it; their denominators are so similar. All you have to do is make sure that you line the decimal places up evenly so you are adding tenths to tenths, hundredths to hundredths, and all that sort of thing.

Just like with fractions, you wouldn't want to combine decimals with different denominators without thinking about it. And adding decimals will be no problem for you.

Just think about money. A dollar is 100 pennies, so a penny is $\frac{1}{100}$ of a dollar or 0.01. So you can think about adding money if you ever get confused as to how things should add up.

To add decimals, line them up along the decimal point and add as you would integers.

$$\begin{array}{r} 0.45 \\ + \ 0.1 \\ \hline \end{array}$$

If, as in the problem above, the numbers don't look as if they're the same length—don't worry about it. Just write in a 0 for any missing place and add.

$$\begin{array}{r} 0.45 \\ + \ 0.10 \\ \hline 0.55 \end{array}$$

Subtracting Decimals

Subtracting decimals works much the same way as adding them. Think of fractions again: You need to add and subtract common denominators, so make sure your decimal places are lined up. When one looks shorter, just throw a few 0s onto the end to make it line up.

$$0.01 - 0.002$$

becomes

$$\begin{array}{r} 0.010 \\ - \ 0.002 \\ \hline 0.008 \end{array}$$

You know from working with fractions that numbers can look different and have the same value, like $1 = \frac{2}{2} = \frac{7}{7}$. The same thing is true of decimals. You can add 0s to the end of a decimal without changing the value of the number, since you are not moving any of the digits with respect to the decimal point. Adding 0s to a whole number *will* change it.

$$12 \quad \text{to} \quad 120$$

In that case, you move the digits farther to the left of the decimal point, which changes the value of the number. This is just something to keep in mind. If you ever get tempted to start throwing 0s onto the ends of numbers to the left of the decimal point, resist.

Multiplying Decimals

Since you know how to multiply regular numbers, you are eminently qualified to begin multiplication of decimals. If you had 4 stacks of 50 cents, how much money would you have?

$$4 \times 0.5 =$$

What you do is first, multiply the numbers as though they were integers.

$$4 \times 5 = 20$$

Then, count the total number of decimal places, counting from right to left, you had in your *first* set-up. You had one place, the tenths, so you make sure you put one decimal place in your product, starting from the right.

$$4 \times .5 = 20$$

You would have $2.00 if you had 4 stacks of $0.50 each.

To figure out where the decimal point goes, just count up the total number of decimal places in the numbers you are multiplying and put them in your product, starting from the right.

$$3.5 \times 1.7 =$$

First, multiply the numbers as though they had no decimals at all.

$$
\begin{array}{r}
35 \\
\times\ 17 \\
\hline
245 \\
350 \\
\hline
595
\end{array}
$$

Then, count the number of decimal places you have in the numbers you are multiplying, and add them together. You have one place in 3.5, and one place in 1.7. Together, that gives a total of two places. Put in the decimal places starting at the right.

5.95

Another way to make sure you have put the right number of decimal places in your answer is to approximate. If you rounded 3.5 and 1.7, what would you have? 4×2. So you know your product will be somewhere near 8. Not 80 or 800.

Dividing Decimals

One of the clearest ways to look at decimal division is to keep this guideline in your head: The divisor should always be in the form of an integer.

$$.3 \overline{).45}$$

Since the divisor must be an integer, you don't want to look at it as .3, but rather 3. You may be thinking, "How do I do that?" Just move your decimal place to the right until you have a whole number. In this case, that means you have to move it to the right only once. Once you have transformed your divisor, give the same treatment to your dividend.

$$3. \overline{)4.5}$$

In the dividend, write the decimal point above the place it sits in the dividend. Then divide as you would normally.

$$3 \overline{)\overset{1.5}{4.5}}$$

To check your work, you can multiply your quotient by your divisor and see if you get your dividend. And you should always practice approximating to see if your answer looks about right. Are there about 1.5 groups of .3 each in .45? Or how many groups of 30 cents are there in 45 cents? About $1\frac{1}{2}$.

PERCENTAGES

Now we get to **percentages**. And guess what. You know how you feel about decimals after looking at fractions? That whole why-they're-just-fractions-over-powers-of-10,-I'm-not-sure-why-they-seemed-so-terrible feeling? Well it's the same thing with percentages. The only difference is that percentages are an even smaller part of fractions. Percentages are fractions over 100. Percent, when you break it down, becomes per and cent. Per as in "there are 3 hats per every 5 children," which means you have $\frac{3}{5}$ of the hats you need. *Per* means for each. *Cent* means 100. Cent is like *cent*ury or *cent*s as in 100 per (there it is again) dollar; so percent means for each 100.

50% means 50 for each 100. It can also look like .5, or $\frac{50}{100}$, or $\frac{1}{2}$ (just reduce the fraction).

100% means 100 for each 100 or $\frac{100}{100}$ which means 1. The whole. If you have 100 percent of something you have the whole thing.

Converting Fractions to Percentages

If a fraction is already over 100, just drop the denominator and add the percent sign.

$$\frac{99}{100} = 99\%$$

If the fraction is over a power of 10, try to convert the denominator to 100 by multiplying by $\frac{10}{10}$, or $\frac{100}{100}$, or reducing to a power of 10 (just move the decimal point on the numerator).

$$\frac{6}{10} = \frac{6}{10} \times \frac{10}{10} = \frac{60}{100} = 60\%$$

$$\frac{5}{1,000} = \frac{5 \div 10}{1,000 \div 10} = \frac{0.5}{100} = 0.5\%$$

And if you are starting from a decimal, translating to a percentage is even easier. The number .68 is 68%, because it is already over 100.

When you want to convert a fraction to a percentage and that fraction is not already over a power of 10, you need to convert the fraction to a decimal. This means dividing the numerator by the denominator, and then moving the decimal place two spaces to the right and adding a percent sign.

$$\frac{3}{8} = 8\overline{)3}$$

$$\begin{array}{r} 0.375 \\ 8\overline{)3.000} \\ \underline{2\ 4} \\ 60 \\ \underline{56} \\ 40 \\ \underline{40} \end{array}$$

Put the decimal point two places to the right, and there is your percent: 37.5%. You can also write it as $37\frac{1}{2}\%$. As a fraction, it is $\frac{375}{1,000}$ or back to your original friend, $\frac{3}{8}$. It's all the same number. Isn't that amazing? See how to work it in the other direction now.

Converting Percentages to Standard Fractions

To convert percentages to fractions, put the percentage over 100 and drop the % sign; then reduce.

$$60\% = \frac{60}{100} = \frac{3}{5}$$

Sometimes percentages have fractions in them, like $66\frac{2}{3}\%$. This means it is $66\frac{2}{3}$ over 100, or $66\frac{2}{3}$ divided by 100 (same thing, remember?). To work with this number more easily, try converting $66\frac{2}{3}$ from a mixed number. Once it is converted, you can divide by 100.

Converting from a mixed number, $66\frac{2}{3} = 3 \times 66 = 198 + 2 = 200; \frac{200}{3}$.

$$66\frac{2}{3} \text{ becomes } \frac{200}{3}$$

$$\frac{200}{3} \div 100 = \frac{200}{3} \times \frac{1}{100} = \frac{2}{3}$$

Converting Percentages to Decimals

To convert percentages to decimals, move the decimal point two spaces to the left and drop the % sign.

$$75\% = 0.75 \text{ and } 2\% = 0.02$$

EXPONENTS AND ROOTS

Exponents are a shorthand way of expressing a number multiplied by itself. For instance, 4^3 is 4 times itself three times.

$$4 \times 4 \times 4 = 64$$

The way to express 4^3 aloud is to say either "four to the third power" or "four cubed."

When a fraction is raised to an exponential power, both the numerator and the denominator get raised to that power. For instance, $\left(\frac{3}{4}\right)^2 = \frac{3 \times 3}{4 \times 4} = \frac{9}{16}$.

Multiplying Exponents

What if you wanted to multiply 4^3 by 4^2? How would you express that using exponents? Take a look at what each of those exponents means.

$$4^3 = 4 \times 4 \times 4, \text{ and } 4^2 = 4 \times 4, \text{ so } 4^3 \times 4^2 = 4 \times 4 \times 4 \times 4 \times 4$$

There are 5 fours, so you have 4^5. Since you see how it works, and now it makes perfect sense, from here on in you can just remember this rule: When multiplying exponents with the same **base**, just add the exponents. And what the heck is the base, you say? It is the number that is being raised to a power. In this particular case, the base is 4.

Dividing Exponents

What about when you are trying—you are getting very ambitious here—to divide exponents? For instance, $\dfrac{3^5}{3^2}$.

Again, just as you did with multiplying exponents, here you should arrange them as multiplication and see what happens.

$$\frac{3 \times 3 \times 3 \times 3 \times 3}{3 \times 3}$$

Two of the threes cancel out, correct? Both $\dfrac{3}{3}$ and $\dfrac{3}{3}$ get counted as 1, because any number over itself is equal to 1 and they both disappear. You are left with $3 \times 3 \times 3$. Or, 3^3. So the rule here is that when you divide exponents with the same base, subtract the exponents.

"But," you ask, "what would have happened if the smaller exponent had been on top, and the larger exponent had been on the bottom?" Well, generally you would leave the larger where it is. $\dfrac{2^4}{2^7} = \dfrac{2 \times 2 \times 2 \times 2}{2 \times 2 \times 2 \times 2 \times 2 \times 2 \times 2}$

Cancel where the $\dfrac{2}{2}$ appears, and you are left with $\dfrac{1}{2 \times 2 \times 2}$ or $\dfrac{1}{2^3}$. So you subtract smaller from larger.

But can you subtract and get 2^{-3}?

Negative Exponents

What happens when you raise 2 to the negative third power (2^{-3})? It is the same as if you had left it $\dfrac{1}{2^3}$. It becomes $\dfrac{1}{2 \times 2 \times 2}$, or $\dfrac{1}{8}$.

Any number raised to a negative power becomes 1 over that number to its exponent's positive power. It all connects.

Adding and Subtracting Exponents

One of the sad things in this world is that there is no real way to add or subtract exponents. Think about it. If you have $2^3 + 2^4$ it is equal to $(2 \times 2 \times 2)$ + $(2 \times 2 \times 2 \times 2) = 8 + 16 = 24$. Unfortunately, you can see that there is no special exponential shortcut, since 24 is not any power of 2, $2^4 = 16$, and $2^5 = 32$.

If you have $2^3 + 2^3$ you can say it is $2(2^3)$, but that is regular old multiplication. Two groups of 2^3 is the same as two times 2^3. Which is 16, by the way. But other than that, there is no way to add exponents with the same base.

Scientific Notation

Numbers can get really huge. Really, really huge. A way to get around it is something called **scientific notation.** Scientific notation uses exponential powers of ten as a way of expressing numbers.

$$56.7 \times 10^2$$

Here is an example of scientific notation. Again, to figure out what is going on, expand it. What is 10^2? 100. So you have 56.7×100. To multiply by 100, move the decimal point two spaces to the right, so $56.7 \times 100 = 5,670$.

That is how scientific notation works. Now that you understand it, here is a simpler way to translate the pieces.

Check the exponent of the 10; then move the decimal point that many places to the *right* if the exponent is *positive.*

$$56.7 \times 10^2 = 56.70$$

The exponent here is 2, so you move the decimal point two spaces to the right to get 5,670.

If you get a scientific notation expression in which the exponent is negative, remember what a negative exponent means. $10^{-2} = \dfrac{1}{100}$. Find the exponent of the ten, and move the decimal point that many places to the *left.*

$$56.7 \times 10^{-2} = 0.567$$

Roots

You know that if you square 3, you get 9.

$$3^2 = 3 \times 3 = 9$$

And you know that if you square –3, you also get 9.

$$-3^2 = -3 \times -3 = 9$$

But what about the famed **square roots**? A square root of a particular number is a number that, when squared, will equal that particular number. For example, a square root of 9 is 3. But –3 is also a square root of 9.

The positive square root of a positive number is called the **principal square root.** The sign for square root, called a **radical sign,** looks like this: $\sqrt{}$.

$\sqrt{25}$ = the square root of 25. You need to ask yourself, "What times itself equals 25?" And the answer is 5.

The numbers 9 and 25 are known as **perfect squares.** This means they are the squares of integers. There are other numbers you will come across that are not perfect squares. For instance, $\sqrt{8}$ is not equal to an integer. This means 8 is not a perfect square. You can approximate, of course, and you should, so you feel comfortable with it. Is $\sqrt{8}$ bigger than 2? Well yes, if it were 2, 2^2 is equal to 4, and 8 is bigger than 4, so $\sqrt{8}$ is bigger than 2. Is it bigger than 3? Well, 3^2 is equal to 9, and 9 is bigger than 8, so $\sqrt{8}$ is smaller than 3. In fact, $\sqrt{8}$ is between 2 and 3.

Another way to handle square roots of numbers that are not perfect squares is to factor them out. This means, find the factors of the number you are taking the square root of, and see if you can take a square root of these factors.

$$\sqrt{8} = \sqrt{4 \times 2}$$

Well, 4 is a perfect square, and the square root of 4 is 2. So, you put the 2 outside the square root sign, and leave what remains that cannot be factored to a perfect square, inside. It looks like this,

$$\sqrt{8} = \sqrt{4 \times 2} = 2\sqrt{2}$$

This also shows you that you can multiply square roots by each other. $\sqrt{4} \times \sqrt{2} = \sqrt{8}$.

Other Roots

Square roots are not the only type of roots; there are as many other kinds of roots as there are numbers. Yikes.

To figure out what kind of root a number is, take a look at the number floating high on the left of the radical sign.

$\sqrt[4]{16}$ = the fourth root of 16. This means some number to the fourth power is equal to 16. Here, the number is 2, because $2 \times 2 \times 2 \times 2 = 2^4 = 16$.

Don't worry though, the ones you will come across most frequently are square roots and **cube roots**. A cube root looks like this: $\sqrt[3]{}$.

The cube root of a particular number is a number that when cubed, equals the particular number. Whew. For instance, the cube root of 8?

$$\sqrt[3]{8} = 2, \text{ because } 2 \times 2 \times 2 = 2^3 = 8.$$

Just like with square roots, cube roots are only positive numbers. And just like square roots, and in fact, everything in the world, you should always try to approximate cube roots so you feel comfortable with them as numbers of a certain type.

$$\sqrt[3]{9}$$

Is it bigger than 2? Well, $2^3 = 8$, and 9 is bigger than 8, so yes, $\sqrt[3]{9}$ is bigger than 2.

Is it bigger than 3? Well, $3^3 = 27$, and 9 is not bigger than 27, so no, $\sqrt[3]{9}$ is a lot smaller than 3, it is some number between 2 and 3, that is closer to 2.

Another way to express roots is as fractional exponents. $27^{\frac{1}{3}}$ is just another way of expressing $\sqrt[3]{27}$, or the cube root of 27, which equals 3. And $36^{\frac{1}{2}}$ is another way of expressing $\sqrt{36}$, or the square root of 36, which equals 6.

KEY TERMS

integers

fractions

decimals

positive number

negative number

whole number

rational number

real number

number line

ordering integers

absolute value

digit

digit place

units digit (ones digit)

tens digit

hundreds digit

algorithm

addition

sum

subtraction

inverse (reverse) operation

multiplication

product

multiplicative identity

distributive law (distributive property)

commutative law
  (commutative property)

factors

prime numbers

division

dividend

divisor

quotient

divisible

remainder

fraction

fraction bar

numerator

denominator

improper fraction

proper fraction

reducing fractions

common denominator

lowest common denominator

mixed number

decimal

decimal point

tenths place

hundredths place

thousandths place

rounding

percentage

exponent

base

scientific notation

square root

principal square root

radical sign

perfect square

cube root

Drill #12

1. Use the number line below to answer the question that follows.

   Which of the following numbers can be represented on the number line between points P and Q?

   A. $\dfrac{24}{12}$

   B. $\dfrac{57}{71}$

   C. $\dfrac{39}{59}$

   D. $\dfrac{2}{100}$

2. Last week Suzanne jogged $9\,\dfrac{1}{2}$ miles. This week she jogged $12\,\dfrac{3}{4}$ miles. What is the difference between the distance she jogged this week and the distance she jogged last week?

   A. 3 miles

   B. $3\,\dfrac{1}{4}$ miles

   C. $3\,\dfrac{1}{2}$ miles

   D. $4\,\dfrac{5}{8}$ miles

3. $\frac{1}{2}$ is how many times greater than $\frac{1}{4}$?

   A. $\frac{1}{2}$

   B. 2

   C. 4

   D. 6

4. Which one of the following expressions finds 20 percent of 130?

   A. $\frac{20}{100} \times 130$

   B. $\frac{130}{20}$

   C. $\frac{130}{.2}$

   D. 130×5

5. Find the sum of 3.468 and 7.397 rounded to the nearest tenth.

   A. 11.0

   B. 10.9

   C. 10.8

   D. 10.0

Please turn the page for answers and explanations
for the questions in this drill.

ANSWERS AND EXPLANATIONS TO DRILL #12

1. **C** Rounding and reducing will lead you to the correct answer on this question. Choice A reduces to two, which is not between P and Q on the number line. Nor is choice D ($\frac{2}{100}$), which is not between points P and Q. Choice B could be rounded to about $\frac{60}{70}$, or about 85%, which seems a bit high for the spot between P and Q, but let's not eliminate it just yet. Choice C can be rounded to about $\frac{40}{60}$, or about 66%. This is the strongest option of the four choices, so choice C is the correct answer.

2. **B** To find the difference, convert all fractions to give them all the same denominator. $12 \frac{3}{4} - 9 \frac{2}{4} = 3 \frac{1}{4}$.

3. **B** Backsolving is the easiest way to solve this problem. Start with answer choice C because it's the middle option as far as number value, and multiply $\frac{1}{4}$ by 4. The result is 1, which is too high, so you know that D is incorrect, too. Try a smaller number—choice B. Multiply $\frac{1}{4}$ by 2 and the result is $\frac{1}{2}$. Choice B is the correct answer.

4. **A** Translate 20 percent as $\frac{20}{100}$. "Of" means multiply. Therefore, $\frac{20}{100} \times 130$ is the correct answer.

5. **B** Before rounding, add the two numbers together. The sum of 3.468 and 7.397 is 10.865. To round to the nearest tenth, look at the digit in the hundredths place, in this case 6. Since the number is 5 or greater, round up. The correctly rounded number becomes 10.9, choice B.

Summary

○ An integer is a number that is not a fraction or a decimal. 0 is an integer.

○ A number line is a visual representation of positive and negative numbers.

○ The absolute value of a number is its distance from zero on the number line.

○ Digits are integers 0 through 9 and the places in a number are called digit places. Decimals are a way to express fractions. The spots to the right of the units digit are called decimal places.

○ For the CSET, you must know the algorithms for addition, subtraction, division, and multiplication.

○ A fraction is comprised of a number in the top part (numerator) and a number in the bottom part (denominator). When working with fractions, reducing and finding the common denominator are helpful tools.

○ Exponents are a shorthand way to expressing a number multiplied by itself.

○ For the order of operations, just remember to Please Excuse My Dear Aunt Sally (Parentheses, Exponents, Multiplication, Division, Addition, and Subtraction.)

Chapter 15
Algebra and Functions

PATTERNS AND FUNCTIONAL RELATIONSHIPS

The Basics

A letter that stands in place of a number is called a **variable.** Why variable? Well, the letter's value varies, meaning that the numerical value which it represents is unspecified. For instance, unless a particular mathematical situation tells you differently, x has no specific numerical value. Variables are also referred to as **unknowns;** they can hold the place of an unknown value within an equation (a very useful function). Variables are italicized, and they can be any letter in the alphabet, though people are generally fond of a, b, c and x, y, z. And while the value of a variable is variable—heh, heh—in any one expression the value can't change. For instance, if you see something like $-a = a^2$, both a's represent the same value, whatever that value may be.

An **algebraic term** is a variable, a number, or a variable and a number combined by either multiplication or division. For instance, $3x$ is a term, $\frac{a}{2}$ is a term, 5 is a term, and x is a term. But $3 + y$ is two terms because the number and the variable aren't combined by multiplication or division, but by addition. A term such as $3x$, in which a variable is multiplied by a number, introduces even more vocabulary: The number 3 is a **coefficient.** The coefficient is the number by which the variable is multiplied. And when terms are combined by addition or subtraction, that combination is called an **algebraic expression.**

Algebraic expressions are more or less the first sentences you are going to speak in your new language. An algebraic expression consists of algebraic terms combined by addition or subtraction. Thus $3x - 4$ is an algebraic expression, as are $x - y$, and $\frac{4}{x} - \frac{x}{4}$. An expression put in terms of a particular variable is said to be in the terms of that variable. For instance, the following algebraic expression is an expression in x.

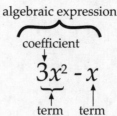

To solve a problem with a variable, you must **isolate the variable.** This is one way of **simplifying.** Take this example:

$$3g = 27$$

You need to get g by itself so that you know its value. The way that you can do this is to move the numbers to one side of the equation and the variable to the other.

You see how equations have two sides? The left side is $3g$, and the right side of the equation is 27. The two sides are separated by the equals sign. You want to end up with just g on one side, and the numbers on the other.

The thing about equations is that you can do anything you want to them, as long as you do it to both sides of the equation. In the case of $3g = 27$, the coefficient 3 needs to be moved in order to obtain the value of g.

The way to move something from one side of the equation to the other is to perform the inverse operation to both sides of the equation. In this case, the 3 is being multiplied by g, so this means that you need to divide by 3. Again, the most important thing is that whatever you do, you must do it to both sides of the equation. So divide away.

$$\frac{3g}{3} = \frac{27}{3}$$

Use the fraction bar to show division.

$$g = 9$$

You can double-check your work by plugging in the value that you just found for g to make sure it works. The original example was $3g = 27$. Does $3 \times 9 = 27$? Yes it is. So your solution that $g = 9$ is exactly right.

Formulas

People also use algebraic expressions to express fixed relationships. These fixed relationships are called **formulas**. You are probably familiar with the old $E = mc^2$ from Einstein. Don't worry—we won't explain $E = mc^2$ here; it's just an example of a formula. Formulas use particular variables to express their components; these variables are usually defined below the formula. A formula is generally presented in this way:

> $E = mc^2$
> in which E stands for energy, m for mass, and c for the speed of light.

Formulas and other algebraic expressions can also contain algebraic terms called **constants**. A constant term has a fixed numerical value within an expression or series of expressions. For example, in the formula $E = mc^2$, c has a constant value, not a variable one; it always represents 299,792,460 miles per second—the speed of light.

Factoring Polynomials

Don't be thrown by the word **polynomials**—it just means that an expression has more than one term in it. "Poly" means many. For example, a polyglot is someone who can speak many languages. The following two expressions are examples of polynomials:

$$3ab + 2b$$

$$4x^2 + 3xy + y^2$$

The term *polynomial* covers all expressions of more than one term (**monomials** contain just one term, like $3g = 27$ that we saw earlier). Polynomials can be **binomials** (with two terms) or **trinomials** (with three terms) or more—anything with more than one term.

When you're factoring a polynomial, you should first simplify it by combining like terms. Like terms are elements of an expression that use identical variables. For example, $7x + 4x + y$ will combine to $11x + y$.

In any expression, x represents one thing the whole way through, so you can combine all information about x. But you cannot combine the information about two unlike terms.

$$7x + 3y \text{ stays } 7x + 3y$$

Think of x as representing hats and y as representing sweaters. The items 7 hats and 3 sweaters don't combine to form 10 hats and 10 sweaters. So combine only like terms. Never try combining unlike terms.

Let's work through a big expression:

$$5x + 7y - z - 2x + 4y - 2z + 10x$$

Here's How to Crack It

Just approach it one step at a time. Take the x terms first, since they come first. The expression includes $5x$, a $2x$ being subtracted, and $10x$. These are all like terms. The $5x$ and $10x$ are being added and the $2x$ is being subtracted. So do this:

$$5x - 2x = 3x \text{ and } 3x + 10x = 13x$$

You now have $13x + 7y - z + 4y - 2z$.

Now take the y terms. You have $7y$ and $4y$. These are like terms, and both are being added to other things, so it's simply

$$7x + 4y = 11y$$

You've simplified the expression down to

$$13x + 11y - z - 2z$$

Now onto the z terms. One thing that you should notice is that algebraic expressions like to have the variables in alphabetical order. It's sort of sweet, really. You have z being subtracted, then $2x$ being subtracted. Luckily, you know how to combine negatives:

$$-z - 2z = -3z$$

Now you can string all of your combined terms together in an expression of three simple terms (a delightful trinomial):

$$13x + 11y - 3z$$

Multiplying Binomials

Multiplying binomials is easy. Just be sure to use FOIL (first, outer, inner, last):

$$
\begin{aligned}
(x + 2)(x + 4) &= (x + 2)(x + 4) \\
&= (x \times x) + (x \times 4) + (2 \times x) + (2 \times 4) \\
&\quad\ \text{FIRST} \quad \text{OUTER} \quad \text{INNER} \quad \text{LAST} \\
&= x^2 + 4x + 2x + 8 \\
&= x^2 + 6x + 8
\end{aligned}
$$

Combine Like Terms First

In manipulating long, complicated algebraic expressions, combine all like terms before doing anything else. In other words, if one of the terms is $5x$ and another is $-3x$, simply combine them into $2x$. Then you won't have as many terms to work with. Here's an example:

$$(3x^2 + 3x + 4) + (2 - x) - (6 + 2x) =$$
$$3x^2 + 3x + 4 + 2 - x - 6 - 2x =$$
$$3x^2 + (3x - x - 2x) + (4 + 2 - 6) =$$
$$3x^2$$

Evaluating Expressions

Sometimes the CSET will give you the value of one of the variables in an algebraic expression and ask you to find the value of the entire expression. All you have to do is plug in the given value and see what you come up with.

Here is an example.

If $2x = -1$, then $(2x - 3)^2 = ?$

Here's How to Crack It

Don't solve for x; simply plug in -1 for $2x$, like this:

$$(2x - 3)^2 = (-1 - 3)^2$$
$$= (-4)^2$$
$$= 16$$

Solving Quadratic Equations

To solve **quadratic equations**, look for direct solutions and either factor or expand when possible.

Here's an example.

If $(x + 3)^2 = (x - 2)^2$, then $x =$

Here's How to Crack It

Expand both sides of the equation using FOIL:

$$(x + 3)(x + 3) = x^2 + 6x + 9$$

$$(x - 2)(x - 2) = x^2 - 4x + 4$$

$$x^2 + 6x + 9 = x^2 - 4x + 4$$

Now you can simplify. Eliminate the x^2 from both sides of the equal sign. Now you have $6x + 9 = -4x + 4$, which simplifies to

$$10x = -5$$
$$x = -\frac{1}{2}$$

Factoring Quadratics

To solve a quadratic, you might also have to factor the equation. Factoring a quadratic basically involves doing a reverse form of FOIL.

For example, suppose you needed to know the factors of $x^2 + 7x + 12$. Here's what you would do:

1. Write down 2 sets of parentheses and put an x in each one because the product of the first terms is x^2.
    $$x^2 + 7x + 12 = (x \quad)(x \quad)$$
2. Look at the number at the end of the expression you are trying to factor. Write down its factors. In this case, the factors of 12 are 1 and 12, 2 and 6, and 3 and 4.
3. To determine which set of factors to put in the parentheses, look at the coefficient of the middle term of the quadratic expression. In this case, the coefficient is 7. So, the correct factors will also either add or subtract to get 7. Write the correct factors in the parentheses.
    $$x^2 + 7x + 12 = (x \underline{\quad} 3)(x \underline{\quad} 4)$$
4. Finally, determine the signs for the factors. To get a positive 12, both the 3 and the 4 are both positive or both negative. But, since 7 is also positive, the signs must both be positive.
    $$x^2 + 7x + 12 = (x + 3)(x + 4)$$

You can always check that you have factored correctly by FOILing the factors to see if you get the original quadratic expression.

Now, try this one.

In the expression $x^2 + kx + 12$, k is an integer and $k < 0$. Which of the following is a possible value of k?

(A) –13

(B) –12

(C) – 6

(D) 7

Here's How to Crack It

First, you can get rid of D because the question says that $k < 0$.

To solve the question, you need to factor. This question is just a twist on the example used above. Don't worry that we don't know the value of k. The question said that k was an integer and that means that you probably need to consider only the integer factors of 12. The possible factors of 12 are 1 and 12, 2 and 6, and 3 and 4. Since 12 is positive and k is negative, you'll need subtraction signs in both factors.

The possibilities are

$$x^2 + kx + 12 = (x - 1)(x - 12)$$

$$x^2 + kx + 12 = (x - 2)(x - 6)$$

$$x^2 + kx + 12 = (x - 3)(x - 4)$$

If you FOIL each of these sets of factors, you'll get:

$$(x - 1)(x - 12) = x^2 - 13x + 12$$

$$(x - 2)(x - 6) = x^2 - 8x + 12$$

$$(x - 3)(x - 4) = x^2 - 7x + 12$$

The correct answer is A, as –13 is the only value from above included in the answers. Of course, you didn't need to write them all out if you started with 1 and 12 as your factors.

Evaluating an Expression

Formulas are sometimes followed by specific values to be put into the formula. A question might look like this:

$$A = \frac{1}{2}bh$$

in which A is the area of a triangle with base b and height h. What is the area of a triangle with a base of 4 and a height of 6?

All you do in a case like this is substitute the values given for the variables and solve it as though it were an arithmetic problem. $A = \frac{1}{2}(4)(6)$ becomes $A = \frac{1}{2}(24)$ becomes $A = 12$.

Solving for specific values as we just did is called **evaluating a formula.** It is one of the basic jobs of algebra students.

Solving Equations That Contain Algebraic Fractions

And what does one do when faced with an equation like this: $\frac{x}{3} + 2 = 4x$? This is an equation that contains an **algebraic fraction.** Well, algebraic fractions follow the rules of all other fractions: To add or subtract them they must have a common denominator (and remember that fractions are just expressions of division).

As for the equation $\frac{x}{3} + 2 = 4x$, there are a number of ways to go about isolating the variable, and we will show you the two most important. First you could simply subtract the variable with the smaller coefficient, in this case the term on the left side where the coefficient is $\frac{1}{3}$. It would look like this:

$$\frac{x}{3} + 2 - \frac{x}{3} = 4x - \frac{x}{3}$$

To subtract on the right side you need a common denominator, and the easiest way to get one is by using the **bow tie**.

The Bow Tie
The bow tie is an easy way to find a common denominator.

$$\frac{4x}{1} - \frac{x}{3}$$

Let's look at it step by step. First multiply up from the denominator of the second fraction to the numerator of the first:

$$12x$$

$$\frac{4x}{1} \quad \frac{x}{3}$$

Then multiply the denominator of the first by the numerator of the second:

$$12x - (x)$$

$$\frac{4x}{1} \times \frac{x}{3}$$

Then multiply the denominators to produce the final denominator:

$$12x - (x)$$

$$\frac{4x}{1} \times \frac{x}{3} = \frac{}{3}$$

Then add or subtract the numerators as directed and you're done!

$$12x - (x)$$

$$\frac{4x}{1} \times \frac{x}{3} = \frac{11x}{3}$$

Now, back to our problem.

$$\frac{x}{3} + 2 - \frac{x}{3} = 4x - \frac{x}{3}$$

Using the bow tie on the right half of the equation makes your equation looks like this:

$$2 = \frac{11x}{3}$$

To isolate the x, do what you would normally do. Perform the opposite operation from what occurs in the equation: Multiply both sides by 3.

$$2 \times 3 = \frac{11x}{3} \times 3$$
$$6 = 11x$$

Finally, divide both sides by 11, and you're left with just your variable.

$$\frac{6}{11} = \frac{11x}{3} \text{ becomes } \frac{6}{11} = x$$

The other way you can isolate the variable in that problem is to get rid of the denominator of the fraction before you even begin adding or subtracting.

Here's the original equation again:

$$\frac{x}{3} + 2 = 4x$$

Instead of just subtracting $\frac{x}{3}$ from both sides, you could multiply the whole equation by 3. The thing to remember here is that you must multiply every part of both sides, like so:

$$3\left(\frac{x}{3} + 2\right) = 3(4x)$$

Remember the distributive law here: When you multiply the left side by 3, you multiply *each term* in the left side by 3. The results are as follows:

$$3\left(\frac{x}{3} + 2\right) = 3(4x) \text{ becomes } x + 6 = 12x$$

Now, proceed to combine like terms and isolate that rascally variable.

$$x + 6 - x = 12x - x$$
$$6 = 11x$$

$$\frac{6}{11} = \frac{11x}{11} \text{ becomes } \frac{6}{11} = x$$

Same right answer, a subtly different way of getting it. And it all goes back to the wonderful distributive law, whose importance and reliability we're sure you're beginning to appreciate.

THE RULES OF LOGARITHMS

Since $\log_3 9 = 2$ can also be written as $\log_3 (3^2) = 2$, we can say, more generally, that $\log_3 (3^x) = x$. So if $\log_3 (3^2 \cdot 3^3) = x$, what is x? Since 3 is the base, the exponent that the whole logarithm is set equal to must be the sum of the exponents that the 3 is raised to within the parentheses. This means that the answer must be 5, since $(3^2 \cdot 3^3)$ is a base of 3 being raised to the 5th power. (Remember the rule of multiplying exponents?)

Logarithmically this means

$$\log_3 (3^x \cdot 3^y) = x + y$$

Since $\log_3 (3^x) = x$, and $\log_3 (3^y) = y$, you know that $x + y = \log_3 (3^x) + \log_3 (3^y)$.

$$\log_3 (3^x \cdot 3^y) = \log_3 (3^x) + \log_3 (3^y)$$

All of the above expressions are equivalent, but the last one most clearly demonstrates the multiplication property of logarithms. The general algebraic form of this property is as follows:

$$\log_a xy = \log_a x + \log_a y$$

For a logarithm of base a where $a > 0$ and $a \neq 1$, the logarithm of the product of two numbers (above we use x and y) is equal to the sum of each of their logarithms.

The next rule relates to division. As you well know, when powers of the same base are divided, their exponents are subtracted. What is x if $\log_3 \left(\dfrac{3^6}{3^2} \right) = x$?

We see that x must be $\log_3 (3^4)$, or 4. Thus $\log_3 \left(\dfrac{3^x}{3^y} \right) = x - y$. As you know, $\log_3 3^x = x$, and $\log_3 3^y = y$. Thus $\log_3 \left(\dfrac{3^x}{3^y} \right) = x - y = \log_3 (3^x) - \log_3 (3^y)$.

Algebraically then, the expression of the logarithmic property of a quotient is this:

$$\log_a \frac{y}{x} = \log_a y - \log_a x$$

The final rule of logarithms that you need to know is the rule regarding logarithms with exponents in them. Since you're so familiar with logarithms of base 3, we'll use one of those. As you've already seen, $\log_3 (3^2) = 2$. Well, you could also express this as $2\log_3 3 = 2$ (the exponent that 3 needs to be raised to in order to yield 3 is 1). This works with larger exponents; actually it works for all exponents (that's why it's a general property, right?). How about simplifying $\log_3 (27^2)$? It's $2\log_3 27$. Which, by the way, is 6. This follows from the rules of raising exponents, of course! When you raise an exponent to another power you multiply the exponents. Thus, the logarithmic equation that produces the exponent is multiplied by the new exponent.

The algebraic expression of this general property is this:

$$\log_a (x^y) = y \log_a x$$

Here's one final example:

What is $\log_3 (9^{27})$?

Here we can use the property of logarithms and exponents. That means going from $\log_3 (9^{27})$ to $27\log_3 9$. Now, what is $\log_3 9$? What power is the base 3 raised to that yields 9? It's raised to the second power, of course, so 27(2) is the answer, or 54.

GRAPHS

Most math questions on the CSET are presented as word problems. The CSET writers also ask you to use graphs to solve various math problems. These graphs can take many forms—a table of information, a bar chart, a line chart, or a pie chart.

Often, questions using graphs can be intimidating to test-takers, simply because of the size or amount of information presented in a graph. Yet graph questions are no more complicated than any other type of math question. Simply find the information that you need from the graph, use the data for any necessary calculations, and you're done. Finally, some test-takers feel that the more complicated the graph, the more difficult the problem will be. Not true! Don't let the size or complexity of the graph intimidate you. Let's use the chart below to evaluate the questions that follow.

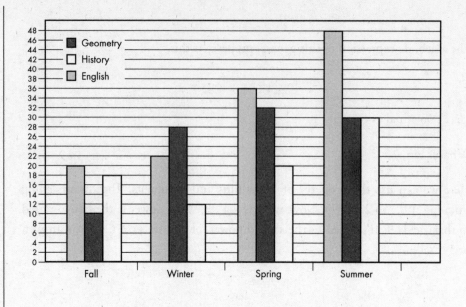

According to the preceding graph, how many more students took geometry in the winter than history in the fall?

A. 3

B. 10

C. 18

D. 28

Here's How to Crack It

In this graph question, you are asked to find the difference between two different values on the graph. First, locate the value of each group: 28 students took geometry in the winter, and 18 students took history in the fall. After finding these two pieces of information, the problem is simple. Subtract 18 from 28 to get 10, or choice B, as the correct answer. Note: Partial answer choices will often appear on problems that use graphs (in this case, choices C and D), so be careful.

In the preceding graph, the percentage
of geometry students who took
geometry in the spring is how much
greater than the percentage of history
students who took history in the spring?

A.   7%

B.   20%

C.   25%

D.   32%

Here's How to Crack It

This question asks us to compare two percents. In the graph above, no percentages are given, so we'll need to calculate the percentages first. To find the percent of geometry students who took geometry in the spring, we need two pieces of information—the total number of geometry students for the year, and the number of geometry students in the spring.

First, add the geometry students for the year (10 + 28 + 32 + 30 = 100). Nice and round number. In the spring, 32 students took geometry. To express this as a percentage, put the number of students who took geometry in the spring in the numerator of a fraction and the total number of students in the denominator: $\frac{32}{100}$ = 32%.

If you follow the same procedure to determine the percent of history students who took history in the spring, you get $\frac{20}{80} = \frac{1}{4}$ = 25%.

The difference between these two values is 32% − 25%, or 7%. Choice A is the correct answer. Again, watch out for partial answer choices.

Relating Data Found in Graphs

In the previous two examples, you had to take information from a graph and perform certain operations on the numbers. On some CSET questions, you will be asked to compare numbers to each other. Here are some sample questions:

- What was the percent increase from year x to year y?
- In order to equal the amount of sales of Company x, Company y needs to increase its sales by what percent?
- What year saw the greatest increase in production for Company x?

The formula for finding **percent change** is

$$\% \text{ change} = \frac{\text{difference}}{\text{original amount}}$$

This formula is often helpful when asked to compare data within a graph. Using the graph from before, let's examine one of these types of questions.

Which class saw the largest percentage change in enrollment from spring to summer?

A. English

B. Geometry

C. History

D. English and History have the same percentage increase.

Here's How to Crack It

We need to find the largest percent change from the spring terms to the summer term. In order to find a percent change, use the percent change formula that we just discussed:

$$\% \text{ change} = \frac{\text{difference}}{\text{original amount}}$$

For English class, the percent change is

$$\frac{(48 - 36)}{36} = \frac{12}{36} = \frac{1}{3} = 33\frac{1}{3}\%$$

For Geometry class, the percent change is

$$\frac{(32 - 30)}{30} = \frac{2}{30} = \text{less than } 10\%$$

For History class, the percent change is

$$\frac{(30 - 20)}{20} = \frac{10}{20} = \frac{1}{2} = 50\%$$

From these calculations, you can see that the correct answer is choice C, History.

Linear Equations

A **linear equation** is an algebraic equation in which each term is either a constant or the product of a constant and (the first power of) a single variable.

A common form of a linear equation in the two variables x and y is

$$y = mx + b$$

This equation is often called the **slope-intercept formula** because m is the slope and b gives the y-intercept (where the line crosses the y plane). Linear equations graph as straight lines, and have simple variable expressions with no exponents on them. An even simpler way to think about slope is as follows:

$$\text{slope} = \frac{\text{rise}}{\text{run}}$$

If a line has a slope of 4, that means that from a given point, you can simply count up 4 units, then over 1 and that is the next point on the line. For example, here is a line with an example of a line with a slope of 4:

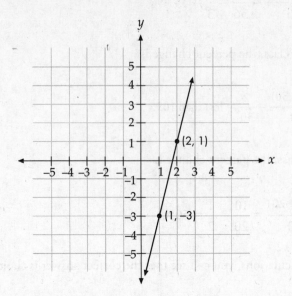

It's very likely that the CSET will throw at least one or two line slope questions at you, so let's take a look at a few sample problems.

What is the equation of the straight line that has slope $m = 4$ and passes through the point $(-1, -6)$?

A. $y = 4x - 2$

B. $y = 2x - 4$

C. $y = -6x - 2$

D. $y = -1x - 2$

Here's How to Crack It

Remember the linear formula, $y = mx + b$. In this case, they've provided the value of the slope ($m = 4$). Also, in giving you a point on the line, they have given you an x-value and a y-value for this line: $x = -1$ and $y = -6$.

So far, the only thing that you don't have a value for is *b* (which gives you the *y*-intercept). Then all you need to do is plug in for the slope and then solve for *b*:

$$y = mx + b$$
$$(-6) = (4)(-1) + b$$
$$-6 = -4 + b$$
$$-2 = b$$

So the line equation must be $y = 4x - 2$

Here's another type of question that CSET loves to test.

Use the graph below to answer the question that follows:

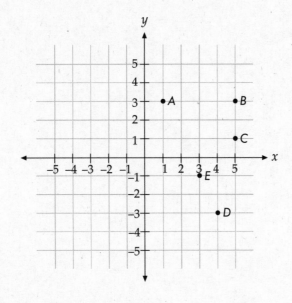

Point E is on a line with a slope of 2 in the *x-y* plane. Which of the following points is also on the line?

A. *A*

B. *B*

C. *C*

D. *D*

Here's How to Crack It

Just remember your rise over run and this question is simple. You know a point and the slope of the line—now all you have to do is tick up two units and over one unit. That takes us to the point (4,1) which isn't a choice (don't fall for trick answer choice C, which is one unit over). Tick up another two units and over one more to (5,3), choice B. There's you're answer.

We worked with a quadratic equation earlier in this chapter. Its title might seem daunting, but quadratic equations are just polynomial equations of the second degree (that is, polynomial equations^2). These are factored out (using FOIL) just like basic binomials.

In Chapter 16, "Measurement and Geometry," we'll delve further into the intersection of geometry and algebra: analytic geometry.

KEY TERMS

variable
unknown
algebraic term
coefficient
algebraic expression
isolate the variable
simplifying
formulas
constants
polynomials
monomials
binomials
trinomials
quadratic equations
evaluating a formula
algebraic fraction
bow tie
exponents
base
power
square
cube
logarithms
percent change formula
linear equations
slope-intercept formula

Drill #13

Each group of questions below is followed by four suggested answers or completions. Select the one that is best in each case.

1. The expression $3x - 5y$ contains how many terms?

   A. 1

   B. 2

   C. 3

   D. 4

2. Translate the following sentence into a formula, using whichever variables you think are appropriate:

   A person's height is equal to the width of her arms from the tip of her middle finger to the tip of her middle finger.

   A. $h = w$

   B. $h = wf_1 - wf_2 + w$

   C. $h = mf_1 + mf_2 + w$

   D. $y = mx + b$

3. If $3z + 6 = 16$, what is the value of $9z$?

   A. 10

   B. 20

   C. 22

   D. 30

4. A television repair person charges a $50 fixed charge plus $25 per hour for time spent working. What is the total bill for a job that requires n hour of work?

   A. ($50 + $25)$n$

   B. 12.50n$ + $50

   C. 50n$ + $25

   D. 25n$ + 50

5. $10y - 36 + 4y - 6 + y = 3$. What is the value of y?

   A. 3

   B. 4

   C. 6

   D. 10

Please turn the page for answers and explanations
for the questions in this drill.

ANSWERS AND EXPLANATIONS TO DRILL #13

1. **B**   Two terms, $3x$ and $5y$

2. **A**   Be careful that you don't make this question unnecessarily difficult. The sentence says that a person's height is equal to her arm span from fingertip to fingertip. It's a simple formula, $h = w$.

3. **D**   If you simplify the equation, you find that $3z = 10$. Rather than solve for z, simply multiply the entire equation by 3. That gives you $9z = 30$. You can save time and calculations by looking for $9z$ only—don't worry about the value of z.

4. **D**   Read the question carefully. If the repair person's rate is \$25/hour and he's working n hours, that part of the equation is \$25n. Remember the fixed charge of \$50 and the answer is clearly D.

5. **A**   Simplify the equation to get

$$15y - 42 = 3$$
$$15y = 45$$
$$y = 3$$

Summary

o A variable is the letter that stands in place of a number and it can vary in value.

o An algebraic term can be a variable, a number, or a variable and a number combined by multiplication or division.

o A coefficient is the number by which a variable is multiplied (for example, in $4y$, 4 is the coefficient).

o Formulas are useful tools for expressing fixed relationships.

o Evaluating a formula means solving for specific values.

o To find a common denominator, use the bow tie method.

o Exponents tell you how many times the base number is multiplied by itself. (x^2 is x squared; x^3 is x cubed.)

o When multiplying powers with the same base, just add exponents.

o To divide powers that have the same base, subtract exponents.

o To raise a power to another exponent, multiply exponents.

o To raise something within parentheses to a power, raise every piece of the term within parentheses to that power.

o Any base raised to the exponent zero always equals 1.

o Use the FOIL system to multiply binomials and solve quadratic equations.

Chapter 16
Measurement and
Geometry

PLANE GEOMETRY

The basic units of plane geometry are **points** and **lines.** Lines continue in both directions to infinity. They are made up of an infinite number of points, each of which occupies a particular space on the line. Lines can be straight, curved, or even broken; for now we will discuss straight lines only.

The unit of measurement that is generally used for lines and angles in plane geometry is the **degree.** A straight line measures 180 degrees.

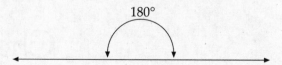

The lines one normally refers to are actually **line segments,** which are cut-up pieces of lines.

Why is this section called plane geometry? Because all of the geometry we'll be talking about occurs in a **plane.** A plane is a two-dimensional space extending infinitely in all directions. Think of a piece of paper that extends, top and bottom, both sides, forever. Then imagine that the paper has no measurable thickness; really cheap, thin paper, for instance. That's a good way to imagine what a plane is.

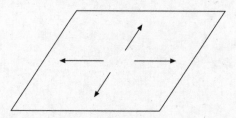

When we say that geometry occurs in a plane, we mean that these shapes and lines are flat; they exist only on the planar level.

Special Lines

Parallel lines are lines that maintain the same distance between them infinitely, and never meet.

The mathematical symbol for parallel lines is two straight lines between the variable for the lines; for example $l_1 \parallel l_2$ is "line one is parallel to line two."

Angles

Lines that *aren't* parallel end up meeting eventually. When two lines meet they form four **angles.**

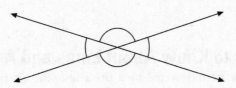

Angles opposite one another are called **vertical angles,** and vertical angles are always equal, meaning they have the same degree measure. The way to mark equal angles is to stick a line into the angle curves; equal angles or sides have the same number of lines through them, like so:

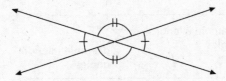

Angles that cut the degree measure of a line in half are said to be **perpendicular,** and are denoted by a small square in the vertex of the angle. The angle formed by perpendicular lines is called a **right angle.**

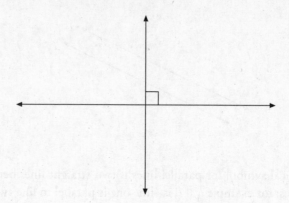

Since the 180° line is cut exactly in half, perpendicular angles measure exactly 90 degrees.

Two angles that together add up to the measure of a line, or 180 degrees, are called **supplementary.** Two **complementary** angles add up to form a perpendicular, or 90 degrees.

Some Things to Know About Lines and Angles

If two parallel lines are intersected by a third line, the **alternate interior angles** formed by that third line are equal, and the corresponding angles—you can see that these are the vertical angles of the alternate interior angles—are also equal. This is called the **rule of alternate interior angles.** Remember: Angles that are exactly the same size are marked with equal numbers of lines through them.

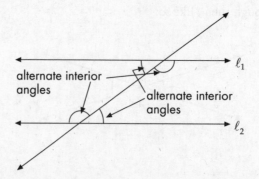

alternate interior angles

alternate interior angles

ℓ_1

ℓ_2

An angle greater than 90 degrees is referred to as **obtuse.** An angle less than 90 degrees is called **acute.**

Quadrilaterals

A **quadrilateral** is a closed, two-dimensional shape that has four sides. Closed means that the four sides meet at the corners rather then opening up, like this:

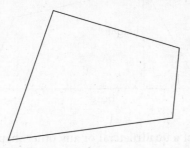

rather than this:

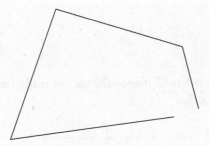

The sum of the degrees of the four internal angles in a quadrilateral is 360. Quadrilaterals are divided into groups according to their more specific properties.

To find the **area** of a regular quadrilateral, multiply its **base** by its **height.** Its area is defined as the number of square units the shape occupies.

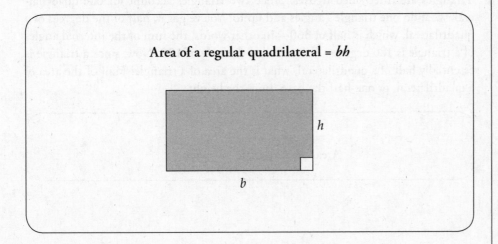

Area of a regular quadrilateral = *bh*

The height of any shape is the vertical distance of a perpendicular line drawn from the highest point of the quadrilateral to its base.

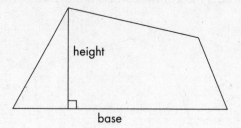

To find the **perimeter** of a quadrilateral or any other shape, add up the sides. The perimeter is the distance around the outside of a shape. When you have a quadrilateral with two pairs of equal sides, you can find the perimeter by multiplying the length by two, multiplying the width by two, and adding these. This is, of course, the same as adding all four sides.

Triangles

When you split a quadrilateral diagonally things really start to happen, because you've created two triangles.

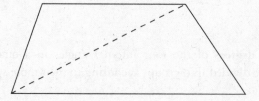

Triangles are three-sided figures. Since two triangles account for one quadrilateral, what do one triangle's angles add up to? You've got it, half of the degrees of a quadrilateral, which is half of 360—in other words, the sum of the internal angles of a triangle is 180 degrees. This is called the **rule of 180**. Now, since a triangle is essentially half of a quadrilateral, what is the area of a triangle? Half of the area of a quadrilateral, or one-half the base times the height.

$$\text{Area of a triangle} = \frac{1}{2}bh$$

The angles of a triangle are directly proportional to the sides opposite them; in other words, the largest angle is always opposite the longest side, and the smallest angle is always opposite the shortest side. When all of the sides of a triangle are equal, all of its angles are equal. A triangle of this type is an **equilateral triangle.**

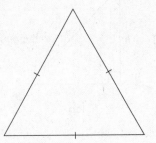

If all of its angles are equal, what is the measure of each angle? Why, 60 degrees of course, because the sum of the angles must be 180°. We'll talk more about this in a minute.

If a triangle has two sides that are exactly equal, then the angles opposite those two sides are also equal. A triangle with two equal sides is an **isosceles triangle.**

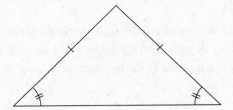

Any **exterior angle** of a triangle is equal to the sum of the two opposite **interior angles,** no matter what type of triangle it is. An exterior angle is an angle abutting but outside the shape; an interior angle is inside the shape. Can you see why this is true (think about the rule of 180°)?

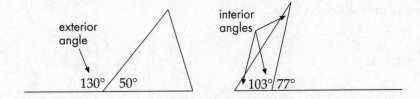

Right Triangles

A triangle that contains a right angle is a **right triangle.**

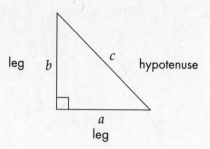

The side opposite the right angle is called the **hypotenuse,** and the other sides of the triangle are called **legs.** The relationship between the length of the legs and the length of the hypotenuse of a right triangle is as follows: $a^2 + b^2 = c^2$, in which c is the hypotenuse and a and b are the legs of the right triangle. This formula is known as the **Pythagorean Theorem.**

Now let's also talk about a group of triangles called **special right triangles.** A special right triangle is a right triangle with some regular feature that makes calculations on the triangle easier. These types of triangles can be either side-based or angle-based. Let's talk about the angle-based ones right now.

A **45-45-90 triangle,** or isosceles right triangle, is a triangle whose three angles measure 90 degrees, 45 degrees, and 45 degrees. For an isosceles right triangle, in which the legs of the triangle are x, the hypotenuse is $x\sqrt{2}$.

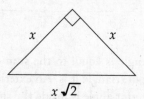

A **30-60-90 triangle** is a triangle whose three angles measure 90 degrees, 60 degrees, and 30 degrees. In this type of triangle, the shortest leg is x, the middle leg is $x\sqrt{3}$, and the longest leg is $2x$.

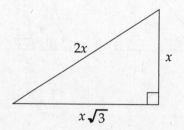

As we saw above, an equilateral triangle is a triangle whose three angles measure 60 degrees, 60 degrees, and 60 degrees.

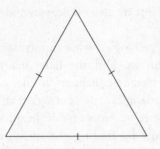

Let's try a problem.

What is the area of the rectangle *ABCD?*

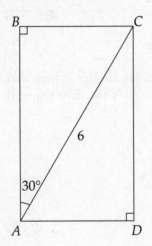

A. $3\sqrt{3}$

B. $9\sqrt{3}$

C. $6\sqrt{3}$

D. $12\sqrt{3}$

Here's How to Crack It

To find the area of the rectangle, the information that's already there needs to be evaluated. Note that by providing the diagonal of the rectangle, the diagram also shows that there are two equal right triangles. Why equal? Well, they share a hypotenuse, they have equal bases and heights, and they have equal angles, because the 30 degree angle shown has a complementary angle of 60 degrees, which means that the angles opposite them are also 60 degrees and 30 degrees.

To find the area of a rectangle, what information is necessary? The base and the height. How can we find the base and the height? Well, the base and the height of the rectangle happen to be equal to the base and the height of these right triangles. By noting that they are 30:60:90 right triangles, which have a specific ratio of side lengths of $x : x\sqrt{3} : 2x$, we can determine all three sides just by finding the measure of one. Do we have the measure of any of these sides? Yes, we have the measure of the hypotenuse, 6. The hypotenuse corresponds to the largest of the edges on the ratio, $2x$. If $2x = 6$, then $x = 3$. Thus, the remaining sides of x and $x\sqrt{3}$ are 3 and $3\sqrt{3}$ respectively.

The area of a rectangle is bh, so the area of this rectangle is 3 times $3\sqrt{3}$, or $9\sqrt{3}$. Choice B is the correct answer.

Similar Triangles

Any two (or more) triangles are **similar** if their corresponding angles are equal. This is because equal angles imply the same shape; thus, these triangles' sides are proportional.

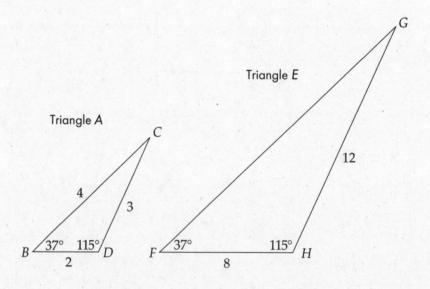

Similar triangles allow you to determine missing information by providing the ratio of the sides. For example, look at triangle A and triangle E. You can tell they're similar because of their equal angles (angle FGH and angle BCD must be 28° because of the rule of 180). You can also tell that their ratio is such that the sides of triangle E are four times the sides of triangle A. This is determined from the ratio of side BD to side FH. Thus, you can determine side FG in triangle E; it must be four times the respective side of triangle A, or 16.

Area of Similar Triangles

How are the areas of two pairs of similar triangles proportional? Well, take a look at the triangles again.

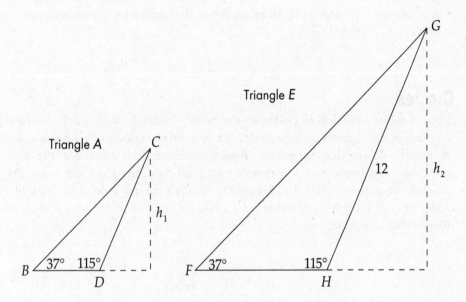

The sides are proportional, which means that they all have the same ratio. Another way of expressing this is $\dfrac{BD}{FH} = \dfrac{BC}{FG} = \dfrac{CD}{GH}$. Since these sides are proportional, you know that the heights are proportional, or $\dfrac{h_1}{h_2}$.

The area of triangle A is $(BD)(h_1)\left(\dfrac{1}{2}\right)$. The area of triangle E is $(FH)(h_2)\left(\dfrac{1}{2}\right)$, so the proportion of the areas is $\dfrac{(BD)(h_1)\left(\dfrac{1}{2}\right)}{(FH)(h_2)\left(\dfrac{1}{2}\right)}$. Thankfully, you can simplify this fraction. The halves cancel out, and you have $\dfrac{(BD)(h_1)}{(FH)(h_2)}$, which can also be seen as

$\left(\dfrac{BD}{FH}\right)\left(\dfrac{h_1}{h_2}\right)$. Of course, since the sides and the heights have the same proportion, you could also write this as $\left(\dfrac{BD}{FH}\right)\left(\dfrac{BD}{FH}\right)$, or better yet as $\left(\dfrac{BD}{FH}\right)^2$. All of which goes to show you that the ratio of the areas of two similar triangles is equal to the square of the ratios of their sides.

Congruence

Triangles that are exactly the same size are **congruent**. This term also applies to angles of the same measure, which we've already seen in isosceles, equilateral, and similar triangles. (Remember?) In an equation, the symbol for congruence is $\cong$, as in angle $ABC \cong$ angle EGH.

Circles

A round figure in which all points on the outside perimeter are equidistant from the point in the center is called a **circle**. The point in the middle of a circle is called the **center**, and any line that passes through the center from one side of the circle to the other is a **diameter**. A line that extends from the center of a circle to an edge is called a **radius**, and since that distance is equal all the way around the edge of a circle, all radii (the plural of radius) of a circle are equal. For the same reason, all diameters of a circle are equal.

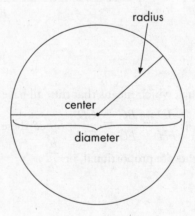

The measurement around the edge of a circle is called the **circumference** (it's called the perimeter for other shapes). All circles are similar in that they have the same proportions, just like similar triangles. The most important of these proportions is the ratio of a circle's circumference to its diameter; this ratio is always 3.1415927..., or approximately 3.14; in fraction form it is approximately $\frac{22}{7}$. This irrational, non-repeating decimal is known as **pi,** the Greek letter π. Pi is extremely important in all circle calculations. Since π expresses the ratio of the circumference to the diameter, the formula for the circumference of a circle is $c = \pi d$, in which c is the circumference and d is the diameter. This is often also depicted as $c = 2\pi r$, because the diameter is always equal to two times the radius. This second formula is sometimes easier to use because many algebraic equations refer to the radius. The area of a circle is expressed as $A = \pi r^2$, in which A is the area of a circle and r is the radius.

Let's try a problem.

List of key formulas:
$A = \pi r^2$
$C = 2\pi r$

What is the area of a circle with a diameter of 16?

A. 256π

B. 64π

C. 32π

D. 16π

Here's How to Crack It
A circle's area is found by using the formula πr^2. At this point, what ingredient are you missing? To find the radius, divide the diameter by two. In this case, the diameter is 16, and half of 16 is 8. So the formula will read $A = \pi 8^2$, or the area is equal to 64π, choice B.

Sections of Circles

A line from one edge of the circle to another that does not go through the center is called a **chord**.

Sections of a circle's actual circumference are called **arcs**. Arcs can be specified by three points along a circle's edge. Arcs of less than 180 degrees are called **minor arcs**.

The length of an arc is proportional to the arc's angle measure. For example, arc *ABD* in the circle below is opposite an angle of 30 degrees.

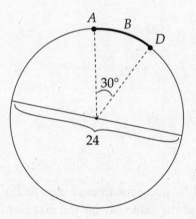

This means that the arc is $\frac{30}{360}$, or $\frac{1}{12}$ of the overall circumference, because the total circle is 360°, and the arc's angle is 30°. Since the diameter is 24, the circumference is 24π, and the length of the arc is $\frac{1}{12}$ of that, or 2π.

The surface measure of an arc is called a **sector**.

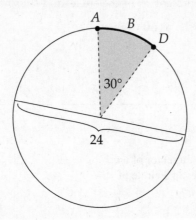

Again, the proportion of the arc to the whole circle is helpful in determining the measure of the area of a sector. Since the diameter of this circle is 24, the radius is 12, so the area is 144π. The 30 degree sector is still $\frac{1}{12}$ of the circle, so the area of the sector is $\frac{1}{12}$ of 144π, or 12π.

Area of a Sector

Is there a formula, and if so, how would you derive it? Well, another way of looking at the proportion is to put the area of the sector, or A_s, over the area of the circle like so: $\frac{A_s}{\pi r^2}$. This is the same proportion as the length of the arc over the circumference of the circle, or $\frac{s}{2\pi r}$. So, $\frac{A_s}{\pi r^2} = \frac{s}{2\pi r}$. To isolate A_s, multiply both sides by πr^2 to get $A_s = \frac{s}{2\pi r} \cdot \pi r^2$. This becomes $A_s = \frac{sr}{2}$, or the length of the arc times the radius, times one-half. And that's the formula for the area of a sector. Do you recognize any similarity to any other area formula, like maybe the one for the area of a triangle?

Of course you can use this information backwards, too. If you're given the length of an arc and the measure of a circle's circumference, you can determine the angle because the proportion is given. For instance, in a circle with circumference 6π, an arc of length π would represent $\frac{1}{6}$ of the circle, and thus have an angle measure of $\frac{1}{6}$ of the 360 degree circle, or 60 degrees.

Let's tackle a sector question.

What is the area of a sector of an angle of 20 degrees in a circle of circumference 36π?

A. 2π

B. 18π

C. 36π

D. 360π

Here's How to Crack It

Here you can use the formula for the area of a sector, which is $A_s = \frac{sr}{2}$. You need to find s, or the length of the sector (the arc part), to use the formula. You know that the sector is opposite a 20 degree angle, so the length is $\frac{20}{360}$, or $\frac{1}{18}$ of the total length of the circle. What is the length of a circle? Its circumference; in this case, 36π. Therefore, the length of the arc is $\frac{1}{18}$ times 36π, or 2π. What else do you need in the formula? The radius. Since you know the circumference is π times the diameter, you know that 36 gives you a diameter of 36π, and a radius of 18. Your formula is thus $\frac{2\pi 18}{2}$ which becomes 18π, choice B.

Another way to find the area is to find the ratio $\frac{1}{18}$ from the degree measure of the sector. Since the radius is still 18, the area of the circle is $\pi 18^2$, and you can see that the area of the sector is just $\frac{1}{18}$ of the total area of the circle. They are, essentially, the same operation, and they give you the same area measure of your sector, 18π. It's just a question of how you'd like to work through the problem.

Inscribing

People just love to place shapes inside circles. Putting a shape inside a circle so that the vertices and ends of the non-circular shape touch the inside edge of the circle is called **inscribing**.

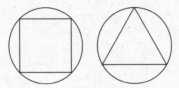

Shapes and angles can be inscribed in semicircles as well. Again, the vertices and ends of the shape or angle must touch the edge of the semicircle. An angle inscribed in a semicircle is, by definition, a right angle. All of the following angles are inscribed in a semicircle; thus they are all right angles.

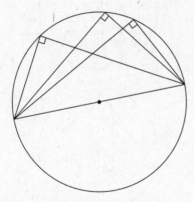

But the following angle is not inscribed in a semicircle; it's merely inside a semicircle, because all of its end points don't touch the edge of the semicircle.

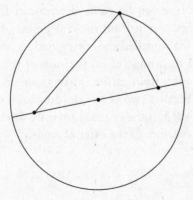

Since any angle inscribed in a semicircle is a right angle, any triangle inscribed in a semicircle is a right triangle.

Inscribed and Corresponding Angles

Angles inscribed in a semicircle are right angles due to a very cool property. An angle inscribed in a circle measures half of the angle formed by taking the ends of the original and joining them at the center.

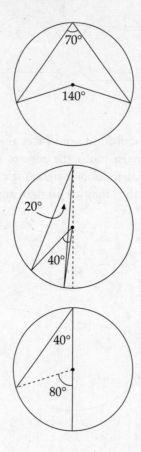

The angle formed by drawing these two new lines is called the **corresponding angle** of the inscribed angle.

The reason that this is true can be easily determined from the last figure. The angle created by the lines drawn from the end points of the first angle through the center of the circle—also called the corresponding angle—forms the exterior angle to a triangle, and thus must equal the sum of the opposite interior angles (remember this information from earlier in the chapter?). Since the triangle here is an isosceles triangle (because two of its sides are radii), the two opposite interior angles are equal; one of them is the original angle we discussed. Thus, this interior angle is one-half of the measure of the exterior angle.

Since a triangle formed from two lines drawn from the center to the edge will always be formed of two radii, you will always be dealing with an isosceles triangle of one sort or another. Take a look at what these triangles look like drawn in on the other figures; note that in the first circle two isosceles triangles are formed.

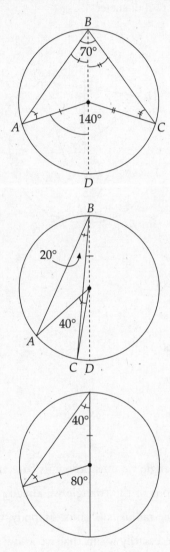

Ready for another problem?

What is the area of triangle *CDE* inscribed in a circle *C*, if diameter *FG* equals 12 units?

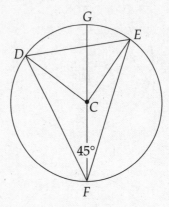

A.   12 square units

B.   18 square units

C.   24 square units

D.   34 square units

Here's How to Crack It

To find the area of the triangle we must know its base and its height. So we must determine which dimensions of the triangle we already have. Since the diameter of the circle is 12 units, the radius is 6 units. Happily, two of our triangle's sides are radii. This does not necessarily mean that we know the height of the triangle in question, though. To find the height we need a perpendicular. Look at the triangle to see what information it contains, and what the measure of angle *ECD* is. Since it's the corresponding central angle of the inscribed angle, it must be twice the inscribed angle's measure, or twice 45, which is 90 degrees. Aha! Our corresponding angle is a right angle, meaning we've got a right isosceles triangle on our hands; the two sides formed by the radii are the height and the base because of the right angle. So the area of the triangle is $\frac{1}{2}(6 \cdot 6)$, or $\frac{1}{2}(36)$, or 18 square units, choice B.

SOLID GEOMETRY

Solid Shapes

As you well know (you solid thing, you), life does not exist solely in a two-dimensional space. So it is for geometric shapes. There are those that exist in a two-dimensional plane that you just studied, and those that exist in space: three-dimensional, or solid, shapes. You're familiar with these shapes on the whole; they are extensions of the ones you encountered in plane geometry. For instance, a square extended by an edge of equal length along a third dimension is a **cube.**

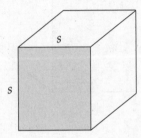

A square or rectangle extends to form a rectangular solid, also known as a **rectangular prism.** A circle in three dimensions so that every point on the outside surface is equidistant from the center is a **sphere.** An isosceles triangle turned around on its central axis forms a **cone.**

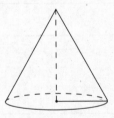

A circle lengthened through space forms a **cylinder.**

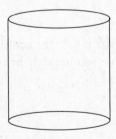

Volume

One of the important measures of a three-dimensional shape is its **volume,** which measures the three-dimensional space that it fills. While area is a measure of square units, volume is a measure of cubic units. Essentially all of the formulas for the volume of a three-dimensional figure are the same: Find the area of a two-dimensional surface of the shape, and then multiply this area by the third dimension. For instance, what is the volume of our base unit itself, the cube? The area of one **face** of the cube, which is just an ordinary square, is s^2.

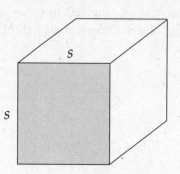

Quick Reference
Cube volume =
surface × third dimension,
or s^3

To find the volume, multiply this area by the third or additional dimension that makes it a cube (the third edge), which is also s. So, $s^2 \cdot s = s^3$. The volume of a cube is s^3.

The same principle applies to a rectangular solid.

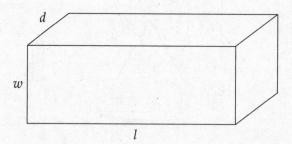

Rectangle area = lw
Rectangle volume = lwd

The area of this rectangle is lw. To find the volume of the solid then, multiply lw by the additional dimension, in this case, depth or d. So the volume of a rectangular solid is lwd.

Cylinder base = πr^2
Cylinder volume = $\pi r^2 h$

For a cylinder, the area of the base is πr^2. The additional dimension is the height of the cylinder, and that's just what you multiply by to find the volume. The volume of a cylinder is $\pi r^2 h$.

The volume of a triangular prism is the area of one face times the third dimension, just as it is in other elongated shapes.

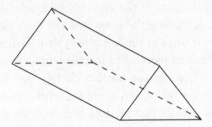

Another way of expressing it is bh, in which b is the area of the triangular base, or $\frac{1}{2}bh$.

The volume of triangular-based pyramids, cones, and spheres are a bit less easily explained. We provide the formulas here; ideas about how the formulas are derived follow in the box below.

The volume of a triangular-based pyramid is $\frac{1}{3}Bh$, in which B is the area of the base; the volume of a cone is $\frac{1}{3}\pi r^2 h$; and the volume of a sphere is $\frac{4}{3}\pi r^3$.

How Does One Find the Volume of These Shapes?

Start with finding the volume of a pyramid with a triangular base. We can do this by taking a shape we know—the triangular prism—and slicing it up to form three pyramids with triangular bases. (Try this with a piece of clay if you happen to have one lying around.) Since the triangular-based pyramids are equal thirds, the volumes are equal thirds of the volume of a triangular prism, or each pyramid formed has a volume of $\frac{1}{3}Bh$. On to the cone.

A cone's relationship to the cylinder is numerically the same as that of the triangular-based pyramid to the triangular prism, so $\frac{1}{3}\pi r^2 h$ as the area of a cone makes a lot of sense. To prove it? Well, that's related to something else; it's related to another form of proof in which the volume formulas for shapes are found by recognizing their equivalence to shapes of the same volume but different compositions. For instance, the volume of a sphere is found by imagining the sphere as a large number of equally thick disks, sliced up sort of like a hard-boiled egg.

Surface Area

Another measure of three-dimensional shapes is **surface area**. Surface area represents the entire exterior surface of an object; you can imagine it as the amount of wrapping paper needed to cover it exactly. For square and rectangular shapes, the surface area consists of the sum of the areas of the faces. This is particularly easy with a cube because each face has the same area and there are six faces; the surface area of a cube of edge s is $6s^2$. For the less obviously measured shapes, try to separate the surfaces into discreet pieces. For instance, in a cylinder the surface area is the sum of the areas of the top and bottom circles—πr^2 times 2—added to the area of the tubular section (sort of like where the label on a can of soup would go). To see how we find the area of that section, first imagine drawing a slit down its side.

For square and
rectangular shapes:
Surface area = sum of
the area of the faces

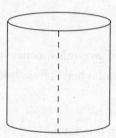

(It's a bit like peeling that soup label off the can.) You end up with a rectangle, which is also called a cylinder's **lateral area**.

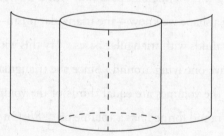

Lateral area is the area of a shape's surface, excluding its top and base. To get the area of the rectangle, multiply the base by the height. And what is the length of the base? Why, the circumference of the circle, of course.

To find the surface area of a cone, you need the area of the circle that is its base, and then the lateral area of the cone itself. The formula for this lateral area is rs, in which s is the **slant height** of the cone, measured from the vertex to an edge of the base circle.

The surface area of a sphere is $4\pi r^2$.

Now let's tackle a surface area problem.

What are the surface area and volume of
the right cylinder pictured?

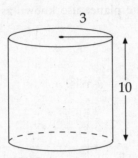

A. 13π, 10π

B. 6π, 10π

C. 60π, 90π

D. 78π, 90π

Here's How to Crack It

We'll start with the surface area simply because that's mentioned first. The area of
the top and bottom circles of the cylinder are part of the overall surface area. The
radius of these circles, which are equal, is 3. So the area of each circle is 9π (from
$A = \pi r^2$). Since there are two of them, their combined area is 18π. Now for the
cylinder's lateral area: We know from the diagram that the height is 10; the length
is the circumference of the circles that form the base and top. Since the radius of
the circle is 3, the circumference is 6π (from $c = 2\pi r$). So the area of the rectangle is 6π
times 10, or 60π. Add this to the area of the circles, which is 18π, and the entire
surface area of the figure is 78π.

As for the volume, it's simply the area of one dimension—the circle—times the
additional dimension. In this case the height of the figure is handy. The area of the
circle is 9π and the height of the cylinder is 10, so the volume is 90π. The correct
answer is choice D.

ANALYTIC GEOMETRY

Coordinating Plane

Now that you know the basic components of geometric shapes and forms, it's time to see the happy place where geometry and algebra meet. The site of this wonderful meeting is the **coordinate plane,** also known as the **Cartesian grid;** it looks like this.

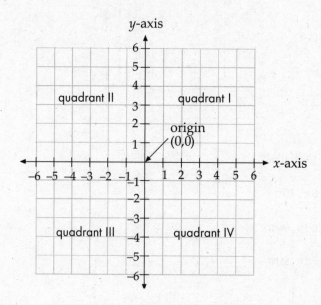

The two lines making up the center of the grid are the **axes** (pronounced ackseeze); the **y-axis** is vertical, and the **x-axis** is horizontal. The place where the two axes meet is at the 0 point on both of them; this point is called the **origin** of the graph or grid. As you can see, the axes split the space into four spaces; these spaces are called **quadrants.** The quadrants are numbered in counterclockwise fashion, starting with the upper right: Quadrants I, II, III, and IV. Grids like this are used to plot points that make up lines and shapes. It's the coordinate *plane,* after all, and planes are made up of an infinity of points. A point is also called a **coordinate pair,** because each point is identified by two coordinates, an **x-coordinate** and a **y-coordinate.** The first coordinate of a pair is the x-coordinate and the second is the y-coordinate. An example might be (3, 5). The x-coordinate of this point is 3, and the y-coordinate is 5. To locate this point on the graph, simply count over three on the x-axis—you'll move to the right to get to the positive 3—and up five on the y-axis. The point you reach is (3, 5) in quadrant I.

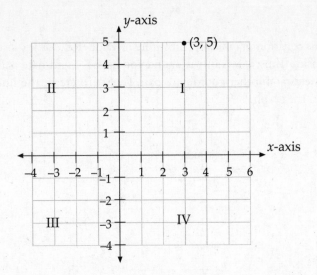

All points with two positive coordinates will be located in quadrant I. Look at the numbers on the axes to get a clear picture of this; you can also see that points in quadrant II have a negative *x*-coordinate and a positive *y*-coordinate. Points in quadrant III have two negative coordinates, and points in quadrant IV have a positive *x*-coordinate and a negative *y*-coordinate.

Lines

What happens when points are joined? They form lines, and the first kinds of lines that we are going to address are straight lines.

Linear Equations

Equations are expressed in lots of different ways. Now is the time to express them graphically. The expression of an equation is called a **graph**, or **locus.** Of course, the space they're drawn on is also sometimes called a graph. Not to worry, the context of a question will almost always show you which type of graph is referred to. The first type of equation we will attempt (and conquer, no doubt) is the **linear equation.** It's called a linear equation because it forms a straight line. Let's look at an example: $y = 3x + 2$

To express this equation graphically, substitute in values for x or y; substituting for x is probably easier. Thus, if x is 0, y is 2, and you have a coordinate pair, (0, 2). If x is 1, y is 5, yielding another coordinate pair, (1, 5). To create the line, plot these two points on the graph.

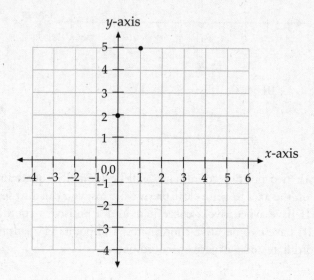

Once you have two points you have a line; simply draw through the two points. Voila. The graph of a linear equation.

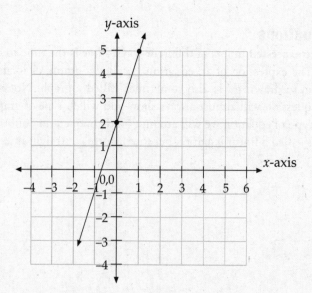

Every (x, y) pair that works in that equation $y = 3x + 2$ exists somewhere on this line.

Simultaneous Equations

When you find the values of x and y for a linear equation system, you are finding the point of intersection of two *different* lines. That's what the values of x and y that worked for both linear equations are; they are the coordinates of the point at which the lines intersect. And lines are exactly what those equations are depicting.

Slope

Slope is the measure of the steepness of a line; mathematically it's represented by the letter m. To calculate the slope of a line, put the difference between two y-coordinates over the difference between two corresponding x-coordinates:

$$m = \frac{y_2 - y_1}{x_2 - x_1}$$

The slope of the line we just graphed, $y = 3x + 2$, can be calculated by the coordinates we identified, $(0, 2)$ and $(1, 5)$. The expression of these coordinate pairs in the formula for slope is $\frac{5-2}{1-0}$, or 3. Thus, the slope of the line is 3.

There is a sneaky little shortcut for finding the slope of certain lines, though. The linear equation we've been working with here is $y = 3x + 2$ which is in the form $y = mx + b$. What is m again? Why, it's the slope. So, if you ever see a linear equation in this particular form, the slope (m) is the coefficient of x. And many times, if the equation isn't already in this form, you can put it in this form.

What is the slope of the line that is represented by the equation $y + 5 = x$?

A.   1

B.   2

C.   −1

D.   3

Here's How to Crack It

There are two ways to find the slope here: You could use the slope formula, or you could put the equation into the form $y = mx + b$. We'll try the second, easier way first, and then go through the formula for good measure. To put the equation into $y = mx + b$ form, what must you do? Well, clearly the y needs to be isolated.

Subtract 5 from both sides.

$$y + 5 - 5 = x - 5$$

This gives you $y = x - 5$. You now have the equation in $y = mx + b$ form. The coefficient for x is 1, so the slope of the line is 1, choice A.

How do we go about putting this equation into the slope formula? Well, the formula needs two coordinate pairs. The line's equation is $y + 5 = x$; if $y = 0$ then $x = 5$, and if $y = 1$ then $x = 6$. The slope formula is the difference in y-coordinates over the difference in x-coordinates. You get $\dfrac{1-0}{6-5}$, also known as 1. Pretty slick, no?

Slippery Slopes

When is a hill not a hill? When it's flat. A flat, or horizontal, line is a line whose y-coordinate is constant. All horizontal lines have the same slope: 0. That's because there is no change in y, so you have a fraction with the numerator 0, which is always equal to 0.

Vertical lines, on the other hand, have an x-coordinate which is constant. This means that they form fractions with 0 denominators, that are undefined; this means that *the slope of a vertical line is undefined.*

A positive slope indicates a line that rises to the right, and a negative slope indicates a line that falls to the right.

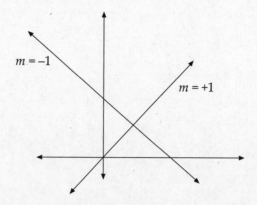

The numerical value of the slope—which is the absolute value if the slope is negative—represents the steepness of a slope and the angle that the slope makes with the x-axis. Thus, a line of slope $\dfrac{1}{2}$ is less steep than a line of slope 1, which in turn is less steep than a line of slope 2.

Parallel lines must have equal slopes, which makes sense if you think about it. So if you come across two distinct lines with the same slope, they must be parallel. Perpendicular lines, on the other hand, must have slopes that multiply together to equal −1. If you see two algebraic lines—linear equations—$y = 2x + 3$ and $y = -\dfrac{1}{2}x + 2$, you now know a geometric fact about them: They're perpendicular, because $\left(-\dfrac{1}{2}\right)(2) = -1$.

What The Heck is The *b*?

In the equation $y = mx + b$, you know that the m is the slope, and the x and y are the x- and y-coordinates. So what the heck is the b? The b is the y-intercept. The **y-intercept** is the point on a line at which it intercepts the y-axis, which is the point at which the x-coordinate equals 0. There is also an **x-intercept**; it's the point at which the line intercepts the x-axis; at which the y-coordinate equals 0. The way to find the y-coordinate if the equation isn't in the form $y = mx + b$ is to substitute $x = 0$ into the equation; this will give you the point at which the line intercepts the y-axis. To find the x-intercept, substitute in $y = 0$.

What is the x-intercept of the line
$3x - y = 2$?

A. $\dfrac{1}{3}$

B. $\dfrac{1}{2}$

C. $\dfrac{2}{3}$

D. 1

Here's How to Crack It

Well, we could put the equation into the form $y = mx + b$, but that won't help us find the x-intercept, because b represents the y-intercept. How do we find the x-intercept? We substitute in $y = 0$. We get $3x = 2$, so $x = \dfrac{2}{3}$. The line intercepts the x-axis at the point at which x equals $\dfrac{2}{3}$, choice C.

Distance

Let's say you have two points on your grid, (1, 3) and (6, 3).

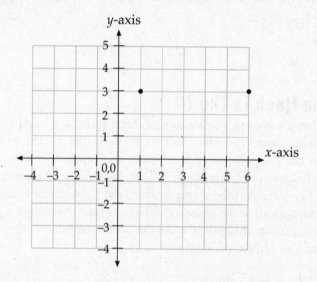

To calculate the distance between them is a fairly easy matter; just count along the x-axis, or subtract the x-coordinates, and you've found the distance between the points. What if, however, the two points did not exist along such an easily countable stretch? Take a look at these points, for instance.

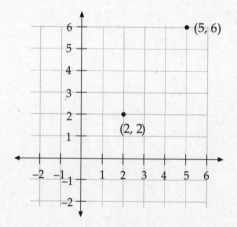

The distance between them does not appear to be so easily measured. However, there is a formula that's designed to determine the distance between two points. There seems to be a formula for everything, doesn't there? Before we get to this specific formula though, let's take a moment to see how it works.

Whenever you have two points on a graph that are not horizontally or vertically aligned, you also have the makings of a right triangle; the line between the two points forms the hypotenuse. You can see it with the two points on the grid below.

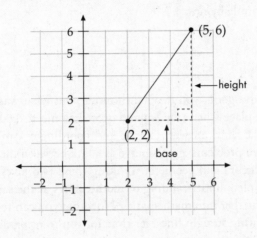

The length of this triangle's legs can be counted out: The height is 4 and the base is 3. To find the length of the hypotenuse, we fall back on that reliable old friend the Pythagorean Theorem: $a^2 + b^2 = c^2$. Thus, in this case $4^2 + 3^2 = c^2$, or $16 + 9 = c^2$, or $25 = c^2$, and $c = 5$. The distance between your two selected points is 5. The **distance formula** simply makes this process more regular; it says that $\sqrt{(x_2 - x_1)^2 + (y_2 - y_1)^2}$ represents the distance between two points, (x_1, y_1) and (x_2, y_2). As you can see, it's exactly how we treated the points above, but by giving it an algebraic formula we can fix it as a more useful truth.

Halfway There

There's one more formula that relates to lines and their equations, and you might want to have it on hand in case anyone ever asks you, "Hey, would you happen to know the midpoint of the line between two points, (x_1, y_1) and (x_2, y_2)?" And how often do you hear that one? On the CSET—you will.

The midpoint of a line between two points (x_1, y_1) and (x_2, y_2) has coordinates

$$x = \frac{x_2 - x_1}{2}, \text{ and } y = \frac{y_2 - y_1}{2}$$

Seems pretty obvious, doesn't it? Well it is. Go ahead and enjoy it, you deserve an easy and obvious formula by now.

Functions

That's all very well and good, you may be thinking, but what was all that hooey about this being the place where algebra and geometry meet? And what's the use of a graph? Here's the short answer: Graphs and coordinates can be used to express and solve algebra problems; graphs serve as a link between the two heretofore separate worlds of algebra and geometry. Linking these two gives you, the eager student, a more complete understanding of mathematics at the same time that it allows you to move further into mathematics. Now that you can recognize certain equations as representing straight lines, it's time for you to recognize another subset of equations: **functions.**

A function is an expression of one variable's dependency on another. Remember back to when you were learning to write formulas. You were expressing interrelationships among variables. For instance, *the retail price of an item is three times its wholesale price* could be expressed as $r = 3w$. The retail price is a function of the wholesale price. The circumference of a circle is a function of its diameter, as $c = \pi d$. The price of a magazine subscription is 67 percent of its newsstand price, $s = 67\%n$, and s is a function of n. All of these can correspond to the statement y is a function of x, which is expressed mathematically as $y = f(x)$. This expression does not mean that f is a quantity or that there is any multiplication going on; it indicates only that the variable y is a function of the variable x. More specifically, the value of y depends on the value of x; thus y is called the **dependent variable** and x is called the **independent variable.** This means that the value of x is assigned without reference to the value of y, and the value of y is a result of this value of x. For each possible value of x, a function presents only one possible value of y. That's important enough to put into a box.

> For each possible value of x, a function presents only one possible value of y.

Perhaps you are already seeing how functions coincide with coordinate planes. It turns out that the most common way of expressing a function is graphically, with each point of the function plotted and joined to form some kind of line. These particular graphs are the graphs of functions.

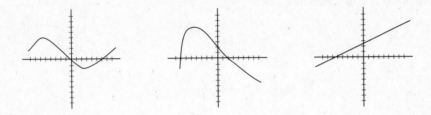

One great way to tell whether a graphed shape or line is a function is to imagine scanning it with a vertical line. If the graph has two points of intersection on a vertical line, it's not a function.

This is called the **vertical line test,** and it shows that you can get a lot of information from a graph itself.

How to Sketch a Graph

The basic way to sketch the graph of an equation, whether it's a function or anything else, is to enter values for the possible coordinates, just as you would with the equation for an ordinary line. For function equations, since the y is dependent, it's easiest to enter values for x and then find the value of y that results. Thus, for the function $f(x) = 3x^3 + 2$, if x is 0, y is 2, and the first plotted point is (0, 2). Enter other values for x, such as x is –1, which means that $y = -1$; then x is 1, which means that $y = 5$; and x is –2, which sends y down and off of the part of our coordinate plane that is visible.

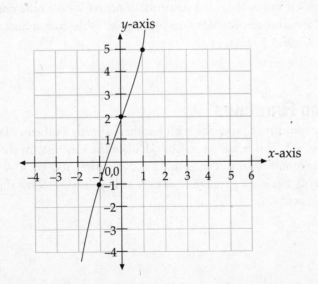

Then draw a line connecting the dots—see, it's almost like a game—in the line or curve that seems appropriate. The more points there are, the easier it is to see the exact shape, but as you become familiar with the shapes that show up over and over, you'll see that usually, even having a few points is enough.

We can express the graph of the function $r = 3w$ (discussed above) on the coordinate plane as a function of x where $y = f(x) = 3x$.

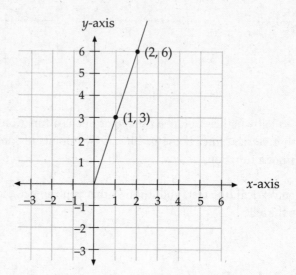

We usually use x and y in order to lend some consistency, though functions can use any letters they care to for variables. For instance, the function itself could be expressed as $r = g(w) = 3w$ or $y = t(x) = 3x$ or just $f(x) = 3x$; if the question makes it clear that you're dealing with a function, it doesn't matter what particular variables are used. The more important issue is being able to tell which of the variables is the dependent variable and which is independent.

The set of possible values for x of a particular function is called the **domain** of the function, and the set of all possible values for x as well as the corresponding values for y is called the **range** of a function.

Evaluating Functions

Functions are sometimes expressed with numbers already in them, like so: $f(4)$ in which $f(x) = x^3 + 2$. This is asking you to calculate the function for the number 4; simply put the number 4 into the formula and evaluate. You get $4^3 + 2$, which is 66. So $f(4)$ is 66. Evaluating functions is easy as long as you follow the directions given and take your time.

MEASUREMENT

The American Measurement System

The **United States Customary System** for measurement is the most widely used measurement system in (not surprisingly) the United States. It originated from the British imperial system of measurement. Although the Metric System discussed later is widely used in other parts of the world, the Customary System remains most popular in the United States.

Linear Measurements

1 foot (ft.)	=	12 inches (in.)
3 feet (ft.)	=	1 yard (yd.)
1 mile	=	1,760 yards

Area Measurements

1 square foot (sq. ft.)	=	144 square inches (sq. in.)
1 square yard (sq. yd.)	=	9 square feet
1 acre	=	4,840 square yards
1 square mile	=	640 acres

Cubic Measurements

1 cubic foot (cu. ft.)	=	1,728 cubic inches
1 cubic yard (cu. yd.)	=	27 cubic feet

METRICS

The **Metric System** is a decimal system of measurement. Metric units are widely used around the world for personal, commercial, and scientific purposes. A standard set of prefixes in powers of ten may be used to note larger and smaller units. Common notations include the following examples.

Linear Metric Measurements

1,000 meters (m)	=	1 kilometer (km)
1.0 meter	=	1 meter
0.1 meter	=	1 decimeter (dm)
.01 meter	=	1 centimeter (cm)
.001 meter	=	1 millimeter (mm)

Mass Measurements

1,000 grams (g)	=	1 kilogram (kg)
1.0 gram	=	1 gram
.001 gram	=	1 milligram (mg)

Volume Measurements

1,000 milliliters (ml)	=	1 liter (l)
1 deciliter (dl)	=	100 ml; 10 cl
1 centiliter (cl)	=	10 ml

KEY TERMS

points
lines
degree
line segments
plane
parallel lines
angles
vertical angles
perpendicular
right angle
supplementary
complementary
alternate interior angles
rule of alternate interior angles
obtuse
acute
quadrilateral
area
base
height
perimeter
triangle
rule of 180
equilateral triangle
isosceles triangle
exterior angle
interior angle
right triangle
hypotenuse
legs
Pythagorean Theorem
special right triangles
45-45-90 triangle
30-60-90 triangle
similar triangles
congruent
circle
center
diameter
radius
circumference

pi
chord
arc
minor arc
sector
inscribing
corresponding angle
cube
rectangular prism
sphere
cone
cylinder
volume
face
surface area
lateral area
slant height
coordinate plane (Cartesian grid)
axes
y-axis
x-axis
origin
quadrants
coordinate pair
x-coordinate
y-coordinate
graph (locus)
linear equation
slope
y-intercept
x-intercept
distance formula
functions
dependent variable
independent variable
vertical line test
domain
range
United States Customary System
Metric System

Drill #14

Each group of questions below is followed by four suggested answers or completions. Select the one that is best in each case.

1. How many degrees is angle *b*?

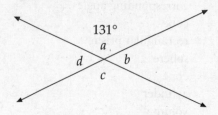

    A.   131°

    B.   90°

    C.   49°

    D.   30°

2. What is the area of a triangle with a base of 2 and a height of 4?

    A.   2

    B.   4

    C.   8

    D.   12

3. What is the measure of *x* if the broken line is parallel to the base?

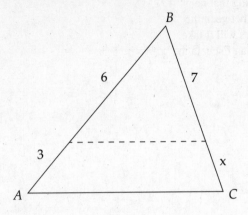

A. 3.5

B. 7

C. 9

D. 16

4. What is the perimeter of the figure below?

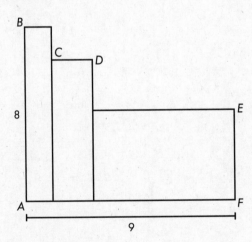

A. 17

B. 33

C. 34

D. 72

5. It is 260 miles between Santa Escuela and Santa Novia. Mr. Lewis drives 40 miles per hour. Assuming that he takes the most direct path between the two cities, how many hours will it take Mr. Lewis to drive from San Escuela to Santa Novia?

    A.   5 hours

    B.   5.5 hours

    C.   6 hours

    D.   6.5 hours

Please turn the page for answers and explanations
for the questions in this drill.

ANSWERS AND EXPLANATIONS TO DRILL #14

1. **B** Remember that one side of a line is 180 degrees total. You know that quadrants *a* and *b* must total 180 degree and you know that quadrant *a* meaures 131 degrees. Now do some simple subtraction: $180 - 131 = 49$ degrees, choice C.

2. **B** Think of the formula for the area of a triangle: $\frac{1}{2} bh$. The base is 2, height is 4, giving us 8. Take half of this for the correct answer, 4 (choice B).

3. **A** These are similar triangles and we know that the sides of similar triangles are proportional. You must use the bowtie method and you get

    $$\frac{6}{6+3} = \frac{7}{7+x}$$

    Cross multiply to get $63 = 42 + 6x$

    Then subtract 42 from both sides, so

    $6x = 21$
    $x = 3.5$

4. **C** Remember that the perimeter is simply the sum of the lengths of the sides of the figure. We know that *AB* is 8; we don't know the measurements of the other vertical lines, but added together, these will sum to 8. (If you can't see this, draw the two lines together—they cover the same distance as segment *AB*). The same is true with the horizontal lines. *AF* is 9 and the two other segments must sum to 9. Thus, the perimeter of the figure is $8 + 9 + 8 + 9 = 34$, choice C.

5. **D** Divide the total number of miles (260) by the number of miles he can drive in one hour (40). 260 divided by 40 is 6.5 hours, choice D.

Summary

- Plane geometry happens in a two-dimensional space, extending in all directions.

- Parallel lines extend infinitely and never meet.

- A quadrilateral is a closed, two-dimensional shape.

- The area of a quadrilateral is base × height.

- The perimeter of a shape is found by adding the length of all sides.

- The area of a triangle is $\frac{1}{2}$ base × height.

- An equilateral triangle has three equal sides.

- An isosceles triangle has two sides that are exactly equal.

- A right triangle has one right angle.

- The hypotenuse of a triangle is the side opposite the right angle. The formula for calculating the hypotenuse is $a^2 + b^2 = c^2$, when a and b are the legs that form the 90 degree angle.

- Triangles of the exact same size are called congruent triangles.

- In a circle, the line that goes from the center to one edge is the radius. Two radii make the diameter of the circle, and the circumference is the measurement of the circle's outside edge.

- The area of a circle is pi × radius^2

- Shapes that exist in space are said to be three-dimensional, or solid, shapes.

- Examples of solid shapes include cubes, spheres, and cones.

- Volume is the space that a three-dimensional shape fills.

- The volume of a rectangular solid is length × width × depth.

o   Surface area is another important measurement of three-dimensional shapes.

o   The coordinate plane is where geometry and algebra come together.

o   The two systems of measurement with which you should be familiar are the United States Customary System and the Metric System.

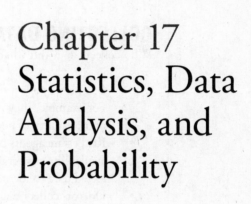

Chapter 17
Statistics, Data Analysis, and Probability

COLLECTION, ORGANIZATION, AND REPRESENTATION OF DATA

Statistics is a science of data. We all use data to estimate unknown quantities, to make decisions, and to develop and implement policies. To draw any sensible conclusions from collected data, we need to summarize the data or examine the patterns that it forms. This chapter begins with a discussion of graphical and numerical methods used to study data.

COLLECTING DATA

Who collects data and what do they do with collected data?

- Businesses collect data on their products and on consumer behavior. For example, they might use the collected data to determine the marketability of new products.
- Real estate agents collect data on market trends and on the availability of certain types of properties. They might use the collected data to identify popular locations for first-time home buyers.
- Doctors collect diagnostic data on their patients. They might use collected data to identify the appropriate treatment for a patient.
- Police collect data on criminal behavior and the frequency of certain crimes. They might use the collected data to determine where to increase police patrols.

Data is rarely collected in a form that is immediately useful for decision making. For example, imagine that a polling group was conducting a telephone survey to estimate the percent of state residents in favor of the governor's new proposal. Five interviewers called a total of 1,800 residents over a period of five days and recorded the result for each resident as "supports" or "does not support." So at the completion of the survey, the polling group had a list of 1,800 responses listed as "supports" or "does not support." What can we say based on the data? Unfortunately, nothing—until somebody takes the time to organize it.

TYPES OF VARIABLES

There are two types of variables: **categorical** and **continuous**. A variable is categorical if it can take on only a fixed number of values. Some examples of categorical data are sex (male or female) and eye color.

A variable is continuous if it can take on any value. Some examples of continuous variables are age, height, and weight. In practice, variables that can take on a great many values are often treated as continuous: For example, IQ can take on any value between about 40 and 200. Technically, that is a fixed number of values, but it is so large that methods for continuous variables can be used. Different methods of analysis must be used for the categorical and continuous variables.

If we take only one measurement on each object, we get **univariate data.** With two measurements on each object, we get **bivariate data.** For example, measuring the heights of a group of children will result in a *univariate* data set of the heights of the children. On the other hand, if we measure the height and the weight of each child, then we will get a *bivariate* data set consisting of the heights and weights of the children.

TYPES OF DESCRIPTIVE METHODS

To use collected data, it needs to be organized and summarized. The different methods for doing this are known as **descriptive methods.** Different descriptive methods might result in different outcomes, leading to different conclusions. Descriptive methods are useful for data presentation, data reduction, and summarization. The best method depends on the type of data being collected.

Descriptive methods are divided into three basic categories:

- numerical methods
- tabular methods
- graphical methods

Different descriptive methods answer different questions about data. Naturally, different questions have different answers. In general, we cannot look at data from all possible angles using only one method. So it's best to use more than one method when we're summarizing a data set, even if the different methods produce some overlap of information.

Numerical, tabular, and graphical methods complement each other. **Numerical methods** are precise and can be used in a wide variety of ways for statistical inference; however, they are full and can be overwhelming. **Tabular methods** allow us to find precise values, but are not as good for grasping relationships among variables. **Graphical methods** allow us to view a large amount of data and a large number of relationships at once, but they are not precise and are often abused.

NUMERICAL METHODS

There are three types of numerical measures:

- measures of central tendency
- measures of variation (spread)
- measures of position

Measures of Central Tendency

Measures of central tendency determine the central point of a variable or the point around which all the measurements are scattered. The two main measures of central tendency are the mean and the median. We'll discuss these further below.

Measures of Variation (Spread)

Measures of variation are also known as measures of spread, and they summarize the spread of a data set. They describe how measurements differ from each other and/or from their mean. This category includes range, which we'll discuss below.

Measures of Position

More Review

For more statistics review, check out *Cracking the AP Statistics Exam* from The Princeton Review.

The **measures of position** are used to describe the position of a value with respect to the rest of the values of the variable. Quartiles, percentiles, and standardized scores are the most commonly used measures of position. Fortunately, these concepts are more in-depth than the CSET will test, so don't worry about them. Let's focus on the basics.

Here's a quick basics review using a sample set of numbers:

2, 3, 5, 8, 10, 13, 13, 17

The **range** of a data set is the difference between the lowest and highest value in a set. In the set above, that is $17 - 2$, which is 15.

The **mean** of a data set is the sum of the data set divided by the number of items in the data set—in short, the average. In this set, the mean is 8.875 (71 divided by 8).

The **median** of a data set is the midpoint of the number range. You can find the median by ordering the data from lowest value to highest value and picking the middle one. If there is an even number of items in the data set, then there is no single middle value. In such cases, the median is defined to be the mean of the two middle values. In this set, that value is 9.

The **mode** of a data set is the value that occurs most frequently. In this set, that value is 13.

TABULAR METHODS

Collected data generally need to be rearranged before analysis. One tabular method is the frequency distribution table. This table facilitates the analysis of patterns of variation among observed data. Typically, the letter n is used to denote the number of observations in a data set.

- The **frequency** of a value is the number of times that observation occurs. Frequency is usually denoted by the letter f.

- The **relative frequency** of a value is the ratio of the frequency (f) to the total number of observations (n). It is usually denoted by rf, and $rf = \dfrac{f}{n}$.

- The **cumulative frequency** gives the number of observations less than or equal to a specified value. It is usually denoted by cf.

A **frequency distribution table** is a table giving all possible values of a variable and their frequencies. The values can be reported in one of two manners: grouped or ungrouped. Additionally, other columns—such as relative frequency, cumulative frequency, the midpoints of groups, and so on—may be added to the frequency distribution table as needed. If the values are reported as they occur, giving a list of all values, then the table is an **ungrouped frequency distribution table.** If the data points are grouped by some scheme into certain categories, also known as **classes,** then the table is a **grouped frequency distribution table.** Let's use grades on an exam as an example.

Ungrouped		Grouped	
Grade	**Frequency**	**Grade**	**Frequency**
100	1	95–100	2
99	1	90–94	3
93	1	85–89	6
92	2	80–84	0
88	3	75–79	0
87	1	70–74	1
85	2		
71	1		

Frequency Distribution Tables

Each group or class is defined by an **upper limit** and a **lower limit.** Values above the lower limit and below the upper limit fall within the group. The point that is halfway between the two endpoints of the class is known as the **class mark,** or **midpoint.**

When we group values, we must define groups so that the entire range of data is covered and so that there are no overlapping groups. For example, consider the following groups used by one teacher to assign letter grades on tests:

Letter Grade	Score on Test
A	90 and above
B	80–87
C	70–82
D	60–69
F	Below 60

Poor Grouping Scheme

Several things are wrong with this grouping scheme:

- No grade is assigned to those who score 88 and 89 on the test. These scores seem to have been forgotten.
- Those who score 80, 81, and 82 will get a B as well as a C. This can't be right!

Here are some guidelines on how to avoid such mistakes while grouping values:

- Groups should not overlap.
- There should be no gaps between groups. However, it is possible that no values will be present for a certain group. The frequency for that group would be 0.
- Groups should cover the entire range of data. No data points should be left out.

It is not essential that all groups be of equal length, as long as the varying group lengths are taken into account when comparing different data sets and making decisions. For example, suppose three teachers are using the following schemes to assign letter grades:

Letter Grade	Score on Test		
	Teacher I	Teacher II	Teacher III
A	Above 90	Above 90	Above 90
B	80–89	76–89	76–89
C	70–79	61–75	61–75
D	60–69	40–60	40–60
F	Below 60	Below 40	Below 40

Grouping Scheme with Multiple Groups

Note that grade distributions for Teachers I and II will not be easy to compare, because the teachers used different grouping schemes. Although Teachers II and III are using unequal group sizes, both of them are using the same grouping scheme. Therefore, the grade distributions for Teachers II and III will be easy to compare.

Let's try a sample problem.

○

The Student Government Association (SGA) at a university was interested in how much students spend per month on housing. Because students who live in dorms pay a fixed housing fee per semester, it was decided not to include those students in the study. The SGA selected a sample of students living off campus and collected data on their housing type and on the amount they spent per month on housing. The collected information is listed in the table below. The columns titled "Exp" (for "Expenditure") give the amount each student spent per month on housing (in dollars). The columns titled "Type" give the type of housing for each student, classified as

A = Apartment   C = Condominium   H = House   T = Townhouse

Exp	Type	Exp	Type	Exp	Type	Exp	Type	Exp	Type	Exp	Type	Exp	Type	Exp	Type
304	C	323	H	529	T	482	A	406	H	628	T	259	C	330	A
342	A	350	A	358	A	423	A	440	H	333	A	424	H	595	C
437	A	349	A	278	A	530	A	384	H	327	A	529	H	383	C
446	A	384	H	482	H	404	H	391	T	581	A	466	H	437	C
362	C	394	A	270	A	393	A	501	T	398	T	834	T	416	C
552	H	296	C	462	H	450	C	550	T	516	T	558	A	351	T
411	C	435	A	503	A	364	T	306	T	478	T	332	C	385	T
330	C	334	A	367	A	264	A	450	H	358	H	317	H	376	T
673	H	525	T	353	H	276	A	309	C	439	H	430	A	408	C
309	H	391	A	760	A	297	T	255	T	377	A	282	T	385	A

Housing Expenditure (in $) and Type of Housing Data

These numbers are useless unless we rearrange and summarize them in a meaningful fashion. Note that data were collected for two variables, namely type of housing and housing expenditure per month. Type of housing is a *categorical* variable and housing expenditure is a *quantitative* variable.

One possible grouped frequency distribution table for housing expenditure is as follows:

Housing Expenditure ($)	Frequency f	Relative Frequency rf=f/n	Percentage 100 rf	Cumulative Frequency cf
250–299	9	0.11	11	9
300–349	14	0.17	17	23
350–399	20	0.25	25	43
400–449	14	0.17	17	57
450–499	7	0.09	9	64
500–549	7	0.09	9	71
550–599	5	0.06	6	76
600–649	1	0.01	1	77
650–699	1	0.01	1	78
700–749	0	0.00	0	78
750–799	1	0.01	1	79
800–849	1	0.01	1	80

Frequency Distribution for Housing Expenditure

Here are some things you should notice about this table:

- Housing expenditures are grouped into different classes. For the class "400–449," the number 400 defines the lower limit and the number 449 defines the upper limit.
- All classes are of length equal to 50.
- The class mark is the halfway point for each class. For class "400–449," the class mark is 424.5.
- The numbers in the frequency column add up to the total number of observations, $n = 80$.
- The numbers in the relative frequency column add up to 0.98. This is due to rounding-off errors. Although the total is not exactly 1, it is very close.
- The numbers in the percentage column add up to 98. As with the proportions, the total should be very close to 100.
- The last entry in the cumulative frequency column is equal to the total number of observations, $n = 80$.

What do the numbers in this table mean? Here are some examples:

- The frequency for group 300–349 is 14. This means that 14 students of those interviewed spend $300 to $349 per month on housing.
- The relative frequency for group 300–349 is 0.17 and the percentage is 17. This means that 17 percent of students interviewed spend $300 to $349 per month on housing.
- The cumulative frequency for group 300–349 is 23. This means that 23 of the students interviewed spend less than or equal to $349 per month.

The frequency distribution table for housing type is as follows:

Type of Housing	Frequency f	Relative Frequency rf = f/n	Percentage 100 rf
Apartment	29	0.36	36
Condominium	14	0.18	18
House	19	0.24	24
Townhouse	18	0.23	23

Frequency Distribution for Housing Type

Notice the following facts from this table:

- The figures in the frequency column add up to the total number of observations, $n = 80$.
- The figures in the relative frequency column add up to 1.01. This is another example of rounding-off error. Although the total is not exactly 1, it is very close.
- The figures in the percentage column add up to 101.
- For this categorical variable, there is no sensible ordering of values. So, cumulative frequency is meaningless.

We can interpret the numbers in this table as follows:

- The frequency for Apartment is 29. This means that 29 of the students interviewed live in apartments.
- The relative frequency for Apartment is 0.36 and the percentage is 36. This means that 36 percent of students interviewed live in apartments.

GRAPHICAL METHODS FOR QUALITATIVE DATA

Presenting data in tables is not always useful and will rarely give a full picture of the data. Almost every statistical problem will benefit from good charts and graphs. With today's technology, it has become much easier to generate useful charts and graphs. To summarize and describe qualitative data, bar charts are particularly useful. Pie charts are frequently used but are not recommended. To summarize and describe quantitative data, dotplots, boxplots, histograms, stemplots, and cumulative frequency charts are often employed.

Examining Graphs

We can describe the overall pattern of the distribution of a quantitative variable set using the following three terms:

- The **center** of a distribution describes the point around which the data points are spread.
- The **spread** of a distribution describes how the data points are spread, using the range of data values and the vastness or narrowness of the spread.
- The **shape** of a distribution can be described in a few different ways. Some distributions have simple shapes; others are more irregular. Some basic shapes of distribution are described by the idea of symmetry. Here are the classifications:

   Symmetric distribution. If one half of the distribution is approximately a mirror image of the other half, then the distribution is described as symmetric. In other words, a symmetric distribution has the same number of observations on its greater half as it does on its lesser half.

   Left-skewed distribution. If the lesser half of the distribution extends further out than its greater half, then the distribution is described as left-skewed. In other words, a left-skewed distribution has a longer left tail than right tail. There are more observations with higher values than there are with lower values. The distribution of scores on an easy exam is generally left-skewed, because there will be more students with higher scores and fewer with lower scores.

   Right-skewed distribution. If the greater half of a distribution extends further out than its lesser half, then the distribution is described as right-skewed. In other words, a right-skewed distribution has a longer right tail than left tail. The distribution of scores on a difficult test is generally right-skewed, because there will be more students with lower scores and fewer with higher scores.

The following three graphs show three basic shapes of distributions.

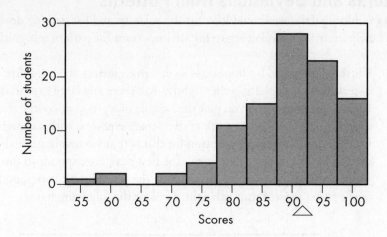

Left-Skewed Distribution

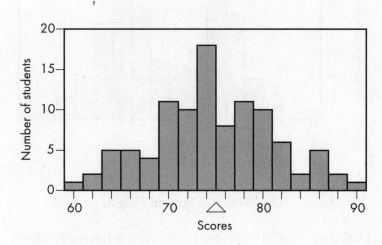

Symmetric Distribution

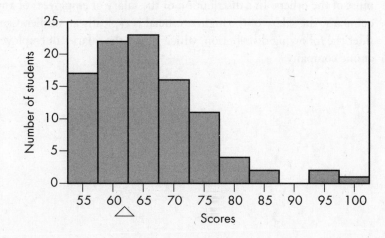

Right-Skewed Distribution

Patterns and Deviations from Patterns

When examining data, we should look for the patterns and for striking deviations from those patterns. The following terms are important for pattern recognition:

- **Clusters and gaps.** It's important to describe clusters and gaps. Are observations grouped together tightly? Are there any large gaps in the values? For example, if you plot the heights of a group of college students, the plot is likely to peak at two separate points, with a trough (or valley) in between. The reason for this is that women in general tend to be a bit shorter than men. The first peak corresponds to the women's most common height, whereas the second peak corresponds to the men's most common height. Look at the following figure:

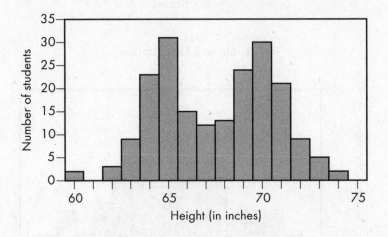

Distribution of Student Heights

- **Outliers.** An outlier is an observation that is surprisingly different from the rest of the data. For example, imagine a class in which most of the students scored between 60 and 98 on a test. But one student scored 18. This score is an outlier, because it's so much different from most of the others. In a distribution of the salary of employees of any company, the salary of the highest official is typically an outlier. Consider the following distribution, which shows the salaries of employees at one company:

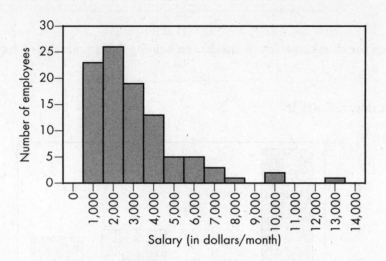

Distribution of Salaries

Note that the distribution is highly right-skewed. A few employees on the higher end earn much more than the rest of the employees. Those higher observations are outliers, because they deviate so much from the rest.

Graphical Methods for Categorical Data: Bar Charts and Pie Charts

Bar Charts

Bar charts are very common. Economists use them to display financial data. The business section of any newspaper usually has at least one bar chart. A bar chart can have either horizontal or vertical bars.

This is how to make a bar chart:

- Draw horizontal (*x*) and vertical (*y*) axes.
- On the horizontal axis, mark the categories of the variable at equal intervals.
- Scale the vertical axis in order to plot frequencies, relative frequencies, or percentages.
- Note that the above three steps would result in a vertical bar chart. For a horizontal bar chart, transpose the *x*-axis and *y*-axis.
- For each category, draw a bar whose height (or whose length, for horizontal bars) is equal to the data plotted, frequency, relative frequency, percentage, and so on.

Let's make one now.

Create a bar chart summarizing the data on housing type in the table on page 419.

Here's How to Crack It

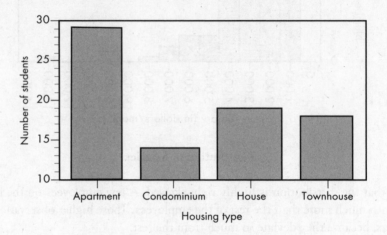

Bar Chart for Type of Housing Data

The bar chart above clearly shows that an apartment is the most popular type of accommodation among these students. There's not much difference in popularity between houses and townhouses, with houses leading townhouses by a narrow margin. The fewest students live in condominiums.

How do we read a bar chart?

- Each bar indicates a different category.
- The height of a frequency bar chart indicates how often that category occurred in the data set. For example, the first bar in the bar chart shown in the preceding figure corresponds to "Apartment." The height of this graph can be read off the vertical axis as 29. This means that 29 students out of all those interviewed live in apartments.

Pie Charts

A **pie chart** displays the groups formed by a data set. It is commonly used to describe the different spending categories of a budget, for example. Businesses use pie charts to display the various components of their entire production output. For example, a paper company producing copying paper, notebook paper, trifolds, and so on, could use a pie chart to describe what proportion of its entire production is made up by each of these products. While popular, they are rarely, if ever, the best method of displaying data, and have been shown to be misleading and hard to read accurately.

This is how to make a pie chart:

- Prepare a frequency distribution table.
- Compute the percentages for each category.
- Equate one percentage point to an angle of 3.6 degrees. For each category, compute angle = 3.6 × percentage.
- Draw a circle of the desired size and then draw one radius within the circle to be used as a starting point.
- Form "slices" of the pie with sizes equal to the corresponding angles computed earlier.
- Go all the way around the circle.

Let's practice.

Create a pie chart summarizing the housing type data in the table on page 419.

Here's How to Crack It
We already created a frequency distribution table on page 421. Now take those percentages and give each percentage point an angle of 3.6 degrees and create the slices.

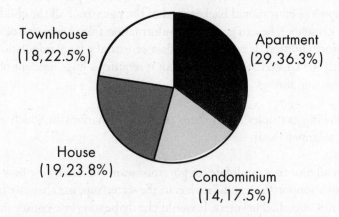

Pie Chart for Housing Type (Frequency, Percentage)

This pie chart shows clearly that the highest percent of students lives in apartments.

How do we read a pie chart?

- Each piece of the pie corresponds to one category.
- The category corresponding to the largest piece is the one that occurs most often.

PLANNING A STUDY

If you want to draw valid conclusions from a study, you must collect the data according to a well-developed plan. This plan must include the question or questions to be answered, as well as an appropriate method of data collection and analysis. This section discusses various techniques for planning a study.

Terms and Concepts

- A **population** is the entire group of individuals or items that we are interested in.
- A **frame** is a list of all members of the population—for example, a list of all account holders in a bank or a list of participants in the Boston Marathon in the year 2010.
- A **sample** is the part of the population that is actually being examined.
- A **sample survey** is the process of collecting information from a sample. Information obtained from the sample is usually used to make inferences about population parameters.
- A **census** is the process of collecting information from all the units in a population. It is feasible to do a census if the population is small and the process of getting information does not destroy or modify units of the population. For example, if a school principal wants to know the educational background of the parents of all the children in his school, he can gather this information from every one of the school children. It is possible to do a census of a large population, as with the United States Census, but it requires a huge amount of work, time, and money.

As the following examples show, there are many situations in which a census is impossible or impractical:

- An advisor to a candidate for governor wants to determine how much support his candidate has in the state. Suppose the state has 4,000,000 eligible voters. It would clearly be too time-consuming to contact each and every voter in this state, and even if it were accomplished, by the time the census was finished, the level of support for the candidate might have changed.
- Suppose an environmentalist is interested in determining the amount of toxins in a lake. Using a census would mean emptying the lake and testing all the water in the lake—obviously not a good way to gather information!
- A manufacturer of lightbulbs is interested in determining the mean lifetime of 60-watt bulbs produced by his factory. Using a census would mean burning all the lightbulbs produced in the factory and measuring their lifetimes. Again, a census would not be practical here.

Clearly, a census is often too costly or too time-consuming, and sometimes damaging to the population being studied. We usually have to take samples instead. How to get those samples is the subject of this section.

Experiments and Observational Studies

An **experiment** is a planned activity that results in measurements (data or observations). In an experiment, the experimenter *creates* differences in the variables involved in the study and then observes the effects of such differences on the resulting measurements. For example, suppose a team of engineers at an automotive factory runs cars at different predetermined and controlled speeds and then crashes the cars at a specific site. Then, the engineers measure the damage to the cars' bumpers. In this example, the team of engineers *creates* the differences in the environment by running the cars at different speeds.

An **observational study** is an activity in which the experimenter *observes* the relationships among variables rather than creating them. For example, suppose an engineering student collects information from car accident reports filed by the local police department. The reports tell the student how fast the cars were traveling when the crashes occurred and how much damage was done to the cars' bumpers. In this example, the experimenter (the student) has no control over the speed of the car. The student observes the differences in speeds as recorded in the reports and the results of the crashes as measured by the amount of damage to the bumpers.

Experiments have some advantages which we describe below, but unfortunately, in some situations it is impossible, impractical, or unethical to conduct an experiment. Sometimes we must instead use an observational study. Here are some examples:

- To study the effect of smoking on people's lungs, an experiment would require that the experimenter get one group of people to smoke and another group not to smoke. But it is clearly unethical to ask some people to smoke so that the damage to their lungs can be measured, and it may not be possible to force a smoker to quit.
- Certain inherited traits affect patients' reaction to medicine. However, it is not possible to create different genetic traits in different patients; they are born with those traits. An experiment in this situation would be impossible.

One of the problems with observational studies is that their results often cannot be generalized to a population because many observational studies use samples (such as volunteers or hospitalized patients) that aren't representative of the population of interest. These samples might simply be easiest to obtain. This problem can be solved by observing hospitalized as well as nonhospitalized patients. Another problem is that of **confounding factors.** Confounding occurs when the two variables of interest are related to a third variable instead of just to each other. For instance, in a study of elementary school children, taller students know more words. The confounding factor here is age; taller students are older, and older students know more words.

PLANNING AND CONDUCTING SURVEYS

Getting Samples

There are many methods of getting a sample from the population. Some sampling methods are better than the others. **Biased sampling** methods result in values that are systematically different from the population values, or systematically favor certain outcomes. Judgmental sampling, samples of convenience, and volunteer samples are some of the methods that generally result in biased outcomes. Sampling methods that are based on a probabilistic selection of samples, such as simple random sampling, generally result in unbiased outcomes.

Biased Samples

Judgmental sampling makes use of a nonrandom approach to determine which item of the population is to be selected in the sample. The approach is entirely based on the judgment of the person selecting the sample. For example, jury selection from an available pool of jurors is not a random process. Lawyers from both parties use their judgment to decide who shall be selected. The result may be a biased jury—that is, a selection of jurors with specific opinions.

Using a **sample of convenience** is another method that can result in biased outcomes. Samples of convenience are easy to obtain. For example, suppose a real estate agent wants to estimate the mean selling price of houses in a Chicago suburb. To save time, he looks up the selling prices of houses sold in the last three months in the subdivision where he lives. Using his own subdivision may have saved him time, but the sample is not representative of all the houses in that suburb.

Volunteer samples, in which the subjects choose to be part of the sample, may also result in biased outcomes. For example, imagine that a local television station decides to do a survey about a possible tax increase to support the local school system. A telephone number is provided and respondents are asked to call and register their opinions by pressing 1 if they support the tax increase and 2 if they oppose it. The television station then counts the number of 1s and 2s to determine the degree of support for the tax increase. But the station may well have inadvertently introduced bias into the results. Only those who feel very strongly about the tax increase (either for or against) are likely to call the number and register their opinions, so the sample may not reflect the true feelings of the whole population.

Simple Random Sampling

Simple random sampling is a process of obtaining a sample from a population in which each member has an equal chance of being selected. In this type of sample there is no bias or preference for one individual over another. Simple random samples, also known just as "random samples," are obtained in two different ways:

1. **Sampling with replacement from a finite population.** An example is the process of selecting cards from a deck, provided that you return each card before the next is drawn. With this scheme, the chance of selection remains the same for all cards drawn—1 out of 52. If you didn't replace the first card before drawing the second, then the chance of selecting a particular second card would be higher (1 out of 51) than the chance of selecting the first one (1 out of 52). When two cards are drawn with replacement, the probability of selecting two cards is $(1/52)(1/52) = 0.0003698$, and is the same regardless of the cards selected.

2. **Sampling without replacement from an infinite population** (or a population that is simply very large compared to the sample size). An example is selecting 2 voters from a list of 200,000 registered voters in a city. Here the population size (200,000) is quite large compared to the sample size (2). Note that when you're sampling without replacement, the available population size decreases as you continue sampling, but because the population size is so large compared to the sample size, the change in the chance of a particular person getting selected is negligible for practical purposes. The chance of selecting the first voter is 1 out of 200,000 (that is, 0.000005). Because the sample is being selected without replacement, the chance of selecting the second voter increases slightly, to 1 out of 199,999 (that is 0.000005000025). But this isn't much of a difference.

To select a simple random sample from a population, we need to use some kind of chance mechanism. Here are some examples:

- Offer prizes at a baseball game. A portion of each ticket collected at the stadium entrance is put into a large box. About halfway through the game, all the ticket stubs in the box are mixed thoroughly. Then a pre-specified number of ticket stubs are picked from the box. The persons sitting in the selected seats (as identified by the ticket stubs) receive prizes.
- A teacher asks each student in a class of 40 to write his or her name on a separate (but identical) piece of paper and drop it into a box. The teacher then mixes thoroughly all the pieces in the box and selects one piece at random, without looking at the name. The student whose name appears on the selected piece of paper is designated as the class representative.
- A teacher wants to select about half of the students in the class for a project, so she asks each student to toss a coin. Those whose tosses result in "heads" are selected for the project.

- A kindergarten teacher wants to select five children to perform a song at the holiday party. The teacher puts two kinds of lollipops in a jar, five of them red and the rest green. He then asks each child to take one lollipop from the jar without looking at it. The five children that pick a red lollipop are selected to sing.

The same random result can be achieved by using **random number tables.** A portion of a random number table is given below:

96410	96335	55249	16141	61826	57992	21382	33971	12082	91970
26284	92797	33575	94150	40006	54881	13224	03812	70400	45585
75797	18618	90593	54825	64520	78493	92474	32268	07392	73286
48600	65342	08640	78370	10781	58660	77819	79678	67621	74961
82468	15036	79934	76903	48376	09162	51320	84504	39332	26922

To demonstrate the use of random number tables, let us again consider the example of the kindergarten teacher. He could number the children using two digit numbers: 01, 02, 03, …, 50. He would then start anywhere in the random number table and read each pair of numbers sequentially (it doesn't matter whether he reads vertically or horizontally). But the teacher is selecting from only 50 children. So he should ignore 00 and the numbers from 51 to 99. Suppose he began at the fourth line. Then he would get 48, 60, 06, 53, 42, 08, 64, 07, and so on. The child numbered 48 would be selected. The number 60 in the sequence would be ignored. The next selected child would be number 06. Number 53 in the sequence would be ignored, and so on. As a result, children numbered 48, 06, 42, 08, and 07 would be selected to participate in the program.

Other Methods of Random Sampling

Besides simple random sampling, there are other sampling procedures that make use of a random phenomenon to get a sample from a population:

- In **systematic sampling,** the first item is selected at random from the first k items in the frame, and then every k^{th} item is included in the sample. This method is popular among biologists, foresters, environmentalists, and marine scientists.
- In **stratified random sampling,** the population is divided into groups called **strata** (the singular is "stratum") and a simple random sample is selected from each stratum. Strata are homogeneous groups of population units—that is, units in a given stratum are similar in some characteristics, whereas those in different strata differ in those characteristics. For example, students in a university can be grouped into strata by their major. If a population is divided into homogeneous strata, then stratified sampling can be useful in reducing variation; that is, it can help make groups more similar and result in a more powerful test.

- In **proportional sampling**, the population is divided into groups called strata and a simple random sample of size proportional to the stratum size is selected from each stratum. The selection of members of Congress in the U.S. House of Representatives is a good example of proportional sampling; the U.S. Senate, on the other hand, is an example of stratified sampling.
- In **cluster sampling**, a population is divided into nonhomogeneous groups called clusters and a simple random sample is obtained from some clusters, but not necessarily all.

Bias in Surveys

For a survey to produce reliable results, it must be properly designed and conducted. Samples should be selected by a proper randomization technique. A nonrandom selection will limit the generalizability of the results. Furthermore, interviewers should be trained in proper interviewing techniques. The attitude and behavior of the interviewer should not lead to any specific answers, because this would result in a biased outcome. Questions should be carefully worded, as the wording of a question can affect the response, and leading questions should be avoided.

Sampling error is a variation inherent in any survey. Even if a survey is repeated with the same sample size and the same questionnaires, the outcome will be different, if only slightly.

A survey is biased if it systematically favors certain outcomes. The following are some sources of bias:

- **Response bias** is caused by the behavior of the interviewer or respondent. For example, if high school children are asked in the presence of their parents whether they've ever smoked a cigarette, then they are likely to deny smoking even if they have smoked. It is possible to reduce response bias by carefully training interviewers and supervising the interview process.
- **Nonresponse bias** occurs if the person selected for an interview cannot be contacted or refuses to answer.
- **Undercoverage bias** may occur if part of the population is left out of the selection process. For example, if you conduct a telephone survey, individuals without a telephone are left out of the selection process. In the United States, almost 98 percent of households have a telephone, so only a small percent of the population would be left out of a telephone survey. But in many African countries, less than four percent of households have telephones, and those that do are often affluent. A telephone survey there would give biased results. In every U.S. census, a certain percent of the population is missed due to undercoverage. This undercoverage tends to be higher in poorer sections of large cities.

- **Wording effect bias** may occur if confusing or leading questions are asked. For example, imagine an interviewer who says, "The American Dental Association recommends brushing your teeth three times a day. How often do you brush your teeth on a typical day?" The respondents may feel compelled to give an answer of three or more, even if they don't brush their teeth that often. So the responses are likely to be higher than the true average of the population. In this situation, the wording effect bias could be reduced or avoided by simply asking, "How often do you brush your teeth on a typical day?"

PLANNING AND CONDUCTING EXPERIMENTS

Terms and Concepts

- A **response,** or a **dependent, variable** is the variable to be measured in the experiment. An **explanatory,** or an **independent, variable** is a variable that may explain the differences in responses. We are interested in studying the effect of independent variables on the dependent variables. For example, a dentist is interested in studying the duration of the effects of different amounts of anesthesia. In this case, the "amount of anesthesia" is the *explanatory* variable and the "duration of the effect" is the *response* variable.
- An **experimental unit** is the smallest unit of the population to which a treatment is applied. In the above example, each patient receiving a dose of anesthesia is an experimental unit. An **observational unit** is the smallest unit for which the measurements are taken. If the observational units are people or animals, they are commonly referred to as "subjects." For example, two different pesticides are to be used to control bugs on pecan trees. Some trees are sprayed with pesticide A and some with pesticide B. After a certain time, a few pecans are selected from each sprayed tree and inspected for infestation. In this situation, each tree is an *experimental* unit, whereas each pecan is an *observational* unit.
- A **confounding variable** is a variable whose effect on the response cannot be separated from the effect of the explanatory variable. In properly constructed experiments, an experimenter tries to control confounding variables. Confounding can be an even more serious problem in observational studies, because the experimenter has no control over the confounding variables.
- A **factor** is a variable whose effect on the response is of interest in the experiment. Factors are of two types: **qualitative**—for example, when studying the effect of education level (as defined by less than high school, high school, undergraduate, and graduate) on the achievement of children, the factor "education level" is a qualitative (or "categorical") factor; **quantitative**—for example, when studying the effect of a car's speed on its stopping distance, the factor "speed" is a quantitative variable. It is possible to redefine quantitative variables into categorical variables. For example, to study the effect of income level on

spending power, we can categorize annual incomes by grouping them into "less than $10,000," "$10,000–$24,999," "$25,000–$49,999," "$50,000–$99,999," and "$100,000 and above."

- **Levels** are the values of a factor used in the experiment. An experiment can have one or more factors. The number of levels used in the experiment may differ from factor to factor. **Treatments** are the factor-level combinations used in the experiment. If the experiment has only one factor, then all the levels of that factor are considered treatments of the experiment.

  Suppose that there is only one medicine on the market for controlling anxiety level, but then two pharmaceutical companies come up with new medicines. A doctor is interested in comparing the effectiveness of the current medicine with that of the two new medicines. Here, "anxiety-controlling medicine" is the only *factor* of interest. There are three *levels* of this medicine, which become three *treatments*, namely, "current medicine," "new medicine A," and "new medicine B."

  Now suppose the doctor also wants to determine the effect of two types of breathing exercises along with the medicines. Let us call the exercises "Exec1" and "Exec2." Now this experiment has two factors, one at three levels and one at two levels, as shown in the following table.

Type of exercise	TYPE OF MEDICINE		
	Current medicine	New medicine A	New medicine B
Exec 1	X	X	X
Exec 2	X	X	X

  Then, as defined earlier, all the factor-level combinations become treatments.

  So there are $3 \times 2 = 6$ treatments of interest to the doctor. They are the following:

  1. Current medicine and Exec1
  2. New medicine A and Exec1
  3. New medicine B and Exec1
  4. Current medicine and Exec2
  5. New medicine A and Exec2
  6. New medicine B and Exec2

- A **control group** is a group of experimental units similar to all the other experimental units except that it is not given any treatment. A control group is used to establish the baseline response expected from experimental units if no treatment is given. For example, the doctor from the example above might want to know what will happen to the anxiety level of patients if no treatment at all (medicine or breathing exercises) is prescribed.

- A **placebo group** is a control group that receives a placebo in experiments involving medicines. A placebo is a medicine that looks exactly like the real medicine, but it does not contain any active ingredients. The patients will not be able to tell the placebo and the real medicine apart by looking at them. People who do not receive any medicine sometimes have different responses from those who receive a placebo. It seems that just the comforting thought of taking medicine has some effect on patients, even when they are not receiving any active ingredients. In other words, belief in the presence or absence of an active ingredient can have an effect on a patient's reaction.

Single-Blind and Double-Blind Experiments

Similarly, it is possible that measurements will be biased if the person taking the measurements knows whether a patient received a placebo or not. **Blinding technique** is used in medical experiments to prevent such a bias. The blinding technique can be used in two different fashions: double blinding and single blinding. In a **single-blind experiment**, either the patient does not know which treatment he or she is receiving or the person measuring the patient's reaction does not know which treatment was given. In a **double-blind experiment**, both the patient and the person measuring the patient's reaction do not know which treatment the patient was given.

Double-blind experiments are preferred, but in certain situations they simply can't be conducted. For example, in an experiment designed to compare the drop in cholesterol level produced by a certain medication to that produced by going on a particular diet, the patients always know which treatment they are given. You can't hide from them the fact that they have been subjected to a medication or a low-cholesterol diet! So a double-blind experiment would not be possible. But a single-blind experiment would be possible, because the lab technician measuring the patients' cholesterol level does not need to know which treatment the patients have been getting.

Randomization

The technique of **randomization** is used to average out the effects of extraneous factors on responses. In other words, it balances the effects of factors you cannot see.

- If each experimental unit is supposed to receive only one treatment, then which experimental unit receives which treatment should be determined randomly. For example, in the experiment above that compares three anxiety-controlling medicines, the doctor should use some kind of randomization mechanism (such as one of the methods described earlier) to decide which participating patient should get each one of the three medicines.

- If each experimental unit is supposed to receive all treatments, then the order of treatments should be determined randomly for each experimental unit. Suppose the doctor is interested in comparing the effects of all three medicines on each patient. Then for each patient, the doctor should use some kind of randomization mechanism to decide the order in which the three medicines will be given. All participating patients will be given all three medicines with some washout period in between the administration of each medicine. But the order in which the three medicines are given will differ with each patient. Some will get "current medicine" first, then "new medicine A," and then "new medicine B." Others will get "new medicine B" first, then "current medicine," and then "new medicine A," and so on.

Blocking

The technique of **blocking** is used to control the effects of known factors—factors that you *can* see. A **block** is a group of homogeneous experimental units. Experimental units in a block are similar in certain characteristics, whereas those in different blocks differ in those characteristics. For example, a doctor might suspect that the effect of a certain medicine is different on women than on men. The doctor could then control this potentially confounding factor by separating patients into two groups by gender. There would then be two blocks, male and female. Blocking may reduce unwanted variation in responses, thus allowing the experimenter to see more clearly those differences in responses due to treatments. Essentially, blocking is another way of describing stratification. In the scenario described above in which three medical treatments are given to each patient, each patient is acting as a block. So, the number of blocks is equal to the number of patients.

Replication

Replication refers to the process of giving a certain treatment numerous times in an experiment or of applying it to a number of different experimental units. Replication reduces chance variation among results. It also allows us to estimate chance variation among results. In the example of comparing three medicines to control anxiety, suppose the doctor prescribes each of three medicines to only one patient each. If the responses of the three patients were different, then we would not know whether the differences were true effects of medicines or due just to chance. Could differences among the patients have led to differences in their responses? Yes, it is possible, but we could not know. What if the doctor were to prescribe each medicine to more than one patient? Each patient could receive one of three treatments selected at random. Then, on the average, the three groups of patients would likely be similar. As the differences among patients are averaged out, the effect of treatment differences will stand out.

Would all patients receiving the same treatment have the same responses? No, not likely. Then how can we explain the differences among the responses of patients receiving the same treatment? The differences are due simply to chance variation among results. Without replication, it would not be possible to estimate this chance variation.

Completely Randomized Design

In a completely randomized design, treatments are assigned randomly to all experimental units or experimental units are assigned randomly to all treatments. This design can compare any number of treatments. There are advantages in having an equal number of experimental units for each treatment, but this is not necessary.

Let's look at a randomized design question.

Suppose a doctor is interested in comparing an anxiety-controlling drug out on the market now (let's call it "current medicine") with two new drugs ("new medicine A" and "new medicine B"). A group of patients from a local clinic is available for the experiment. Design an experiment to compare the effects of these three drugs.

Here's How to Crack It

In this experiment, there is one factor of interest with three levels.

- Factor of interest: anxiety-controlling medicines
- Number of levels: 3
- Treatments: "current medicine," "new medicine A," and "new medicine B"
- Experimental unit: each patient
- Response variable: the anxiety level measured for each patient

Use the group of patients available from the local clinic and design the experiment as follows:

- Measure the anxiety level of each patient.
- Use a randomization scheme to divide the patients into three groups. For example, throw a six-sided die for each patient. If the numbers 1 or 2 show, then assign the patient to group 1; if the numbers 3 or 4 show, assign the patient to group 2; otherwise, assign to group 3. Or fill a jar with blue, red, and green beads, with the total number of beads equal to the total number of participating patients. Ask each

patient to take out one bead without looking in the jar. If the patient selects a blue bead, assign that patient to group 1; if the patient selects a red bead, assign to group 2; if the patient selects a green bead, assign to group 3.

- Prescribe current medicine to all patients in group 1.
- Prescribe new medicine A to all patients in group 2.
- Prescribe new medicine B to all patients in group 3.
- After a designated time period, measure the anxiety level of each patient.
- Compare the results.

This scheme is also described in the following diagram.

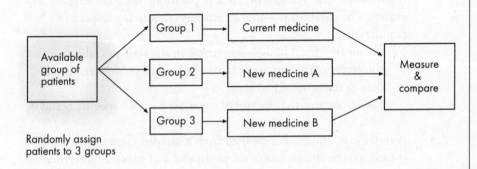

Randomly assign patients to 3 groups

Schematic Diagram of a Completely Randomized Experiment

INFERENCES, PREDICTIONS, AND ARGUMENTS ON DATA

Important information about a population of interest is often unknown, but we can take samples from the population and gather and summarize the information from the samples. Such summary statistics can then be used to

- estimate unknown population characteristics
- make inferences about unknown population characteristics

This section discusses the use of estimation and statistical inference.

PARAMETERS AND STATISTICS

In a telephone survey conducted by a local newspaper, 400 randomly selected residents of a county on the Gulf of Mexico were asked, "Are you in favor of spending tax money on measures to prevent the erosion of private beaches?" The answers were recorded as "yes," "no," or "no opinion." The newspaper found that 76 percent of respondents were against spending tax money to support private beaches. This percentage, known as a statistic, was calculated from the information obtained from a random sample of county residents and not the entire population of that county. Still, it provides a reasonable estimate for the unknown parameter, namely, the percentage of *all* county residents who oppose such action.

- A **parameter** is a characteristic of a population. The following are all examples of parameters—that is, numbers describing respective populations:
  - the mean annual household income in the state of California
  - the percentage of voters in favor of a certain presidential candidate in the state of Florida
  - the variance of the amount of sugar per can of a specific brand of soda
- A **statistic** is a number computed from a sample. Generally, a statistic is used to estimate an unknown parameter and make an inference about it. The following are all examples of statistics:
  - the mean annual household income computed from 500 randomly selected households in the state of California
  - the percentage of voters in favor of a certain presidential candidate in a sample of 385 randomly selected voters in the state of Florida
  - the variance of the amount of sugar per can of a specific brand of soda in 12 randomly selected cans

ESTIMATION

Generally, population characteristics (parameters) are unknown. To estimate them, we take samples from the population and use information from those samples to make our best guess. This procedure of guessing an unknown parameter value using the observed values from samples is known as an **estimation process**. A specific guess or value computed from a sample is known as an **estimate**.

To estimate the mean annual income per resident of Los Angeles County, we would probably use the mean annual income per resident of a random sample of residents of Los Angeles County. The sample mean would estimate the unknown population mean. Similarly, if we were interested in estimating the proportion of voters in favor of a candidate in the state of Louisiana, then we would use the proportion of voters in favor of this candidate from any random sample of voters from Louisiana. Again, the sample proportion would estimate the population proportion.

There are two estimation methods:

- **Point estimation** gives a single value as an estimate of the unknown parameter and makes no allowance for the uncertainty of the value's accuracy.
- **Interval estimation** recognizes the uncertainty of the estimate's accuracy and compensates for it by specifying a range of values around the estimate within which the population parameter may actually lie.

For example, Paul is planning a trip to Florida during his spring break. He collects information about the trip and prepares a budget. Using the collected information, he concludes, "This trip will cost me $1,000, give or take $100." Paul is expecting the cost of his trip to be somewhere between $900 and $1,100. Because he does not know all the exact costs for the different components of this trip, his estimation procedure does not guarantee that the actual cost of the trip will be within the estimated range, but still he believes that there is a very good chance that it will be within those limits. His estimated cost of $1,000 is a point estimate of the unknown cost of the trip. The range of $100 around the point estimate of the cost is known as the **margin of error (MOE)**. The estimated range of cost ($900, $1,100) is an **interval estimate** of the cost of his trip.

PROBABILITY

Words referring to probability or chance are commonly used in conversation. For example, we often come across statements like these:

- It is likely to rain today, so please take your umbrella with you.
- It was an easy test. I'll probably get an A on it.
- The Yankees have a much better chance of winning than the Mets.

Words like "probably," "likely," and "chance" carry similar meanings in conversation. They all convey uncertainty. By using probability, we can also make a numerical statement about uncertainty. For example, bank managers can never know exactly when their depositors will make a withdrawal or exactly how much they'll withdraw. Managers also know that though most loans they've granted will be paid back, some of them will result in defaults—but they can't know exactly which ones. In other words, a variety of outcomes is possible, and therefore bank managers can never know exactly how much money the bank will have at any given moment in the future. However, the bankers can use the rules of probability and their past experience to make a reasonable estimation, and then use that estimation when making business decisions.

What Is Probability?

Probability is a measure of the likelihood of an event. Consider a fair coin toss. What makes this coin toss "fair"? We call it fair if the coin's chance of showing heads when flipped is the same as its chance of showing tails—in other words, if there is a 50 percent chance of its showing heads and a 50 percent chance of its showing tails. Suppose we tossed the coin twice and got two heads. Does that mean this coin toss was not fair? What if we toss the coin three times? What do we expect to happen? Let's toss a coin 5, 10, 15, 20, 25, and more times and count the number of heads. Then we can calculate the probability of getting heads in a toss and plot that figure on a graph:

$$P(\text{Heads in a toss}) = \frac{\text{Number of heads}}{\text{Number of tosses}}$$

$$P(\text{Percent Heads}) = \frac{\text{Number of heads}}{\text{Number of tosses}} \times 100$$

The table below lists the results of one such experiment.

Number of Tosses	Number of Heads	P(Heads)	Percent of Heads	Number of Tosses	Number of Heads	P(Heads)	Percent of Heads
2	0	0	0	35	17	0.48571	48.571
3	2	0.66667	66.667	40	18	0.45	45
4	3	0.75	75	45	18	0.4	40
5	5	1	100	50	23	0.46	46
6	3	0.5	50	60	32	0.53333	53.333
7	5	0.71429	71.429	70	29	0.41429	41.429
8	5	0.625	62.5	80	34	0.425	42.5
9	7	0.77778	77.778	90	48	0.53333	53.333
10	4	0.4	40	100	49	0.49	49
15	10	0.66667	66.667	150	74	0.49333	49.333
20	9	0.45	45	200	106	0.53	53
25	12	0.48	48	500	264	0.528	52.8
30	17	0.56667	56.667	1,000	508	0.508	50.8

Number of Heads in Different Numbers of Tosses

This figure graphically plots the results from the table.

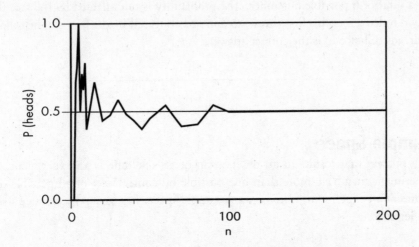

P(heads) Estimated from Different Numbers of Tosses

Notice that as the number of tosses increases, the percent of times that the coin lands on heads gets closer and closer to 50 percent. In other words, in the long run, the relative frequency of getting heads approaches 0.5, which is what we expected it to be. This relative frequency reflects the concept of probability. In fact, in the long run, the relative frequency of the occurrence of any specific event will always approach the expected value, also known as the probability.

George throws a six-sided die and gets a 3. What is the probability that his next throw will not be a three?

A. $\frac{1}{6}$

B. $\frac{1}{4}$

C. $\frac{1}{2}$

D. $\frac{5}{6}$

Here's How To Crack It

The probability of not getting a three is $\frac{5}{6}$. There are five rolls (the desired outcome) which will not give George three, namely if he rolls 1, 2, 4, 5, or 6. There are a total of 6 possible outcomes. The probability is not affected by the fact that David rolled a 3 on his first throw, so don't be confused by the fact that he rolled a 3 already. Choice D is the correct answer.

Sample Space

Any process that results in an observation or an outcome is an experiment. An experiment may have more than one possible outcome. A set of all possible outcomes of an experiment is known as a **sample space.** It is generally denoted using the letter S.

- Tossing a coin will result in one of two possible outcomes, "heads" or "tails." Therefore, the sample space of tossing a coin is

$$S = \{\text{Heads, Tails}\}$$

- Throwing a die will result in one of six possible outcomes. The resulting sample space is

$$S = \{1, 2, 3, 4, 5, 6\}$$

- Tossing two coins will result in one of four possible outcomes. We can indicate the outcome of each of the two tosses by using a pair of letters, the first letter of which indicates the outcome of tossing the first coin and the second letter the outcome of tossing the second coin. H is for heads and T for tails. Then the resulting sample space is

$$S = \{(H, H), (H, T), (T, H), (T, T)\}$$

The outcomes listed in a sample space are never repeated, and no outcome is left out. Two events are said to be equally likely if one does not occur more often than the other. For example, the six possible outcomes for a throw of a die are equally likely.

A **tree diagram** representation is useful in determining the sample space for an experiment, especially if there are relatively few possible outcomes. For example, imagine an experiment in which a die and a quarter are tossed together. What are all the possible outcomes? The six possible outcomes of throwing a die are 1, 2, 3, 4, 5, and 6. The two possible outcomes of tossing a quarter are heads (H) and tails (T). The figure below is a tree diagram of the possible outcomes.

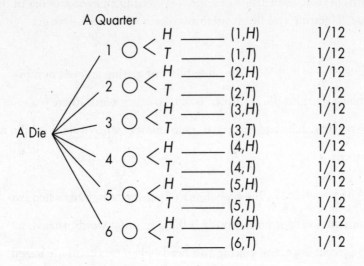

A Quarter

A Die

H —— (1,H)	1/12
T —— (1,T)	1/12
H —— (2,H)	1/12
T —— (2,T)	1/12
H —— (3,H)	1/12
T —— (3,T)	1/12
H —— (4,H)	1/12
T —— (4,T)	1/12
H —— (5,H)	1/12
T —— (5,T)	1/12
H —— (6,H)	1/12
T —— (6,T)	1/12

Tree Diagram

Looking at the tree diagram, it is easy to see that the sample space is

$$S = \{(1, H), (2, H), (3, H), (4, H), (5, H), (6, H),$$
$$(1, T), (2, T), (3, T), (4, T), (5, T), (6, T)\}$$

The number in each pair represents the outcome of throwing the die, and the letter (H or T) represents the outcome of tossing the coin. All 12 outcomes are equally likely. Therefore, the probability of each outcome is $\dfrac{1}{12}$.

It is common practice to use capital letters to indicate events. For example, one may define

A = getting an even number when a die is thrown = {2, 4, 6}
B = getting two heads when two coins are tossed simultaneously =
   {(H, H)}

The probability of an event is generally denoted by a capital "P" followed by the name of the event in parentheses: P(the event). If all the events in a sample space are equally likely, then by using the concept of relative frequency, we can compute the probability of an event as

$$P(\text{An event}) = \frac{\text{Number of outcomes that lead to the event}}{\text{Total number of possible outcomes}}$$

Applying this to the events defined earlier—A (getting an even number in the toss of a die) and B (getting two heads when two coins are tossed)—we get

- $P(A) = \dfrac{3}{6} = \dfrac{1}{2} = 0.5$. The probability of getting an even number when a six-sided die is thrown is 0.5. In other words, there is a 50 percent chance of getting an even number when a six-sided die is thrown.

- $P(B) = \dfrac{1}{4} = 0.25$. The probability of getting two heads when two coins are tossed simultaneously is 0.25. In other words, there is a 25 percent chance of getting two heads when two coins are tossed simultaneously.

Basic Probability Rules and Terms

There are two rules that all probabilities must satisfy:

- **Rule 1:** For any event A, the probability of A is always greater than or equal to 0 and less than or equal to 1.

$$0 \leq P(A) \leq 1$$

- **Rule 2:** The sum of the probabilities for all possible outcomes in a sample space is always 1.

As a result, we can say the following:

- If an event can never occur, its probability is 0. Such an event is known as an **impossible event.**
- If an event must occur every time, its probability is 1. Such an event is known as a **sure event.**

The **odds in favor of an event** is a ratio of the probability of the occurrence of an event to the probability of the nonoccurrence of that event.

$$\text{Odds in favor of an event} = \frac{P(\text{Event } A \text{ occurs})}{P(\text{Event } A \text{ does not occur})}$$

or

$$P(\text{Event } A \text{ occurs}) : P(\text{Event } A \text{ does not occur})$$

When tossing a die, what are the odds in favor of getting the number 2?

A. $\dfrac{1}{6}$

B. $\dfrac{5}{6}$

C.   2:5

D.   1:5

Here's How to Crack It
When tossing a die,

$$P(\text{Getting the number 2}) = \frac{1}{6} \text{ and}$$

$$P(\text{Not getting the number 2}) = P(\text{Getting the numbers 1, 3, 4, 5, or 6}) = \frac{5}{6}.$$

Thus, the odds in favor of getting the number 2 are $\dfrac{1}{6} : \dfrac{5}{6}$ or 1 to 5 (or 1:5), choice D is correct.

Terms Related to Venn Diagrams

Venn diagrams illustrate some terms related to statistics. The rectangular box indicates the A' sample space. Circles indicate different events.

The **complement** of an event is the set of all possible outcomes in a sample space that does not lead to the event. The complement of an event A is denoted by A'.

See the figure below.

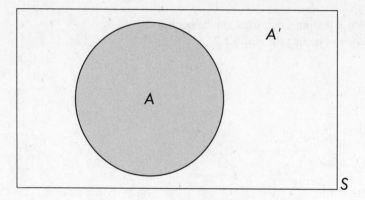

Event *A* and Its Complement

Disjoint, or **mutually exclusive, events** are events that have no outcome in common. In other words, they cannot occur together. See the figure below.

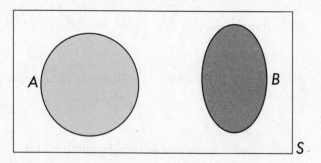

Disjoint Events *A* and *B*

The **union** of events *A* and *B* is the set of all possible outcomes that lead to at least one of two events *A* and *B*. The union of events *A* and *B* is denoted by $(A \cup B)$ or $(A$ or $B)$. See the figure below.

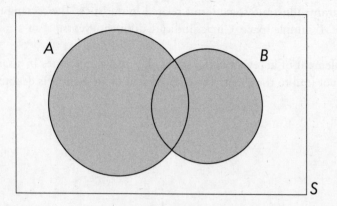

Union of Events *A* and *B*

The **intersection** of events A and B is the set of all possible outcomes that lead to *both* events A and B. The intersection of events A and B is denoted by $(A \cap B)$ or $(A$ and $B)$. See the figure below.

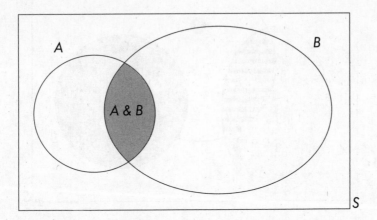

Intersection of Events A and B

In a **conditional event**, A given B is a set of outcomes for event A that occurs if B has occurred. It is indicated by $(A|B)$ and reads "A given B."

Two events A and B are considered **independent** if the occurrence of one event does not depend on the occurrence of the other.

Independence versus Dependence

Imagine that you shuffle a standard deck of cards and then draw a card at random. The chance of your getting an ace is the same across all four suits (hearts, clubs, diamonds, and spades). In other words, the likelihood of your getting an ace does not depend on the suit of the card. So we can say that the events "getting an ace" and "getting a particular suit" are *independent*.

Now consider a doctor examining patients in an emergency room. The likelihood of a patient being diagnosed for a knee injury is higher if that patient is a football player, because football players are more likely to suffer knee injuries than non-football players. Therefore the event "knee injury" *depends* on the event "football player."

The sample space for throwing a die is $S = \{1, 2, 3, 4, 5, 6\}$. Suppose events A, B, and C are defined as follows:

A = Getting an even number = $\{2, 4, 6\}$
B = Getting at least 5 = $\{5, 6\}$
C = Getting at most 3 = $\{1, 2, 3\}$

How do we use the terms defined above to describe these events?

Here's How to Crack It

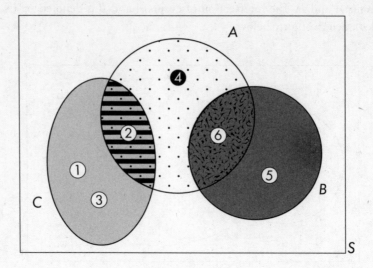

Venn Diagram

- **Probability:** $P(A) = \dfrac{3}{6} = 0.5$, $P(B) = \dfrac{2}{6} = 0.333$, and $P(C) = \dfrac{3}{6} = 0.5$

- **Complement:** $A' = $ Getting an odd number $= \{1, 3, 5\}$

$$P(A') = \frac{3}{6} = 0.5$$

$B' = $ Getting a number less than 5 $= \{1, 2, 3, 4\}$

$$P(B') = \frac{4}{6} = 0.667$$

$C' = $ Getting a number larger than 3 $= \{4, 5, 6\}$

$$P(C') = \frac{3}{6} = 0.5$$

- **Union:** $(A \cup B) = $ Getting an even number or a number greater than or equal to 5 or both.

$$= \{ 2, 4, 5, 6\}$$

$$P(A \cup B) = \frac{4}{6} = 0.667$$

$(A \cup C) = $ Getting an even number or a number less than or equal to 3 or both.

$$= \{1, 2, 3, 4, 6\}$$

$$P(A \cup C) = \frac{5}{6} = 0.833$$

$(B \cup C)$ = Getting a number that is at most 3 or at least 5 or both.

$$= \{1, 2, 3, 5, 6\}$$

$$P(B \cup C) = \frac{5}{6} = 0.833$$

- **Intersection:** $(A \cap B)$ = Getting an even number that is at least 5 = $\{6\}$

$$P(A \cap B) = \frac{1}{6} = 0.167$$

$(A \cap C)$ = Getting an even number that is at most 3 = $\{2\}$

$$P(A \cap C) = \frac{1}{6} = 0.167$$

$(B \cap C)$ = Getting a number that is at most 3 and at least 5 = $\{ \}$

$$P(B \cap C) = \frac{0}{6} = 0.000$$

In other words, B and C are disjoint or mutually exclusive events.

- **Conditional event:** $(A|C)$ = Getting an even number given that the number is at most 3 = $\{2\}$

$$P(A|C) = \frac{1}{3}$$

$(A|B)$ = Getting an even number given that the number is at least 5 = $\{6\}$

$$P(A|B) = \frac{1}{2}$$

$(B|C)$ = Getting at least 5 given that the number is at most 3 = 0

$$P(B|C) = 0$$

KEY TERMS

descriptive methods

categorical variable

continuous variable

univariate data

bivariate data

numerical methods

tabular methods

graphical methods

measure of central tendency

measure of variation (spread)

measure of position

range

mean

median

mode

frequency

relative frequency

cumulative frequency

frequency distribution table

ungrouped frequency distribution
  table

classes

grouped frequency distribution
  table

upper limit

lower limit

class-mark (midpoint)

center

spread

shape

symmetric distribution

left-skewed distribution

right-skewed distribution

clusters

gaps

outliers

bar chart

pie chart

population

frame

sample

sample survey

census

experiment

observational study

confounding factors

biased sampling

judgmental sampling

samples of convenience

volunteer samples

simple random sampling

random number table

systematic sampling

stratified random sampling

strata

proportional sampling

cluster sampling

sampling error

response bias

nonresponse bias

undercoverage bias

wording effect bias

response (dependent) variable

explanatory (independent) variable

experimental unit

observational unit

confounding variable

factor

qualitative factor

quantitative factor

levels

treatments

control group

placebo group

blinding technique

single-blind experiment

double-blind experiment

randomization

blocking

block

replication

parameter

statistic

estimation process

estimate

point estimation

interval estimation

margin of error (MOE)

interval estimate

probability

sample space

tree diagram

impossible event

sure event

odds in favor of an event
Venn diagram
complement
disjoint (mutually exclusive) events
union
intersection
conditional event
independent event

Drill #15

1. Denise takes three tests and scores a 90, 80, and 82. What is her average score for the three tests?

    A. 83

    B. 84

    C. 85

    D. 252

2. Ron scores an average of 74 in his history class, and has a total of 296 points. How many tests did Ron take?

    A. 3

    B. 4

    C. 5

    D. 6

3. Anne, Sue, and Jen want to go to the amusement park together. They agree to combine their money. Anne has $11.00, Sue has $15.00, and Jen has $16.00. Admission is $21/person. How much more money will they need to obtain, on average, in order for everyone to be able to go to the amusement park?

    A. $5.00

    B. $6.00

    C. $7.00

    D. $10.00

4. Use the chart below to answer the following question:

VOTES RECEIVED IN COUNTY W	
Candidate	**Number of Votes**
Peter	150
Derek	10
Grant	80
Chris	60

What percent of votes did Peter receive in the election?

    A. 15%

    B. 33%

    C. 50%

    D. 60%

5. An event with a probability of 0 is known as:

    A. an impossible event.

    B. a sure event.

    C. the odds in favor of an event.

    D. the complement of an event.

Please turn the page for answers and explanations
for the questions in this drill.

ANSWERS AND EXPLANATIONS TO DRILL #15

1. **C** Fill in what you know. The total of her three test scores (90 + 80 + 82) = 252. To find the average, divide the total by the number of scores. 252 ÷ 3 = 84.

2. **B** You know two pieces that will lead you to the answer. First, you know that the points total is 296, and second you know that the average is 74. Simply divided the total by the average. 296 ÷ 74 = 4, choice B.

3. **C** Together, the three girls have $42.00 (11 + 15 + 16). The total amount of money they need is $63.00 ($21.00 × 3). Together, they need a total of $21.00 (because $63.00 − $42.00 = $21.00), which works out to $7.00 per person.

4. **C** To find the percentage of votes that Peter received, you need to find the total number of votes. The four numbers sum to 300. Peter received 150 votes, and 150/300 = 50%, choice C.

5. **A** An event with a probability of 0 is known as an impossible event. A probability of 1 is known as a sure event, and all probabilities exist between 0 and 1.

Summary

o   Statistics is the science of data. Different methods for summarizing and organizing data are known as descriptive methods.

o   There are two types of variables: categorical and continuous.

o   Descriptive methods are divided into three categories: numerical methods, tabular methods, and graphical methods.

o   The most basic ways to analyze data are by finding the mean, median, mode, and range.

o   Charts and graphs are useful ways to express statistical analysis.

o   Experiments and observational studies are useful ways to measure or observe a population.

o   When getting samples from a population, one must be careful to avoid biased sampling methods.

o   Probability is a numeric way to express uncertainty.

o   The set of all possible outcomes of an experiment is known as the sample space.

o   A Venn diagram is a useful way to visually illustrate some terms related to statistics.

Subtest III: Physical Education, Human Development, Visual and Performing Arts

Chapter 18
Physical Education

IT'S NOT JUST DODGEBALL ANYMORE

Elementary school Physical Education classes may incorporate which of the following activities?

A.   swimming, water ballet, kayaking, and fishing
B.   juggling, stilt walking, unicycle riding, and tightrope walking
C.   tennis, golf, fencing, and croquet
D.   all of the above

The correct answer is D, all of the above.

You mean they actually plan that stuff?

You may recall "gym," "P.E.," or "Phys. Ed." as nothing more than a teacher in shorts and a T-shirt blowing a whistle while you ran or climbed or jumped until you were gasping for air—or until the bell rang, whichever came first. But just like any other class, Physical Education requires careful planning, extensive subject matter knowledge, and no small amount of creativity.

I LIKE TO MOVE IT, MOVE IT

Basic Movement Skills

Stand up and walk across the room. Good! Now sit back down and read about how your body worked to make it happen.

Basic movement skills are the foundation to more complex skill sets needed to exercise and play games and sports. The three main categories of movement skills are **traveling**, **stabilizing**, and **control** (of objects).

Movement Concepts

In Physical Education, students learn to become aware of their bodies and movements. Movement concepts are often referred to as the *how*, the *where*, and the *what* of body movement.

- **Body awareness** teaches children about body shapes, body parts, and relationships.
- **Space awareness** refers to personal and shared space, and the body in relation to dimensions in space.
- **Effort awareness** is awareness of the way the body moves: speed, rhythm, force, and coordination.

Locomotor Skills

The term **locomotor** indicates the movement of the body from one place to another—in other words, you use your feet to get you someplace.

Locomotor skills are used to walk, run, leap, jump, hop, skip, gallop, and slide.

Activities

Physical Education teachers build their lessons around the fundamentals of basic skills. Even the simplest of activities requires multiple skills. For example, two students tossing a ball back and forth have to throw, catch, balance, adjust force and speed, and gauge distance. It's the teacher's job to help them to become aware of all of those components, and to assess their progress.

HEALTH AND PHYSICAL FITNESS

In Physical Education, students learn how physical fitness affects their health.

Health Benefits

The benefits of regular exercise include

- weight management
- better sleep patterns
- heart and lung (cardiovascular) efficiency
- higher energy levels
- stress relief

Exercise Principles

A mnemonic device will help you remember some of the basic principles of exercise. Think **FITT**:

- **F**requency of exercise
- **I**ntensity of exercise
- **T**ype of exercise
- **T**ime spent exercising

Other principles of exercise vary slightly in terminology but can include the following:

- **Balance:** To be effective, exercise should require the use of different muscles and parts of the body.
- **Variety:** Varying activities reduces boredom and aids or increases motivation.
- **Recovery:** During recovery, muscles are given a chance to rest.
- **Overload:** To achieve a training effect, the workload must exceed the normal demands placed on a body.

Physical Fitness Components

There are two types of physical fitness components: **health-related components** and **skill-related components.**

The following are health-related components:

- body composition
- cardiovascular fitness
- muscular endurance
- muscle strength
- flexibility

The following are skill-related components:

- agility
- balance
- coordination
- power
- speed
- reaction time

CURRICULUM

You're expected to be able to take your knowledge of movement and physical fitness and apply it to teaching Physical Education through a strong curriculum.

Activities

We weren't kidding at the beginning of the chapter—it's standard now for Physical Education teachers to incorporate a wide variety of activities into the curriculum. It's important for a number of reasons, including employing all of the components of physical fitness, and keeping the students interested and motivated.

Rules and Etiquette

You should familiarize yourself with as many sports and games as you can: Make sure you know the basic rules and social etiquette. If you're not familiar with a sport, you might want to watch it on TV or join a league to learn the game and have fun.

Rules are the mechanics of a game, including details like scoring, game length, rounds, and timing. For example, here are some rules in baseball: one point is scored when a player makes it all the way around the bases, a team's inning ends when the team has three outs, a runner is safe if he or she reaches the base before it is tagged by a defensive player.

Social etiquette is about manners and fairness. In baseball, it might mean not arguing with an umpire over a close call at the base, or backing off to allow another outfielder to catch the ball if he or she calls for it.

Content Areas

Anytime a Physical Education teacher can integrate activities with other content areas, it's beneficial to everyone. It helps students build on prior knowledge, and reinforce concepts learned in other disciplines.

- Math: hurrying to form groups in the number called out by the teacher
- Science: using weights to balance bottles and then attempting to knock them down
- Social Science/History: jousting, Native American hand wrestling, capoeira, lacrosse
- Language Arts: creating words or sentences while throwing and catching a ball

---

Which of the following is not an example of effort awareness?

A. timing a run

B. checking your heart rate

C. serving a volleyball

D. walking on a balance beam

Here's How to Crack It

Effort awareness is the consciousness of how the body moves, and, well, the effort it can exert (hence, the term). Which of the above activities doesn't show some type of bodily effort? Running (choice A), hitting a volleyball (choice C), and walking on a balance beam (choice D) take some type of effort: speed, force, and coordination. Determining your heart rate (choice B), though, is a form of body awareness.

WATCH THEM GROW

Physical Growth and Development

Picture a group of kindergarteners walking in a line. All of the students are about the same height and weight, give or take a few inches and pounds. Now picture a group of sixth graders walking in a line: They could conceivably vary by up to two feet and 100 pounds. And those are just the superficial differences.

Gross Motor Skills

Gross motor skills are the basic skills acquired by children in the early stages of development, using the large muscle groups. They include major bodily skills like walking, climbing, and throwing. Skills are acquired in a natural progression. Children learn to stand before they can jump, walk before they can run. In healthy children, gross motor skills are fully developed by age five or six.

Fine Motor Skills

Fine motor skills are sometimes referred to as hand skills, because that's what they are: skills you can perform with your hands. Again, as with gross motor skills, they are acquired in a natural progression. Babies first reach for things, then learn to grasp, and later learn to hold and carry.

Fine motor skills are much more complex and continue to develop well into the school years. Fine motor skill development varies more by age than does gross motor skill development, which progresses at generally the same rate—think about things like writing, drawing, and cutting. By first grade, some children are adept at all of those skills, while others are still in the early stages of development.

Growth Spurts and Puberty

The most rapid growth occurs in infancy. By one year old, average babies triple their birth weight and grow up to a foot in length. After that, children grow slowly and steadily until adolescence. And then…welcome to puberty.

The onset of **puberty** in healthy girls can occur anywhere from age 8 to age 13. The actual growth spurts usually start around age 11 or 12 and last until age 15 or 16.

Boys' **growth spurts** start a little later, usually around age 12 or 13, and can last until age 19. Some boys don't reach their full height until they're in college.

Puberty includes many body changes: the appearance of pubic and underarm hair, weight gain, voice changes, development of sex organs, and, in girls, menstruation.

All of these factors affect students' physical abilities. Growth spurts can lead to awkwardness and discomfort, which in turn may hinder movement. Adolescents have to learn to adjust to different heights, weights, and hand and foot sizes. This adjustment makes it difficult for them to do some physical activities they previously performed with confidence and skill, like running, jumping, and playing certain sports.

SELF-IMAGE

Children's emotional development is similar to their physical development. Most children have a pretty healthy **self-image** as they begin school. As they progress through the early grades, many remain secure and confident in themselves, some begin to develop higher levels of self-esteem, and others start to lose self-esteem. Then puberty hits like an explosion, and sends them all careening in different directions.

Most adolescents develop insecurities about something, whether it be physical features, personality traits, academic capabilities, physical skills, or any number of other factors about themselves. And even though it's not logically possible, it seems that all adolescents go to school feeling insecure and worried that everyone else is staring at and judging them.

Physical Activity

Exercise and fitness play a major part in children's self-image. Staying active relieves stress, burns off excess energy, both physical and emotional, and builds confidence. It can also build and strengthen friendships, because many physical activities available to children involve other people. Even for those activities in which a child might compete alone, like gymnastics and running, training is usually done in a group setting and can have great social benefits.

Psychological Skills

There are a number of skills children can learn and use to build self-esteem, including

- helping others
- thinking positively
- joining groups or clubs
- having healthy family relationships
- taking on responsibilities
- goal setting
- working hard to succeed academically

Parents, teachers, coaches, and other adults in a child's life should help foster these skills.

Which activity would most challenge a person's fine motor skills?

A. bowling

B. basketball

C. origami

D. swimming

Here's How to Crack It

When you see the term *fine motor skills*, focus on the word *fine*. What does the word make you think of? Small? Precise? Refined? Those are all good descriptions of fine motor skills. If you don't have a confident grasp on the word, take a different route and remember the other type of motor skills, *gross motor skills*. Those refer to large muscle groups and movements. While all of the activities above require some measure of fine motor skills, all primarily utilize gross motor skills. The delicate art of origami, choice C, would be the biggest challenge for fine motor skills.

SOCIAL DEVELOPMENT

Physical Education class can be considered the most important class of the day when it comes to students' social development. Students interact far more in Physical Education than they do in traditional academic classes. It's important for teachers to factor in social dynamics when planning curriculum and structuring class sessions.

Class Setting

Teachers can promote healthy social relationships in their classrooms by using the following strategies:

- Encourage a gender balance, regardless of the sport or activity.
- Choose activities, games, and sports from different cultures.
- Plan a wide range of activities in which all students have the opportunity to showcase their skills.
- Frequently change and mix groups so that students interact with as many other peers as possible.
- Monitor students' verbal and nonverbal attitudes toward themselves and their peers.

Team Sports

Team sports in Physical Education classes are used to teach students the rules and regulations of a variety of games, to give students an opportunity to learn and practice different types of movements and skills, and to provide enjoyment and exercise.

Teachers need to be mindful of social interaction during team sports. With younger children, it's common practice to remove the competition aspect of sports, which in essence means that no one keeps score. Students learn to cheer each other for good plays and encourage those who aren't doing as well, no matter which team the players are on.

In the upper grades, competition is factored back in, and this is where it's especially important for teachers to promote **sportsmanship.** On one hand, good sportsmanship means that students should be polite and respectful to players on the opposing team, as well as to all coaches and officials, but it also refers to supporting other members of their own team instead of simply focusing on their individual skills and performance.

One of the most important things teachers can do when incorporating team sports into the curriculum is to maintain a fair balance. Students should regularly rotate among positions and between teams. Each student should have a turn at being a team captain. Teams should be heterogeneously formed: a mix of genders, cultures, and skill levels.

KEY TERMS

traveling
stabilizing
control
body awareness
space awareness
effort awareness
locomotor skills
FITT
balance
variety
recovery
overload
health-related components
skill-related components
rules
social etiquette
gross motor skills
fine motor skills
puberty
growth spurt
self-image
sportsmanship

Drill #16

1. Which of the following would most likely be considered poor sportsmanship?

    A. a baseball player loudly cheering a home run by a member of his team

    B. a football team captain designating player positions based on her team members' strengths

    C. a skilled soccer player scoring as many goals as she can in order to ensure her team's win

    D. a basketball player consistently blocking an opponent's attempt to shoot baskets

2. A child whose locomotor skills are slower to develop might be the last one in his peer group to be able to:

    A. use scissors.

    B. hop on one foot.

    C. write the alphabet.

    D. make a noise like a train.

3. In order to effect positive changes to the body through exercise, it is best to:

    A. stop before you are out of breath.

    B. exercise for at least one hour.

    C. work to the point of exhaustion.

    D. push yourself slightly farther than you've gone before.

4. In general Physical Education classes, students should usually be grouped:

    A. by gender, because there will be less discomfort and embarrassment.

    B. according to skill level, to keep activities moving at a steady pace and to prevent boredom.

    C. in a variety of ways, to promote equality and interaction.

    D. randomly, because it is the most fair.

5. Approximately what percentage of carbohydrates, protein, and fats would make up the healthiest diet?

    A. 50% carbohydrates, 25% protein, 25% fats

    B. 75% protein, 15% carbohydrates, 10% fats

    C. 50% carbohydrates, 45% protein, 5% fats

    D. 50% fats, 25% carbohydrates, 25% protein

ANSWERS AND EXPLANATIONS TO DRILL #16

1. **C** Let's break it down. The only reason cheering loudly for his own teammate (choice A) might be considered poor sportsmanship by a baseball player would be if he countered it by jeering or booing the other team, but there's no indication of that here. The football team captain (choice B) has the prerogative to designate positions, and playing on her teammates' strengths will allow all of them to showcase their skills; there's not much wrong with that. One of the basic rules of basketball is to block opponents' attempts to score (choice D), so there's nothing unsportsmanlike about simply following the rules. But a soccer player taking it upon herself to score all or most of the goals indicates that she's not giving her teammates the same opportunity, which makes choice C the correct answer.

2. **B** To answer this question, think of a motor, which powers a vehicle to move from one place to another. *Locomotor skills* are those which enable bodies to move from one place to another. Using scissors (choice A) is a fine motor skill, not a locomotor skill. Writing the alphabet (choice C), along with cognitive skills, also requires fine motor skills. Making a noise like a train (choice D) might be considered, well, a loco*motive* skill. Hopping on one foot (choice B) is the only answer choice that actually refers to the movement of the full body.

3. **D** The reference here is to the term *overload* that you read about earlier. To achieve maximum training results, you should exert yourself more than you can comfortably withstand (choice D). Stopping before you're out of breath (choice A) indicates that you're not putting forth enough effort. Exercising for at least an hour (choice B) doesn't mean much: The health benefits would depend on the type and intensity of exercise, and the person's body composition and size. And it's never healthy to work to the point of exhaustion (choice C).

4. **C** The question asks for the best grouping in general Physical Education classes. You can usually interchange the words *general, average, usual, normal, most common,* and similar terms, and they all mean the same thing: Don't think about the exceptions. Go with the majority. Most of the time, teachers would avoid grouping students by gender (choice A) or skill level (choice B), because both promote inequality and separatism. And beware of choice D: Choosing groups at random—by methods such as "counting off" or drawing names—is just as dangerous, because it's possible that the groups will end up with a majority of one gender, or one culture, or a higher skill level, leaving one or a few "different" others feeling singled out. It's best for teachers to regroup frequently, and to try to make the groups as heterogeneous as possible. Therefore, the correct answer is choice C.

5. **C**   They're asking for the healthiest diet of the answer choices listed—and *diet* doesn't just mean something you do to lose weight; it means your daily nutritional intake. You can immediately rule out choice D as ridiculous. There's no way that consuming 50% of your calories from fat could be considered healthy. By the same token, you can also rule out choice A: That's still too much fat. Choice B is also too heavily weighted: A diet this high in protein is too extreme, regardless of what some diet plans tout. A well-balanced diet should have a more even balance of carbohydrates, for energy, and protein, for strength, with a small percentage allowed for healthy fats, as in avocados and some nuts. Choice C is the best choice.

Summary

o   Basic movement skills are the foundation from which more advanced physical skills develop.

o   When developing curriculum, Physical Education teachers should draw from a wide variety of sports, games, and activities.

o   Children grow and develop at very different rates and in very different ways.

o   Exercise and fitness are good for children both physically and emotionally.

o   Physical Education is greatly beneficial to students' social development.

Chapter 19
Human
Development

NO TAXONOMY WITHOUT REPRESENTATION
Read the example; then answer the two questions that follow.

At the end of a Social Studies unit on the Colonial Era, Mr. Yeh asked his students, "A family of Quakers who had left England because of religious persecution would probably have chosen to settle in which of the Middle Colonies?"

1. The correct answer is:

   A. New York.

   B. New Jersey.

   C. Pennsylvania.

   D. Delaware.

Because you'll have studied your history, you'll remember that Pennsylvania was founded by William Penn, a Quaker, so the first question will be a breeze. But then…

2. Which level of Bloom's taxonomy does Mr. Yeh's question represent?

   A. knowledge

   B. application

   C. analysis

   D. synthesis

Unfortunately, *Huh?* is not one of the answer choices. The answer is choice B *Application*, but that won't do you any good if you have no idea why.

TEACHING TO THE TEST

Above all, the CSET is an exam for teachers, and as a teacher, you'll be tested not only in subject matter, but also on your understanding of how to apply that knowledge in the learning environment.

COGNITIVE DEVELOPMENT

You'll need to know the basic developmental theories and theorists in cognitive, social, and moral development. Here's an overview of the big ones.

Piaget's Theory

Jean Piaget was a Swiss psychologist whose theory of **cognitive development** may be alluded to in CSET questions. You should be familiar with the basics of this theory and some common examples used to illustrate its principles.

Piaget believed that learning happens as people adapt to their environments. He suggested that cognitive development proceeds as follows: When faced with a situation, you first try to use or apply what you already know, and if that doesn't work, you figure out something else based on what's new or different about that situation. The first idea, using your existing **framework** or **schema**, he called **assimilation;** the second, developing new frameworks, he called **adaptation.** He believed that we are constantly refining our frameworks.

Based on his observations, Piaget theorized that this ongoing process of assimilation and adaptation leads all children to pass through identical stages of cognitive development, but not necessarily at identical times. He identified four stages; let's review them in order.

Sensorimotor Stage (approximate age 0 to 2 years)

Because most children pass through the **sensorimotor stage** by the time they reach the age of formal instruction, it's unlikely that you'll see questions dealing with it. You should know, however, that things that babies do and the types of games that parents typically play with babies are all relevant to this stage. For instance, one of the characteristics of the sensorimotor stage is understanding **object permanence**—the concept that things continue to exist even though you can't see them. Some educational psychologists and social anthropologists agree that the game of peek-a-boo is practically universal in human cultures specifically because it reinforces the concept of object permanence. Another hallmark of the sensorimotor stage is the early development of **goal-oriented behavior.** For example, a very young child who is able to roll over at will, but not yet able to crawl, may consciously roll over multiple times to reach a bottle or favorite toy.

Preoperational Stage (approximate age 2 to 7 years)

At the **preoperational stage,** children are developing language skills quickly. They also begin to use symbols to represent objects. Children in this stage will be able to think through simple problems, but only in one direction—that is, they won't be able to reverse the steps mentally. They also will have difficulty seeing things from another person's point of view. This idea is called **egocentrism.** Although this sounds like a negative quality, it's best understood as the child's assumption that everyone else sees things the same way that he does. For example, a child may assume that everyone likes orange juice simply because he likes orange juice.

Concrete Operational Stage (approximate age 7 to 11 years)

Children in the **concrete operational stage** develop the ability to perform a mental operation and then reverse their thinking back to the starting point, a concept called **reversibility**. They demonstrate the concepts of **transitivity** (they can classify objects according to a specific characteristic, even if the object has many different characteristics) and **seriation** (they can put objects in order according to a given criterion such as height or volume). One important concept is that of **conservation**—the idea that the amount of a substance doesn't change just because it's arranged differently. For example, conservation of mass might be demonstrated by taking a large ball of clay and creating several smaller balls of clay out of it. A child in the concrete operational stage will understand that the total amount of clay hasn't changed, while a child in the preoperational stage might think that there is more clay (because there are more balls). Children in the concrete operational stage also understand the concept of **class inclusion**—they can think about a whole group of objects while also thinking about the subgroups of those objects. For example, while thinking about the whole class, a child could also think about how many girls or boys are in the class. At this stage, children can solve concrete, hands-on problems logically.

Formal Operational Stage (approximate age 11 years to adulthood)

Not all students reach the **formal operational stage**. In fact, some theorists estimate that only about 35 percent of the adult population ever achieves this stage. It's characterized by the ability to solve abstract problems involving many independent elements. The thought process necessary to frame and solve such problems is called **hypothetical-deductive reasoning**.

Vygotsky's Theories

Lev Vygotsky was a Russian educational psychologist in the early twentieth century whose theories you should be familiar with. You might see questions about his four major ideas.

Culture

Vygotsky believed that environmental and cultural factors have an enormous influence on what children learn. Piaget argued that children are constantly developing methods of adapting to the world around them; Vygotsky argued that **environment** and **culture** dictate what methods the children will find useful, and what their priorities will be.

Private Speech

To Vygotsky, language use is a critical factor in cognitive development. Young children frequently talk to themselves as they play or solve problems. This is called **private speech.** While Piaget would cite private speech as evidence of egocentrism in the preoperational stage, Vygotsky believed that private speech allows children to use language to help break down a problem and solve it—in effect, the children talk themselves through it. He believed that a fundamental stage in development comes when children begin to carry on this speech internally, without speaking the words aloud. Children who routinely use private speech learn complex tasks more effectively.

Zone of Proximal Development

At any given stage, there are problems that a child can solve by herself, and there are other problems that a child couldn't solve even with prodding at each successive step. In between, however, are problems that a child could solve with the guidance of someone who already knows how. That range of problems is what Vygotsky referred to as the **zone of proximal development.** He believed that real learning takes place by solving problems in that zone.

Scaffolding

Scaffolding is another idea fundamental to Vygotsky's notion of social learning. It's about providing children with help from more competent peers and adults. Children are given a lot of support in the early stages of learning and problem solving. Then, as the child is able, he takes on more responsibility, and the supporter diminishes the support. Supportive techniques include clues, reminders, encouragement, breaking the problem into steps, providing examples, and anything that helps a student develop learning independence.

CONSTRUCTIVISM

Piaget's and Vygotsky's theories (among others') led to an educational philosophy called **constructivism,** which essentially says that learning is a constant assimilation of new knowledge and experiences into each student's unique worldview. Because each student's point of view will be different from everyone else's, a strict constructivist would be in favor of guided hands-on learning rather than traditional lecture-based teaching, because hands-on learning would more likely be related to a student's own experience.

Bloom's Taxonomy

Bloom's taxonomy is broadly encouraged and utilized in teacher preparation and instruction—in other words, if you don't know it already, you should! It's broken down into the six levels in which students develop thinking skills: In order, they are knowledge, comprehension, application, analysis, synthesis, and evaluation. In the early grades, students are limited to facts and other rote knowledge. As they develop, they're capable of processing information at levels of greater and greater complexity. In general, teachers should try to develop higher-order thinking skills (those at the end of the list). Let's take a look at the types of questions that would stimulate these types of thinking. Remember Mr. Yeh, and his unit on the colonization of the United States?

Bloom Taxonomy Level	Description	Question Example
Knowledge	Recalling factual information	What were the names of the New England colonies?
Comprehension	Using factual information to answer a specific question	What crops were common to the New England Colonies and the Southern colonies? What were the major religious differences between the New England colonies and the Middle Colonies?
Application	Taking an abstract concept together with specific facts to answer a question	In which area of the colonies would a Freethinker have been most likely to find like-minded people?
Analysis	Breaking down a question into concepts and ideas in order to answer a question	What characteristics of the New England colonists made them the most likely to rebel against British rule?
Synthesis	Connecting concepts and ideas to create a new product or idea	What steps could the king have taken to appease the New England colonists that might have prevented the American Revolution?
Evaluation	Making considered judgments by breaking down and reconnecting ideas, concepts, and facts and comparing the judgments to standards	In which area of the colonies did the colonists have the best natural resources from an economic standpoint?

In planning the unit, Mr. Yeh built a base of facts and concepts and then developed lessons that would encourage students to ask and answer increasingly complicated types of questions based on those facts and concepts.

Cognitive, Affective, and Psychomotor Domains

Bloom's taxonomy deals with skills in the cognitive area, or domain. The other two widely recognized areas are the affective and psychomotor domains.

The **affective domain** includes class participation, including listening as well as speaking, defending positions, and recognizing the opinions of others.

The **psychomotor domain** includes abilities related to physical prowess ranging from reflexes through basic motions such as catching and throwing a ball, to skilled motions such as playing tennis and playing the piano. It also includes the ability to communicate through motion, as in dancing or miming.

Which of the following examples best demonstrates Vygotsky's theory of the zone of proximal development for a sixth-grade student?

A.   She reads a chapter in her geometry textbook, and is asked to define the key terms.

B.   She is given a book to read in French, even though she has never studied the subject.

C.   She can already solve one-variable algebra equations, and is asked to solve multi-variable algebra equations.

D.   She is asked to complete a spelling assignment, which reviews words that she learned last year.

Here's How to Crack It

Remember that the *zone of proximal development* refers to a situation in which the student is asked to build upon prior learning, and has a reasonable chance to solve the problem, with some assistance. To crack this question, look to see which answer fits each part of that theory and use POE to eliminate the rest. The first answer you can rule out is choice B, which is obviously wrong because the student has no prior knowledge to build on. Choice D is incorrect for the opposite reason: The student is using prior knowledge, but she is not building anything new out of it. Technically, both choice A and choice C can be considered within the student's zone of proximal development, but remember, the CSET asks for the "best" example. Choice A is too vague. Choice C is specific and shows very clearly the student's current knowledge base as well as the logical next learning stage, and that is how you know it is the correct answer.

SOCIAL DEVELOPMENT

Erikson's Eight Stages of Psychosocial Development

You should be familiar with **Erik Erikson's** stages of psychosocial development. Erikson, a German-born American psychologist, identified eight stages of personal and social development, each of which takes the form of a resolution of an identity crisis. Here they are in chronological order.

1. Trust vs. Mistrust (birth to 18 months)

If children are well cared for during this time, they will become naturally trusting and optimistic. The goal is for infants to develop basic trust in their families and the world. Again, due to the age range involved, you will probably not see questions dealing with this stage.

2. Autonomy vs. Doubt (18 months to 3 years)

Children learn the mechanical basics of controlling their world, including walking, grasping, and toilet training. The "terrible twos" fall into this stage, with common traits including stubbornness and willful behavior as the child pushes the limits of control and develops autonomy. Children want to become independent and still rely on their support system. Ideally, parents need to be supportive of the children's needs so that they come out of this stage proud of their abilities rather than ashamed.

More Review

For more in-depth coverage of this content, check out *Cracking AP Psychology* from The Princeton Review.

3. Initiative vs. Guilt (3 to 6 years)

After becoming autonomous, children start wanting to do things. They have ideas and plans and carry out activities. Some activities aren't allowed, and it's important for children to feel that their activities are important and valued by adults. If this feeling isn't there, children believe that what they do is wrong, and guilt develops, which restricts growth.

4. Industry vs. Inferiority (6 to 12 years)

In these elementary-school years, children are expected to learn and produce. Parental influence decreases. Teachers and peers become more important. Success creates high self-esteem, while failures lower self-image. Just the perception of failure can cause children to feel inferior, even if the failure is not real. If children can meet the expectations of themselves, parents, and teachers, they learn to be industrious. If they do not, they risk feeling inferior.

5. Identity vs. Role Confusion (12 to 18 years)

During this stage, adolescents answer the question "Who am I?" It's quite common for teenagers to rebel, some very strongly. Erikson believed that the social structure of the United States was a healthy one for teenagers. They are offered the opportunity and leeway to try out different personalities and roles, and decide which ones suit them best. Acceptance by peer groups is of extreme importance.

Because the last three stages, described below, are stages that adults go through, it is unlikely that you will see any questions about them on the exam. They're listed here only for the purpose of completing the list.

6. Intimacy vs. Isolation (Young adulthood)

Being able to form mutually beneficial intimate relationships is the defining characteristic of this stage.

7. Generativity vs. Self-Absorption (Middle adulthood)

Adults need to be productive in helping and guiding future generations, both procreatively and professionally. If adults don't, they risk being self-absorbed.

8. Integrity vs. Despair (Late adulthood)

Finally, adults need to feel complete and comfortable with themselves and the choices they've made in their lives. They need to accept their eventual deaths.

Mildred Parten's Stages of Play Development

Play is an important way in which children learn to socialize. Mildred Parten, a child psychologist in the 1930s, was one of the first people to study children at play. Here are **Mildred Parten's stages of play development**, which are linked to different levels of social interaction.

1. Solitary Play

During this stage, children play by themselves. While children may continue to do this throughout their childhoods, in the context of social interaction, this is usually observed in children less than two years of age.

2. Onlooker Play

At around two years, children watch others play without doing anything themselves or making any effort to join in. This is closely followed in the same time frame by parallel play.

3. Parallel Play

In parallel play, children do the same thing that other children are doing. There is no interaction between the children.

4. Associative Play

Normally, by age four or five, children engage in associative play. Associative play is similar to parallel play, but there is increased interaction. Children share, take turns, and are interested in what others are doing.

5. Cooperative Play

Finally, usually by age five to seven, children play together in one activity.

MORAL DEVELOPMENT

Lawrence Kohlberg was a developmental psychologist at Harvard University in the late twentieth century. He conducted extensive research in the field of moral education. You should be familiar with **Kohlberg's stage theory of moral reasoning**. He split moral development into three levels, each of which contains two stages.

Level 1: Preconventional Moral Reasoning (Elementary School)

Rules are created by others.

Stage 1: Punishment and Obedience Orientation

Young children obey rules simply because there are rules, and they understand that they risk punishment by breaking them. Whether an action is good or bad is understood in terms of its immediate consequences.

Stage 2: Instrumental Relativist Orientation

Children internalize the system from Stage 1 and realize that following the rules is generally in their best interests. An action is right or good if it gets you what you want. A simple view of "fair's fair" develops, so that, for example, favors are done with the expectation of something in return.

Level 2: Conventional Moral Reasoning (Junior High–High School)

Kohlberg called this level conventional because most of society remains at this level. Judgment is based on tradition and others' expectations and less on consequences. Individuals adopt rules and sometimes put others' needs before their own.

Stage 3: Good Boy–Good Girl Orientation

An action is right or good if it helps, pleases, or is approved by others.

Stage 4: "Law and Order" Orientation

An action is right or good if it's expected out of a sense of duty or because it supports the morals or laws of the community or country. This reflects the common sentiment "It's right because it's the law."

Level three is unlikely to be tested because Kohlberg believed that it's not fully attained until adulthood, if it's ever attained at all. It's included here for completeness.

Level 3: Post-Conventional Moral Reasoning
People determine their own values and ethics.

Stage 5: Social Contract Orientation
An action is right or good if it meets an agreed-upon system of rules and rights (such as the United States Constitution). Unlike stage four, this phase recognizes that rules can be changed for the betterment of society.

Stage 6: Universal Ethical Principle Orientation
Good and right are relative, not absolute, and require abstract thinking in terms of justice, equality, and human dignity. One's conscience determines right from wrong. (In his later years, Kohlberg decided that stages 5 and 6 were actually the same.)

STUDENTS AS DIVERSE LEARNERS
Not all students learn the same way, and students have strengths and weaknesses in a variety of areas. The major ideas you should be familiar with are multiple intelligences, different learning styles, gender-based and culture-based differences, and exceptional students.

Multiple Intelligences
What is intelligence? This question may never be fully answered. Nonetheless, you should be familiar with Howard Gardner's work because it might show up on the CSET. **Howard Gardner** is a developmental psychologist at Harvard University who categorized the following nine **types of intelligence:**

1. **Logical-mathematical intelligence** relates to the ability to detect patterns, think logically, and make deductions. Scientists and mathematicians tend to be logical-mathematical thinkers.
2. People who have **linguistic intelligence** are particularly sensitive not only to words themselves, but also to the relationship between the meanings and sounds of words and the ideas and concepts that words represent. Poets and journalists tend to possess linguistic intelligence.
3. **Musical intelligence** is the ability to recognize and reproduce rhythm, pitch, and timbre—the three fundamental elements of music. Obviously, composers and musicians possess musical intelligence.

4. People with **spatial intelligence** have the ability to create and manipulate mental images. They also perceive spatial relationships in the world accurately and can use both the mental and actual perceptions to solve problems. Both artists and navigators use well-developed spatial intelligence.

5. **Naturalist intelligence** relates to being sensitive to natural objects like plants and animals and making fine sensory discriminations. Naturalists, hunters, and botanists excel in this intelligence.

6. **Bodily-kinesthetic intelligence** is the ability to consciously and skillfully control and coordinate your body's movements and manipulate objects. Athletes and dancers need a strong bodily-kinesthetic intelligence.

7. **Interpersonal intelligence** is the ability to understand and respond to the emotions and intentions of others. Psychologists and salespeople make good use of interpersonal intelligence.

8. **Intrapersonal intelligence** is the ability to understand and respond to your own emotions, intentions, strengths, weaknesses, and intelligences.

9. **Existential intelligence** is the sensitivity and capacity to tackle deep questions about human existence, such as the meaning of life, why we die, and how we got here.

Gardner believes that we all possess some degree of these intelligences, and that each of these must be relatively well developed in order for us to function well in society.

Although the intelligences are categorized separately, we rarely use them strictly independently. It is difficult to think of a profession or activity that wouldn't combine some of these intelligences. For instance, a pianist needs not only musical intelligence, but also interpersonal (to be able to relate to an audience) as well as bodily-kinesthetic (to control the actions of her hands on the keyboard).

Different Learning Styles

Not all people learn the same way. Different students process information differently depending on how it's presented. Many theorists split learning styles into the following three categories:

1. **Visual learners** learn by seeing. They prefer graphs and charts to summarize information, rather than text or a spoken summary. They prefer maps and diagrams to step-by-step directions. They're more likely to remember faces than names when they meet someone. Traditional lecture-based lessons can be good for visual learners as long as the teacher makes good use of visual aids.

2. **Auditory learners** learn by hearing. They're more likely to remember what was said about a painting they've studied than to be able to describe its appearance. Traditional lecture-based lessons are effective with aural learners.

3. **Kinesthetic learners** learn by doing. They remember things best if they try them out and see for themselves. They're more likely to remember what they were doing when they met someone than what they talked about. Traditional lecture-based lessons are not good for kinesthetic learners. Lessons that involve laboratory work or hands-on experimentation tend to be effective.

Theorist Lawrence Kohlberg would most likely agree with which of the following statements about first-grade students?

A. Children have no clear morality.

B. Children show concern for others and try to live up to expectations.

C. Children are able to differentiate between legality and morality.

D. Children have a generalized sense of respect for rules and expectations.

Here's How to Crack It

You know that Kohlberg split moral development into three levels, and as soon as you read the words "first grade," you know the question refers to Level 1: preconventional moral reasoning. Choices B and C are farthest from that level—much too advanced. When you look at the two choices that are left, though both seem plausible, remember that Kohlberg designated Level 1 for elementary school students. First graders are pretty low on the elementary school totem pole, so he most likely would agree with the statement that refers to the most basic stage of moral reasoning, which is choice A.

STUDENT MOTIVATION AND THE LEARNING ENVIRONMENT

Now that we've looked at how children develop and how they learn, let's take a look at how motivation and the classroom environment can have an impact. There are several major theorists you should be familiar with: Edward Lee Thorndike, Ivan Pavlov, Abraham Maslow, B. F. Skinner, and Albert Bandura.

Thorndike's Laws

Edward Lee Thorndike was an early behavioral psychologist whose work led him to three major conclusions:

- Law of effect: An action that produces a positive result is likely to be repeated.
- Law of readiness: Many actions can be performed in sequence to produce a desired effect.
- Law of exercise: Actions that are repeated frequently become stronger.

Pavlov's Conditioned Responses

Ivan Pavlov, a Russian psychologist, proved through experimentation that behavior could be learned according to a system of stimulus and response. His most famous experiment conditioned dogs to salivate at the sound of a bell. He did so by noting that dogs normally salivate at the smell of food, an unconditioned (that is, innate or reflexive) response to an unconditioned stimulus. The ringing of a bell has no natural meaning for dogs. Such a signal is called a neutral stimulus. He introduced the sound of the bell at feeding time, thereby linking the sound of the bell and the smell of the food in the dogs' minds. Eventually, the dogs salivated at the sound of the bell alone, which was now a conditioned (that is, learned) response to a conditioned stimulus.

Maslow's Hierarchy of Needs

Abraham Maslow was an educational theorist who believed that children must have certain needs met before they're ready to learn and grow. He organized these needs into a hierarchy, and taught that you couldn't progress to the next level until you'd achieved the previous one. Here's the hierarchy from low to high:

Deficiency Needs

Physiological needs—food, sleep, clothing, and so on
Safety needs—freedom from harm or danger
Belongingness and love needs—acceptance and love from others
Esteem needs—approval and accomplishment

Growth Needs

Cognitive needs—knowledge and understanding
Aesthetic needs—appreciation of beauty and order
Self-actualization needs—fulfillment of one's potential

Maslow called the first four **deficiency needs.** They are the basic requirements for physical and psychosocial well-being. Desire for these declines once you have them, and you don't think about them unless you lack them. He called the other three **growth needs.** They include the need for knowing, appreciating, and understanding. People try to meet these needs only after their basic needs have been met. He believed that meeting these needs created more desire for them. For example, having adequate shelter and food doesn't make you crave more shelter and food. By contrast, learning and understanding sparks the desire to learn and understand more.

Skinner's Operant Conditioning

B. F. Skinner was a psychologist who believed that you could use a system of positive and negative reinforcements to affect voluntary behavior. He called a positive reinforcement a **reinforcing stimulus,** or **reinforcer,** and the behavior that leads to the positive reinforcement an **operant.** The classic lab scenario is that of a rat pressing a bar in a cage in order to receive food. The pressing of the bar is the operant and the food is the reinforcer. If, after a time, the operant no longer leads to positive reinforcement, the behavior will decrease, and eventually stop. That process is called **extinction.**

A **negative reinforcement** is the removal of an unpleasant stimulus after a certain desired behavior occurs. For instance, a parent wishing to reward a teenager for consistently following a 10:00 P.M. curfew might extend the curfew until 10:30 P.M.

Presentation punishment is what we normally think of as being punished for bad behavior. For instance, a teenager that violated curfew rules might be grounded.

Bandura's Concept of Reinforcement

Albert Bandura, a psychologist, theorized that people learn behavior by watching others, trying the behavior themselves, and deciding whether the behavior is beneficial or detrimental. A positive result means that the behavior is **reinforced**, and therefore likely to be repeated. Bandura believed that peer group modeling and images from the media provided very strong suggestions for new behavior patterns.

EXTRINSIC AND INTRINSIC MOTIVATION

One important idea with respect to classroom management is **extrinsic**, or **external**, **motivation** (motivation that comes from outside factors) versus **intrinsic**, or **internal**, **motivation** (motivation that comes from within). In general, while external motivation can be used, the long-term goal is that students' motivation for learning be intrinsic.

Putting all this together means that children learn best in an environment in which they are encouraged to reach their potential, are inwardly motivated to learn, and are exposed to positive behaviors that allow learning to happen. Sounds easy, right?

Here are important things to keep in mind.

Consistency

Whatever approach you take to classroom management, you must be consistent. Rules that aren't followed consistently cease to have any weight. There should be consistent, regular procedures for daily activities (such as putting chairs on the top of desks at the end of the day).

Structure

Students need structure and direction. Lessons or tasks should have clear, well-articulated goals. Students should always know what they're supposed to be doing at any given point during the day.

Discipline

Discipline techniques that are too harsh and autocratic run the risk of suppressing students' internal motivation. Discipline techniques that are too laissez-faire run the risk of not providing enough structure. Striking that balance is challenging, but can be made easier by establishing guidelines immediately. Guidelines should be age-appropriate. First graders can simply be told that they need to raise their hands and wait for a teacher to call on them before they can start speaking. A sixth-grade teacher might use part of the first day of school having the class as a whole decide what types of behavior should be prohibited, and what consequences should arise from prohibited behavior.

Inappropriate behavior should be dealt with immediately, consistently, and in a manner that does not unwittingly provide positive reinforcement. For instance, a verbal reprimand should occur out of earshot from the rest of the class. A trouble-maker who craves attention will continue to act out if the teacher gives him/her attention for each inappropriate behavior. For the student, the teacher's attention is positive reinforcement.

Time on Task

It's easy to lose the forest for the trees, but remember that students are there to learn. Structure and discipline serve to make sure there's as much time as possible available for actual learning.

Transitions

Procedures should be in place for getting students from one task to another in an efficient manner. Suggestions include agreed-upon signals such as flipping the lights on and off or clapping your hands.

CREATIVE THINKING VS. CRITICAL THINKING

Good teachers promote both **critical** and **creative thinking** in their students. The difference between the two might best be described by thinking about the following questions:

- How many different ways can you think of to get from New York to San Francisco?
- What's the best way to get from New York to San Francisco?

Answering the first question involves creative thinking. Answering the second involves critical thinking. Let's compare the two.

Creative Thinking

The first question involves **divergent thinking**—there are many possible answers, and no particular answer is necessarily right or wrong. One technique that a good teacher can use to help with questions such as these is **brainstorming**, in which students are encouraged to come up with as many solutions as possible without stopping to evaluate their merits. Imagine posing the question to a group of active sixth graders. At first, you'd probably get some relatively predictable responses that you'd write down as the students came up with them:

- You could fly; you could drive; you could take a train.

Then, you could start to expect some more "outside the box" ideas:

- You could bike; you could run; you could walk; you could take a boat around the tip of South America and come back up the other side.

And some with less critical thought behind them:

- You could hitchhike. How about a hot air balloon? You could drive to Florida and take the space shuttle. You could wrap yourself up and have yourself FedExed. Could you dig a tunnel?

And after a while the responses would taper off, and you'd be left with a large list of possibilities on the board.

You should be familiar with two other important ideas regarding creative thinking:

- **Restructuring** is a term that describes the process of thinking about an old problem in a new way. Many educational psychologists believe that time away from the problem is an important element that encourages restructuring—some believe that dreaming is also an important component.
- Also, play encourages creative thinking, and good teachers use well-designed in-class games for this purpose.

Critical Thinking

Let's go back to the results of the brainstorming exercise. There's a large list of possibilities on the board, and you're now ready to ask the second question:

What's the best way of getting from New York to San Francisco?

This question requires **convergent thinking**—from many possible answers the student is expected to choose and defend the best one. A good teacher will use this opportunity to show how the answer to this question depends on the criteria used. Does "best" mean "cheapest"? If so, then hitchhiking might be a good choice, but you'd have to factor in the cost of food and shelter, because the trip would take longer than it would if you flew. Does "best" mean "quickest"? If so, then flying is probably the best way to go. A good teacher would also seize the opportunity to allow for **transfer,** the application of previously learned skills or facts to new situations. For example, if the class had recently completed a unit on the environment, the teacher could ask, "What if 'best' means 'most environmentally friendly,' but you have to get there within three days?"

Two important aspects of critical thinking are inductive and deductive reasoning.

Inductive Reasoning

Inductive reasoning occurs when, after viewing several examples, students perceive underlying rules or patterns. For example, students could be given many different parallelograms, and asked what they all have in common. Through measurement and comparison, students might induce that opposite sides of parallelograms are parallel, and that the sum of any two adjacent angles in a parallelogram is 180 degrees.

Deductive Reasoning

Deductive reasoning works in the opposite direction. For example, students might be told that if the sum of any two adjacent angles in a given quadrilateral is 180 degrees, then that quadrilateral is a parallelogram. Then, they'd be given many quadrilaterals, and asked to determine which ones are parallelograms. Both inductive and deductive reasoning are important cognitive skills.

INSTRUCTIONAL STRATEGIES

Different teaching approaches should be taken to stimulate different types of thinking. You should know what options are available to you and which strategies are most likely to accomplish a given educational goal.

Direct Instruction

Direct instruction is the most common form of teaching, the traditional model in which the teacher stands in front of the room, presents new material, and guides the class toward understanding. You should be familiar with the following concepts:

Hunter's Effective Teaching Model and Mastery Learning

Madeline Hunter, an educational psychologist, expanded on the basic idea of direct instruction and broke the process down into discrete steps:

1. Prepare students to learn:
   - Review the previous day's material with a question or two.
   - Get the students' attention with an **anticipatory set,** a question or problem designed to spark students' curiosity and imagination.
   - Outline the lesson's objectives.
2. Use input and modeling:
   - Teach well.
   - Organize your presentation.
   - Present the information clearly.
   - Connect new ideas to old ideas.
   - Use examples and analogies.
   - Demonstrate and model new techniques.

3. Make sure students understand. Ask both individual and group questions.
   - Have students apply new techniques immediately.
   - Work several short examples—**guided practice.**
   - Monitor student ability—**independent practice.**

Ausubel's Advance Organizers

David Ausubel's theory expands on some aspects of Hunter's model. **Advance organizers** are the structure (also known as **scaffolding** or **support**) and information that students will need to learn new material effectively. They fall into two categories:

1. A **comparative organizer** relates previously mastered material to the material that's about to be presented. For example, a middle-school lesson about sonnet form might begin with a comparative advance organizer that reminds students of a previous lesson on iambic pentameter or simple ABAB rhyme schemes.
2. An **expository organizer** is a new idea or concept that needs to be understood before a specific lesson can be understood. For example, a high-school literature class already familiar with rhyme schemes might need an expository advance organizer that discussed the purpose of analyzing poetry and showing that rhyme scheme analysis is just one method of doing so.

Demonstrations

Visual learners in particular respond well to **demonstrations.** Showing is more effective than simply telling. New computer technology allows for imaginative and compelling demonstrations. Good teachers take advantage of all tools at their disposal.

Mnemonics

Provide students with memory devices to help them retain factual information. For instance, "Please excuse my dear Aunt Sally" is a common **mnemonic** for the order of mathematical operations: parentheses, exponents, multiplication, division, addition, and subtraction. We have seen quite a few mnemonics throughout this book.

Note-Taking

Students need to be taught how to take notes effectively. One important technique involves giving students a general outline of the major points to be discussed and having them fill in the blanks as the lesson progresses.

Outlining

A clear order of presentation with a well-defined hierarchy of ideas is crucial so that students have an understanding of what the most important parts of a lesson are.

Use of Visual Aids

As with demonstrations, visual aids can make new information stick in students' minds better than it would if it were presented through lecture alone.

Student-Centered Models

In contrast to direct instruction, **student-centered models** make students, not teachers, the center of attention while new material is being learned. These methods do not lessen the demands on the teacher; in fact, use of student-centered models requires more planning and as much active participation by the teacher as does use of direct instruction. Here are some important student-centered models.

Emergent Curriculum

In **emergent curriculum,** students are given a strong voice in deciding what form the curriculum will take. For instance, students could decide that they were interested in studying leaves. It would then be incumbent upon the teacher to find useful leaf-related activities and experiments that would meet established educational goals. Alternatively, the teacher could present a variety of possible topics, and the students could choose which they wanted to study.

Cooperative Learning

In **cooperative learning**, students are split into mixed-ability groups, assigned well-defined tasks to accomplish or problems to analyze, and are given individual roles within the group (such as note-taker or illustrator). Students learn from each other and interact in a way that is not possible with direct instruction. One well-known method of organizing cooperative learning in the classroom is called **STAD (student teams achievement divisions)** in which cooperative learning cycles through the following stages:

1. teaching, in which the teacher presents basic material and gives teams a task;
2. team study, in which students work on the project;
3. test, in which students take individual quizzes; and
4. team recognition, in which the best-performing teams are rewarded.

In another model, called the **think-pair-share method,** students research a topic on their own, discuss their theories and ideas with one other student, and then participate in a classroom discussion.

Discovery Learning

Discovery learning is closely aligned with inductive reasoning. Students are given examples and are expected to find patterns and connections with minimal guidance from a teacher during class. Students are encouraged to use **intuitive thinking,** and then make an effort to prove or disprove their intuition given the available information.

Concept Models

Concept models are part of an organizational strategy that helps students to relate new ideas to old ideas. There are three aspects that you should be familiar with:

- Concept development: The concept is promoted by the identification of a prototype, or stereotypical example of the concept. For example, if the concept is polygons, a prototype might be a square or a triangle. From the prototype, students generate the definition, in this case, a closed plane figure with a finite number of straight-line sides.
- Concept attainment: Students learn to identify examples (pentagons, right triangles) and non-examples (circles, open figures) and sub-define the category according to given criteria (a rectangle is a special polygon having four sides and four equal angles).
- Concept mapping or webbing: Students draw a pictorial representation of the concepts or ideas about some topic and the links between them. Teachers can look over these maps and discern areas of misunderstanding. There are several different types of methods that currently go by names like **concept mapping, mental mapping,** and **concept webbing.**

Inquiry Method

The **inquiry method** is related to discovery learning. A teacher poses a question, and the students have to gather information and then formulate and test hypotheses in order to answer it. Although this method could conceivably be used in teaching almost any discipline, it's particularly well-suited to teaching science and math. For instance, a teacher could pose the question "Do all triangles have 180 degrees?" Students could then try to find different ways of proving or disproving the statement (drawing triangles, measuring the angles, and adding them up; comparing the degree measures to a straight line; and so on), and eventually conclude that yes, all triangles have 180 degrees.

Metacognition

Teachers can also encourage students to think about their own learning processes. This is called **metacognition.** For example, a teacher might assign a journal assignment in which students would answer the questions "What did I learn today?" and "How did it relate to things I've learned earlier?"

QUESTIONING

Good teachers ask good questions that encourage different kinds of thinking in students. Use Bloom's Taxonomy as a sorting mechanism for different types of questions.

In addition to asking good questions, teachers should also be aware that how questions are asked can have a large impact on student learning. You should be familiar with the following concepts.

Frequency

Frequency simply refers to the number of questions you ask. Socrates notwithstanding, if everything you say is a question, it's difficult for students to learn. On the other hand, nothing is duller than a lecture with no questions. Strike a balance and use questions well to enhance learning.

Equitable Distribution

Call on individual students to ensure that all students are participating. Gear specific questions to specific students, ensuring that a question will be challenging for a given student, but will be something the student has a good chance of answering correctly.

Cueing

Cueing is further prompting by the teacher after the initial question is met with silence or an incorrect or partially correct response. For a rote-memory sort of question such as "What's the capital of Kansas?" a teacher might cue with a reference to a previously learned mnemonic such as "Remember: 'Everyone in Kansas wears sandals, so…,'" thereby eliciting the student response of "Topeka!" More complicated questions could require more extensive cueing.

Wait-Time

Wait-time is the amount of time a teacher waits for a response after asking a question. Students need time to process the question, think of the answer, and formulate a response. A wait-time of three to five seconds is shown to have a strong positive impact on student learning.

Further, a good teacher can use questioning as a mechanism to support classroom management techniques. One common technique is called **group alerting,** in which the teacher asks the whole class the question, waits, and then selects one student to answer. Naming the student before the question is asked increases the likelihood that the other students will stop paying attention.

Ms. Barabian finds that her fourth-grade class loses focus when she switches from subject to subject. Which of the following techniques would help Ms. Barabian manage her class more effectively?

A. modeling

B. guided practice

C. transitions

D. assertive discipline

Here's How to Crack It

This is really a common sense question. You know that choices A and B are teaching techniques, but the question is looking for a classroom management technique. You're left with two choices, and in this case, the easiest way to determine the right answer is to look for key words within the question. The phrase *switches from subject to subject* tells you that the problem Ms. Barabian is having relates to choice C, transitions.

PLANNING INSTRUCTION

How does a teacher decide what to teach? Ideally, teachers have long-term and short-term objectives for their students. It's important that these objectives are well-defined, because planning instruction and assessment is easier and more meaningful if goals are clearly specified.

There are two fundamental approaches to defining objectives. Good teachers apply both.

Teaching Objectives

Teaching objectives are defined in general terms. A cognitive objective might be, "Students will understand the hierarchical relationships among the different types of quadrilaterals." The advantage to a teaching objective is that it's general enough to encompass a wide variety of teaching approaches and techniques. The disadvantage is that it's difficult to measure student understanding of any given concept in all its various forms. Could you write a test that would measure whether students understood all "the hierarchical relationships among the different types of quadrilaterals"?

Learning Objectives

Learning objectives are defined in concrete terms, and can be directly observed. Students are expected to exhibit the desired behavior at the end of the lesson(s). For example, "Students will be able to construct a perfect square of a given length using a compass and straightedge." These goals are easy to assess—you can simply watch a student perform the construction—but their specificity makes it difficult to include large-scale concepts. For instance, imagine how long the list of learning objectives would be to describe the body of knowledge and skills covered in the first semester of a geometry class.

The type of objective a teacher will use depends on the plan he/she is creating. A daily lesson plan will require learning objectives; a unit or monthly plan will include teaching objectives. Here's an example:

Type of Lesson	Type of Objective	Example of Objective
Unit lesson plan	Teaching objective	Students will understand the hierarchical relationships among the different types of quadrilaterals.
Daily lesson plan	Learning objectives	Students will recite the definition of a quadrilateral. Students will be able to demonstrate the hierarchical distinction between squares and rectangles. Students will be able to prove that every rhombus is a parallelogram.

ASSESSMENT STRATEGIES

Just as you'd use different teaching strategies to teach different ideas, you should use different assessment strategies to measure student achievement. Here are some terms you should be familiar with.

Norm-Referenced Tests

If you've ever been graded on a curve, then you've experienced a **norm-referenced test**. That means that your grade depended on how well you did compared to everyone else who took the test.

Criterion-Referenced Tests

Your driver's license test was probably a **criterion-referenced test**. Perhaps there were 25 questions, and you needed to answer 20 of them correctly in order to pass. It didn't matter how many people had aced the test and how many people had answered only 10 questions correctly. You needed to prove a certain proficiency in order to pass.

Standardized Tests

If you're reading this book, then we probably have a pretty good idea about what you think of **standardized tests**. The term *standardized* means that test content, conditions, grading, and reporting are equivalent for everyone who takes the test. We tend to think of them as purely multiple-choice, but that's not true.

- Achievement tests—Most standardized tests given are achievement tests, given to measure specific knowledge in a specific area.
- Aptitude tests—These tests purport to measure how well a student is likely to do in the future.

Remember, of course, that you don't have to give standardized tests to your students. You have a much wider range of options, including the following.

Assessments of Prior Knowledge/Pretesting

It's important to take into account the level of knowledge a student had before beginning a given lesson or semester. Would it be fair to hold a recent immigrant to the same standards as a native English speaker on an oral grammar test? Probably not. Some curricula are designed so that a specific set of knowledge and skills is necessary before instruction in a new area can occur. Such a set of knowledge and skills is called a **prerequisite competency.**

Structured Observations

These are particularly well-suited to situations in which cooperative learning is taking place. The teacher can observe the interactions within a group and evaluate student performance accordingly. This is an example of an **informal assessment,** meaning that there is no grading rubric or checklist that a teacher follows. An informal assessment is more subjective and situation-specific than it is during a **formal assessment** such as a standardized test.

Student Responses during a Lesson

This shouldn't necessarily be considered the same as grading on class participation, but a teacher can get a strong sense of student understanding (or lack thereof) based on responses during classroom discussions. This is another example of an informal assessment.

Portfolios

Portfolios aren't just used in art classes. They're are often used to give students a place to collect their best work over a longer period of time, such as a unit or even a semester. Teachers can get a sense of the level of student work holistically, without placing undue influence on a specific test. Portfolios allow teachers to assess learning growth over a period of time.

Essays Written to Prompts

While these take longer to grade, and depend upon students possessing sufficient writing skills, essays give insight into student thought in a way that multiple-choice tests cannot.

Journals

Many good teachers use **journals** not only as tools to promote individual self-expression, but also to gauge understanding.

Self-Evaluation

Sometimes, a good teacher will give students an opportunity to grade their own work. While it's not usually binding, the grade a student chooses to give himself (along with the explanation of why it's deserved) can provide the teacher valuable insight.

KEY TERMS

Jean Piaget

cognitive development

framework (schema)

assimilation

adaptation

sensorimotor stage

object permanence

goal-oriented behavior

preoperatonal stage

egocentrism

concrete operational stage

reversibility

transitivity

seriation

conservation

class inclusion

formal operational stage

hypothetical-deductive reasoning

Lev Vygotsky

environment

culture

private speech

zone of proximal development

scaffolding

constructivism

Bloom's taxonomy

affective domain

psychomotor domain

Erik Erikson's stages of psychosocial development

Mildred Parten's stages of play development

Lawrence Kohlberg's stage theory of moral reasoning

Howard Gardner's multiple intelligences

logical-mathematical intelligence

linguistic intelligence

musical intelligence

spatial intelligence

naturalist intelligence

bodily-kinesthetic intelligence

interpersonal intelligence

intrapersonal intelligence

existential intelligence

visual learners

auditory learners

kinesthetic learners

Edward Lee Thorndike's laws

Ivan Pavlov's conditioned responses

Abraham Maslow's hierarchy of needs

deficiency needs

growth needs

B. F. Skinner's operant conditioning

reinforcing stimulus (reinforcer)

operant

extinction

negative reinforcement

presentation punishment

Albert Bandura's concept of reinforcement

extrinsic (external) motivation

intrinsic (internal) motivation

creative thinking

critical thinking

divergent thinking

brainstorming

restructuring

convergent thinking

transfer

inductive reasoning

deductive reasoning

direct instruction

Madeline Hunter's effective teaching model and mastery learning

anticipatory set

guided practice

independent practice

David Ausubel's advance organizers

scaffolding (support)

comparative organizer

expository organizer

demonstrations

mnemonics

student-centered models

emergent curriculum

cooperative learning

STAD (student teams achievement divisions)

think-pair-share method

discovery learning

intuitive thinking
concept models
concept mapping
mental mapping
concept webbing
inquiry method
metacognition
frequency
cueing
wait-time
group alerting

teaching objectives
learning objectives
norm-referenced tests
criterion-referenced tests
standardized tests
prerequisite competency
informal assessment
formal assessment
portfolios
journals

Drill #17

1. Jean Piaget stated a theory of four stages of cognitive development in young children. Which stage is most associated with a fourth-grade student whose thinking becomes organized and logical?

   A. sensorimotor

   B. preoperational

   C. concrete operational

   D. formal operational

2. Students in third grade are given a spelling test. The skills measured in this test are aligned with what stage in Bloom's taxonomy of learning?

   A. knowledge

   B. comprehension

   C. synthesis

   D. evaluation

3. Students in Mr. Meyer's class were having trouble remembering the names of the five Great Lakes, so Mr. Meyer told them, "Think of all of the people who have homes on the shores of the Great Lakes. That will help you remember the first letter of each lake: Huron, Ontario, Michigan, Erie, and Superior."

   Mr. Meyer employed which of the following instructional strategies?

   A. demonstration

   B. mnemonic

   C. outlining

   D. allegory

4. After presenting a lecture on the human circulatory system, Ms. Burns demonstrated how blood travels toward and away from the heart. Ms. Burns is in what stage of Madeline Hunter's effective teaching model?

   A. anticipatory set

   B. input

   C. modeling

   D. guided practice

5. Which of the following is typically not addressed in a lesson plan?

   A. objectives

   B. assessment

   C. practice

   D. punishments

Please turn the page for answers and explanations
for the questions in this drill.

ANSWERS AND EXPLANATIONS TO DRILL #17

1. **C** During the concrete operational stage, students' thinking becomes operational, which means that concepts become organized and logical, as long as they are working with or around concrete materials or images.

2. **A** In the knowledge stage, students are asked to remember specifics, recalling terms, formulas, and theories.

3. **B** Mr. Meyer gave the class a mnemonic, which is a tool to help the students retain factual information.

4. **C** In the modeling stage, the skills or procedures are being taught or demonstrated. Notice the clue in the question, which indicates that a lecture had already been given. A lecture would qualify as *input*, or the presentation of new information.

5. **D** And just so you know, *consequences* is the politically correct term anyway.

Summary

- For the CSET, you should know a few theories of cognitive development: Jean Piaget, Lev Vygotsky, and Bloom's taxonomy.

- Social development is extremely important. You should be familiar with theories from Erik Erickson, Mildred Parten, and Lawrence Kohlberg.

- There are many types of intelligence, according to Howard Gardner's list of eight types of intelligence.

- As a teacher, you should also be aware that your students will have different learning styles.

- You should be familiar with major theorists of student motivation and the learning environment: Edward Lee Thorndike, Ivan Pavlov, Abraham Maslow, B.F. Skinner, and Albert Bandura.

- Teachers should promote both critical and creative thinking in their students.

- There are many different instructional strategies that can be used to stimulate different types of thinking in students.

- When planning instruction and assessment, teachers should think about both teaching objectives and learning objectives.

- Many different types of assessment strategies can be used, including norm-referenced tests, criterion-referenced tests, standardized tests, pretesting, journals, self-evaluation, and more.

Chapter 20
Visual and Performing Arts

IS THAT PAINT-BY-NUMBER?

The painting reproduced above depicts:

A.   an ancient game of tag.

B.   an unfortunate Superglue incident.

C.   the earliest known experiment
     with static electricity.

D.   the creation of Adam.

ART IMITATES LIFE

A comprehensive arts program in schools includes four disciplines: dance, music, theatre, and the visual arts. For each grade level, the standards are grouped under five strands.

Artistic Perception

Artistic perception, the first of the five strands, refers to the way students learn to respond to, process, and analyze sensory information. They learn and use the vocabulary and skills unique to each of the disciplines.

Creative Expression

In **creative expression**, students are expected to participate and perform. They learn to create their own works, using a variety of means to communicate intent and meaning, and apply processes and skills in composing, arranging, and performing their works.

Historical and Cultural Context

Students study the time and place of creation of works of art, and understand the historical and cultural impacts on a work. They learn about artists in each discipline.

Aesthetic Valuing

Through the process of **aesthetic valuing**, students analyze, interpret, and critique works in each discipline, including works of their own creation.

Connections, Relationships, and Applications

The final strand is called **connections**, **relationships**, and **applications**. Students connect and apply what they learn in each discipline to other arts disciplines and to other subject areas. They learn about careers in and related to arts disciplines.

DANCE

Elements of Dance

While ballet and breakdancing may not appear to be similar, they have more in common than you might think. All dance is based on the same basic elements.

Space

Space in dance refers to the area covered by movements.

- Level: the distance from the floor
- Directions: up, down, forward, backward, and so on
- Shape: the "design" of the body
- Pathways: patterns made by the body as it moves

Time

Time has several designations.

- Duration: the length of time the movement takes
- Tempo: the speed of the dance
- Beat: even or uneven

Force

Force, or **dynamics,** refers to the amount of energy the movement takes. In both ballet and breakdancing, for example, a fast spin uses a great amount of force.

Relationship

Relationship in dance identifies with whom or what the body is moving. Every dance is comprised of some kind of relationship. Dances may be made in any kind of grouping, such as **solo** (in which the dancer is considered to have a relationship with the space), **duet,** and **ensemble,** for example.

Dance Techniques

Each style or genre of dance has its own specific techniques, or physical skills required to perform the movements and steps. Of course, many skills overlap between genres. Basic techniques include

- balance
- weight shift
- alignment
- patterns
- mirroring
- positioning

While teachers should try to incorporate as many different styles of dance as possible, some genres are taught most frequently to children, in part because of the basic movement skills utilized. Those genres include ballet, line dancing, jazz, tap, folk dancing, modern dance, and ballroom dancing.

Cultural and Historical Context

You should be familiar with types of dances developed in different historical eras and geographical settings, and purposes of dance in various cultures.

Purpose

These are some examples of how dance is used.

- Ceremonies and celebrations: Native American, Japanese, Greek
- Artistry: Japanese, Russian, Mexican
- Communication: African, Chinese, Indian
- Recreation: American, Spanish

Origins

Here are some of the historical and geographical origins of the more well-known forms of dance.

- Ballet: Renaissance Italy and France
- Jazz: early- to mid-twentieth-century African Americans
- Tap: based on Irish step dancing, African drum rhythms, and English clog dance; popularized during Vaudeville era
- Flamenco: Spanish gypsies, strongly influenced by Indian and colonial African dance
- Tango: Argentina, developed centuries ago but modernized and popularized in the early to mid-twentieth century
- Waltz: seventeenth-century Austria
- Modern dance: early twentieth-century North America and Germany

---

Which of the following dances allows a dancer the widest range of levels?

A. tap

B. ballet

C. cha-cha

D. line dancing

Here's How to Crack It

Level in dancing refers to how high or low a dancer is in relation to the floor. To help you determine the answer, pull up a mental video of each of the types of dances. Tap dancing (choice A), cha-cha (choice C), and line dancing (choice D) are all generally performed in an upright position, with some bending at the knees and waist. On the other hand, it is entirely common to see a ballet dancer lying on the floor or leaping high in the air, which is how you know that ballet, choice B, is the best answer choice.

MUSIC

Elements of Music

There are eight basic elements of music.

Musical Instruments

In its broadest definition, a **musical instrument** is considered to be any device used to produce sound.

Timbre

Timbre is the quality of sound that distinguishes one instrument or voice from another. It is also referred to as **tone color**.

Dynamics

Dynamics are symbols or abbreviations used to indicate the volume of, or change of volume within, a piece of music. Examples of dynamic signs include the following:

- *p* : piano (soft)

- *ff* : fortissimo (very loud)

- > : decrescendo (gradually softer)

Melody

Melody refers to a tune created by playing a series of notes or chords.

Harmony

Harmony is the sound that results when two or more tones are played or sung at the same time. Harmony works in tandem with melody to give music texture.

Rhythm

Rhythm is the pattern or placement of beats in music. Beats are characterized as weak or strong and are grouped in measures.

Meter

Meter refers to the rhythmic patterns developed in groups of strong and weak beats.

Tempo

Tempo is the speed at which a piece of music is played. The following are examples of different tempos:

- allegro: fast and lively
- adagio: slow
- moderato: moderate
- grave: very slow

Musical Notation

The CSET will ask you some questions that require you to read and interpret short excerpts of sheet music, so you should be able to recognize some of the more common signs and symbols of **musical notation.**

Staff

The **staff** is the five-line foundation on which notes are written.

The **treble staff** opens on the left with a **treble clef,** which looks a little like the "and" symbol on your keyboard. From the bottom line up, the lines represent the musical notes E, G, B, D, F. You can remember them with the mnemonic device "Every Good Boy Does Fine." From the bottom up, the spaces between the lines represent the notes F, A, C, E—which lends itself to an easy mnemonic device, "FACE."

Remember these Mnemonics!
Every Good Boy Does Fine
and
F A C E

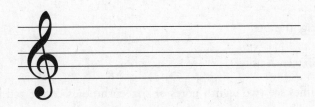

The **bass staff** opens with a **bass clef.** The bottom line represents G, and the lines follow the same upward order. A mnemonic device to remember the lines in the bass staff is "Good Boys Don't Fight Anyone." To remember the spaces, which start with the note A, you can use "All Cows Eat Grass."

Another Mnemonic!
Good Boys Don't Fight Anyone
and
All Cows Eat Grass

The **grand staff** is what you'd normally see in piano music, because of the range of pitches on that instrument. It is a combination of the treble staff (top) and the bass staff (bottom).

Notes
Musical notes represent the length of beats.

- ○ Whole note

- ♩ Half note

- ♩ Quarter note

- ♪ Eighth note

- ♪ Sixteenth note

You'll sometimes see two eighth notes or sixteenth notes connected by a straight line on the top.

Measures
Measures, which divide the music, are marked by vertical lines. Sometimes there will be numbers at the top of each line to better navigate the piece of music.

The **time signature,** or **meter signature,** determines the number of beats allowed in each measure. It is represented by one number on top of another, like a fraction. The top number tells you how many beats to count per measure. The bottom number tells you what kind of notes to count for one beat: Each number represents a note—2 represents a half note, 4 represents a quarter note, 8 represents an eighth note, and 16 represents a sixteenth note. For example, a 3/4 time signature indicates that there are three beats in every measure, and that each beat is one quarter note long.

Key Signature

The **key signature** is a set of either sharp symbols, which look like tilted number signs, or flat symbols, which look like pointed b's, located at the beginning of a musical staff. It tells you which notes will be sharp or flat throughout the piece.

Musical Instruments

There are several accepted systems of classifying musical instruments, though all base the categories on the same basic features, and many instruments fall under more than one classification.

Wind

Wind instruments use air as a vibrating medium to produce sound. In brief, they're the instruments you blow into.

Wind instruments are often split into **brass instruments** and **woodwinds.** The terms originally described the material the instruments were made from, but now they are indicators of the way sound is produced.

In brass instruments, tone is produced by the vibration of the lips, and valves are used to change the pitch. Brass instruments include tubas, trombones, and French horns.

Woodwinds produce sound when air is blown against an edge or opening in the instrument, usually past a thin piece of wood called a **reed,** causing the air to vibrate. Clarinets, oboes, and saxophones are all woodwinds.

Keyboard

Keyboard instruments produce sound when keys are pressed. Some instruments, like the piano, use hammers to strike strings and cause vibrations. Others, such as the pipe organ, release compressed air through pipes when the keys are pressed.

Percussion

Percussion instruments are sounded by striking, plucking, shaking, or scraping. Drums, bells, tambourines, maracas, and cymbals are all examples of percussion instruments.

String

String instruments produce tone by vibrating taut strings. The strings can be plucked, as with a guitar or harp; bowed, as with a violin or cello; or struck, as with a dulcimer or piano.

Origins

Beyond the classifications, you should be familiar with the historical and cultural origins of musical instruments, such as the ones listed below.

- Drums: dating back to 5,000–6,000 B.C.E. in many parts of the world
- Piano: developed from the clavichord and harpsichord, and perfected in Italy, Germany, and Austria during the early 1700s
- Guitar: based on early Egyptian and Mesopotamian stringed instruments; the modern version first appeared in sixteenth-century Italy and Spain
- Flute: earliest known version traced to China, approximately 900 BCE; popularized in Western Europe in the early fifteenth century
- Violin: originated in Italy in the early 1500s
- Harmonica: nineteenth-century Germany
- Trumpet: originally used as a signaling device in ancient Greece, Egypt, and parts of Asia; first used as a musical instrument in sixteenth-century Germany
- Tambourine: can be traced back to its use in festivals and processions by civilizations in many parts of the world, including Ancient Egypt, Greece, and Rome; China; Eastern Europe; and Native Americans in Canada; popularized in Western Europe in the mid-eighteenth century
- Saxophone: mid-eighteenth-century Belgium

Which of the following is a woodwind instrument?

A.   bassoon

B.   timpani

C.   cello

D.   tuba

Here's How to Crack It

Narrow down the answer choices based on what you know. A woodwind instrument produces sound when the player blows air through a thin opening in the instrument, causing the air to vibrate. Based on that, you can eliminate choice B, the timpani, which is a type of kettle drum, and choice C, the cello, which is a large string instrument. You're left with two wind instruments, and you know one of them has to be a brass instrument. One of the defining characteristics of a brass instrument is the use of valves to control pitch; the tuba (choice D) has valves, so you can rule it out. The correct answer is choice A, the bassoon.

THEATRE

In schools, theatre is often referred to as drama (not to be confused with what ensues during recess when someone decides to change best friends without warning).

Elements of Theatre

Acting

Actors bring characters to life by conveying emotions through words that elicit responses from an audience. Acting comes in many forms, including

- improvisation
- monologue/soliloquy
- pair or group scenes
- singing
- mime

When reading **dialogue**, actors have to take into account not only the words, but the emotions, relationships, and situations involved. Take the following sample lines of dialogue. Read them with the assumption that Lance is Tori's fiancé and has come home early from a business trip to surprise her. She wasn't home, so he checked with her roommate, Fiona, and tracked her down at work with a giant bouquet of flowers.

> TORI: Lance! What are you doing here?
> LANCE: I just had to see you.
> TORI: How did you find me?
> LANCE: Fiona told me where you were.

Now, read the lines over again, but this time, imagine that Lance is Tori's psychotic ex-boyfriend. He has escaped from prison and managed to find her, even though she has changed her name and moved hundreds of miles away. Fiona is Tori's sister, and the only person who knows where Tori lives. Tori knows Fiona would never betray her unless her life had been threatened.

After these two very different readings, you should see how much the context, relationships, and **backstory** (background story) affect the delivery of dialogue.

Directing

The **director** of a play or film takes his or her vision of the script and guides the cast and crew into making it a reality.

A director has a lot to do with how actions are expressed and how the actors play their characters. For example, in William Shakespeare's scripts, there is virtually no stage direction: no movement, no expressions of emotion. Every now and then, there will be a "He falls" or "Exeunt" (all exit). The director of a Shakespeare play has the enormous task of creating the setting, the action, and the character development based almost solely on the dialogue.

Scriptwriting

Scripts should have all of the elements of any type of story: theme, setting, character development, and a solid plot. The challenge in scriptwriting is to move the action along by primarily using dialogue.

Design

Design is the setting of the play or film. It includes elements such as shapes, colors, props, costumes, pictures, and background.

Styles of Theatre

Theatrical styles, or **genres**, can be categorized by a number of aspects, including theme and dialogue style. Some plays and playwrights overlap more than one genre.

Realism

Realism is grounded in fact. Plays of this genre depict real people in real situations, without any idealism or appeal to the imagination. Henrik Ibsen's *A Doll's House* (1879) is one example.

Classicism

Classicism, **classicalism**, or **neoclassicism** in theatre exemplifies the aesthetic principals rooted in ancient ("classic") Greek and Roman art: an emphasis on simplicity, formality, and restraint. *The Discovery* (1763) by Frances Sheridan is considered a play of this genre.

Romanticism

Romanticism developed as a rebellion against classicism. Romantic plays emphasized emotion and feeling rather than form and restraint. Shakespeare (1564–1616) was a Romantic playwright.

Modernism

Modernism is a genre that breaks from the past; it focuses on the contemporary, drawing a distinction between itself and previous genres. T.S. Eliot's play *The Cocktail Party* (1949) is an example.

Expressionism

Expressionism in theatre is a style of presentation, both in content and in design, focusing on symbolic and abstract representations of reality. Emphasis is placed on the emotions and reactions of the characters. Eugene O'Neill's *The Hairy Ape* (1922) is an expressionist play.

Existentialism

Existentialism is the belief that each person is wholly responsible for his or her own feelings, thoughts, and actions, and that it is up to the individual to make sense of the universe. An example of an existentialist play is Samuel Beckett's *Waiting for Godot* (1952).

Absurdism

Absurdism is similar to existentialism in that it is a philosophy based on the idea that there is no meaning in the universe in relation to humanity, and any attempt by humans to find any sense or logic out of this chaos is absurd. One of the most well-known plays of this genre is Tom Stoppard's *Rosencrantz and Guildenstern Are Dead* (1966).

Epic Theatre

Epic theatre is probably the most difficult theatrical style to explain. It follows a familiar story, such as a historical event or a fable, but is presented in loosely connected episodes. Epic theatre employs what is called the **alienation effect,** which refers to a technique intended to detach the audience's emotions from the drama. Bertolt Brecht was possibly the most famous playwright of this genre; one of his more well-known plays is *Mother Courage and her Children* (1938).

Historical and Cultural Context

Forms of theatre date back to ancient times, when primitive peoples performed rituals and ceremonies by creating actions, or early **scenes,** through dance.

Egypt

There is evidence of dramatic productions in Egypt dating back to about 2000 B.C.E. Most likely, these were passion plays, which depicted the suffering and sacrifices of gods.

China

Though historians have pieced together evidence of ceremonial dances and theatrical performances well before the Common Era, the commonly recognized "first period" of Chinese drama occurred in the eighth century, when dramatic productions focusing on extraordinary themes and heroic characters were performed before the Imperial Court.

India

Indian and Hindu theatre developed from an ancient custom whereby the national poetry was recited at social and religious gatherings. Dramatic gestures and music were gradually added to the recitations; eventually, religious legends and stories, usually featuring Krishna or Shiva, were transformed into performances.

Greece

Greek drama originated in the worship of Dionysus, the god of wine and agriculture, now recognized as the patron god of the Greek stage. Dramatic performances developed through choral songs and dances.

Native American

Native American theatre began with ceremonies and rituals regarding gods and nature. It utilized symbolism, engaged all of the senses, and incorporated active audience participation.

Which would be the best choice for a third-grade teacher to use as a culminating project in a theatre unit?

A. Pairs or small groups of students write and perform short plays.

B. Students watch scenes from various plays and identify the genres.

C. Pairs or small groups of students memorize and perform famous one-act plays.

D. Students memorize and perform monologues.

Here's How to Crack It

First, consider the age group you're given: third-grade students. That should help you eliminate some answers; for example, identifying genres, choice B, is too advanced. Choice C, memorizing and performing one-act plays is also too difficult; you should know that *one-act* is not necessarily synonymous with *short*. Now that you're down to your last two choices, switch to teacher mode. For many reasons, including teamwork and writing across the curriculum, choice A is the best choice.

VISUAL ARTS

The area of **visual arts** is comprised of many sub-disciplines, such as drawing, painting, sculpture, and photography. We'll focus here on the general principles and elements, most of which apply to more than one category.

Elements of Art

Line

A **line** is a continuous mark going from one point to another. Lines can be used to express a variety of things such as feelings, moods, and movement.

Color

Color has three characteristics: **hue,** which is the shade of color; **value,** which represents the lightness or darkness; and **intensity,** which refers to the dullness or brightness of a color.

Space

Space gives depth by creating visual perspective. Space can be positive, negative, or three-dimensional.

Shape

Artists use a variety of **shapes,** such as circles, rectangles, and triangles, to enclose areas of specific lengths and widths.

Form

A **form** has three dimensions and encloses volume. A sphere and a cube are examples of forms.

Texture

Texture is usually created by shading and lines to represent the quality of a surface. Texture can be actual, simulated, or invented.

Value

Value refers to changes in color, either by varying degrees of intensity or of light.

Principles of Art

Balance

Balance refers to the way the elements of art are arranged within a piece. Balance can be symmetrical, asymmetrical, and radial.

Emphasis

Artists often use the principle of **emphasis** to make one or more features of the piece stand out, or catch the viewer's eye. In a predominantly black-and-white drawing, for instance, an artist may use a splash of a bright color in one spot.

Contrast

Contrast refers to a method of stressing the difference between particular artistic elements. For example, an artist may combine bright and dark colors, or different shapes.

Unity

Unity, or **harmony,** gives a sense of belonging to a piece. Artists use similar elements to create a cohesive look or feel.

Rhythm

Rhythm is also referred to as **pattern** or **repetition**. Artists use repeated elements, such as lines and shapes, to give the piece a visual rhythm.

Movement

Artists can use the elements of art to create a sense of **visual movement,** causing the viewer's eye to move from one place to another.

Proportion

Proportion usually refers to the size of images in relation to each other. For example, an artist may draw a large flower in the center of a piece, then a very small building to one side, which gives the sense that the flower is much closer than the building.

Variety

Artists create **variety** by combining different artistic elements to create complex and intricate relationships.

Styles of Visual Arts

Historical Context

Art history dates back to ancient times. The following list contains some early forms of art from the various regions of the world:

- Prehistoric times: cave and rock painting, simple sculptures
- Egypt: colorful drawings
- Mesopotamia: pottery, jewelry, sculpture, architecture
- China: bronzeware, terracotta, silk drawings
- Japan: pottery
- India: rock paintings, petroglyphs
- Persia: jewelry, animal art
- Mexico: ceramics, jade carvings
- Rome: busts, architecture
- Greece: ceramics, frescoes, jewelry, architecture

Art Movements

The following list contains a few of the major art movements and the artists and cultures commonly associated with each:

- Gothic: thirteenth- and fourteenth-century France; linear, graceful style
- Renaissance: fifteenth- through seventeenth-century Europe; associated with Leonardo and Michelangelo; balance, harmony, scientific perspective, secular subjects
- Baroque: seventeenth- and early eighteenth-century Europe; strong emotion, dramatic lighting, violent movement
- Neoclassicism: late eighteenth- and early nineteenth-century Europe; revived order and harmony of ancient Roman, Greek art
- Romanticism: late eighteenth- and early nineteenth-century Europe; spontaneous expression, energy, brilliant colors
- Impressionism: late nineteenth-century France; associated with Renoir and Monet; often painted from nature with an emphasis on changing effects of light and color
- Cubism: early twentieth-century Europe; associated with Picasso; fragmentation, multiple viewpoints
- Surrealism: early twentieth-century France; associated with Dali and Magritte; dreams, spontaneity, juxtaposition
- Expressionism: early twentieth-century Europe; communication of emotion with emphasis and distortion
- Pop art: mid-twentieth-century Britain and United States; associated with Lichtenstein and Warhol; images and techniques of mass media and irony

Interpretation

The CSET may present an image of a work of art and ask you to derive meaning, or make an interpretation. This is a tough one, because interpretation is very subjective. Your best bet is to use what you know to gather as many details as you can. Ask yourself questions such as

- What type of art is it?
- Which artistic elements seem to be most predominant?
- How well does the artist present the principles of art?
- How old does the piece seem to be?
- What culture might the piece be from?
- What art movement might the piece be indicative of?
- What does the purpose of the piece seem to be?

KEY TERMS

artistic perception
creative expression
aesthetic valuing
connections
relationships
applications
force (dynamics)
relationship
solo
duet
ensemble
level
musical instrument
timbre (tone color)
dynamics
melody
harmony
rhythm
meter
tempo
musical notation
staff
treble staff
treble clef
bass staff
bass clef
grand staff
measure
time signature (meter signature)
key signature
wind instruments
brass instruments
woodwinds
reed
keyboard instruments
percussion instruments
string instruments
dialogue
backstory

director
design
genres
realism
classicism
classicalism
neoclassicism
romanticism
modernism
expressionism
existentialism
absurdism
epic theatre
alienation effect
scenes
visual arts
line
color
hue
value
intensity
space
shape
form
texture
value
balance
emphasis
contrast
unity (harmony)
rhythm (pattern, repetition)
visual movement
proportion
variety

Drill #18

1. Which of the following is not an example of recreational dancing?

   A. ballet

   B. square dancing

   C. tango

   D. twist

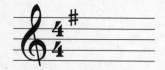

2. The numbers in the music staff above are used to indicate:

   A. key.

   B. harmonics.

   C. instrumentation.

   D. meter signature.

3. Which term refers to the intended volume of a piece of music?

   A. timbre

   B. harmony

   C. dynamics

   D. tempo

4. In theatre, a soliloquy is a type of:

   A. pantomime.

   B. monologue.

   C. plot.

   D. costume.

5. Which principle of art is most apparent in the work represented above?

   A. movement

   B. rhythm

   C. proportion

   D. variety

Please turn the page for answers and explanations
for the questions in this drill.

ANSWERS AND EXPLANATIONS TO DRILL #18

1. **A**   Recreational dancing is dancing for fun, exercise, and social interaction. Square dancing (choice B), tango (choice C), and the twist (choice D) all fall into one or more of those categories. Ballet (choice A), however, is a classical and artistic form of dance.

2. **D**   The two vertical numbers at the beginning of a music staff represent the meter signature, or time signature. The top number indicates the number of beats in each measure, and the bottom number indicates the duration of each beat. In this staff, there are four beats in each measure, and each beat is one quarter note in length.

3. **C**   Timbre (choice A) is the quality of sound that distinguishes one voice or instrument from another. Harmony (choice B) refers to combinations and relationships. Tempo (choice D) refers to the speed at which a piece is played. The correct answer is choice C, dynamics.

4. **B**   The word *soliloquy* should make you think "solo." A soliloquy is a speech given when an actor is alone on the stage. Pantomime (choice A) is performed without words, so you can eliminate that answer choice. Plot is the overall action of the play, which rules out choice C as well. And costume (choice D) has nothing to do with spoken lines. A soliloquy is a type of monologue (choice B); the main difference is that monologues can be performed within the context of a conversation with other characters on stage.

5. **A**   Use your basic knowledge of the principles, and one of the answers should stand out to you. Choice B, rhythm, indicates repetition or pattern, and there is nothing particularly indicative of that here. The same holds true for proportion (choice C), which does not appear to have been altered or skewed in any way, and variety (choice D), of which there is nothing striking. The position of the figure, bent and twisted, with the arm back, draws the eye up and out, giving the piece a great sense of movement (choice A): One almost expects to see him uncoil and spring forward to throw the disc.

Summary

o   The four art disciplines are dance, music, theatre, and the visual arts.

o   The five strands of standards for each discipline are artistic perception; creative expression; historical and cultural context; aesthetic valuing; and connections, relationships, and applications.

o   Elements of dance include space, time, and force.

o   Elements of music include instruments, timbre, dynamics, melody, harmony, rhythm, meter, and tempo.

o   Four basic classifications of musical instruments are wind, keyboard, percussion, and string.

o   Elements of theatre include acting, directing, scriptwriting, and design.

o   There are many theatrical styles, including realism, existentialism, classicism, and romanticism.

o   Elements of art include line, color, space, shape, form, texture, and value.

o   Principles of art include balance, emphasis, contrast, unity, rhythm, movement, proportion, and variety.

Chapter 21
Writing Skills
Review

ANOTHER TEST!?

The CSET: Writing Skills is a separate test (administered along with the CSET: Multiple Subjects) that offers an option for meeting the basic skills requirement. In short, if you are taking the CSET: Multiple Subjects, you can meet the basic skills requirement by passing the CSET: Writing Skills. If you've already passed all three sections of the CBEST (California Basic Educational Skills Test™), you don't need to take the CSET: Writing Skills.

CONSTRUCTED-RESPONSE QUESTIONS VS. CSET: WRITING SKILLS

Both the constructed-response questions found in CSET: Multiple Subjects Subtests I, II, III and the CSET: Writing Skills require you to do some expository and expressive writing. So whatever path you take to meet the basic skills requirement, you'll need some writing skills. Let's break down these two sections.

Constructed-Response Questions

Subtests I, II, and III require you to complete a total of 11 constructed-response questions. The subjects are all over the map: questions about reading, language, and literature; history and social science; science and mathematics; physical education, human development, and visual and performing arts. Phew! Fortunately, you've already reviewed that subject matter in the preceding chapters.

Now let's talk about how you'll write these constructed responses. According to the California Commission on Teacher Credentialing (CTC—the folks who run the CSET), the constructed-response assignment score is based on the following criteria:

- purpose: the extent to which the response addresses the constructed-response assignment's charge in relation to relevant CSET content specifications
- subject matter knowledge: the application of accurate subject matter knowledge as described in the relevant CSET content specifications
- support: the appropriateness and quality of the supporting evidence in relation to relevant CSET content specifications

As you can tell, the constructed-response questions are intended to assess your subject matter knowledge, not necessarily your writing ability. But a clear, well-written essay can't hurt. You must communicate your thoughts and ideas clearly enough so that the readers can adequately judge your knowledge and skills. Don't let sloppy organization or a few spelling mistakes distract the reader from seeing that you know your stuff.

Keep these three items in mind: purpose, subject matter knowledge, and support. Basically, don't stray from the question.

For example, suppose you are answering the constructed-response question within the math section of Subtest II. The question asks you about number theory and geometry using the example of a tile design. Perhaps that question prompts you to think about the tile designs of the Byzantine Empire and the recurring themes of religion and imperial powers. That sounds like an interesting classroom tie-in—teaching students about math and history simultaneously—fantastic! But on the CSET, nobody cares. Stick with the prompt and remember where you are: in the math section. Show off your math subject matter knowledge and utilize strong supporting points to buttress your argument, but don't go too far off topic.

Also, remember to tailor your writing to your audience: other educators in the field. Don't write as though you are teaching young students or having a casual conversation with coworkers. Write for your peers in academia.

If writing is not your strong suit and the thought of crafting a constructed response makes your skin crawl, take heart in this fact: On the CSET: Multiple Subject, the constructed-response questions account for only 30% of your score.

CSET: Writing Skills

The CSET: Writing Skills is comprised of two constructed-response questions. Just two questions!? Yup. One is an expository writing prompt, which asks you to analyze a given situation or statement. The other is an expressive writing prompt, which asks you to write about a specified personal experience. Unlike the constructed-response questions that we discussed above, the writing skills questions don't require you to demonstrate any specialized knowledge. In this section, simply show off your writing skills.

The Writing Skills section is scored holistically by qualified California educators. Holistic scoring is a method by which trained readers evaluate a piece of writing for its overall quality. The readers are trained not to focus too much on any one aspect of writing but rather to look at a response as a whole.

For the CSET, the readers are looking for the following performance characteristics:

- rhetorical force: the clarity with which the central idea or point of view is stated and maintained; the coherence of the discussion and the quality of the writer's reasoning
- organization: the clarity of the writing and the logical sequence of the writer's ideas
- support and development: the relevance, depth, and specificity of supporting information

- usage: the extent to which the writing shows care and precision in word choice
- structure and conventions: the extent to which the writing is free of errors in syntax, paragraph structure, sentence structure, and mechanics (that is, spelling, grammar, punctuation, and capitalization)
- appropriateness: the extent to which the writer addresses the topic and uses language and style appropriate to the given audience and purpose

As you can see, this is the section where you wow them with your fantastic vocabulary, skilled organization, and phenomenal supporting ideas. Does that sound daunting to you? Fear not—we'll break it down for you below.

GUIDE TO ESSAY WRITING: FORMAT

All essays can be divided into a basic template shown below. You might find it hard to believe that all essays fit this format, but they do. Take note of this format as you read articles and essays in newspapers and magazines in your daily life.

Basic Writing Template

Introduction

Examples or reasons (body of an essay)

Conclusion

Introduction

An introduction can be a few sentences or a paragraph. It is simply a response to the question or prompt. Essentially, the introduction is the response you would give if you weren't forced to write an entire essay on the subject. The introduction is where you should outline your thoughts and what you are going to say in the subsequent essay.

Examples or Reasons

The body of an essay includes in most cases three (sometimes more or fewer) paragraphs, with specific examples in support of the answer you present in your introduction.

Conclusion

The conclusion is a restatement of your introduction, with some notes on how the intervening examples clearly support your contention. It wraps up the essay and should always connect back to the beginning for a cohesive feel.

HOW TO WRITE IT

Step 1: Prepare

You're already doing the right thing by reading this book: You're preparing and studying. The CSET: Writing Skills expository writing question can be about anything from physical education to Roman history to geometry to communication theory to California history. So studying for the CSET: Multiple Subjects will prepare you for the CSET: Writing Skills. Then you will be able to craft thorough opinions (your introduction and conclusion) and support them with clear evidence (the supporting paragraphs and examples that make up the body of your paper). These are the essential aims of studying, anyway.

Step 2: Outline

The essay questions deserve very brief outlines. The outlines need not even be written down; nevertheless, they must be thought through. Do not make life needlessly difficult for yourself by writing without knowing what you are writing. Figure out your topic sentence, then your three (or more) examples; then you can begin. Let's take a look at a fun example:

> "Compare and contrast Patrick Ewing and Shaquille O'Neal as they performed over the course of the 1992–1993 basketball season, and decide which of the two you think should have been the starting center of the All-Star game."

Here's a strong outline for this question:

> *Ewing was a better center.*
>
> (1) *Better leadership of team*
>
> (2) *More control over whole game, not just his performance*
>
> (3) *Not a show-off*

Now that your outline is complete, you can start writing.

Step 3: Write

Essays written under timed conditions leave less room for posturing. The pressure of a time limit forces you to think of what you want to say, say it, and move along. This can lead to better writing in general, because you are forced to be concise and say what you mean. Do not be intimidated by those who sit near you and seem to be writing tomes. Length is not in and of itself a virtue. The more succinctly you express yourself, the better your essay will be, so don't spend time thinking about the fanciest way to write something; just write it.

In the paragraphs that make up the body of the essay, you must clearly present the supporting evidence and then show how that evidence supports your point. For example, suppose you're writing about incidents that led to the American Revolution. It's not enough to say that there were high taxes on tea at the time and people in Boston were unhappy. You must also note that, because of ongoing tensions with Britain, Boston was fertile ground for a revolution.

Let's take a look at a sample essay:

INTRO

Two of the most important centers in the Eastern conference over the 1992–93 season were Patrick Ewing of the New York Knickerbockers, and Shaquille O'Neal of the Orlando Magic. Both are magnificent athletes, and they have similarities as well as differences, but in any comparison, Patrick Ewing is a better center and deserved to start in the All-Star game.

COMPARE AND CONTRAST

The two players were very similar. Both were high-scoring centers, both excelled in the college game, and both were the number-one draft picks of their respective years. Yet it is important to note that these years were very different. O'Neal came out of the draft in 1992, so the 92–93 season was his first. Ewing was drafted in 1985. During the 1992–93 season Ewing was just reaching the height of his considerable powers. His experience and maturity would lend an important resonance to the Eastern All-Star team.

They both played the role of the outstanding player of their particular teams. But this role, and the ways they performed in it, also demonstrates some of their differences, and shows why, and how, Ewing was the more appropriate choice for All-Star center.

EWING BETTER

As the star of his team, Ewing did an outstanding job in scoring, rebounds, and assists. Thus, he not only played well for himself, making himself a better player, but he made his team a better team. One of the most important developments of the 92–93 season was the offensive presence of John Starks. Clearly, Starks could not have come to the fore unless Ewing had played in such a way as to help develop another outstanding player.

REASON 1

While some may say that Ewing was surrounded by better players, this is not enough to prove that the centers' differences resulted solely from their teams. Most glaring among O'Neal's weaknesses of that season was his self-congratulatory play. A smashed backboard may have looked impressive at the time, but it was only another piece of evidence showing that O'Neal wanted his *playing* to be noticed. Contrast that with Ewing, who never asked for attention, but worked his absolute hardest so that his *team* would be noticed, and win.

REASON 2

The many reasons mentioned here—experience in the National Basketball Association, leadership ability, and generous play—provide sufficient evidence that during the 1992–93 season, Patrick Ewing was a better center, and a better player, than Shaquille O'Neal, and thus would have been the best choice for the starting center for the Eastern All-Star team.

CONCLUSION

Step 4: Proofread

While proofreading is always a part of writing, it takes a slightly different form in a test setting. You do not have much time, so you must restrict your check to spotting flagrant errors of meaning and form. A sentence that expresses what you mean in a slightly awkward form does not have to be rewritten in a testing environment. You want your CSET: Writing Skills to be well-written and correct, but don't pull your hair out with a proofread. The majority of your time should be focused on the initial brainstorming and writing, with a quick proofreading pass.

HOW TO MAKE IT EASY FOR THE READER TO GIVE YOU A HIGH SCORE

The most important part of your essay is the content. There are just a few vital things you must do to let your excellence come shining through with full impact. These basics have to do with the surface of your writing. That might seem cheap, but it's not. If the surface of your essay is clean and clear, the reader can see through to the depths.

Neatness Counts

Studies have shown that neatly written essays earn higher scores on holistically graded tests, such as the CSET. It's not fair, but it's a fact of life. Do everything in your power to make your essays readable. Write slowly. Write in large letters. Write dark. Your writing doesn't have to be pretty, but it must be legible.

Indent

Your reader's first impressions are crucial. Think about the person at a job interview with gum in his hair. If his battle isn't already lost, it's definitely an uphill fight the rest of the way. The overall look of your essay is a first impression. It's the smile on your face as you walk in the door. Your essay should look neat, organized, and clear. Make your paragraphs obvious. Indent twice as far as you normally would. When in doubt, make a new paragraph. Ever look at a book, flip it open, and see nothing but one long paragraph? Your next thought is usually, "Oh please, don't make me have to read this!" That's exactly what readers think when they see essays without paragraphs. Make sure your reader can see the paragraphs right away. Neat presentation, clear handwriting, paragraphs just screaming out "I'm so organized, it's scary!" will have the reader thinking, "Now here's a high-scoring student" before he or she has even read a word.

Write Perfectly...for the First Paragraph

Your second first impression (that's an oxymoron...just trying to keep things lively!) is the first paragraph of the essay. Take triple care with your first paragraph. If you're unsure about the spelling of a word, don't use it. If you're unsure how to punctuate a sentence, rewrite it in a way that makes you feel confident. Don't make any mistakes in the first paragraph. Don't worry about the rest of the essay; the readers expect mistakes. If you try to write the entire essay perfectly, you'll write so slowly, or fill up your brain with so much worry, that you'll either run out of time or write such stilted, dull prose that your reader will wish you had made a mistake just for some relief.

All you need are a few good sentences to convince the reader that you can write a good sentence when you want to. The glow of a good beginning carries over to the whole essay. Mistakes later on look like little, minor errors not even worth bothering with. After all, the reader has already seen that you can write well. Mistakes at the very beginning look just the opposite—they appear to be telling signs of inability and a weak grasp of fundamental English mechanics. Take extra care at the beginning of your essay; then relax and just write (neatly!)

Show Off Your Vocabulary

Readers do not give great scores to students who merely parrot the prompt. A good way to show that you understand what the question is asking is to paraphrase the prompt in your response. Be sure to do this by selecting strong words that showcase your fantastic vocabulary.

Check out The Princeton Review's great vocabulary book *WordSmart*.

Use Snappy Verbs and Tasty Nouns

Juice up your writing. Try to write with some pizzazz. Try. That's all there is to it. Don't let the test environment, the tension, or anxiety over writing for a stranger take over your brain. Take risks: You may fall flat every so often, but the reader will appreciate your effort and reward it. When you've gotten our essay techniques down, you'll understand that 90 percent of dull writing on the CSET: Writing Skills comes from confusion about what to write, which leads to inhibition. Don't be inhibited. Jazz it up a little.

A FEW NOTES ABOUT PERSONAL ESSAYS

In the expressive writing half of the CSET: Writing Skills test, you can share a personal experience or story. Let's review a few things about personal essays before we go any further.

Common Pitfalls of Personal Essays

Day by Day by Day by Day by…(Day?)

Don't feel tied to chronology. You are asked to produce a personal essay because the reader wants to know something further about you. This doesn't necessarily mean that your essay must include a detailed biography. In fact, you can share more about yourself by discussing your thoughts on current events or morality or scientific ethics. You can tell a story about your life, but it does not have to be set as a straight biography beginning with the day you were born and detailing each event to the present. Stick to what really interests you and you'll have a much more interesting essay.

Having No Point

A personal essay is not a mandate to list the events of your life. Before you start writing, have an idea of how you will respond to the expressive writing prompt. You must have a main point. Your main point can be that you learned through many years of shopping for shoes that shopping was, for you, an opportunity to understand the nature of capitalism and American culture. Your main point can be that by watching the film *Bambi* you realized how transitory and powerful the idea of life on this earth is for you. Whatever you write about, you must have a point in mind. Simply listing the events of your life will lead you to write a journal entry, not an essay.

Being Kooky

Most people fear that they are boring and that the CSET reader will look over their essay and say, "Well, I've seen a million expressive writing essays about the same topics over and over." To make themselves stand apart, these test-takers think of the oddest, craziest thing that they've ever done and somehow fit that experience to the writing prompt.

Before you run out and write your essay about your encounter with space aliens, remember our guideposts: clarity and honesty. If you don't really believe that eating fried fire ants in the desert was important to you, for goodness sake, don't write about it. Not only will you misrepresent yourself, but you will also be writing about something you don't really care about, which leads to muddled, messy work.

Your perspective on your subject—not the subject itself—makes an essay interesting. While many phenomena are common, people are unique, and your particular experience and the angle from which you saw it can be duplicated by no one else on this earth. Therefore, that view, that particular perspective is what you should aim to convey in your expressive writing essay.

Getting Too Detailed

When you write a personal essay, you may get into territory that most readers are not familiar with: your family, your hometown, and other personal information. While it is necessary to introduce characters or settings with which your reader may be unfamiliar, "my best friend Toby," or "the dump down the hill from my house," it is not helpful to describe anything in greater detail than the essay calls for. It is probably unnecessary to inform the reader of Toby's hair color unless you are writing an essay regarding a major hair-dyeing trauma that you experienced.

Being Overly Dramatic

"The day I dyed my hair so that I would look more like Toby was the most momentous day of my life." Think for a moment. Is this really true? Or are you trying to get your reader interested by yelling, in effect, "Over here! Over here! Big things!" When you reread your essay, be sure to check for words such as *ever, never,* and *the most.* Allow your thoughts and ideas to be the drama and truth of the moment. By being overly dramatic, you make your writing seem desperate to be noticed, which is no more attractive in prose than it is in people.

Avoid Redundancy

People are tempted to begin sentences with "I think" or "I believe." In a personal essay, this wording is unnecessary. Anything that you write in the expressive writing essay is something you think, feel, or believe. To say so explicitly is redundant.

Avoid Excessive Informality

Just because you are writing about something personal is no reason for your prose to become casual or intimate. While there is room for a certain relaxation in a personal essay, do not let your writing become a mere record of a conversation. Your aim is clarity, so avoid excessive folksiness. Your ideas will allow the reader to view you as you are, and the way to present them clearly is to write them clearly.

RECAP OF SCORING

Constructed-Response Questions

The constructed-response section of the CSET: Multiple Subjects accounts for only 30% of your score. The other 70% is the multiple-choice section of the test. Just remember the bullets that we mentioned above. The readers are looking at your essays for clear purpose, subject matter knowledge, and support.

CSET: Writing Skills

The CSET: Writing Skills is scored on a 1–4 scale, with "U" (unscorable) and "B" (left blank) as options. Here's a breakdown of exactly what each score point means:

Score Point	Score Point Description
4	**A "4" is a well-formed writing sample that effectively communicates a whole message to the specified audience.** • The writer clearly presents a central idea and/or point of view and maintains focus on that topic; the response is well reasoned. • Ideas or points of discussion are logically arranged, and their meaning is clearly communicated. • Generalizations and assertions are well supported with relevant, specific, and detailed development. • Choice of words is precise; usage is careful and accurate. • The writer composes sentences of syntactic complexity and variety and constructs coherent paragraphs, although the response may contain minor flaws in mechanical conventions. • The response completely addresses the topic and uses language and style appropriate for the given audience and purpose.
3	**A "3" is an adequately formed writing sample that communicates a message to the specified audience.** • The writer presents a central idea and/or point of view, and the focus is generally maintained; the response is adequately reasoned. • Organization of ideas is generally clear and effective, and the meaning is generally clear. • Generalizations and assertions are adequately supported, although perhaps unevenly. • Word choice and usage are adequate; some errors exist but do not impede meaning. • The writer's response may have errors in paragraphing, sentence structure, and/or mechanical conventions, but they are neither serious nor frequent enough to distract or confuse the reader. • The response may not fully address the topic (i.e., one of the tasks in the assignment may be neglected or may be vaguely or incompletely addressed), but language and style are appropriate for the given audience and purpose.
2	**A "2" is a partially formed writing sample that attempts to communicate a message to the specified audience.** • The writer may state a central idea and/or point of view but loses focus on that idea; the response is simplistically reasoned. • Organization of ideas may be evident, but is largely ineffective, and the response is generally unclear. • Generalizations and assertions are only partially supported; the response may contain irrelevant, insufficient, or imprecise details. • Word choice and usage are generally imprecise and distracting. • The writer's response may have distracting errors in paragraphing, sentence structure, mechanical conventions, and/or dependence upon short, choppy sentences with minimal modification. • The response incompletely addresses most tasks of the assignment and/or inadequately uses language and/or style appropriate for the given audience and purpose.
1	**A "1" is an inadequately formed writing sample that fails to communicate a message to the specified audience.** • The writer fails to state and/or to remain focused on a central idea and/or point of view; the response lacks coherence and reason. • Organization of ideas is ineffective and seriously flawed; meaning is unclear throughout. • Generalizations and assertions are not supported or are severely underdeveloped; the presentation of details is confused. • Word choice and usage are largely imprecise, and there are severe distracting errors. • The writer commits serious and numerous errors in paragraphing, sentence structure, and/or mechanical conventions. • The response demonstrates little or no understanding of any of the assignment's tasks; language and style may be inappropriate for audience and purpose.
U	**The response is unscorable because it is off topic, illegible, primarily in a language other than English, or of insufficient length to score.**
B	**The essay response sheet is blank.**

Summary

- o Do everything in your power to make your essays readable.

- o Write carefully, in large, dark handwriting. Your writing doesn't have to be pretty, but it must be clear.

- o Make your paragraph indentations easy to spot.

- o When in doubt, create a new paragraph.

- o Your first paragraph should be grammatically perfect. Your reader will make a very quick judgment about your ability to write. Once the reader has decided you can write a sentence, he or she will cut you some slack later on (as long as you write neatly).

- o Have a solid vocabulary. You'll express yourself with greater clarity.

About the Authors

Kate Smith taught all subjects in elementary and middle schools in New York and California from 1999–2007; most recently, she taught seventh- and eighth-grade English Language Arts/Reading and Journalism at Bowditch Middle School in Foster City, California. She served as Lead Teacher for the San Mateo-Foster City School District middle school level summer school program in 2006 and 2007. She now teaches courses in Education and English/Language Arts at Notre Dame de Namur University in Belmont, California, and at Skyline College in San Bruno, California. She has supervised Notre Dame de Namur University teaching credential candidates in student teaching placements, and she is a PACT Scorer for Teaching Events in Single Subject: English Language Arts. She holds a Bachelor of Arts in English from the University of the Pacific, a Master of Science in Teaching: Elementary Education from Fordham University, and a Master of Arts in English from Notre Dame de Namur University. She is a member of Mensa and writes fiction as well as journalistic and educational reference materials. Ms. Smith lives in Foster City, California, with her daughter, Elena.

Riley Dacosta is a teacher, practicing attorney, and law professor. She holds an undergraduate degree from the University of California at Berkeley and a law degree from Santa Clara University. Riley also holds a Master of Fine Art in Literature and Writing from the University of San Francisco. She resides in the Bay Area with her family.

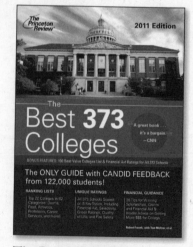